MW00651819

ENFU INKS

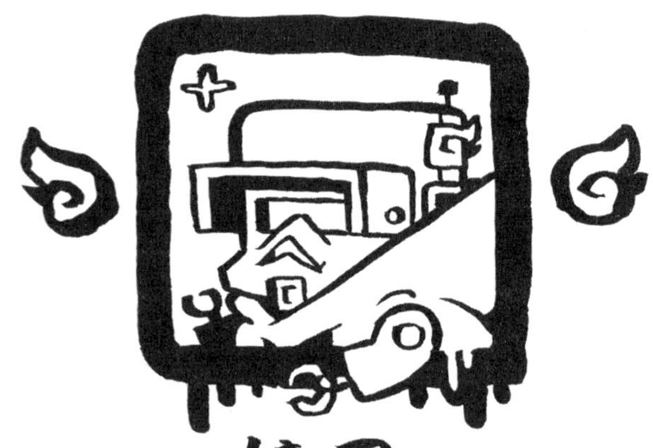

猿風
えん ふう
ENFU
シカゴ生まれシアトル育ち
「ENFU INKS」
2020年
@enfu
enfu.com

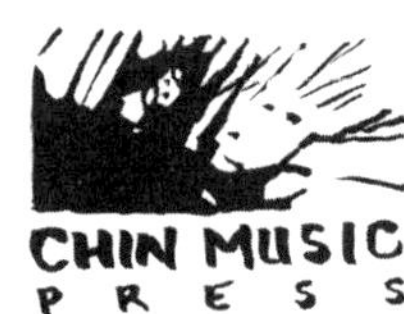

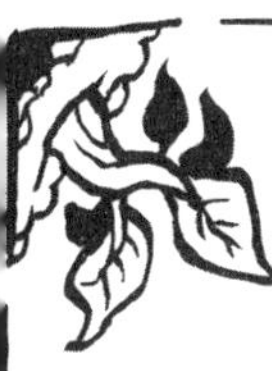
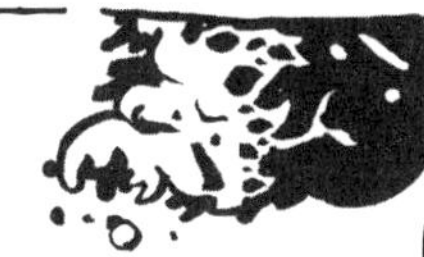

ENFU INKS

ideas are cheap

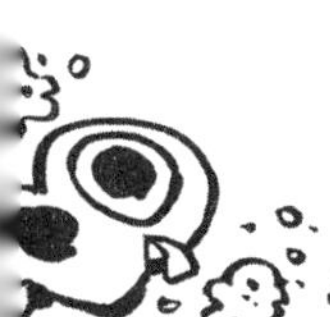
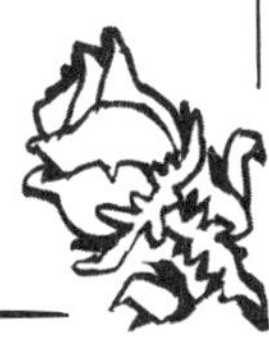

CHIN MUSIC PRESS

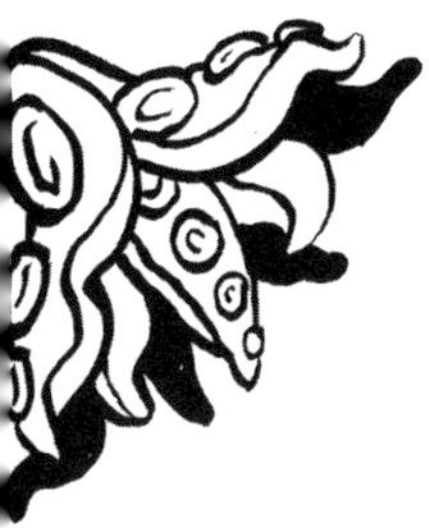

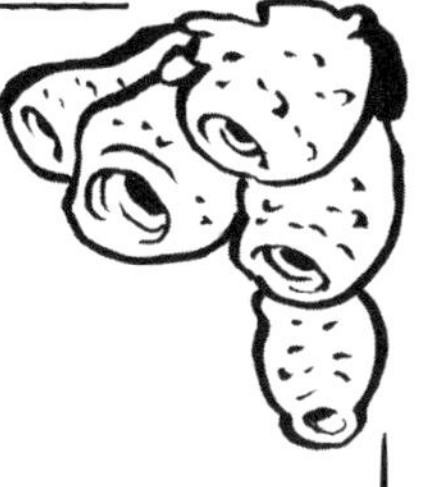

this book is dedicated to my house tribe:

minoru
makiko
ikuko
erika
satoko
michio
shigenobu
emiko
yoko
tim
di
naomi
noelle
isaiah

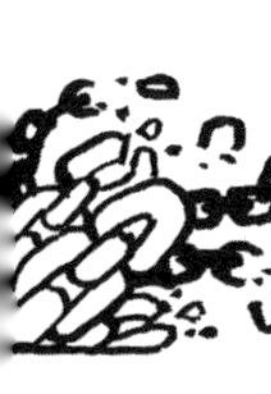

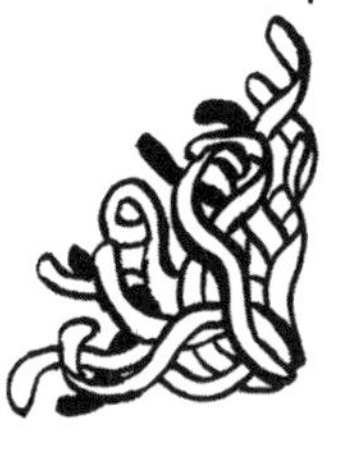

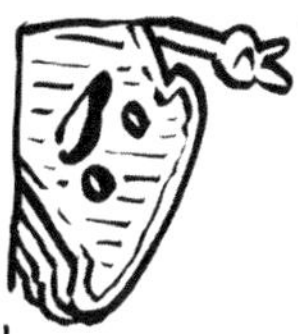
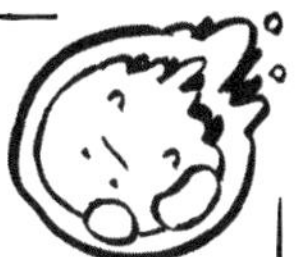

ideas are cheap execution is expensive

Starting as a thought, evolving to pages of pencil sketches, then finding its way as ink brushed on shikishi, none of these pages are that precious. All these original characters were an exercise for me to attempt to quickly execute the simplest reduction of these ideas. There are no under sketches to these inks, these strokes are mindful but swift, letting all mistakes remain in play and embracing imperfection.

I've listened to many talkers and watched many doers, I prefer working with the doers.

If you're an "idea guy" or someone who works on ideating or the concepting phase, the "ideas are cheap" assertion is not meant to denigrate your role, but only to enforce its importance. You'd know that to get that great idea or concept, so many have to self cull or throw away a concept mid draft. All these half baked ideas and concepts must be explored to get to the great idea. "Fail fast, fail cheap," and "kill your darlings" are comments you'd hear often in game development, and I also apply to my art.

Nonetheless, I hope you enjoy my cheap ideas.

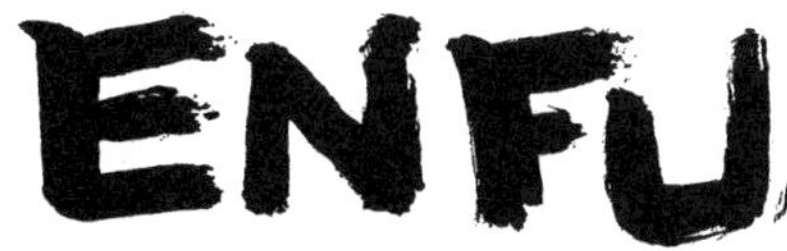

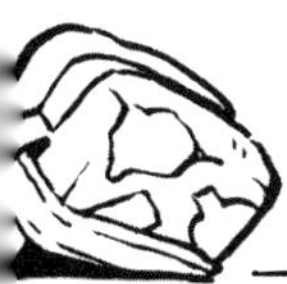
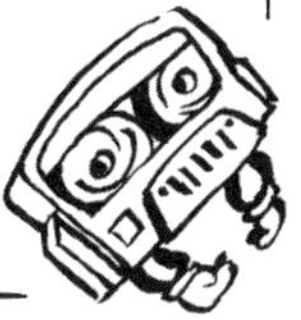

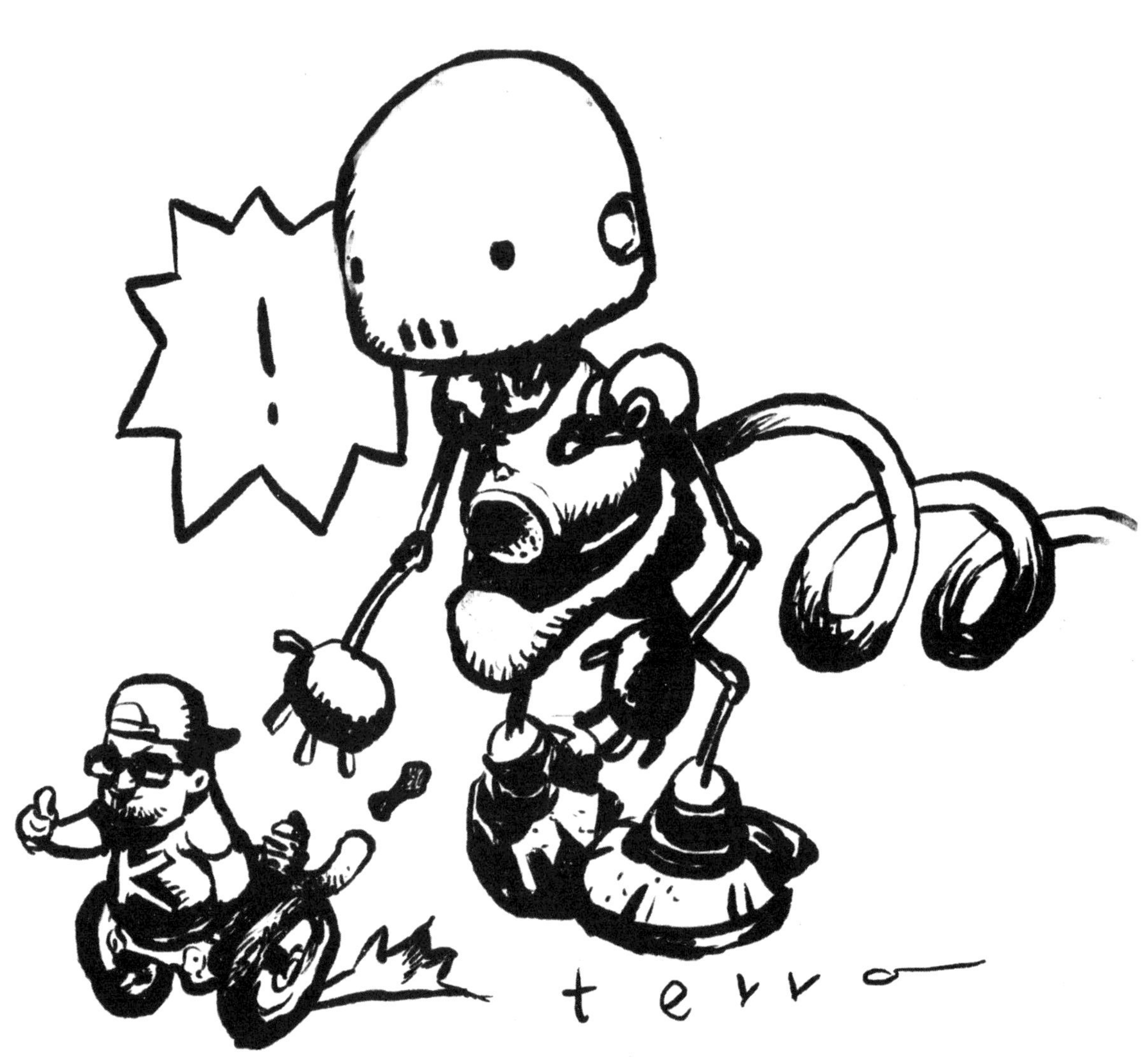
!
terra

INTRODUCTION

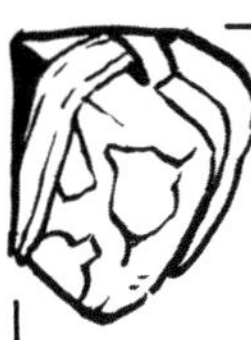

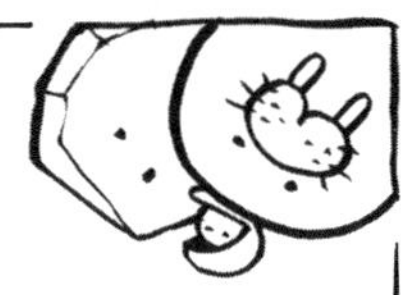

才能は、それを生み出す「量」が育てる部分も大きい。

Ken Tayaがそれを証明してると思う。この量の凄さといったら！！

それぞれが高いレベルでキャラクター化されていて、縦横無尽に動き回っている。

そのキャラクターになる対象も、これまた縦横無尽でモンスターはもちろん、私達の身の回りにあるもの、それはナチョスだったり、瓶だったり自由だ。

さらにその対象は森羅万象に及び、雲と山までが

彼の筆先からキュートなキャラクターとして動き出す。

「質」と「量」がKenの中から溢れだしている。

この本を手に取った人は、ぎっしりとページに詰め込まれたKen Tayaのキャラクター達が命を得て本からはみ出す勢いで跳ね回っている姿をたのしめるハズだ。

そして自分もその中で一緒に踊りたい衝動が沸き起こる。

ほらその証拠に私もついスケッチしてしまう！

寺田克也

Talent is largely responsible for the quantity of an artist's output. I think Ken Taya proves that. I mean look at the prodigious volume of his work!! These high-level characterizations cover such a wide range. The objects he turns into characters come from all over. Of course, there are monsters, but he also uses things around us, like nachos, bottles, whatever he likes. His subjects come from everywhere in the universe. Clouds and mountains are transformed into cute characters by his brushtip. Ken overflows with quality and quantity.

Anyone who flips through this book will enjoy watching the characters crammed into every corner of these pages come to life and energetically bounce around. You'll want to burst into these pages and dance along with them. Hey, I'll show you what I mean in a sketch!

KATSUYA TERADA
Illustrator

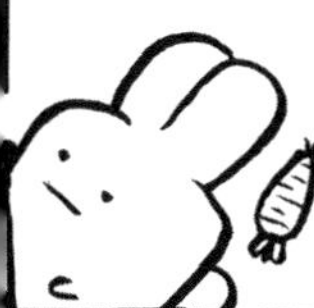

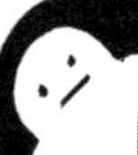

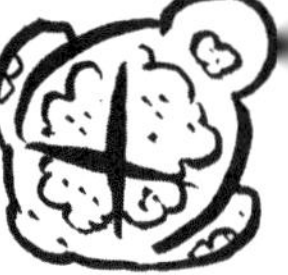

INDEX OF INKS

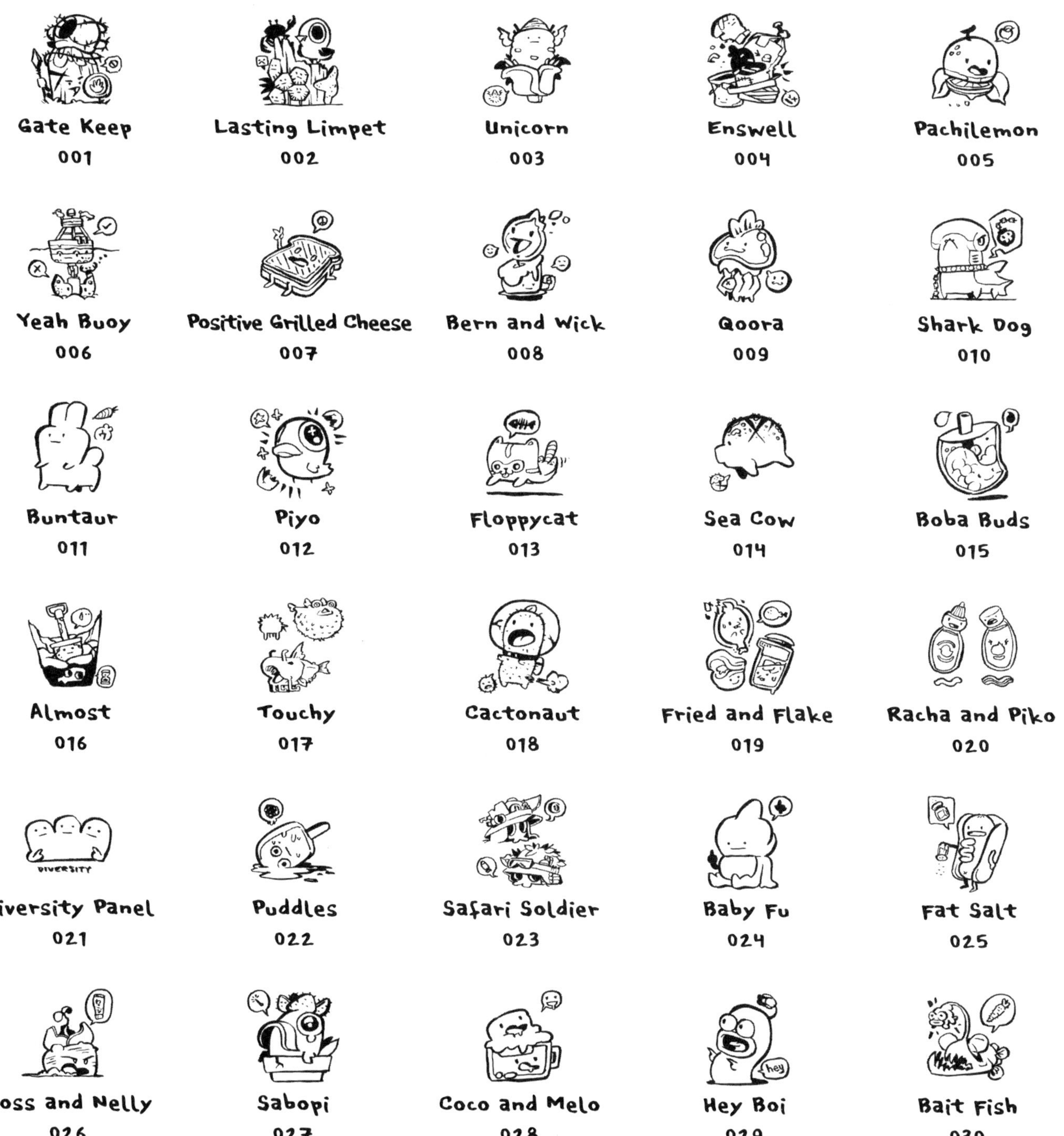

Gate Keep
001
Lasting Limpet
002
Unicorn
003
Enswell
004
Pachilemon
005
Yeah Buoy
006
Positive Grilled Cheese
007
Bern and Wick
008
Qoora
009
Shark Dog
010
Buntaur
011
Piyo
012
Floppycat
013
Sea Cow
014
Boba Buds
015
Almost
016
Touchy
017
Cactonaut
018
Fried and Flake
019
Racha and Piko
020
DIVERSITY
Diversity Panel
021
Puddles
022
Safari Soldier
023
Baby Fu
024
Fat Salt
025
Ross and Nelly
026
Sabopi
027
Coco and Melo
028
hey
Hey Boi
029
Bait Fish
030

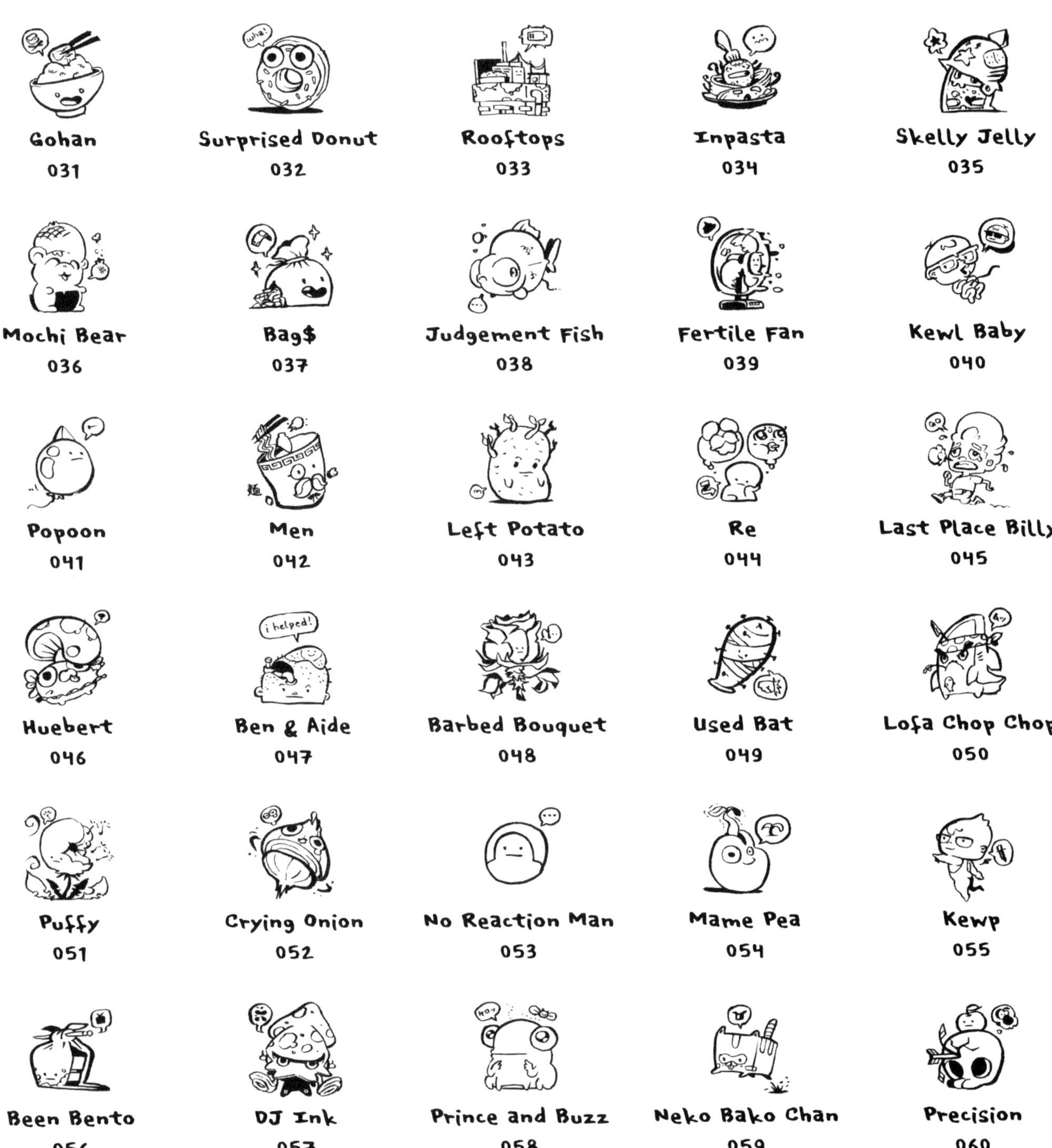

wha?
Gohan
031
Surprised Donut
032
Rooftops
033
Inpasta
034
Skelly Jelly
035
Mochi Bear
036
Bag$
037
Judgement Fish
038
Fertile Fan
039
Kewl Baby
040
Popoon
041
Men
042
Left Potato
043
Re
044
Last Place Billy
045
Huebert
046
i helped!
Ben & Aide
047
Barbed Bouquet
048
Used Bat
049
Lofa Chop Chop
050
Puffy
051
Crying Onion
052
No Reaction Man
053
Mame Pea
054
Kewp
055
Been Bento
056
DJ Ink
057
Prince and Buzz
058
Neko Bako Chan
059
Precision
060

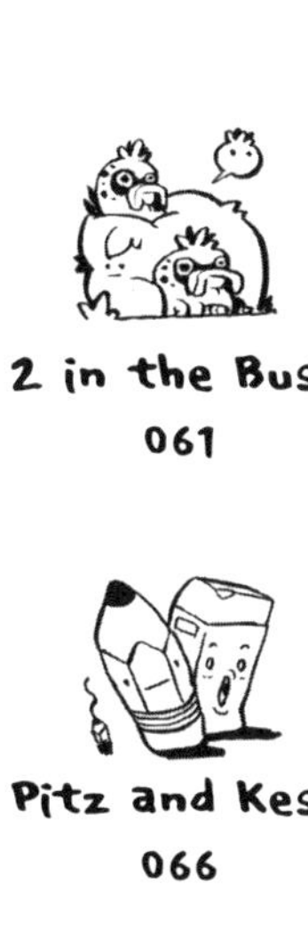

2 in the Bush
061

Friendly Waves
062

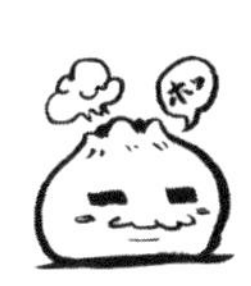

Dim Sum Kids
063

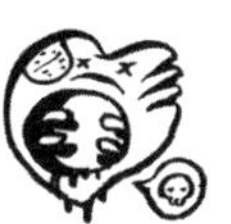

Blue Heart
064

Panki
065

Pitz and Kesh
066

Jam Jam
067

BFF
068

Peckish
069

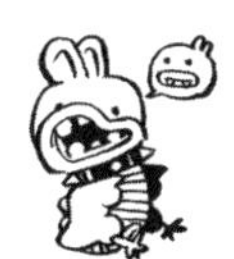

Busausa
070

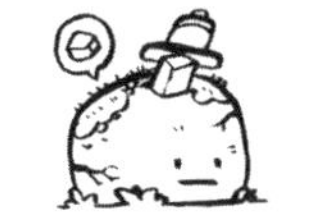

Quest Rocks
071

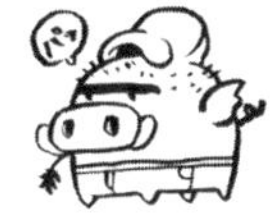

Pantsu
072

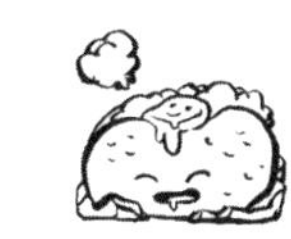

Spuds and Pat
073

Count Toofula
074

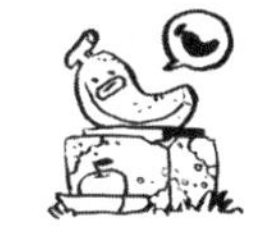

Empty Gesture
075

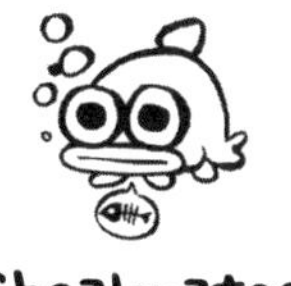

Shoalmates
076

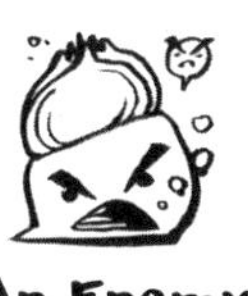

An Enemy
077

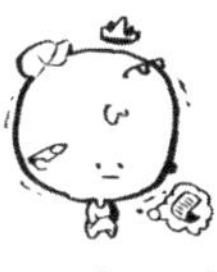

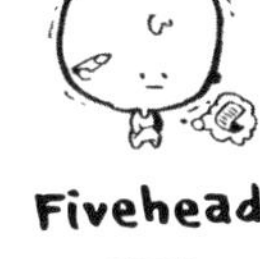

Fivehead
078

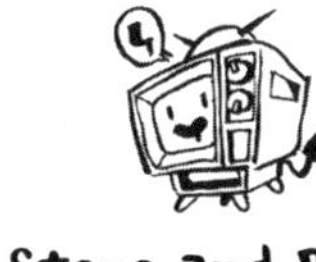

Steve and Paige
079

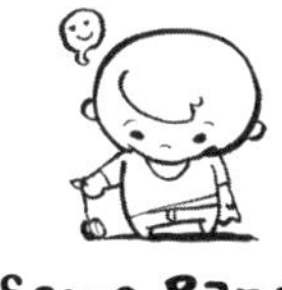

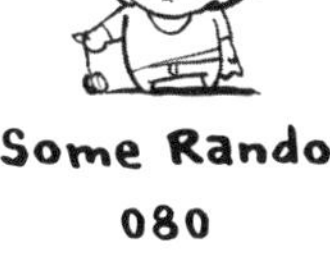

Some Rando
080

Bye Bob
081

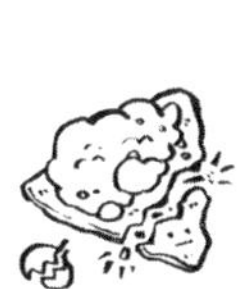

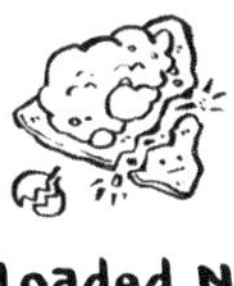

Overloaded Nacho
082

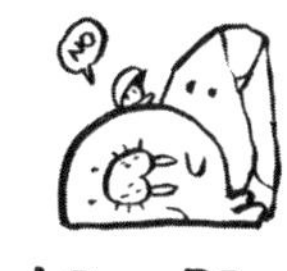

Lazy Dayz
083

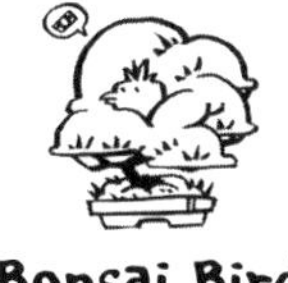

Bonsai Bird
084

Tamachan
085

Imagine
086

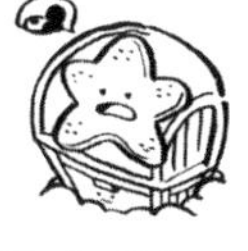

Selfish Starfish
087

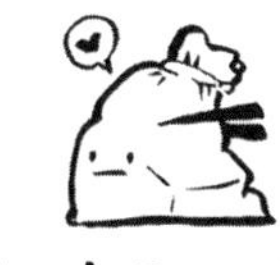

Trash Dumpling
088

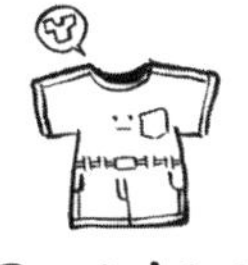

Pantshirt
089

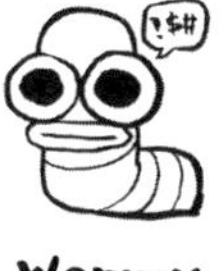

Wermy
090

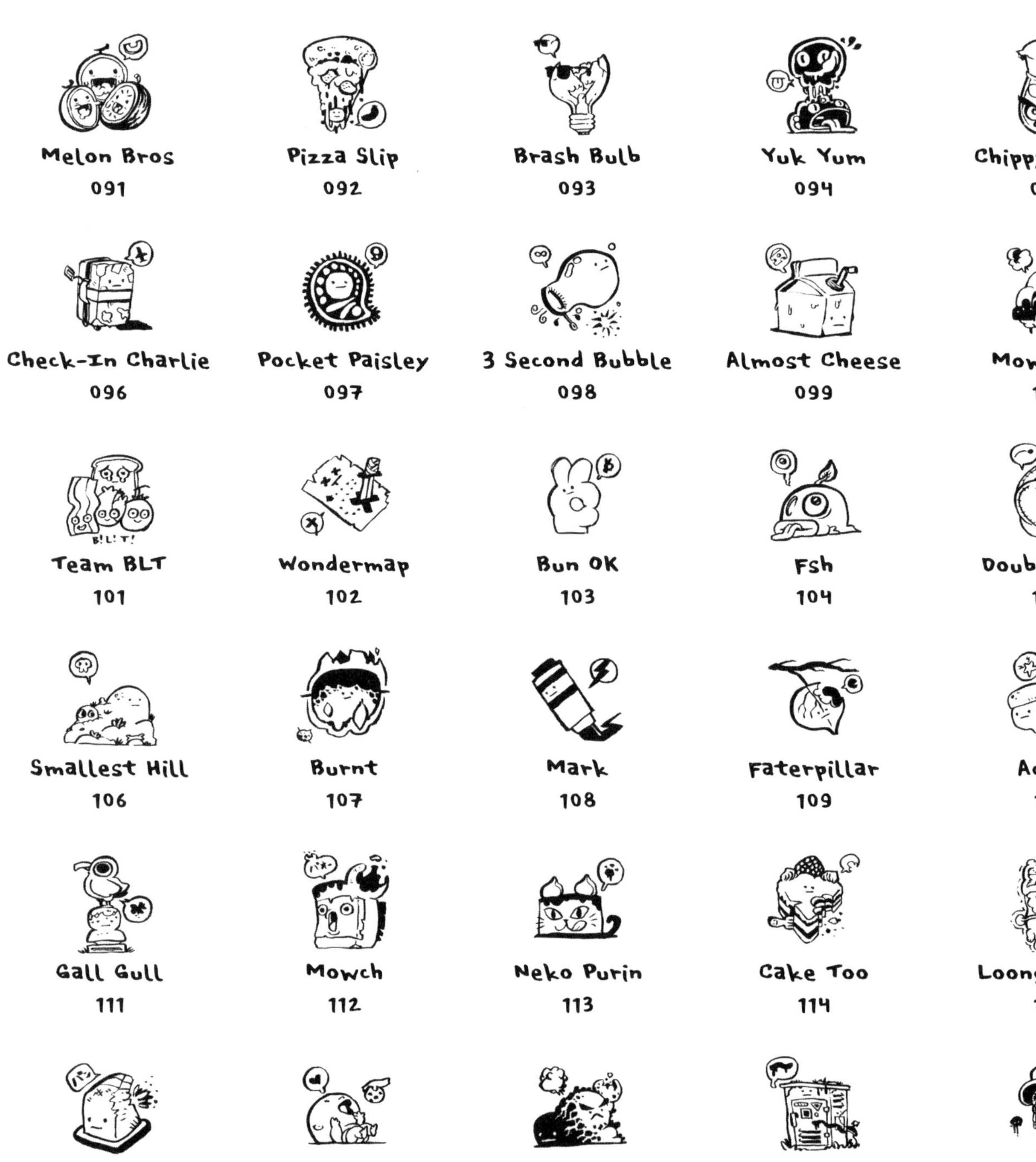
Melon Bros 091
Pizza Slip 092
Brash Bulb 093
Yuk Yum 094
Chippy Shoyu 095
Check-In Charlie 096
Pocket Paisley 097
3 Second Bubble 098
Almost Cheese 099
Mowhawk 100
B!L!T!
Team BLT 101
Wondermap 102
Bun OK 103
Fsh 104
Double Play 105
Smallest Hill 106
Burnt 107
Mark 108
Faterpillar 109
Acorn 110
Gall Gull 111
Mowch 112
Neko Purin 113
Cake Too 114
Loong Otter 115
Hit Cone 116
All By Myself 117
Iggy & Maggy 118
City Camo 119
Death Jr. 120

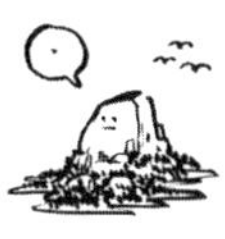

Isle 121	Glass Houses 122	Berg 123	Kororin 124	Leaky Linus 125
Pichasu 126	Ninja Fields 127	Melty Crisp 128	Propane Pete 129	Amped 130
Nailed 131	Keep Scrap 132	OJ 133	Arms Race 134	Overcast 135
Rocklet 136	Brick Message 137	Tank Tank 138	Old School 139	Chipped Chime 140
Past Future 141	Sand Surety 142	Fauntleroy 143	U.O.K? 144	Solopus 145

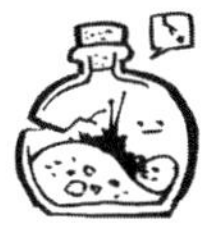

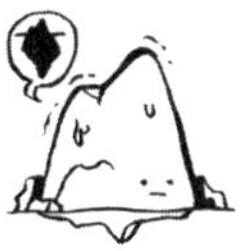

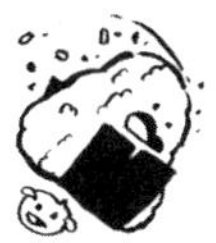

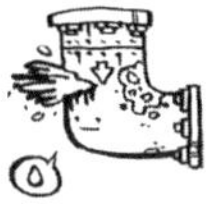

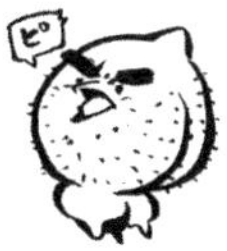

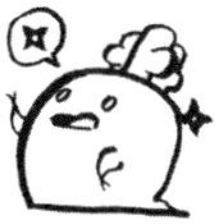

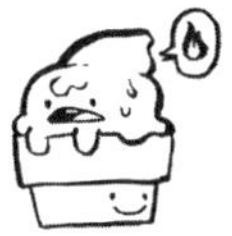

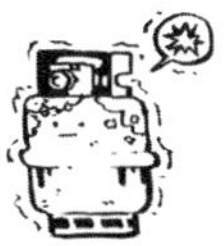

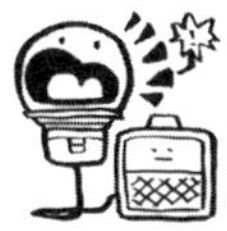

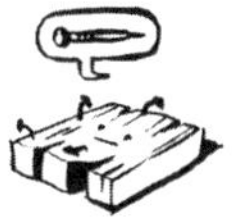

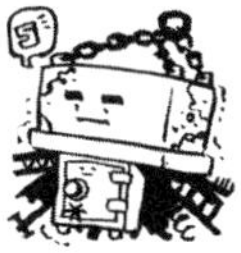

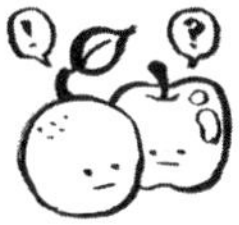

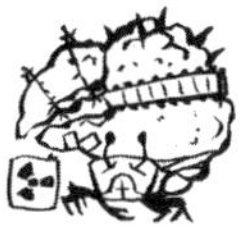

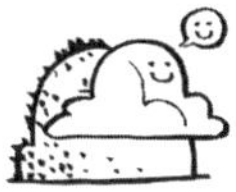

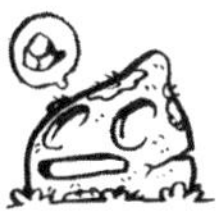

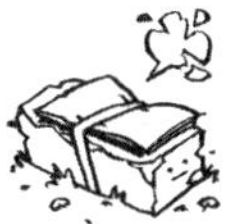

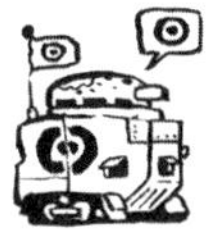

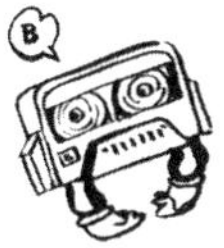

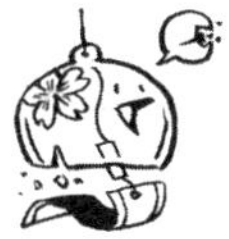

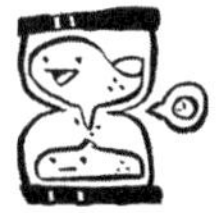

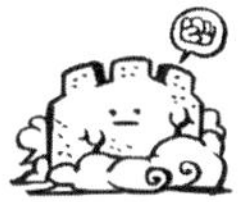

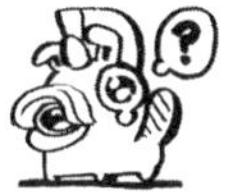

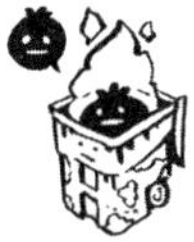

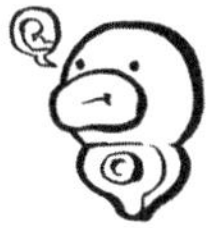

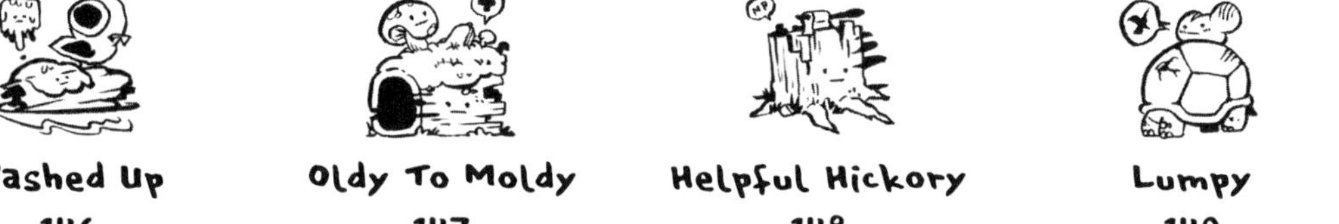

Washed Up 146	Oldy To Moldy 147	Helpful Hickory 148	Lumpy 149	Good Enuf 150

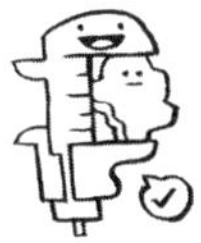

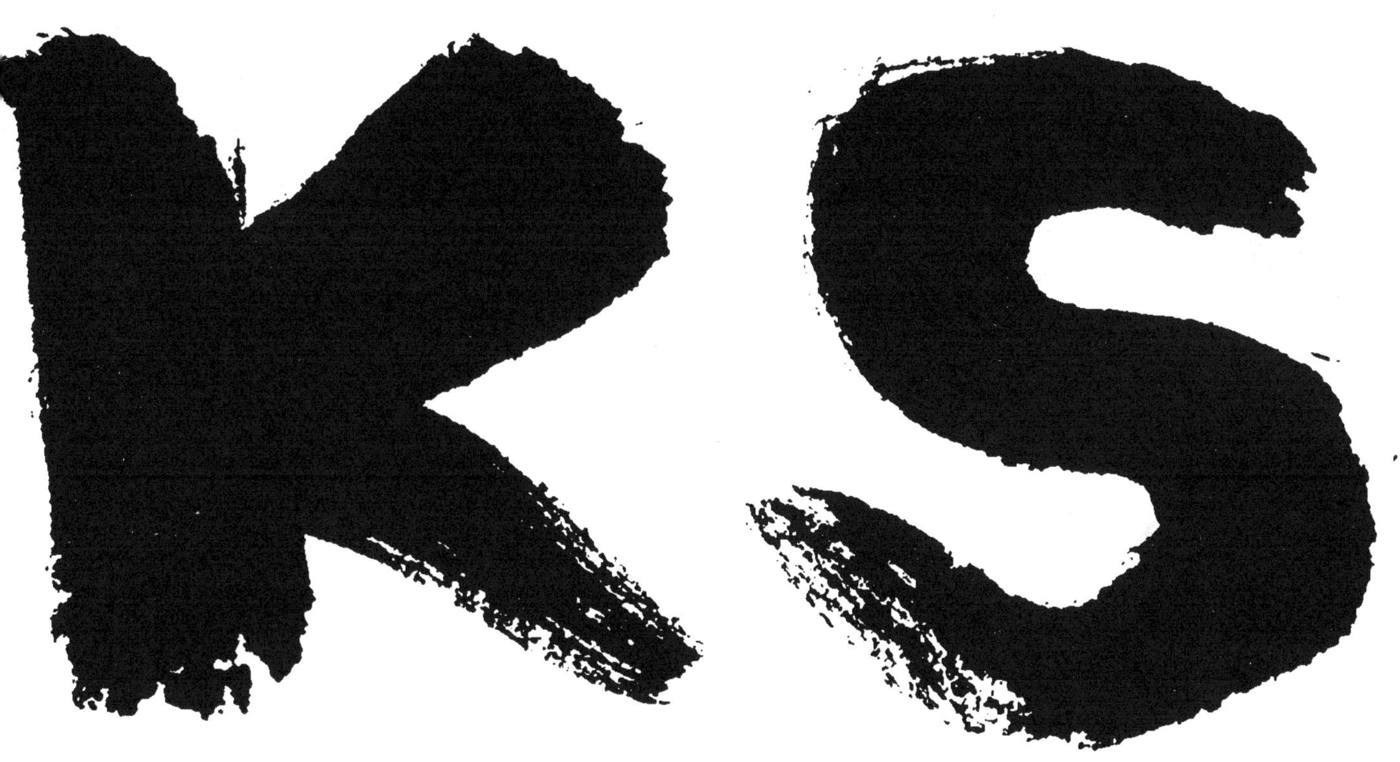
KS

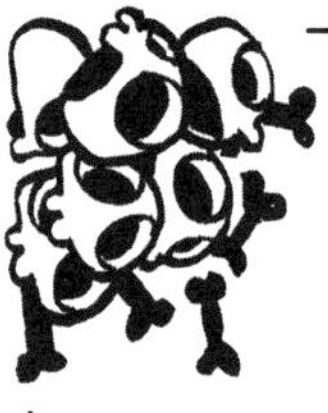

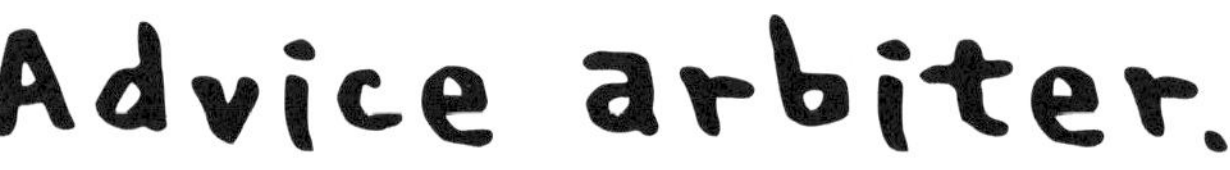
Advice arbiter.

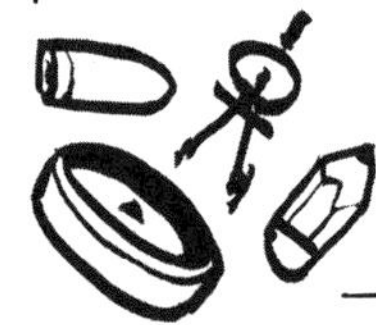

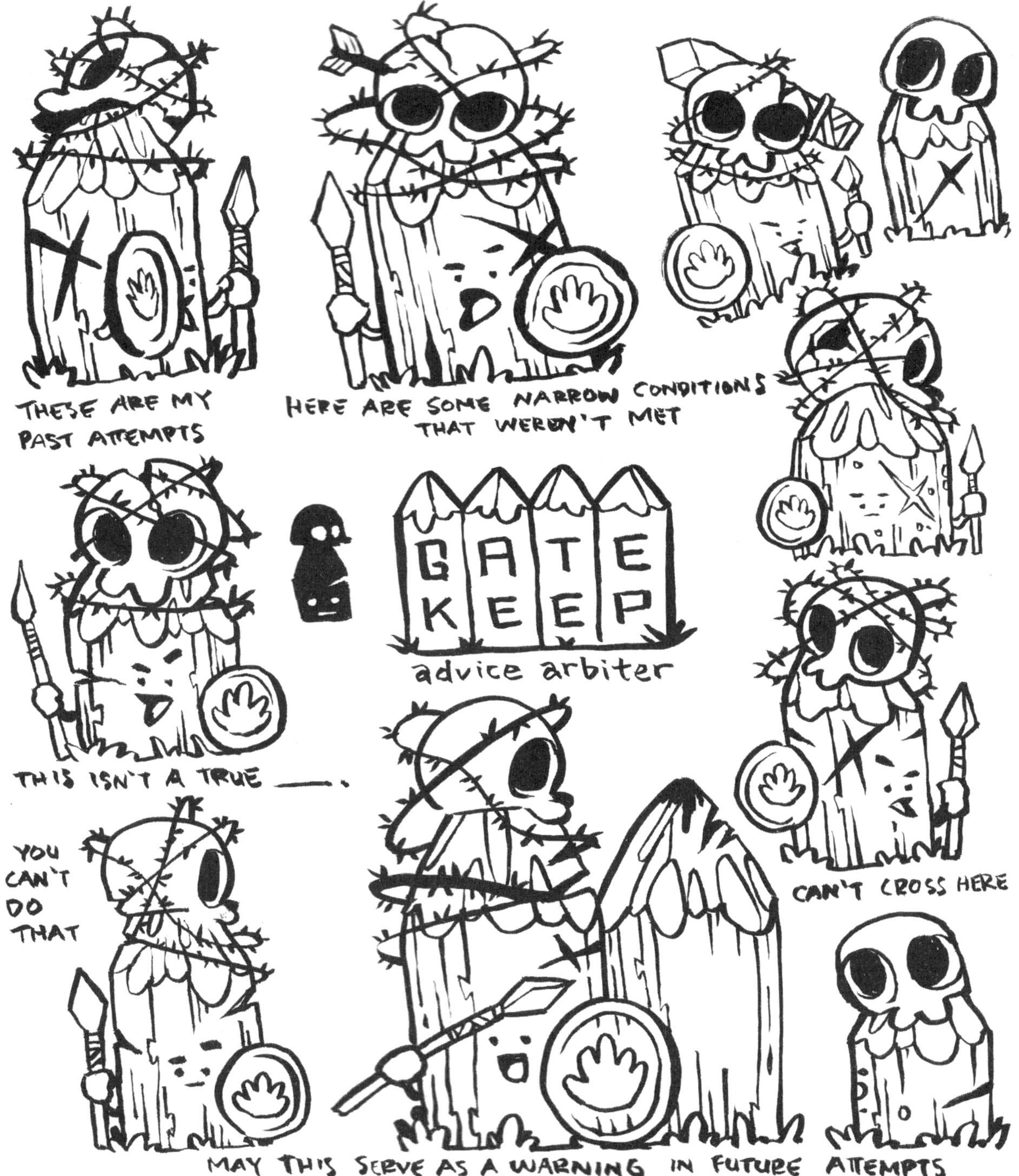
THESE ARE MY PAST ATTEMPTS
HERE ARE SOME NARROW CONDITIONS THAT WEREN'T MET
GATE KEEP
advice arbiter
THIS ISN'T A TRUE ___.
CAN'T CROSS HERE
YOU CAN'T DO THAT
MAY THIS SERVE AS A WARNING IN FUTURE ATTEMPTS

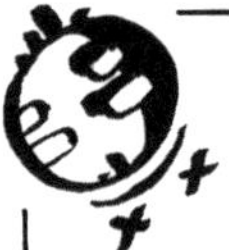

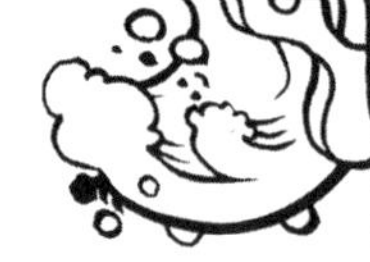

Hanging in there.

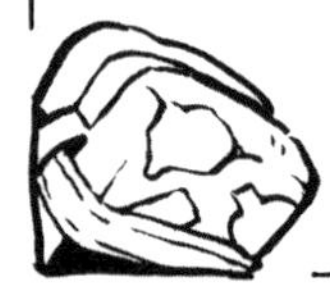

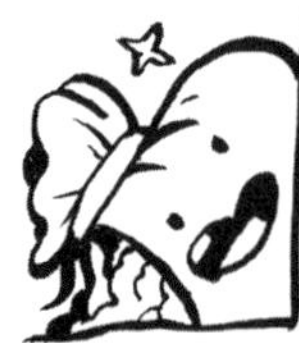

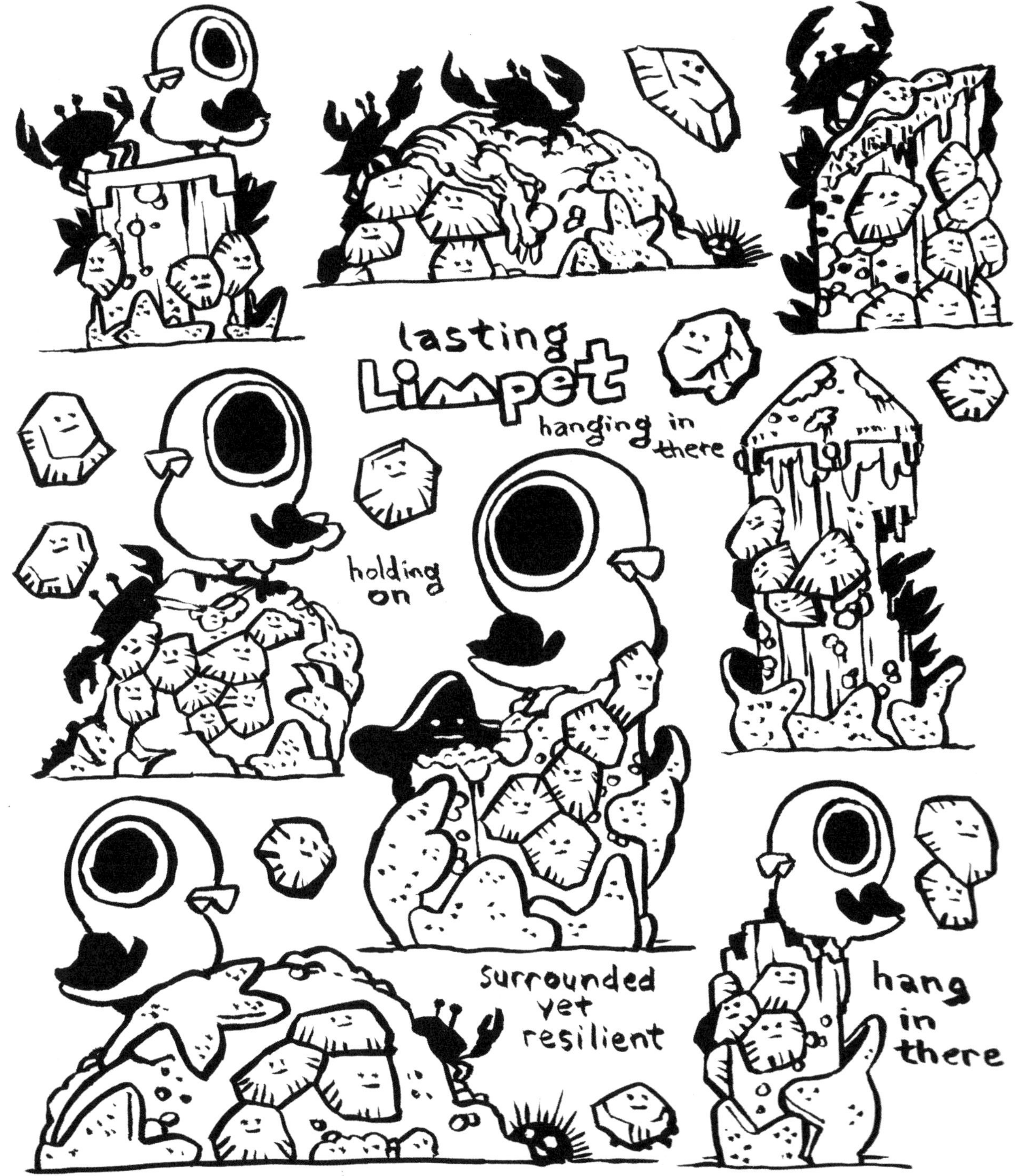
lasting
Limpet
hanging in there
holding on
surrounded yet resilient
hang in there

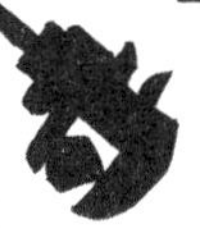

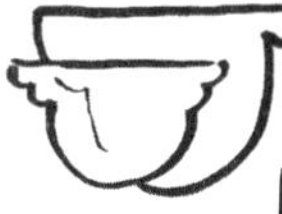

You've never seen
one like it.

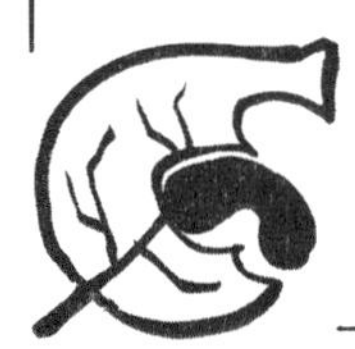

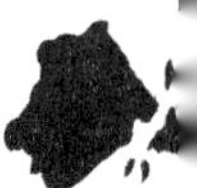

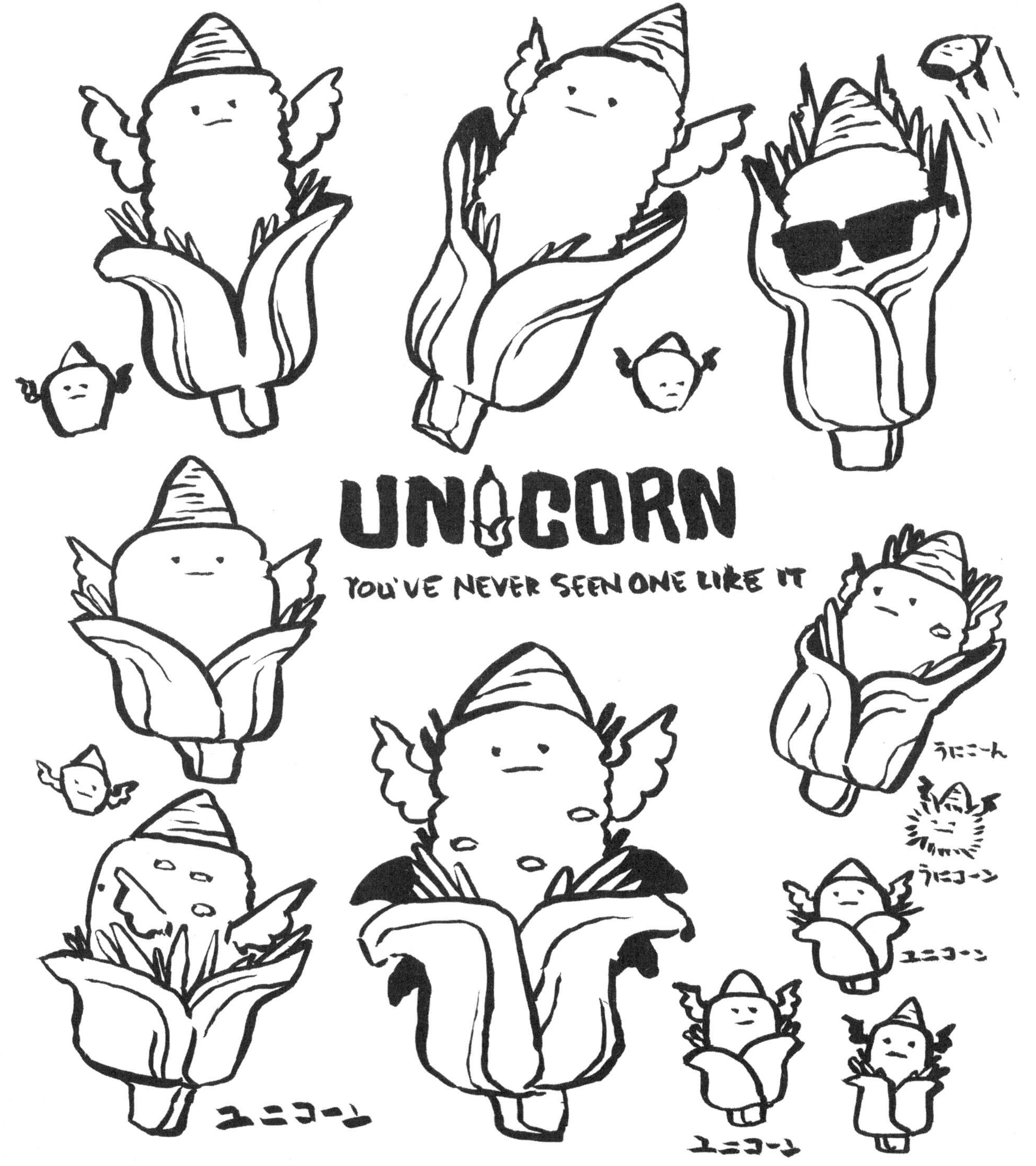
UNICORN
YOU'VE NEVER SEEN ONE LIKE IT
うにこーん
うにコーン
ユニコーン
ユニコーン
ユニコーン

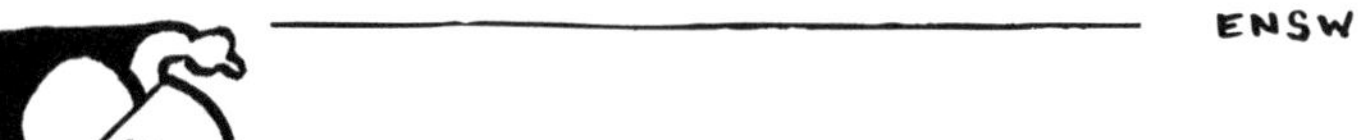

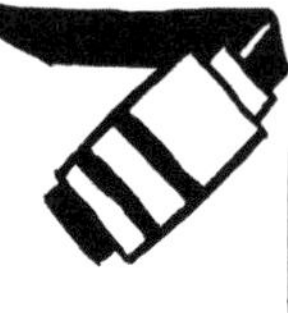

All's well that ends well.

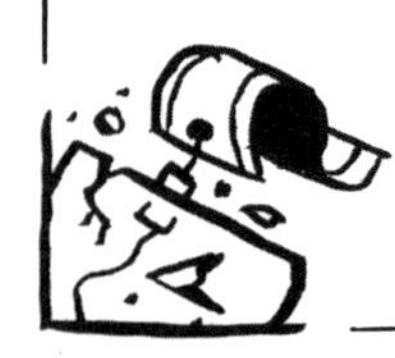

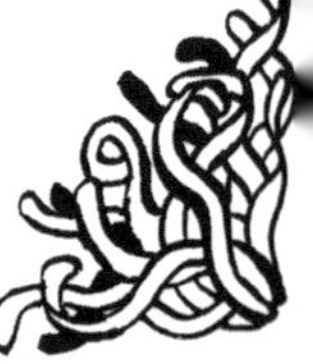

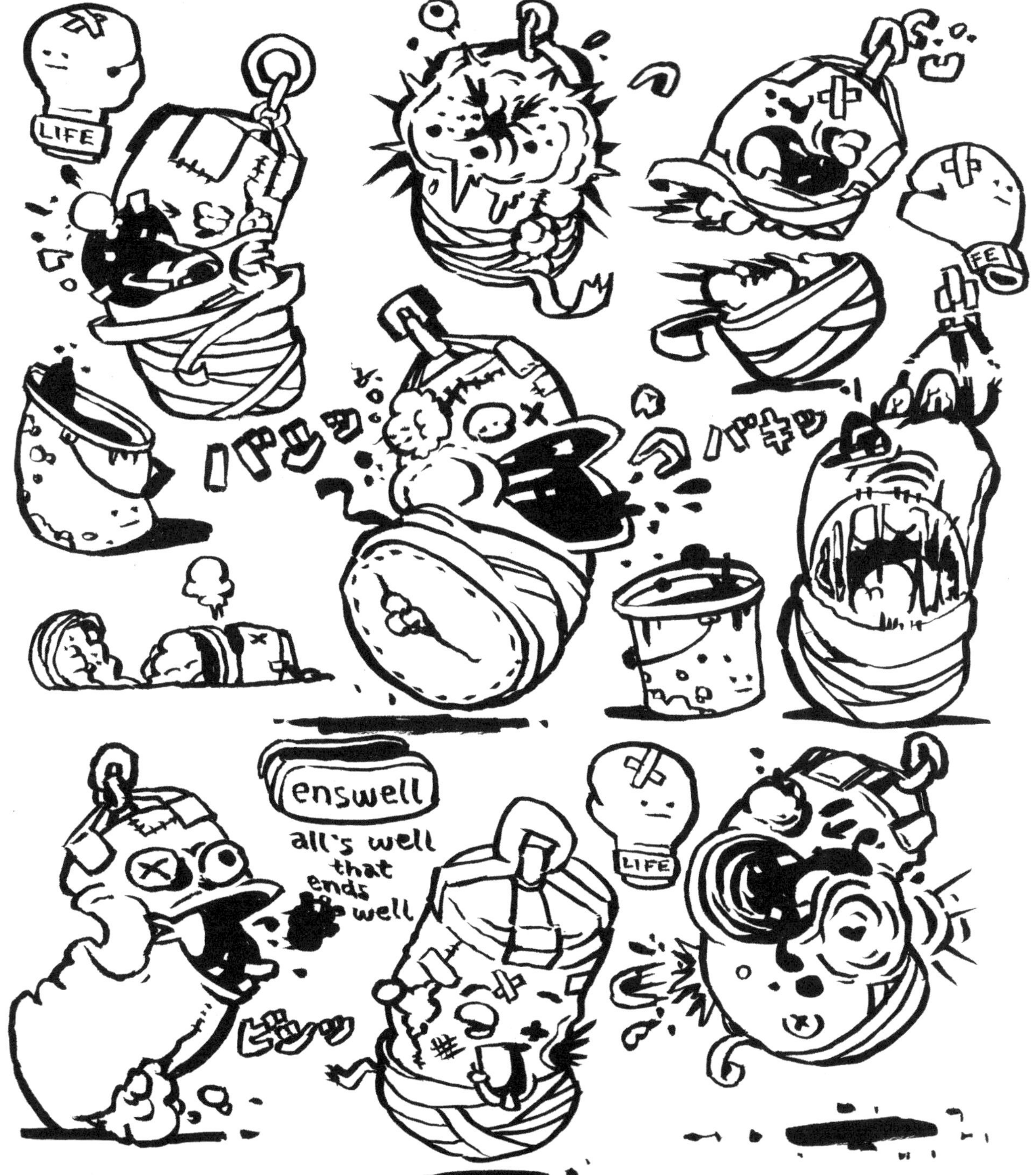
LIFE
パキッ
enswell
all's well
that
ends
well
LIFE

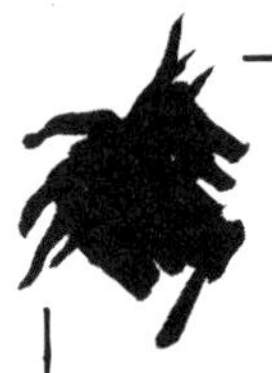

Protect your
local flying citrus.

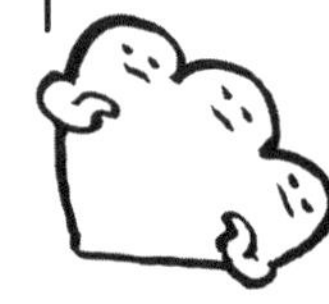

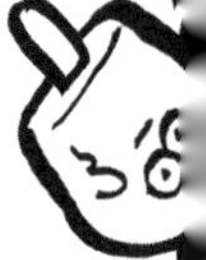

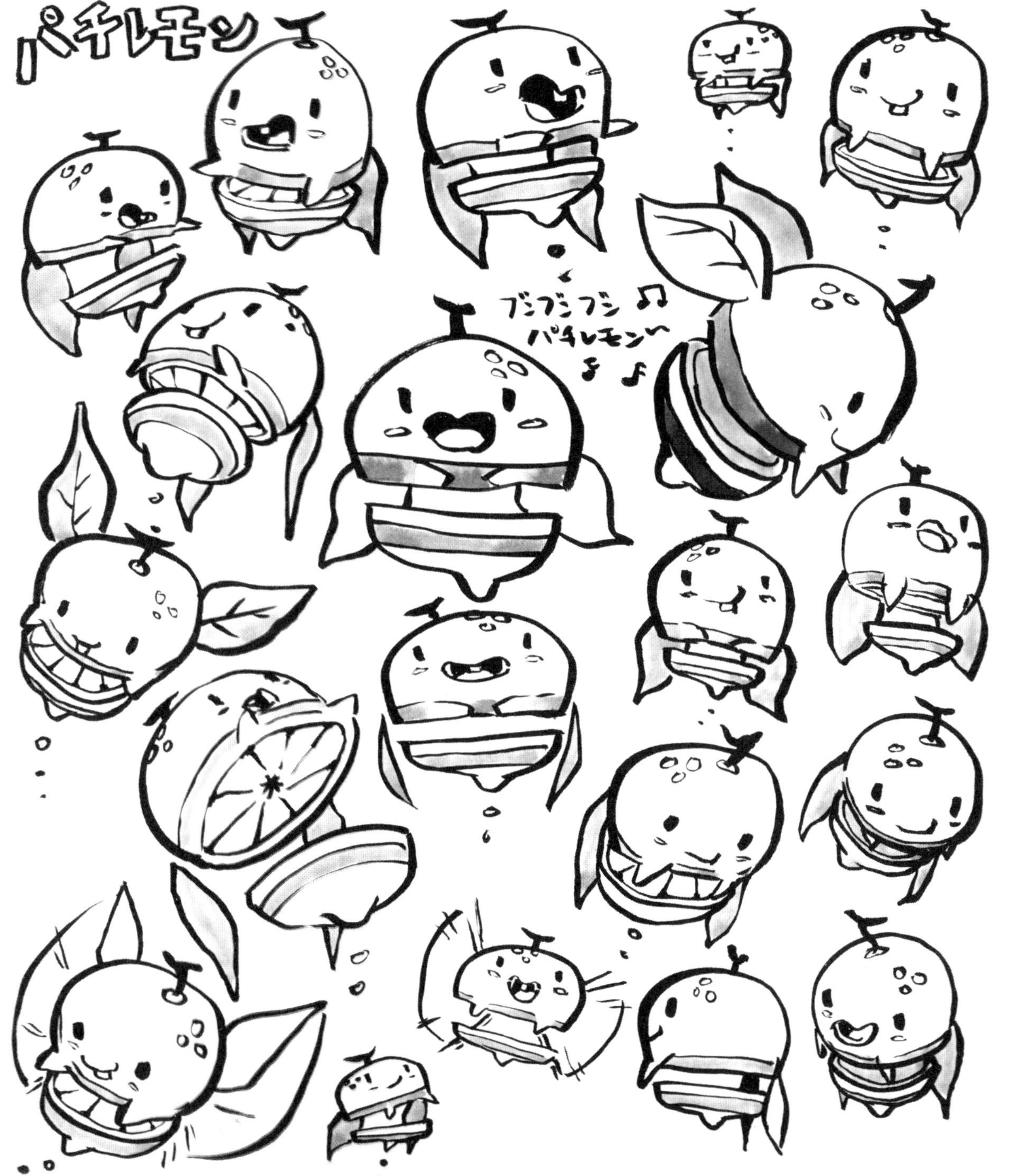
パチレモン
ブンブンブン♫
パチレモン〜♪

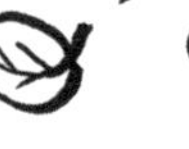

Choppy waters.

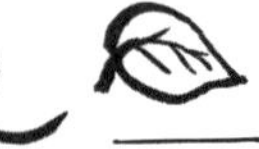

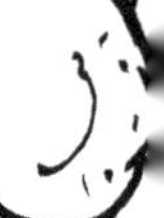

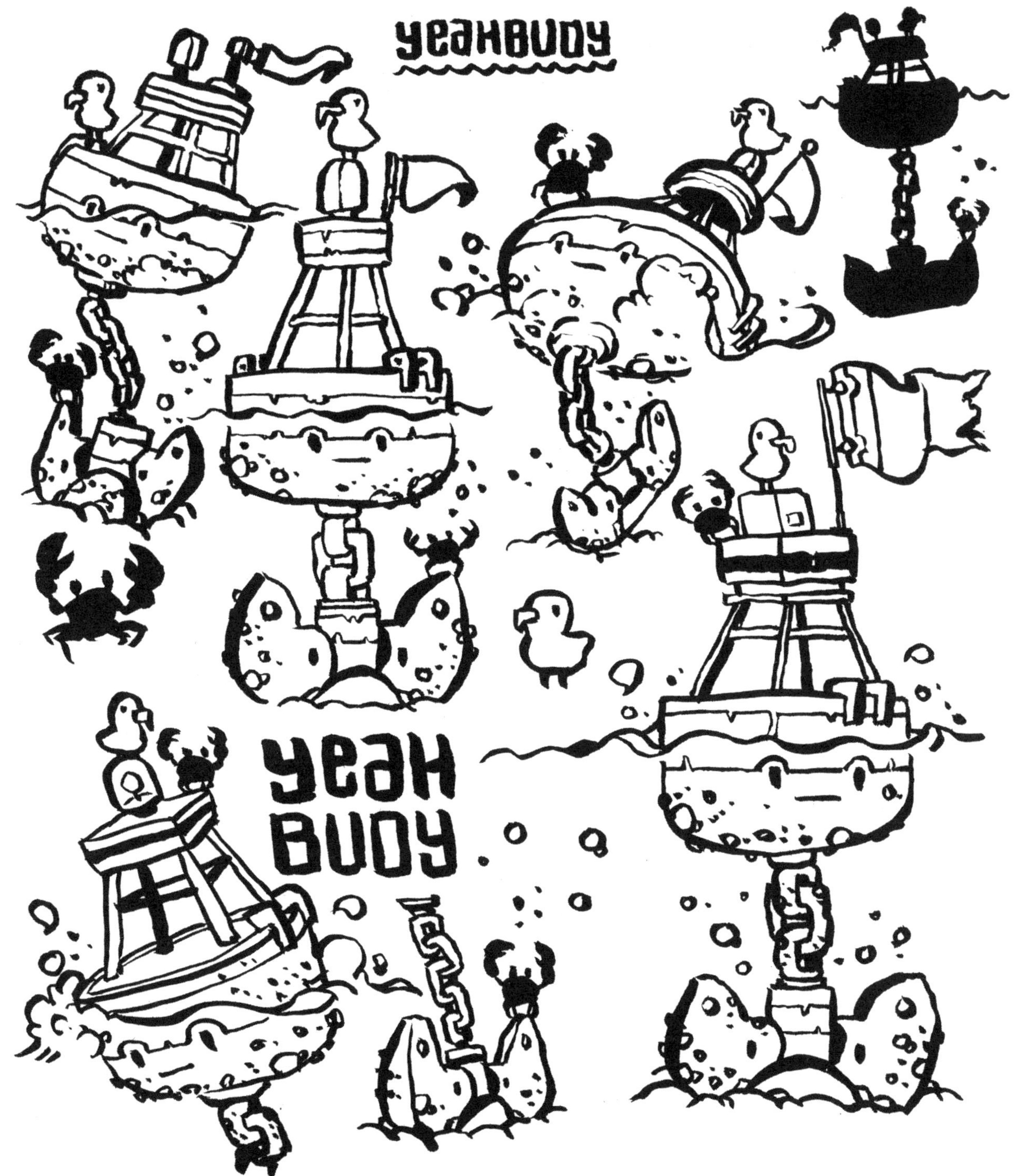
YEAHBUDY
YEAH BUDY

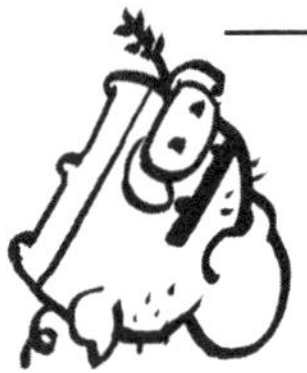

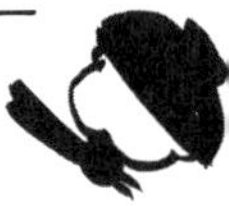

Positive Grilled Cheese oozes cheese and positivity, doing its best to cheer up Salty Tomato Soup.

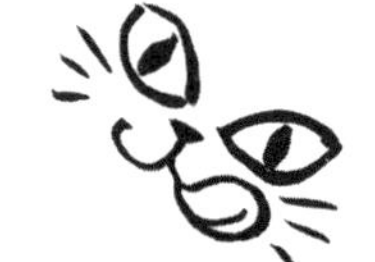

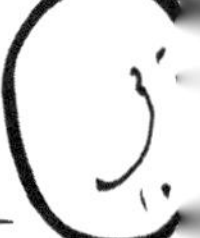

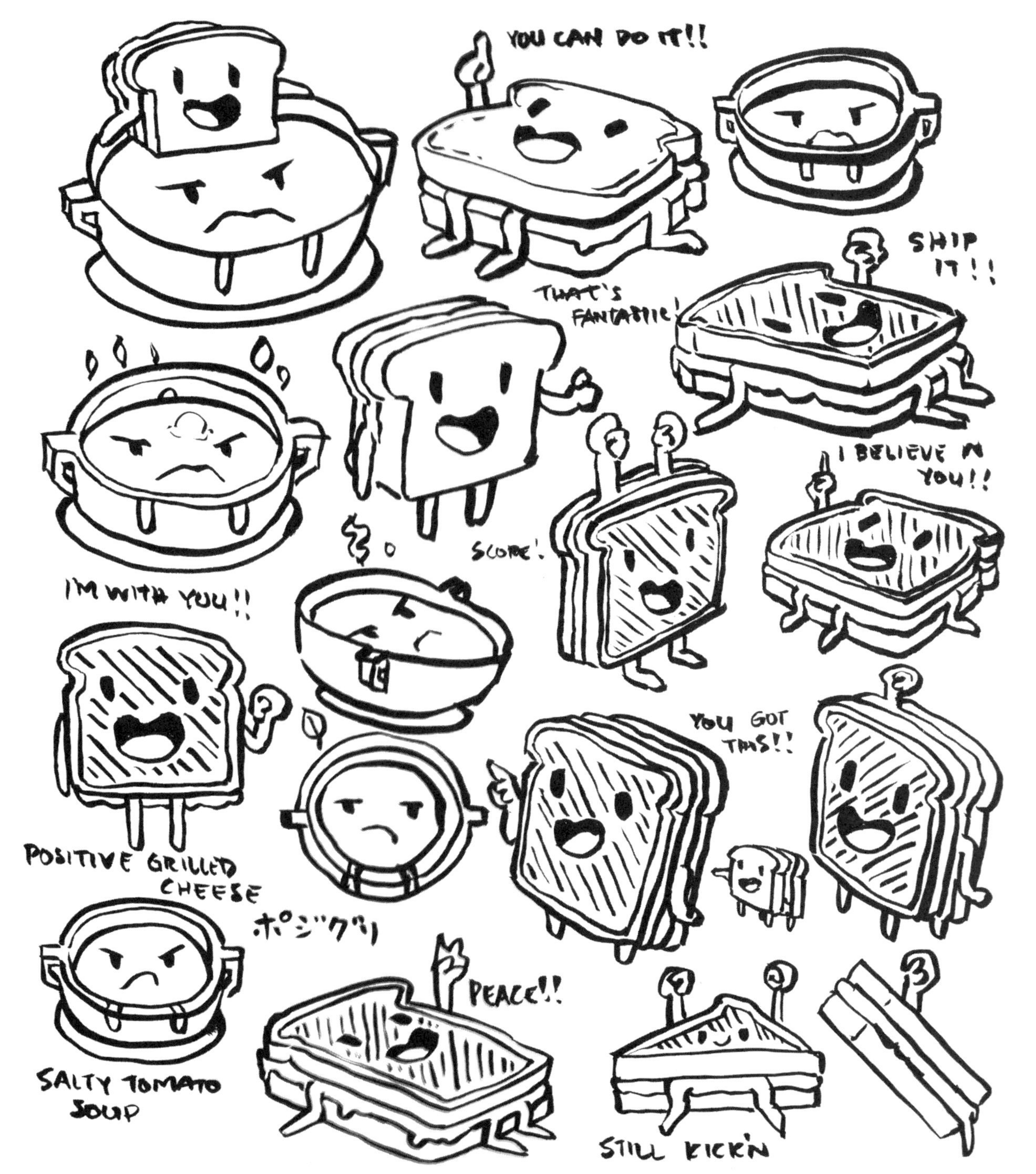
YOU CAN DO IT!!
SHIP IT!!
THAT'S FANTASTIC!
I BELIEVE IN YOU!!
SCORE!
I'M WITH YOU!!
YOU GOT THIS!!
POSITIVE GRILLED CHEESE
ポジグリ
PEACE!!
SALTY TOMATO SOUP
STILL KICK'N

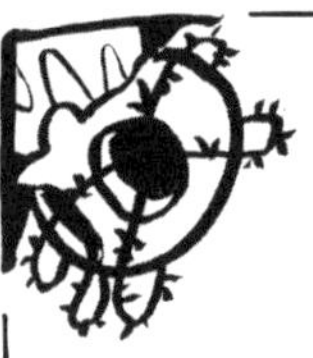

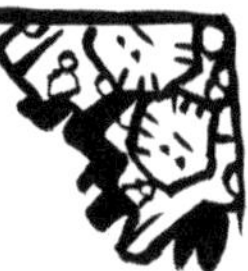

Opportunities cost.

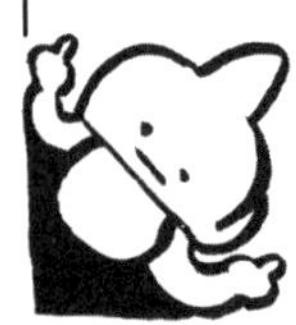

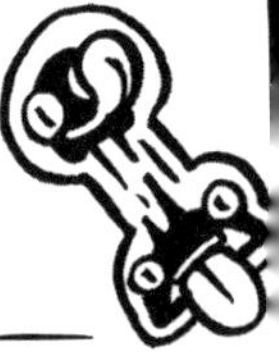

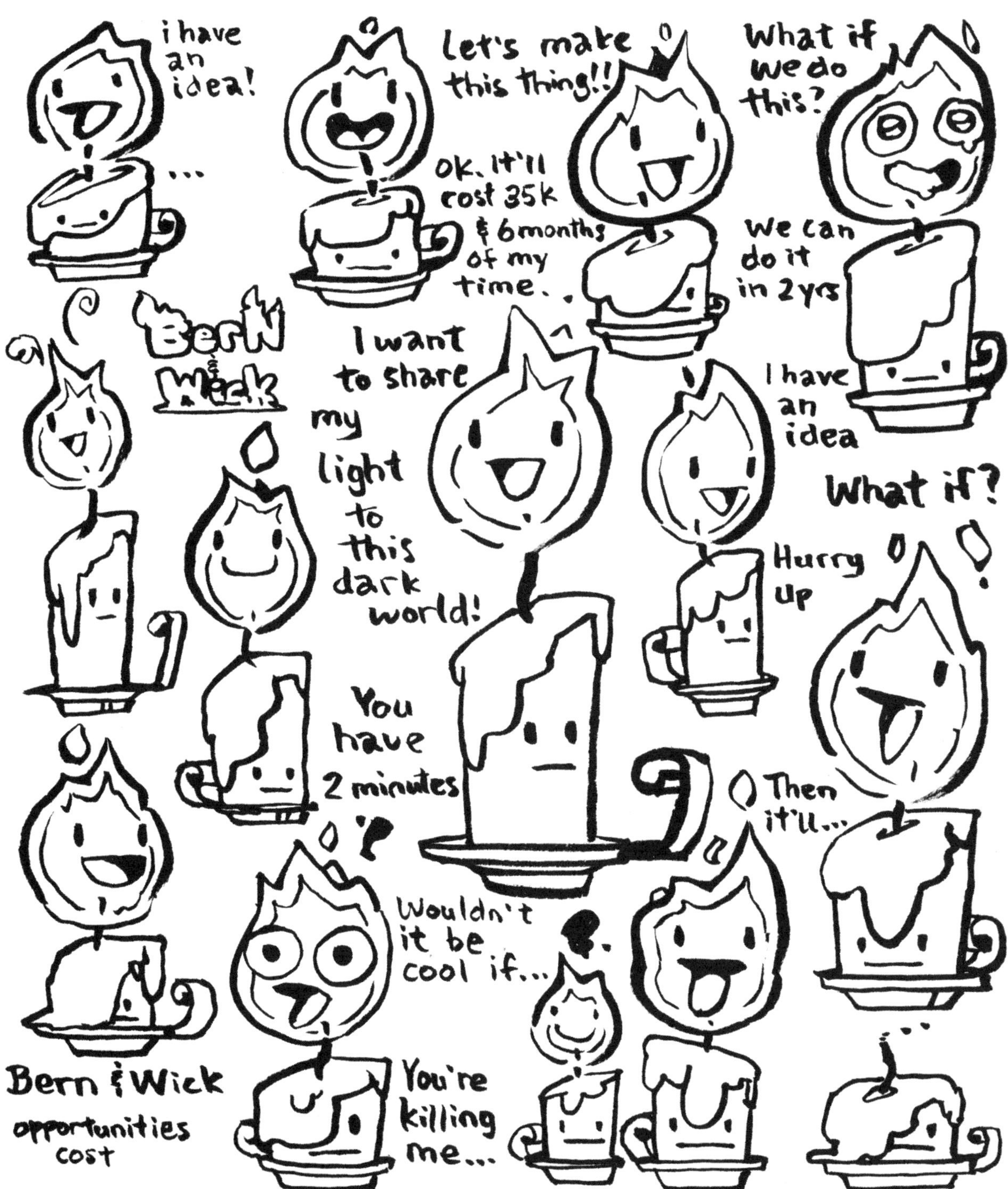
i have an idea!
...
Let's make this thing!!
OK. It'll cost 35K & 6months of my time..
What if we do this?
We can do it in 2yrs
Bern & Wick
I want to share my light to this dark world!
I have an idea
What if?
Hurry up
You have 2 minutes
Then it'll...
Wouldn't it be cool if...
Bern & Wick
opportunities cost
You're killing me...
...

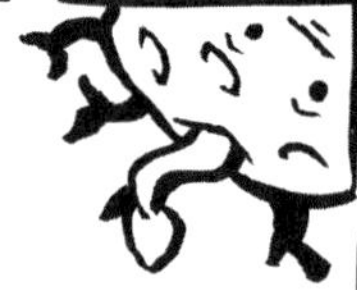

The friendly and unknowing assassin keeps inviting guests over for dinner.

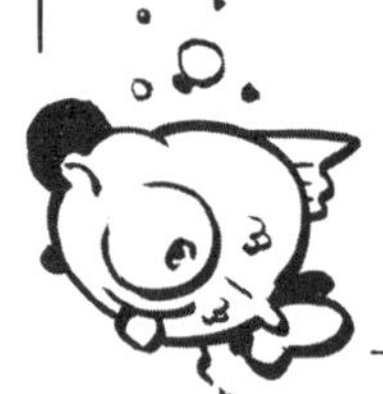

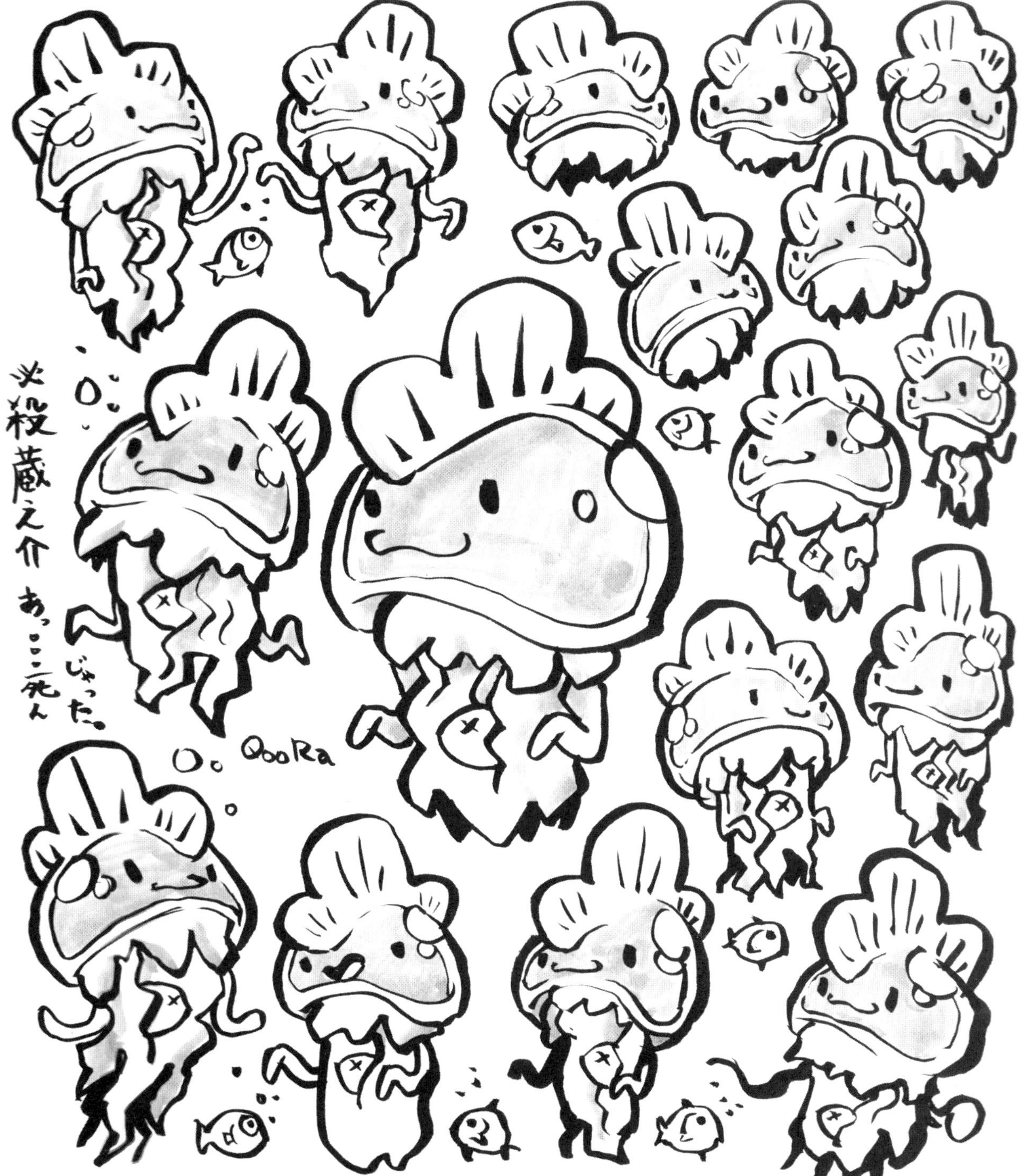
炎殺蔵之介
あっ…死んじゃった。
QooRa

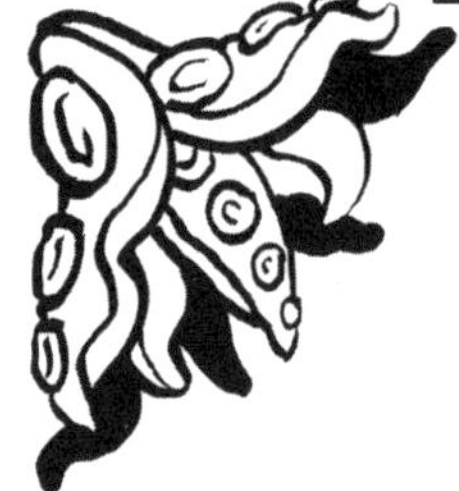

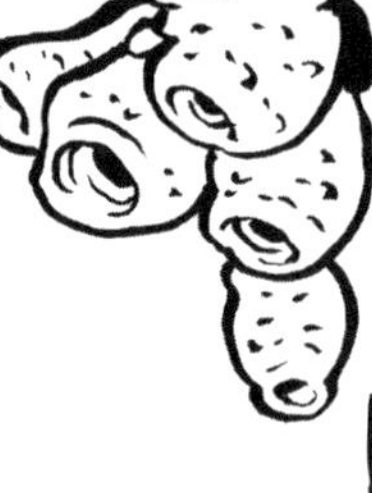

Misunderstood.

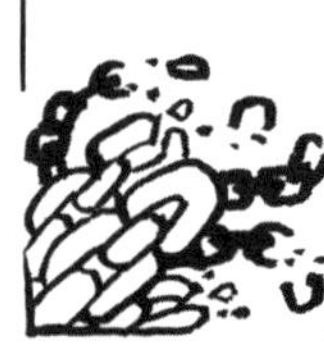

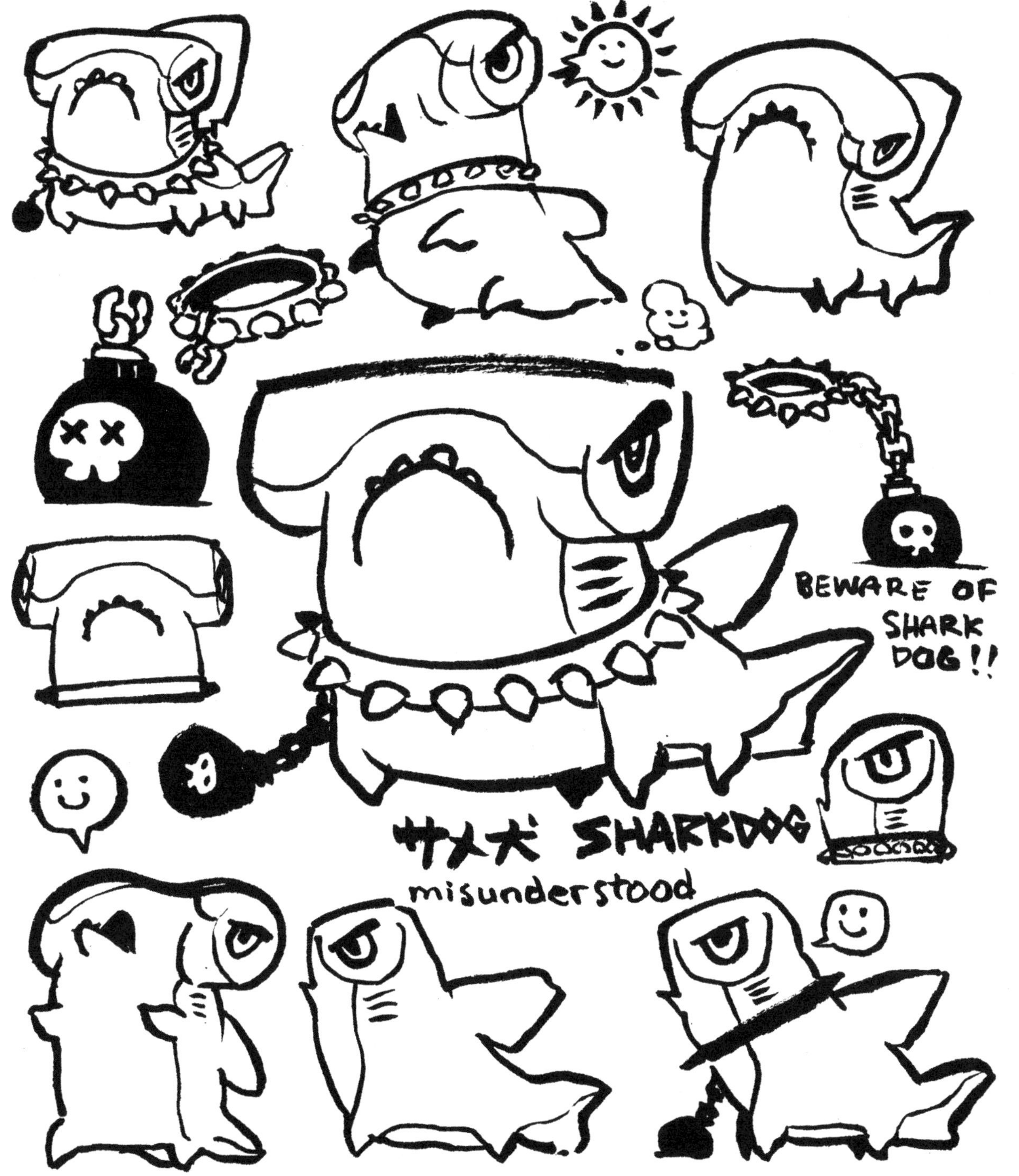
BEWARE OF SHARK DOG!!
サメ犬 SHARKDOG
misunderstood

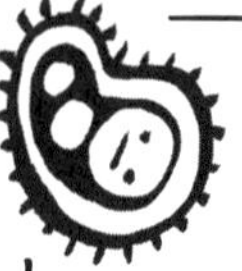

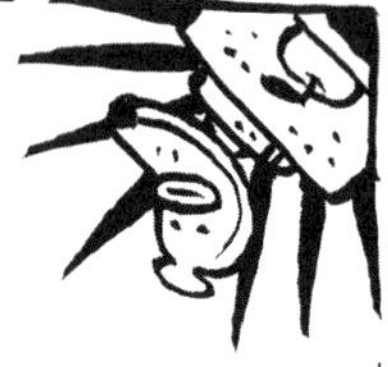

Motivated solely by a carrot, this mini pet is easy to please.

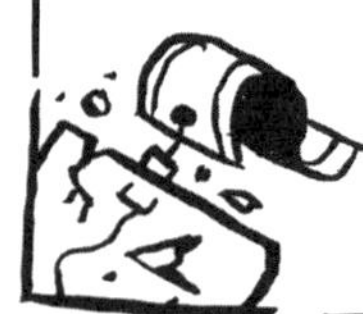

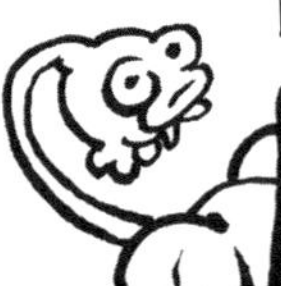

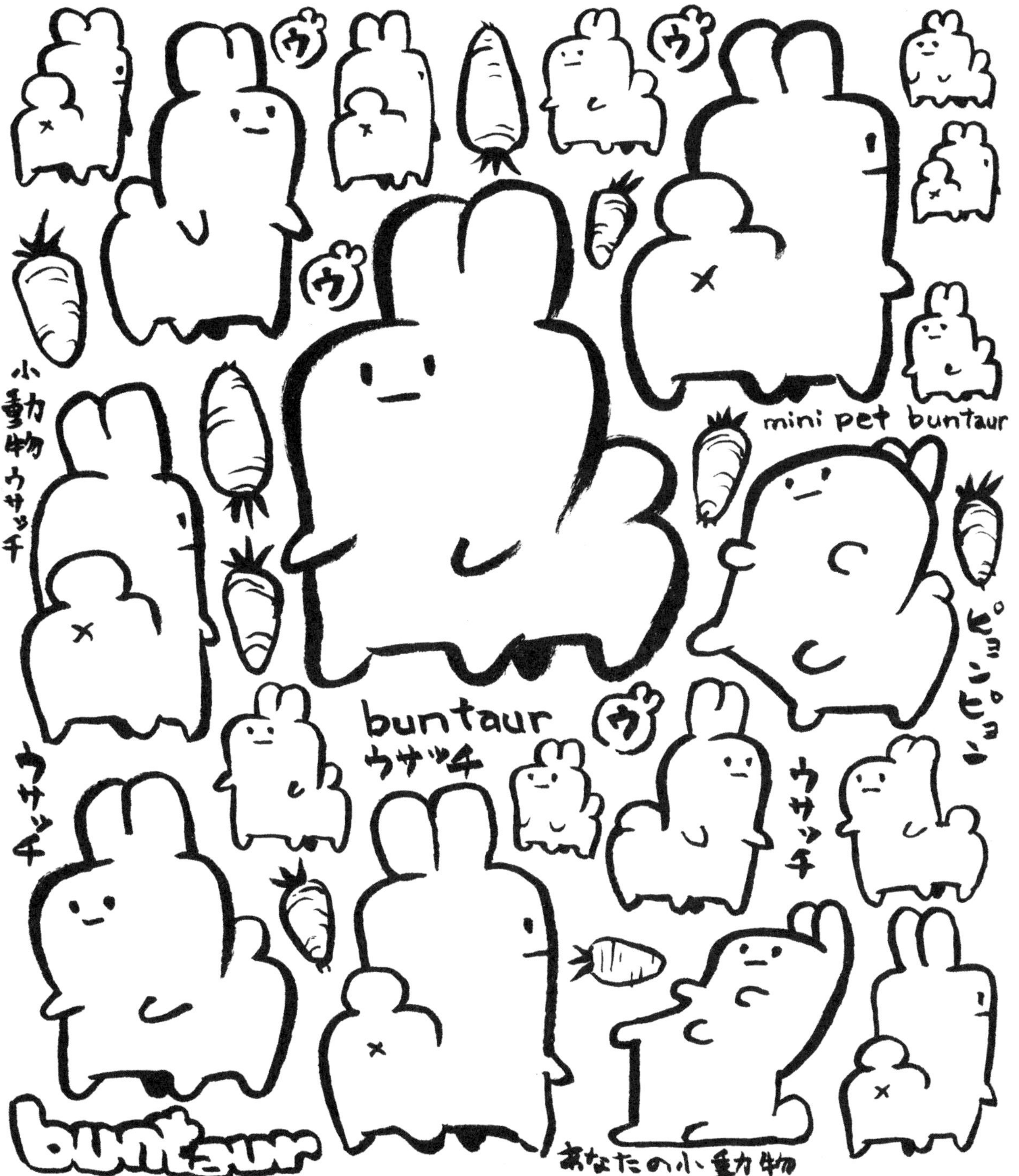

ウ
ウ
ウ
小動物ウサッチ
mini pet buntaur
ピョンピョン
buntaur
ウサッチ
ウ
ウサッチ
ウサッチ
buntaur
あなたの小動物

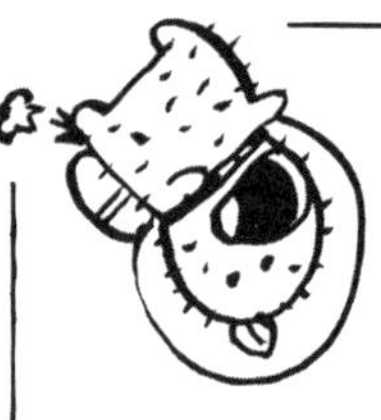

A chick who just hatched and the whole world is ahead of it.

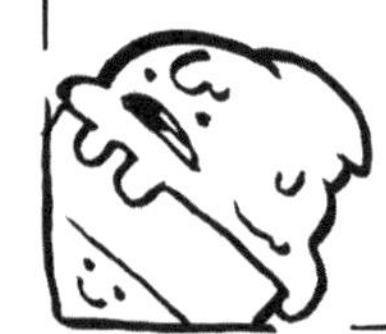

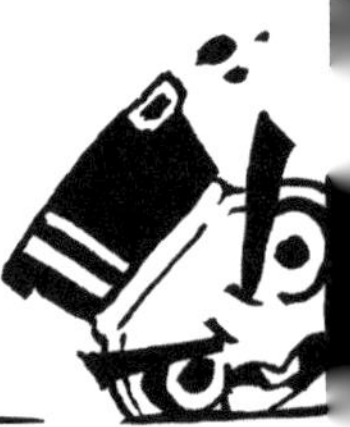

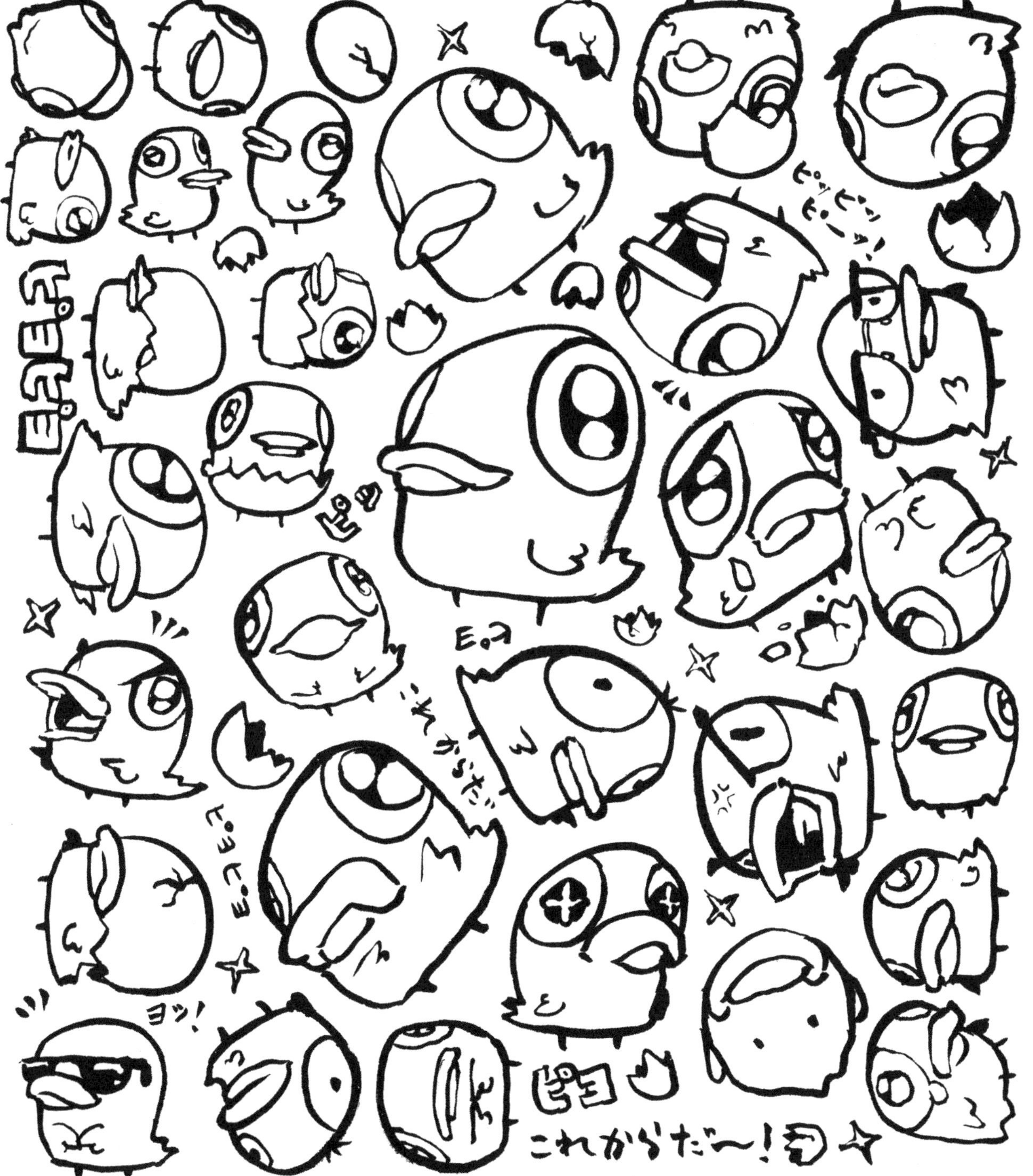

ピッピッ
ピーッ!
ピヨピヨ
これからだ!
ピヨピヨ
ヨッ!
ピヨ
これからだ〜!

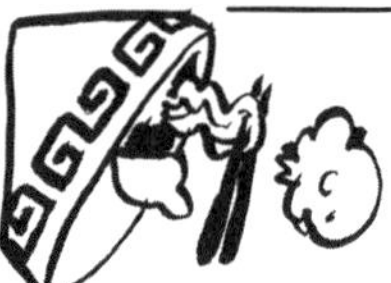

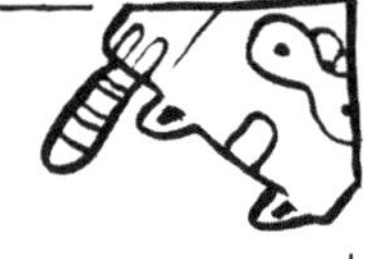

Floppycat enjoys
catching the wind and
flying about to
the next adventure.

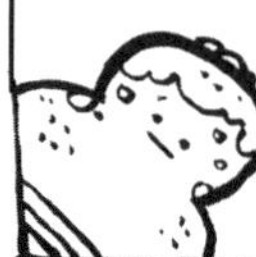

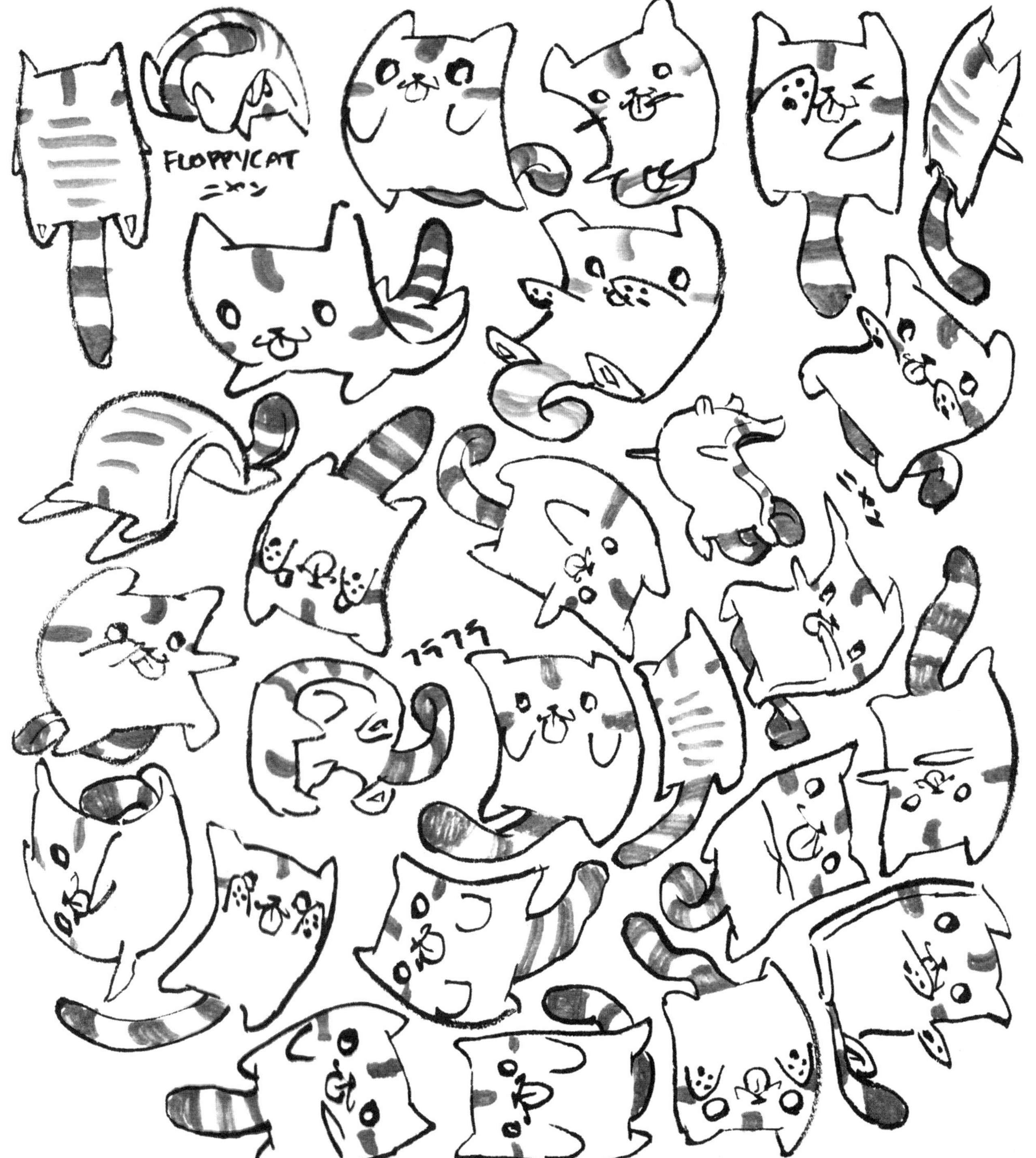
FLOPPYCAT
ニャン
ニャン
フラフラ

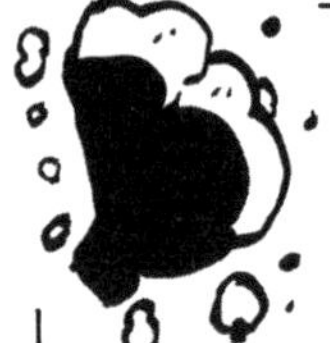

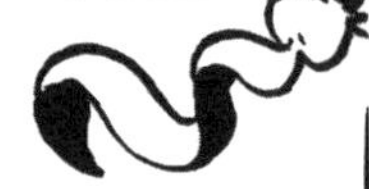

Now you see it...

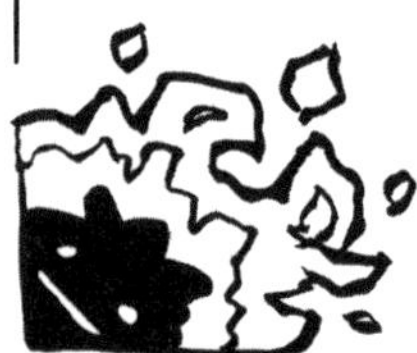

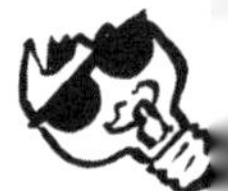

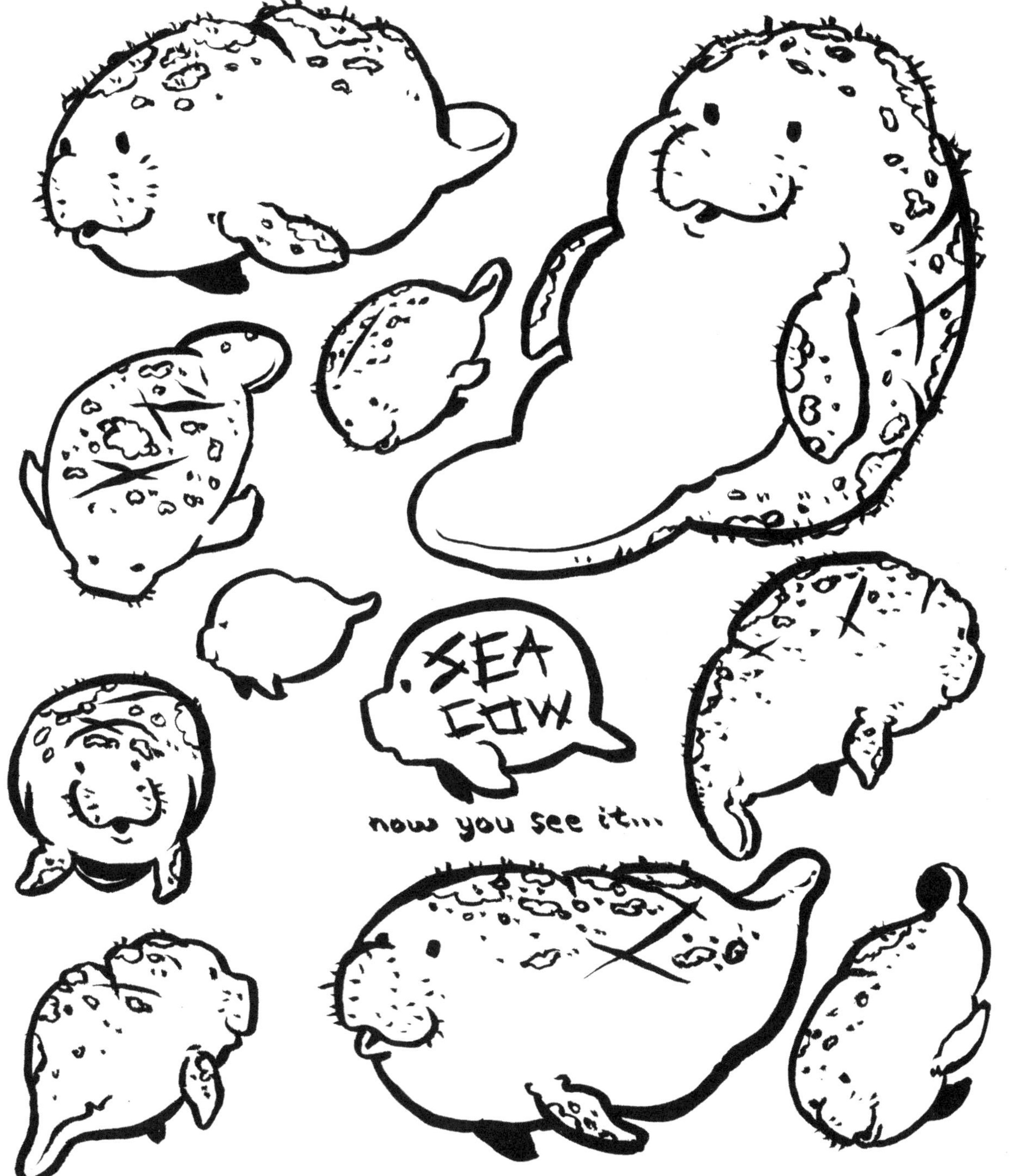

SEA COW
now you see it...

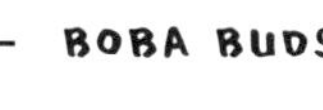

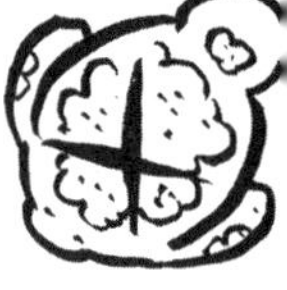

Tappy, Kory, and Bob are friends of summer.

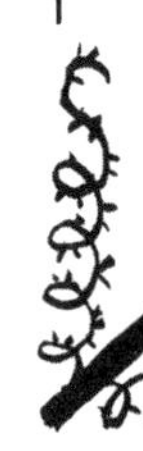

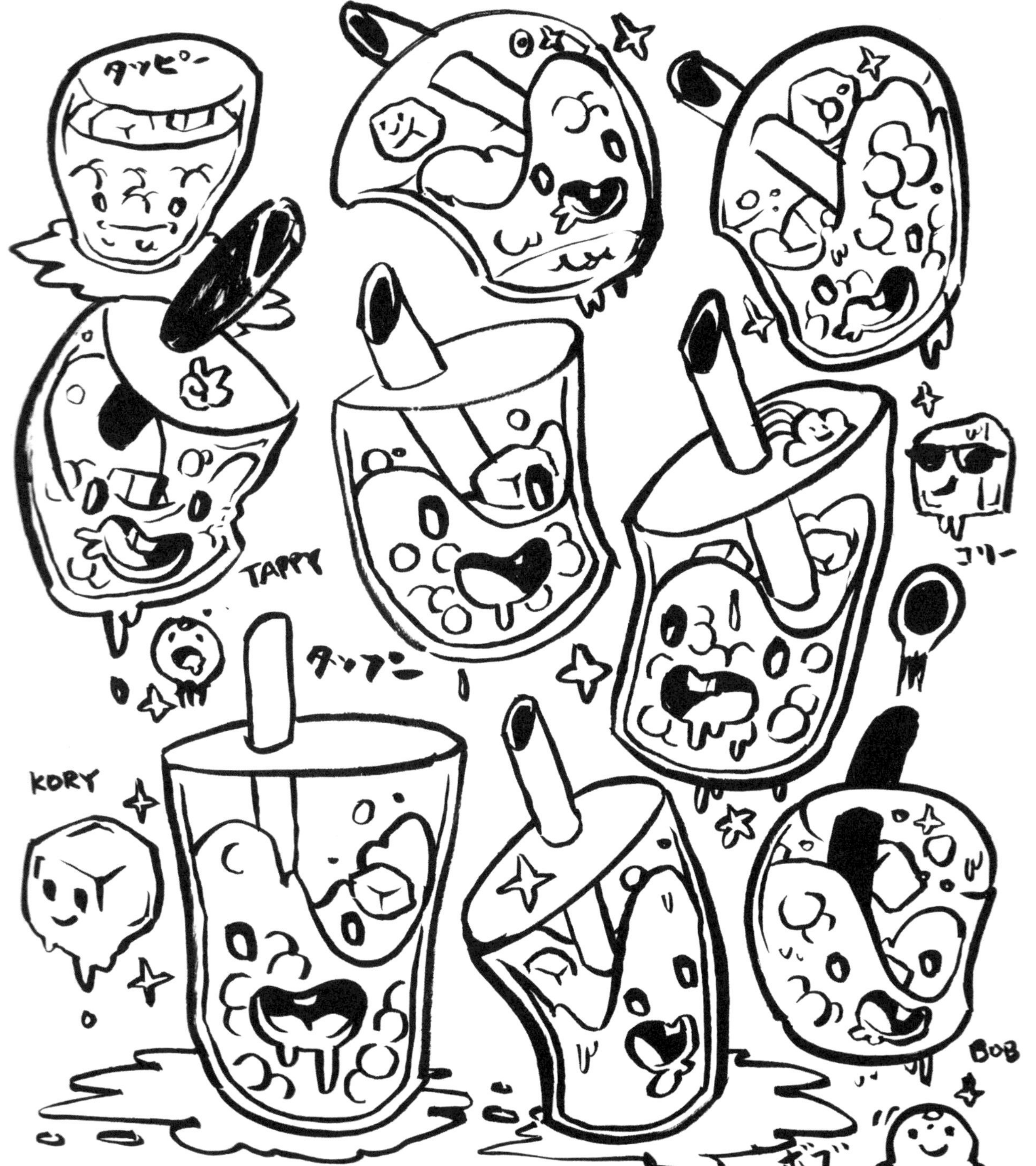
タッピー
TAPPY
コリー
KORY
BOB
ボブ

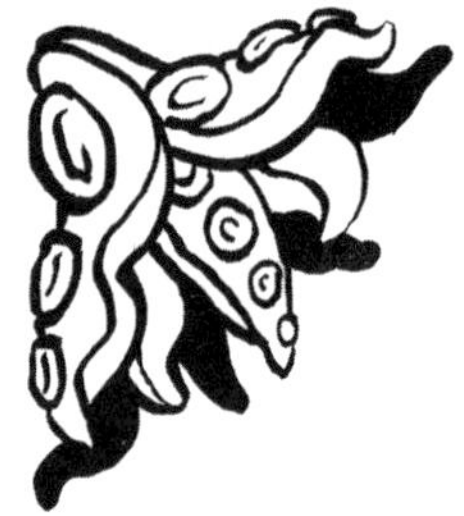

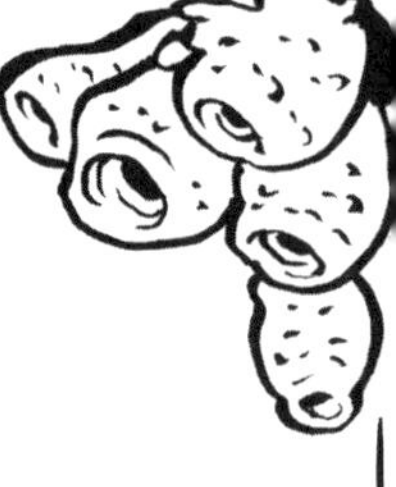

Undiscovered
greatness.

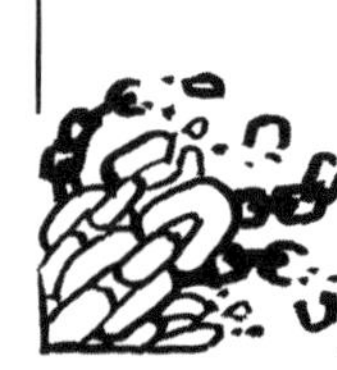

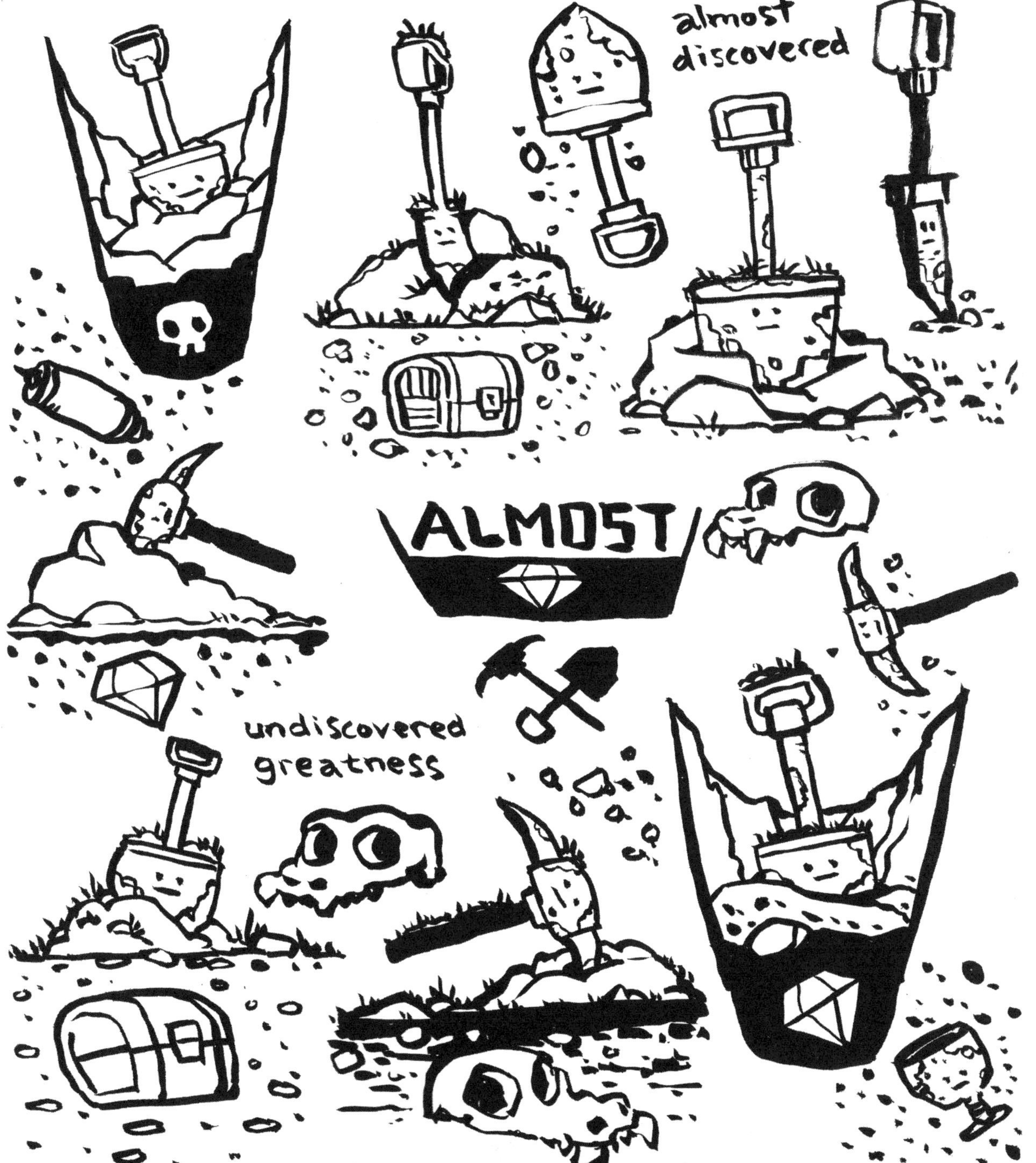
almost discovered
ALMOST
undiscovered greatness

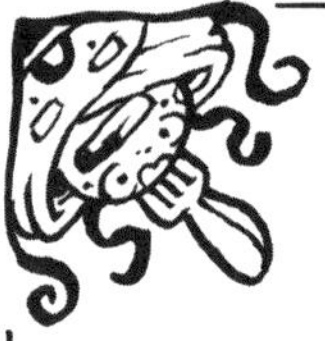

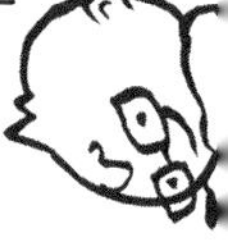

Fish of a feather.

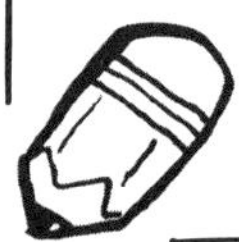

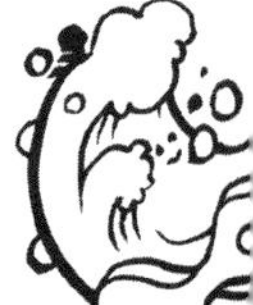

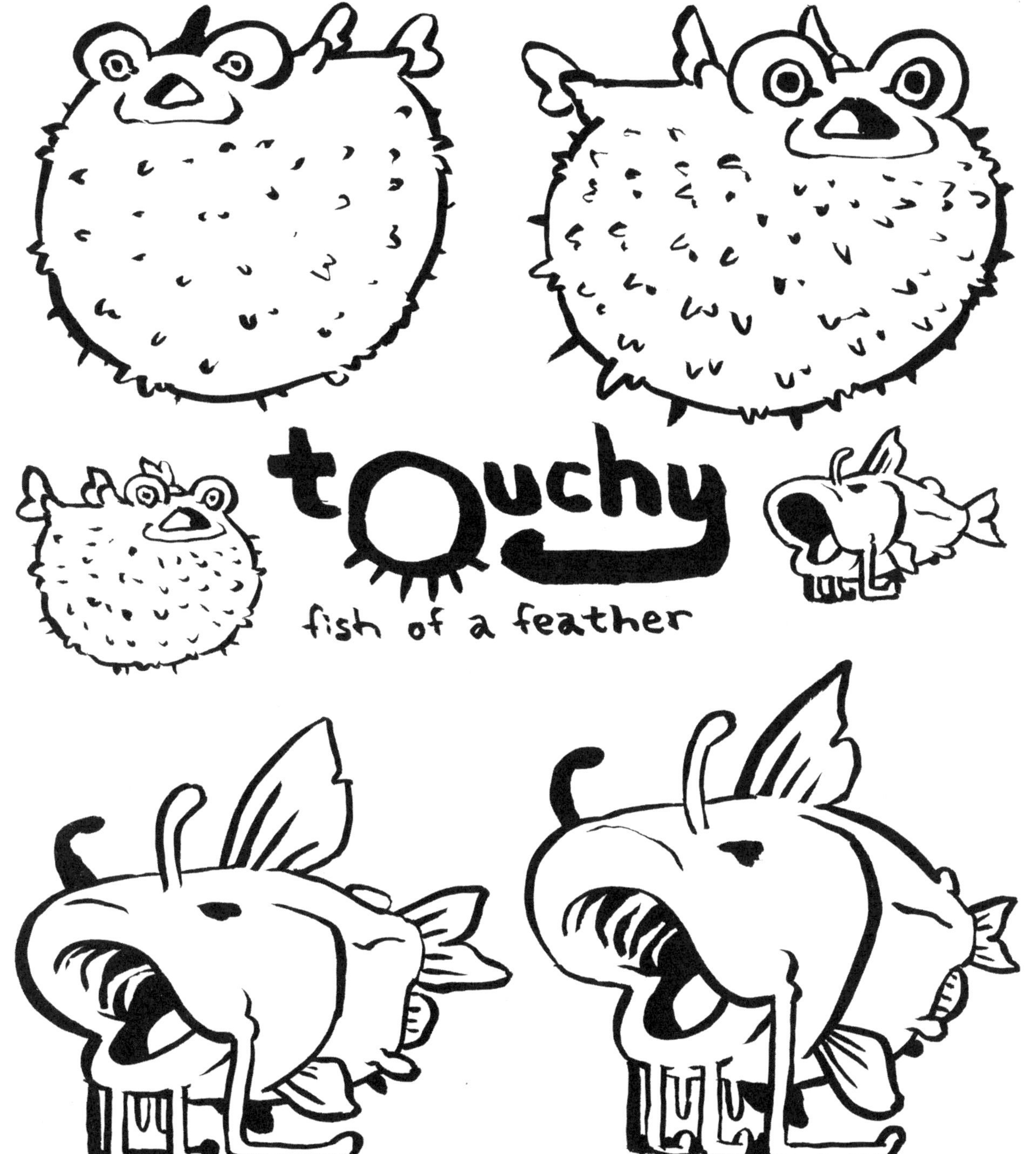
touchy
fish of a feather

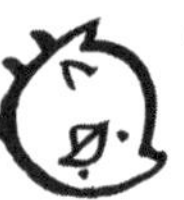

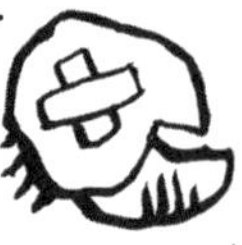

Spacesuit tester,
poking holes.

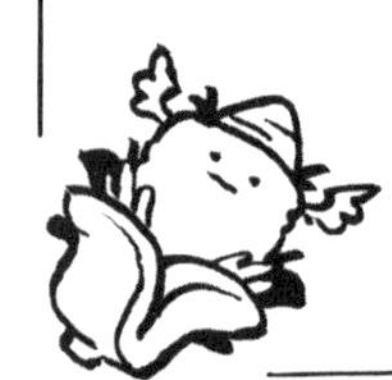

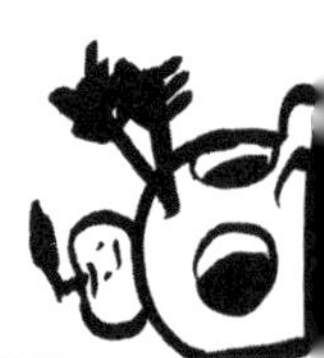

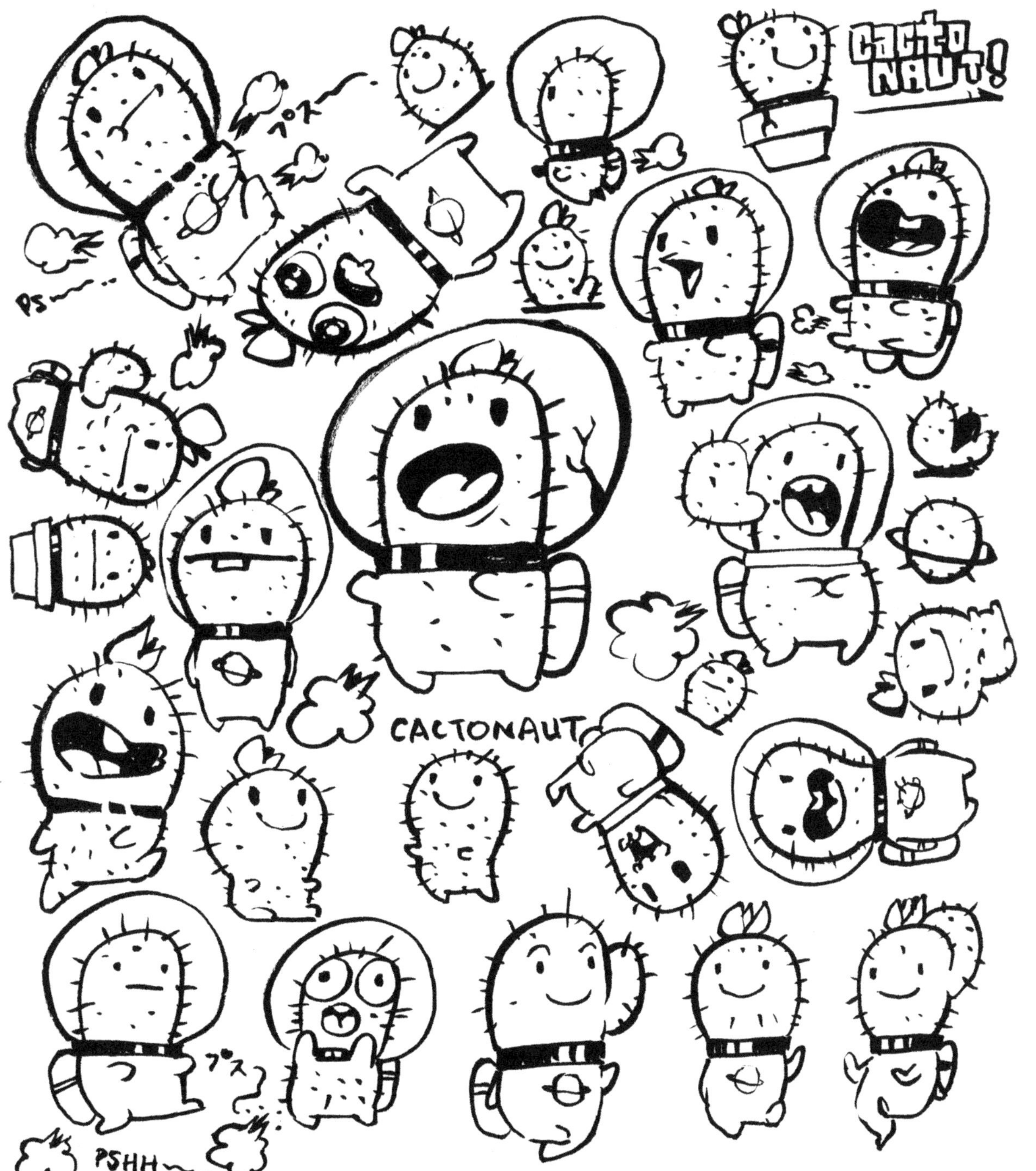

cacto NAUT!
プスー
PS
CACTONAUT
プス
PSHH

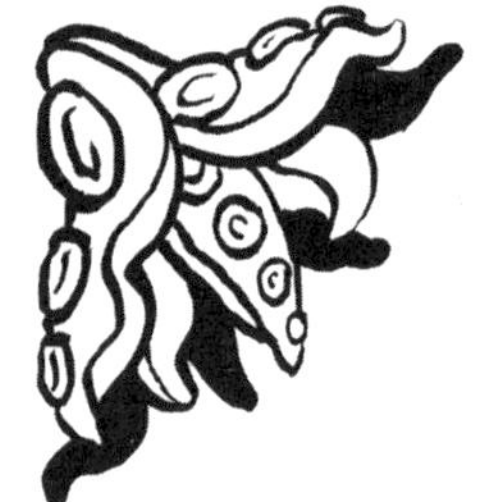

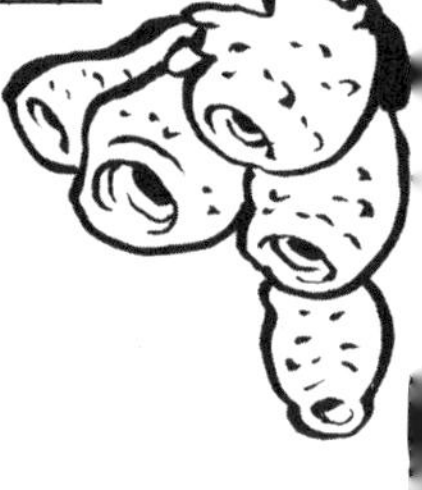

Mr. Crisp, Sweetie,
and Flake. The trio
that'll plump... you up!

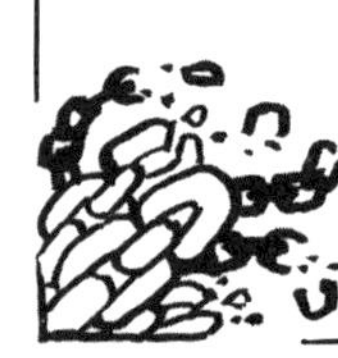

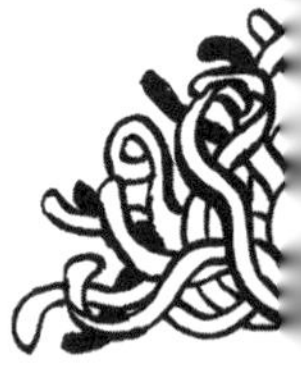

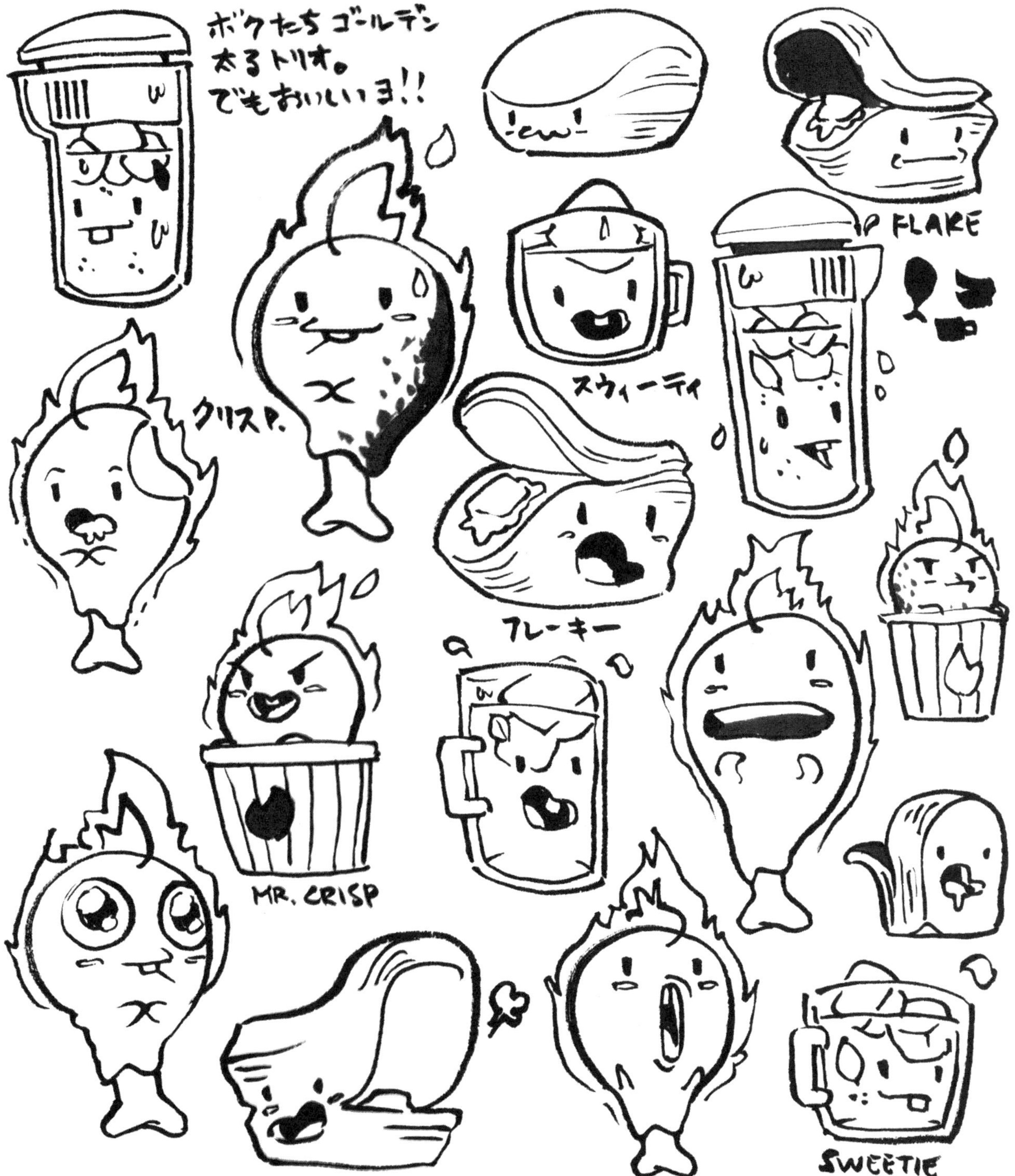

ボクたち ゴールデン
太るトリオ。
でもおいしいヨ!!
FLAKE
クリスP.
スウィーティ
フレーキー
MR. CRISP
SWEETIE

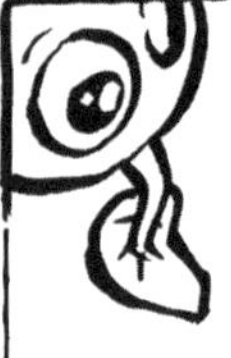

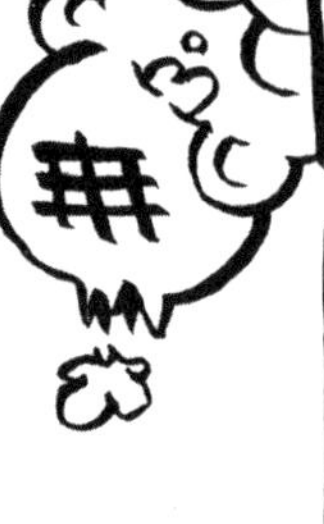

Welcome to
flavortown.

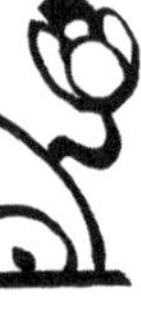

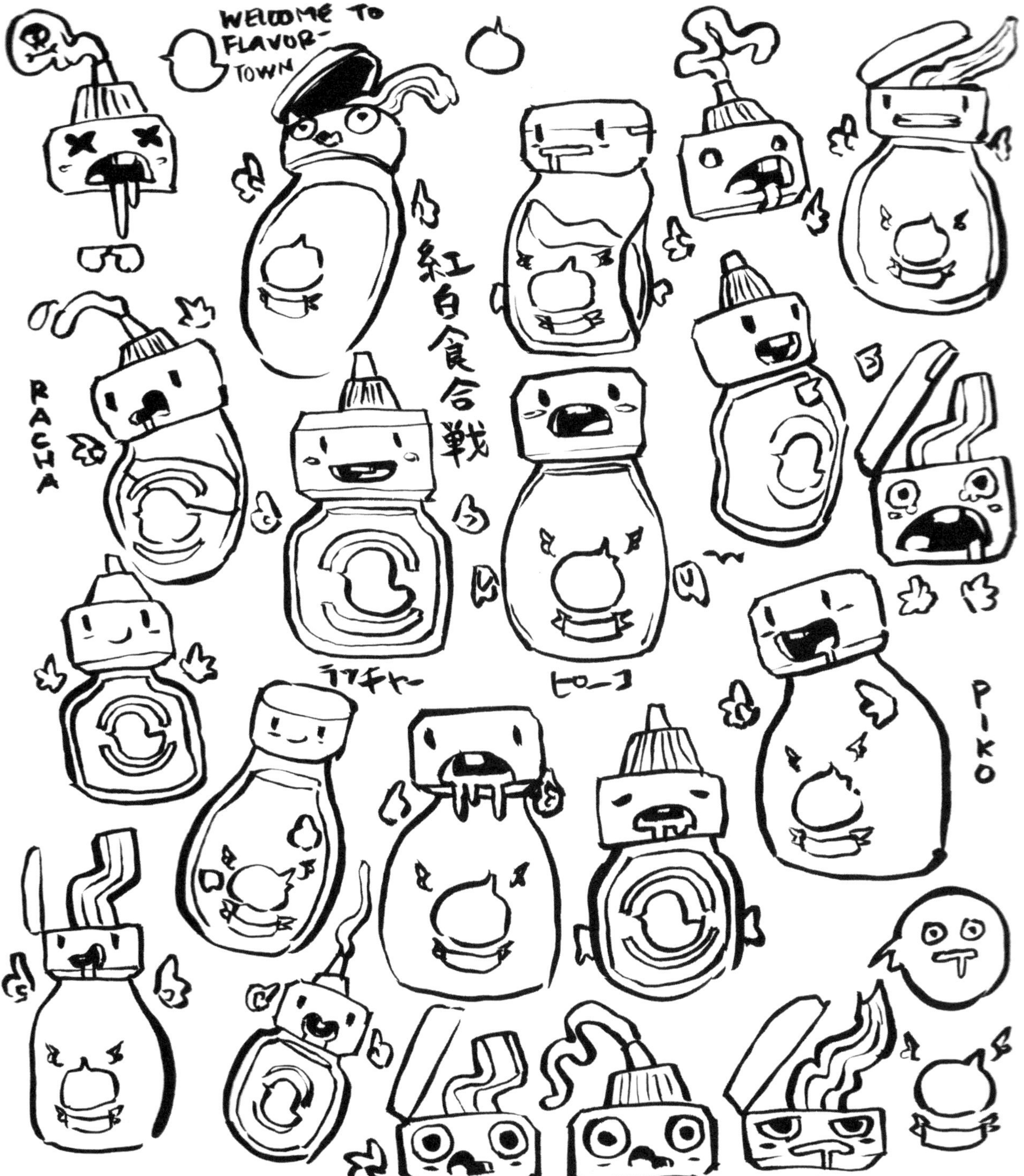
WELCOME TO FLAVOR-TOWN
紅白食合戦
RACHA
ラァチャー
ピーコ
PIKO

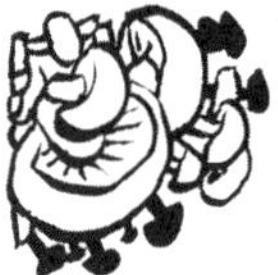

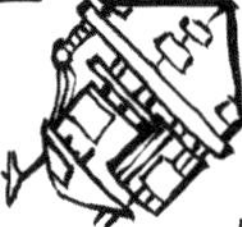

Representing all.

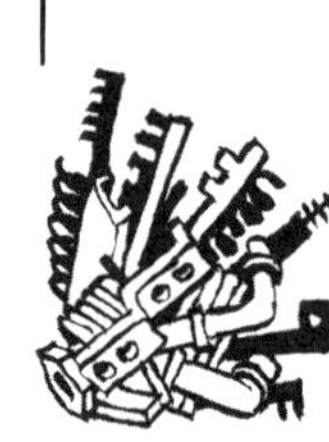

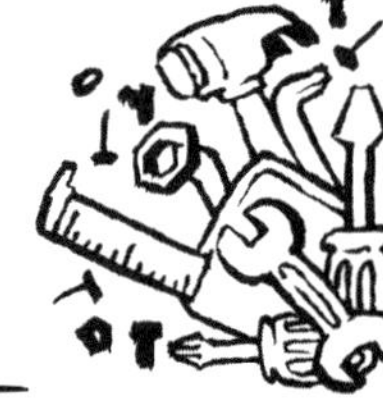

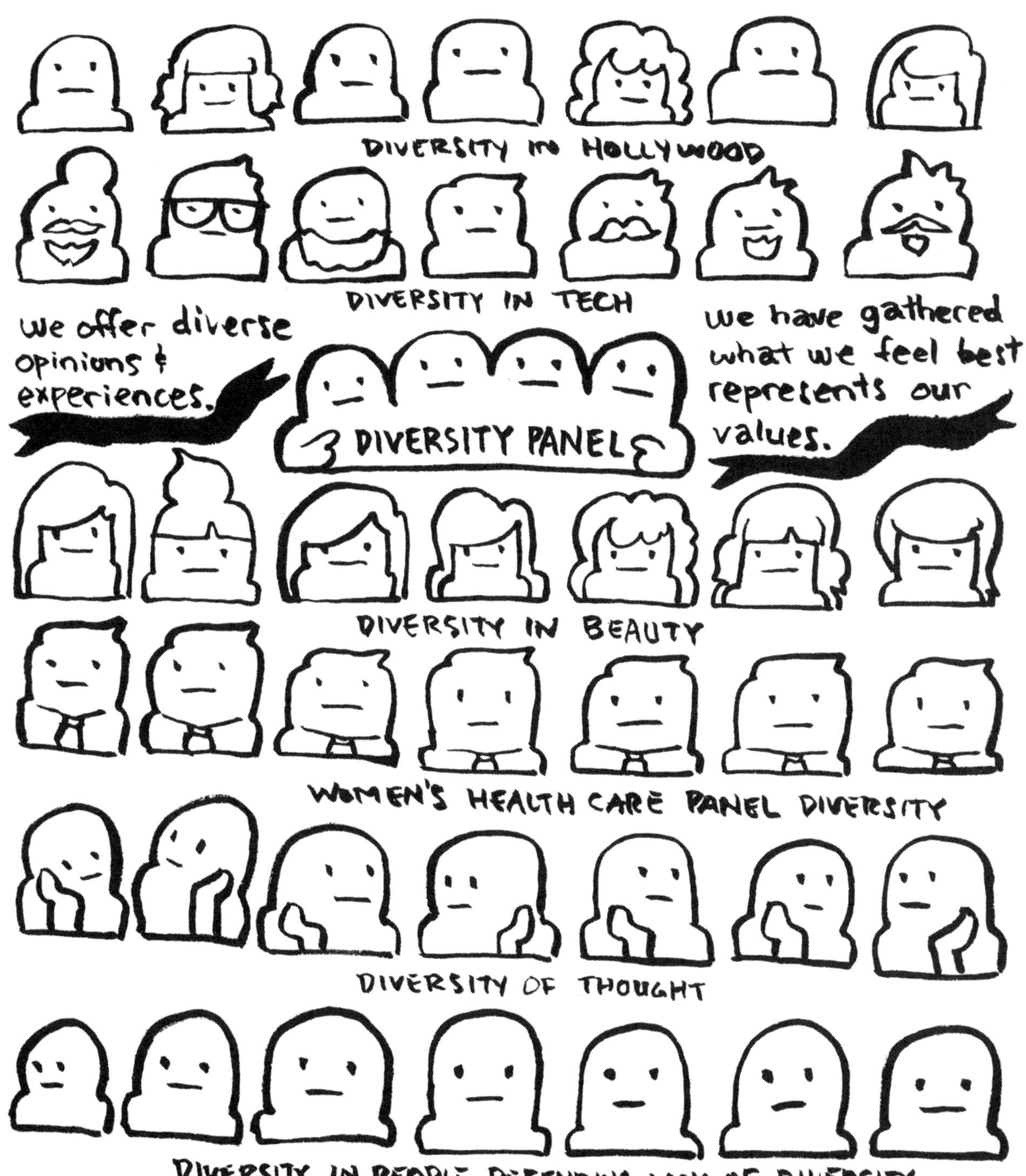
DIVERSITY IN HOLLYWOOD
DIVERSITY IN TECH
we offer diverse opinions & experiences.
DIVERSITY PANEL
we have gathered what we feel best represents our values.
DIVERSITY IN BEAUTY
WOMEN'S HEALTH CARE PANEL DIVERSITY
DIVERSITY OF THOUGHT
DIVERSITY IN PEOPLE DEFENDING LACK OF DIVERSITY

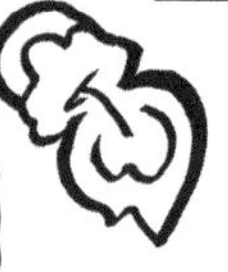

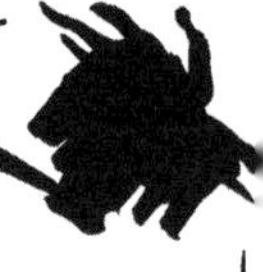

Abandoned dreams.

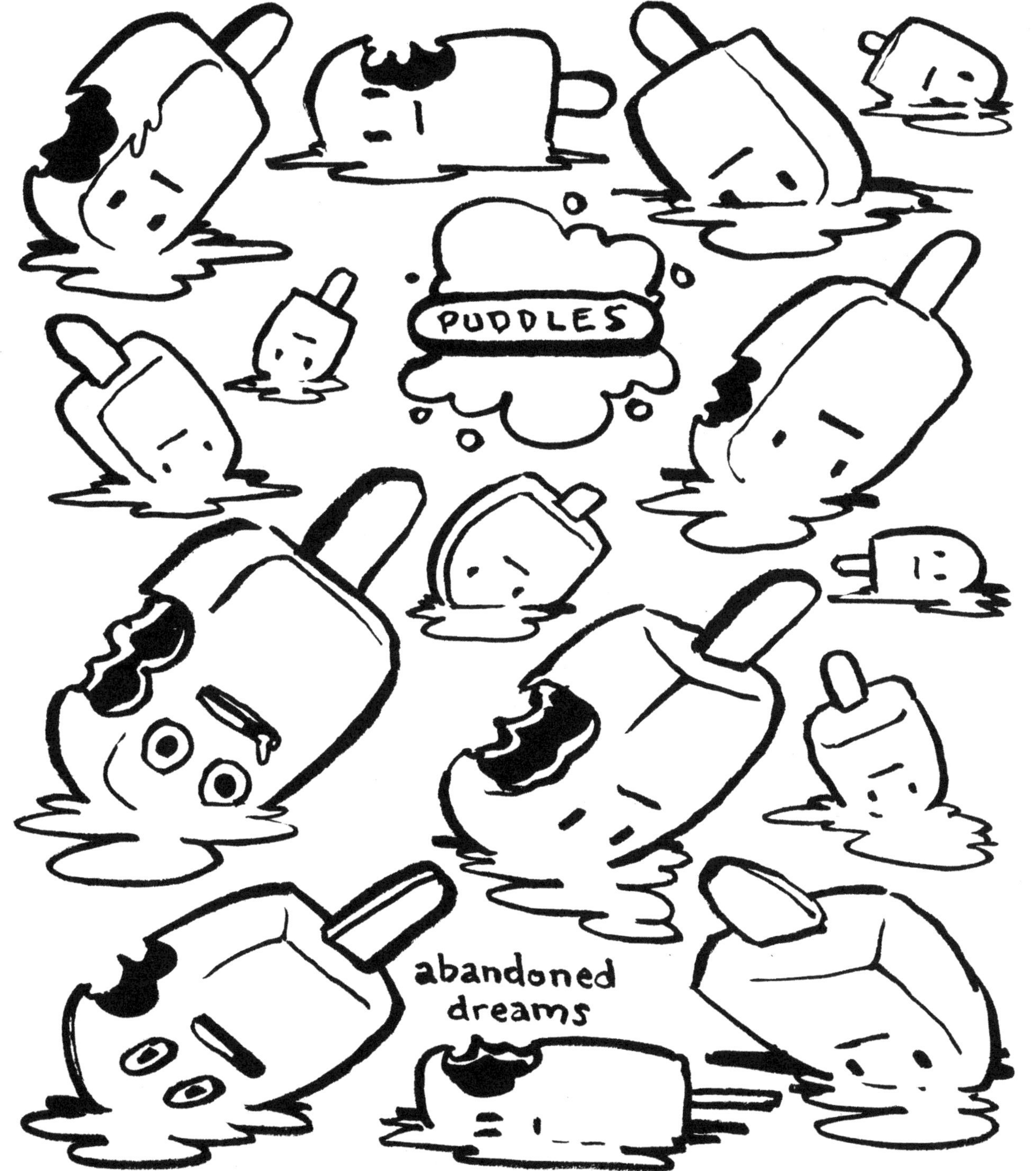
PUDDLES
abandoned dreams

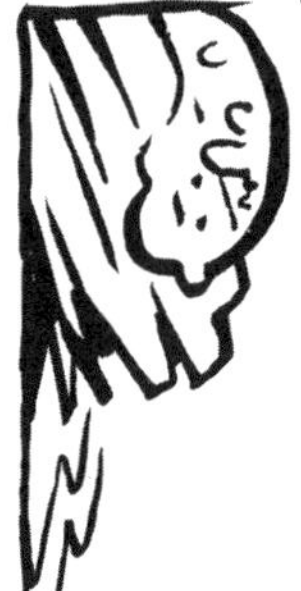

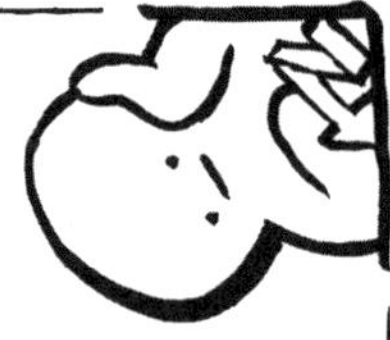

Unknown known.

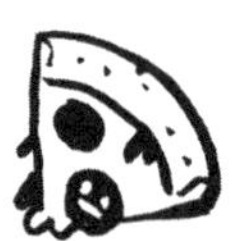

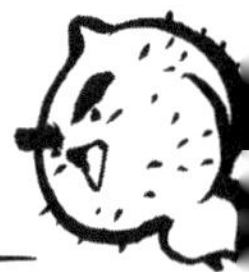

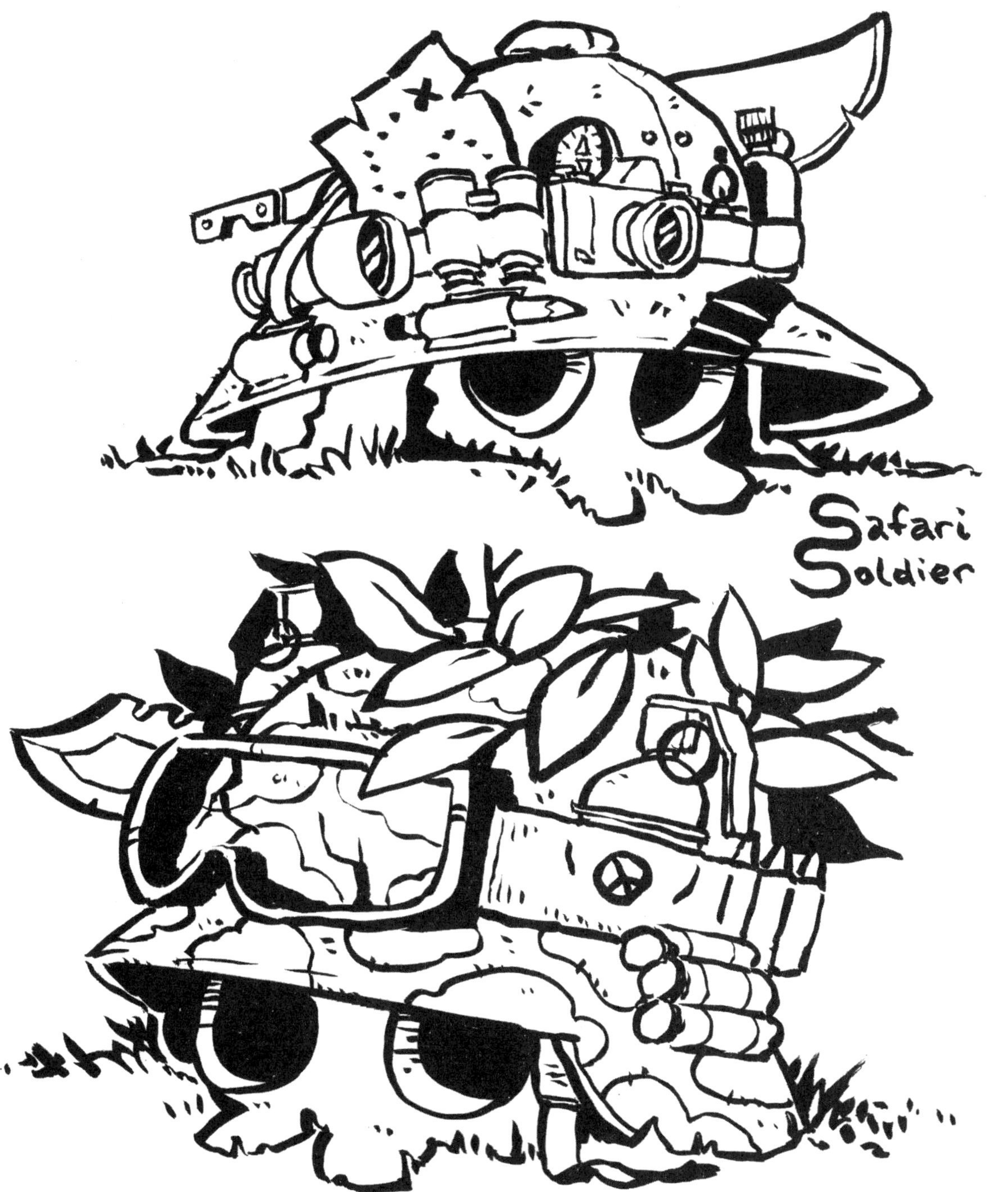
Safari
Soldier

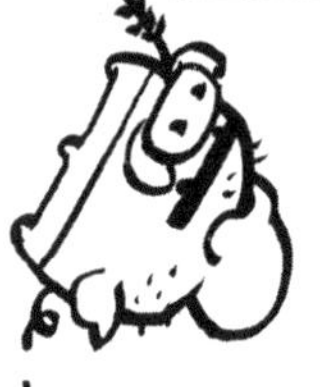

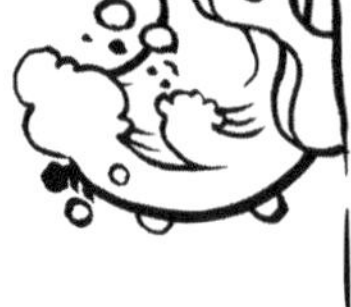

One digit dance.

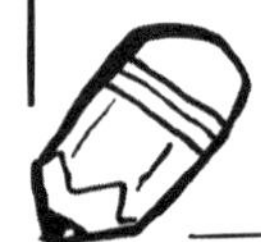

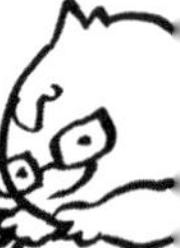

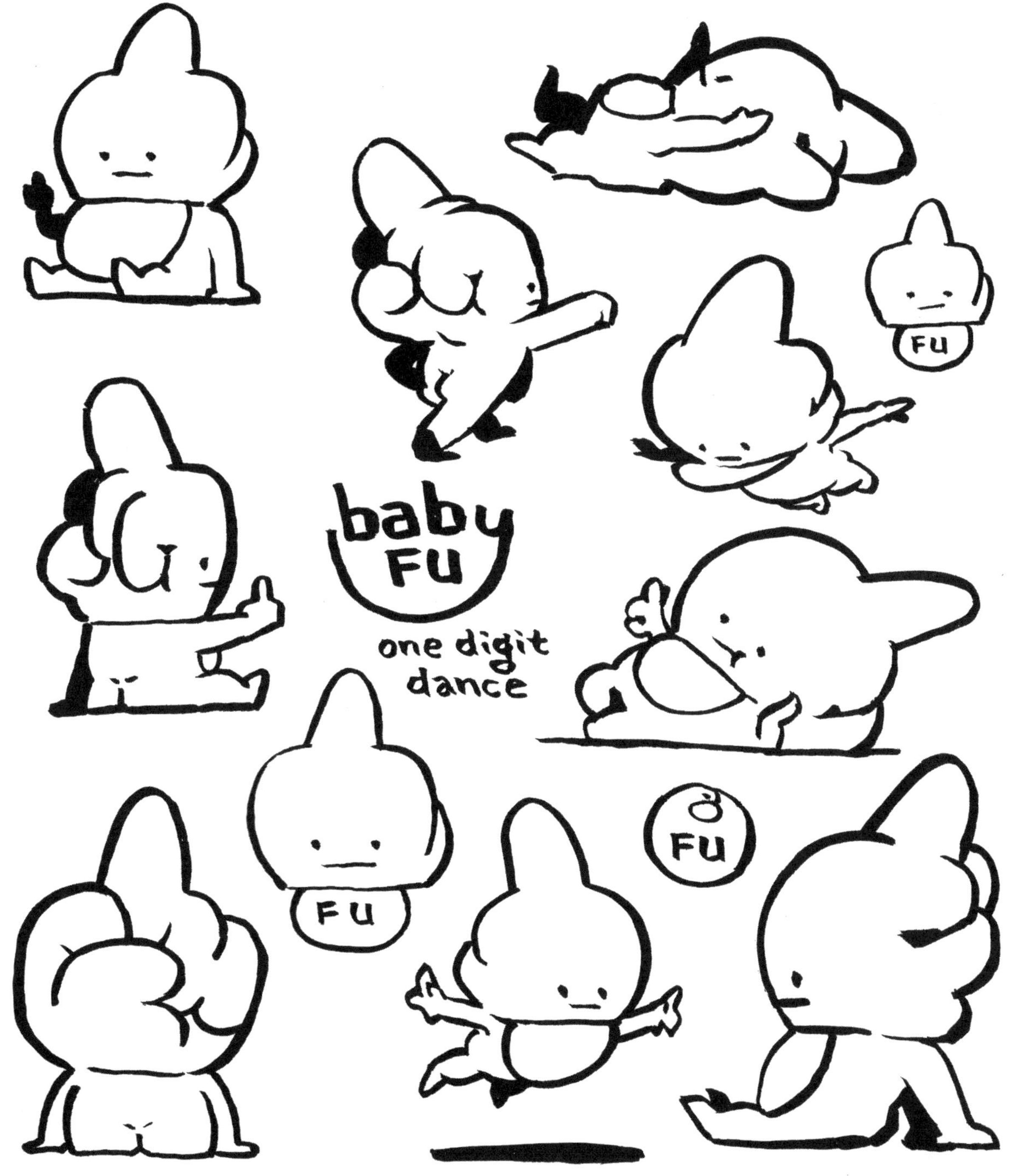
FU
baby
FU
one digit
dance
FU
FU

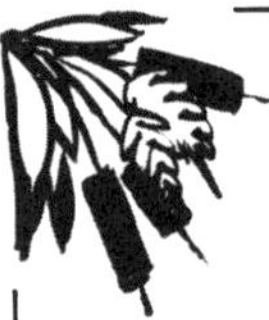

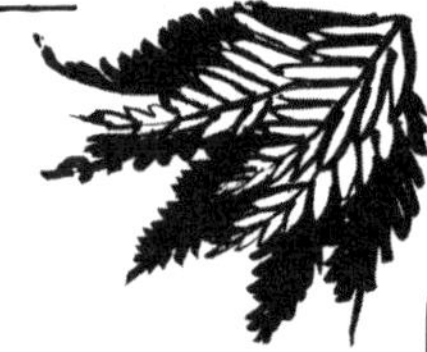

Fat Salt.

This dog sweats.

Fat Salt.

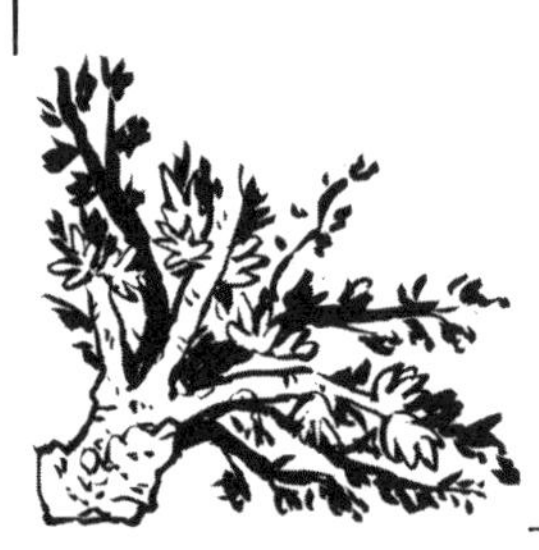

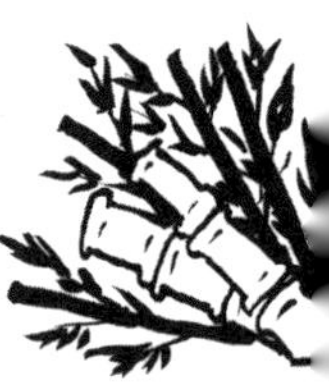

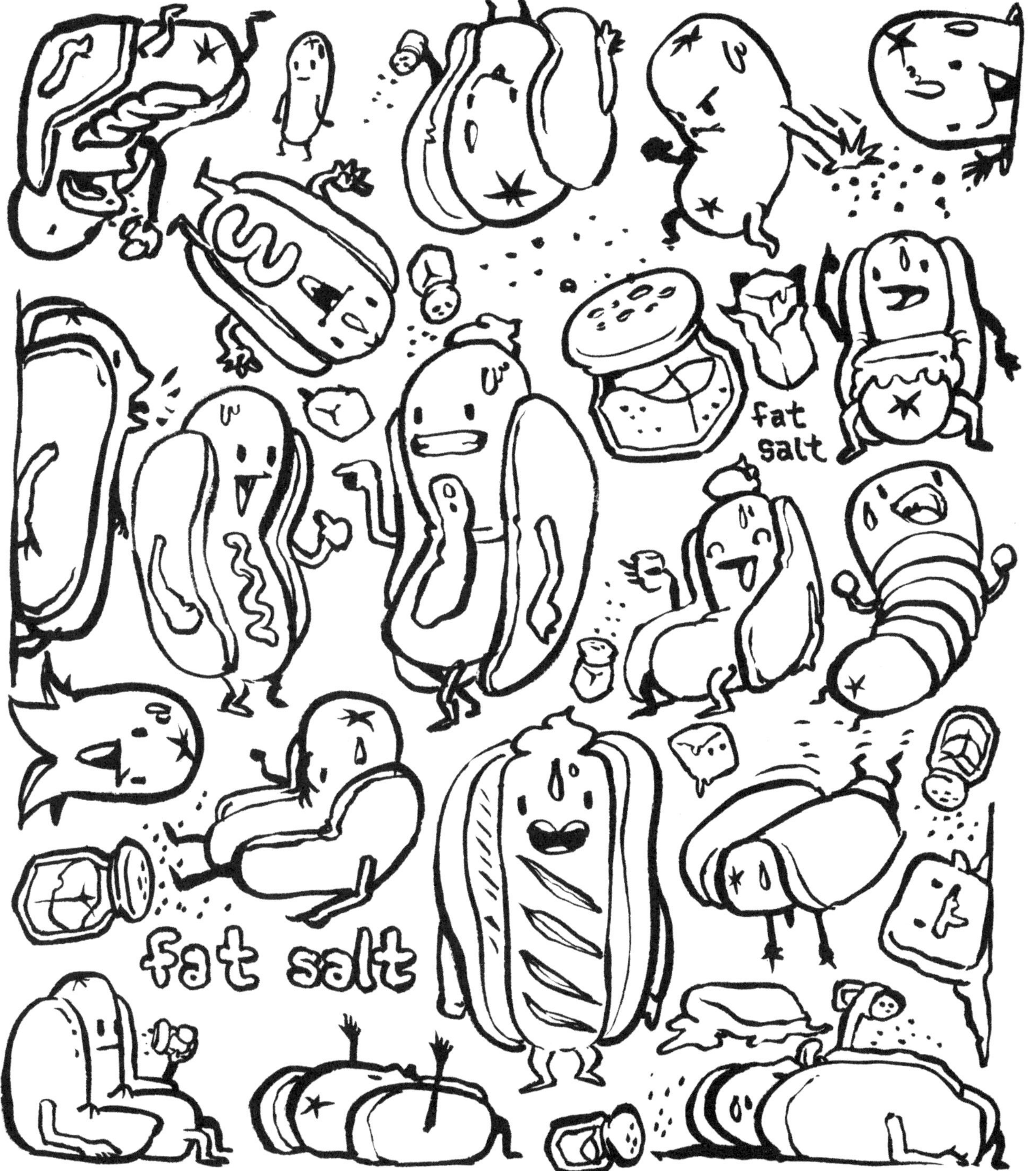
fat
salt
fat salt

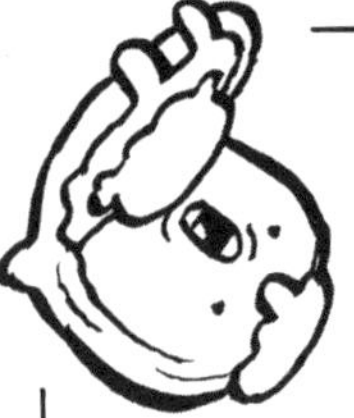

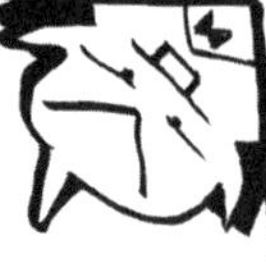

Authentic

vs

imitation.

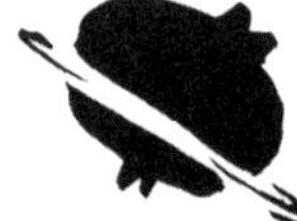

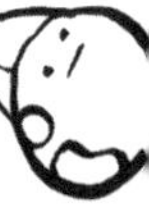

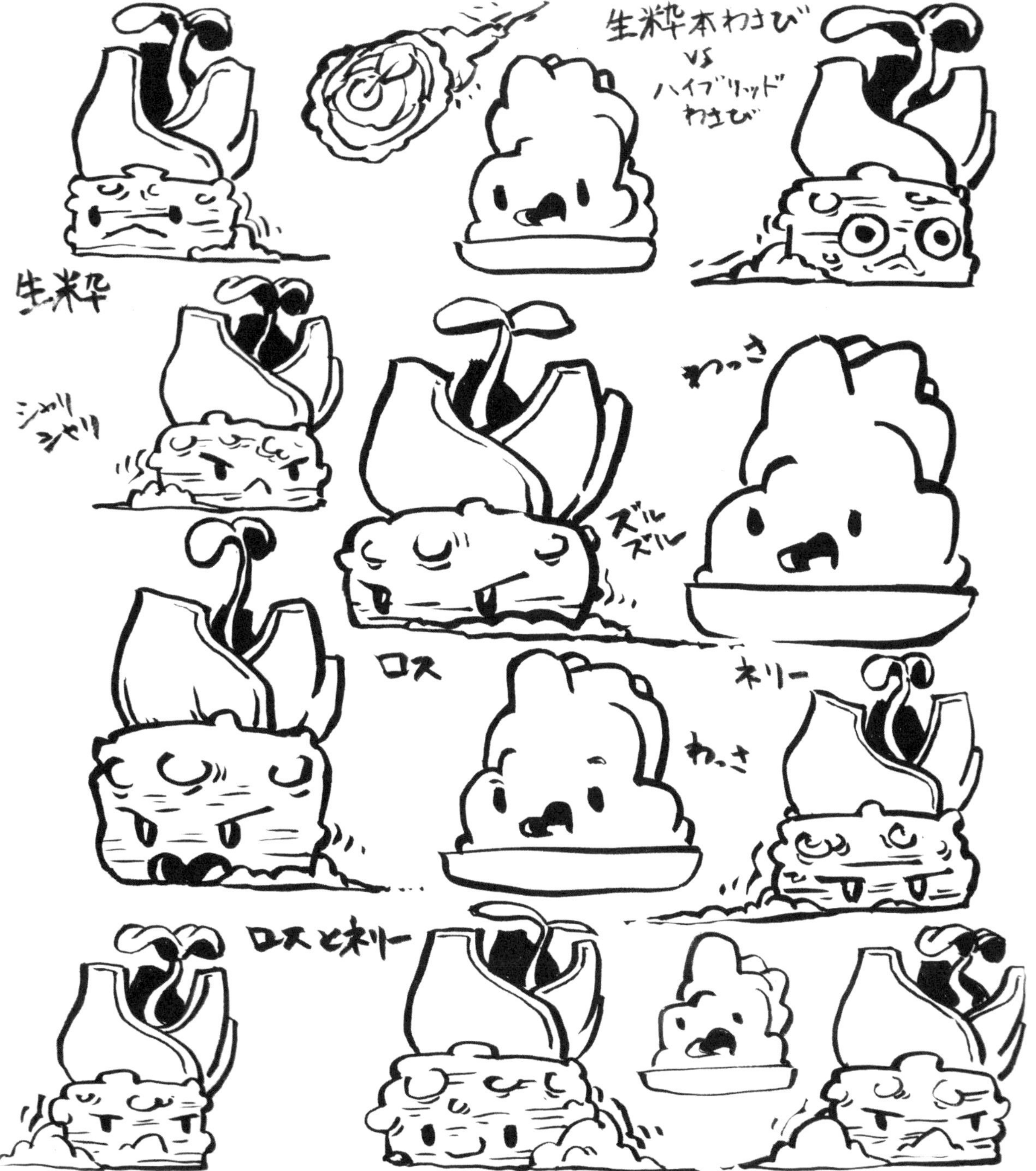
生粋本わさび
vs
ハイブリッド
わさび
生粋
シャリ
シャリ
わっさ
ズル
ズル
ロス
ネリー
わっさ
ロスとネリー

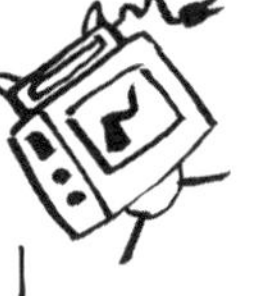

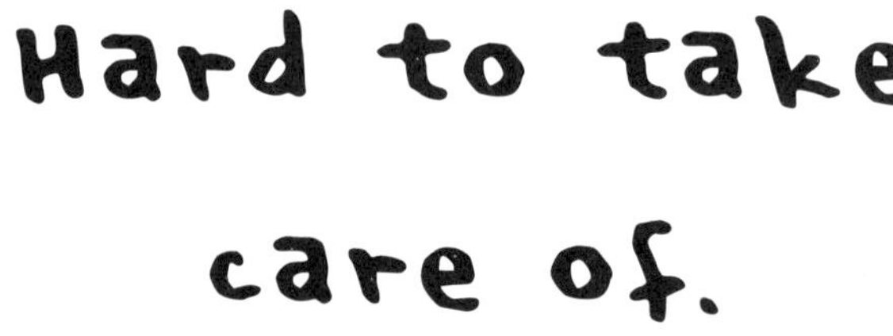
Hard to take
care of.

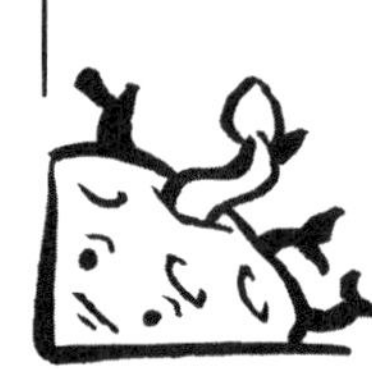

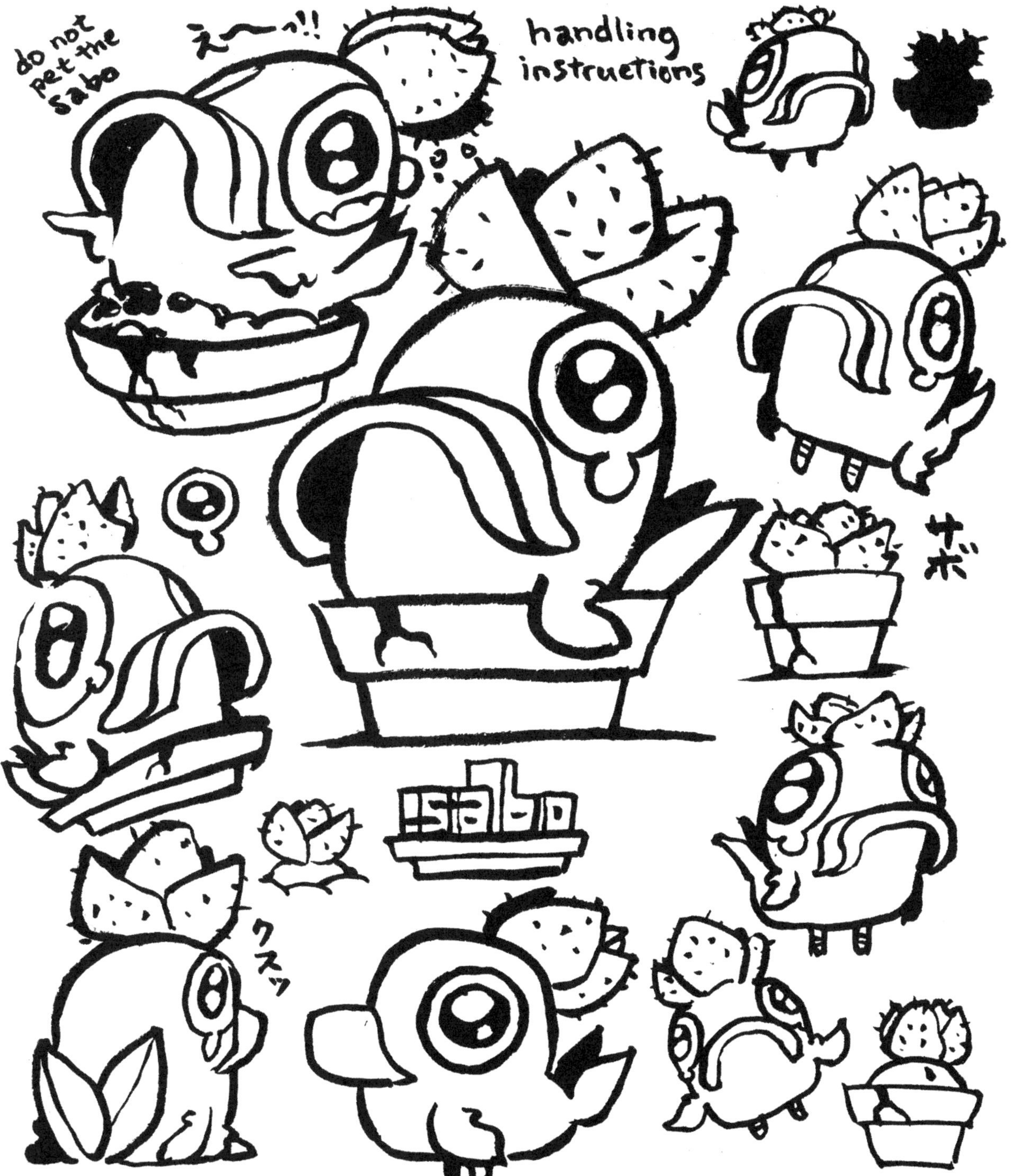
do not pet the sabo
え〜っ!!
handling instructions
サボ
sabo
クスッ

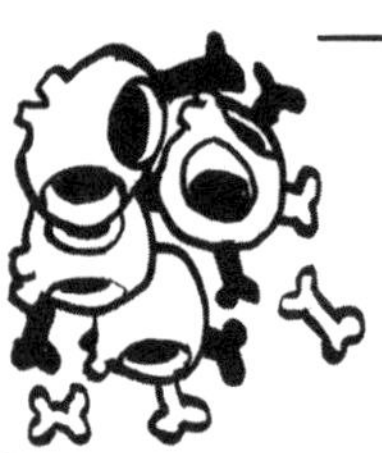

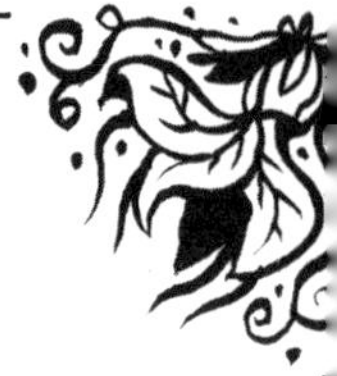

A sweet
friendship.

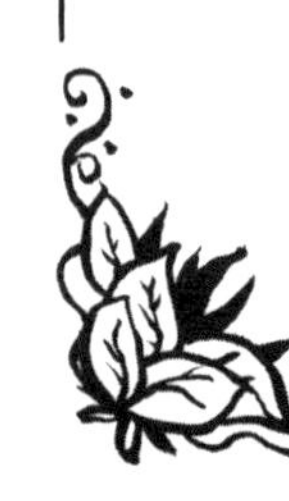

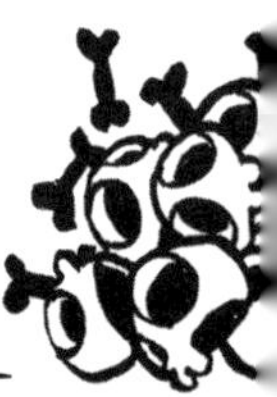

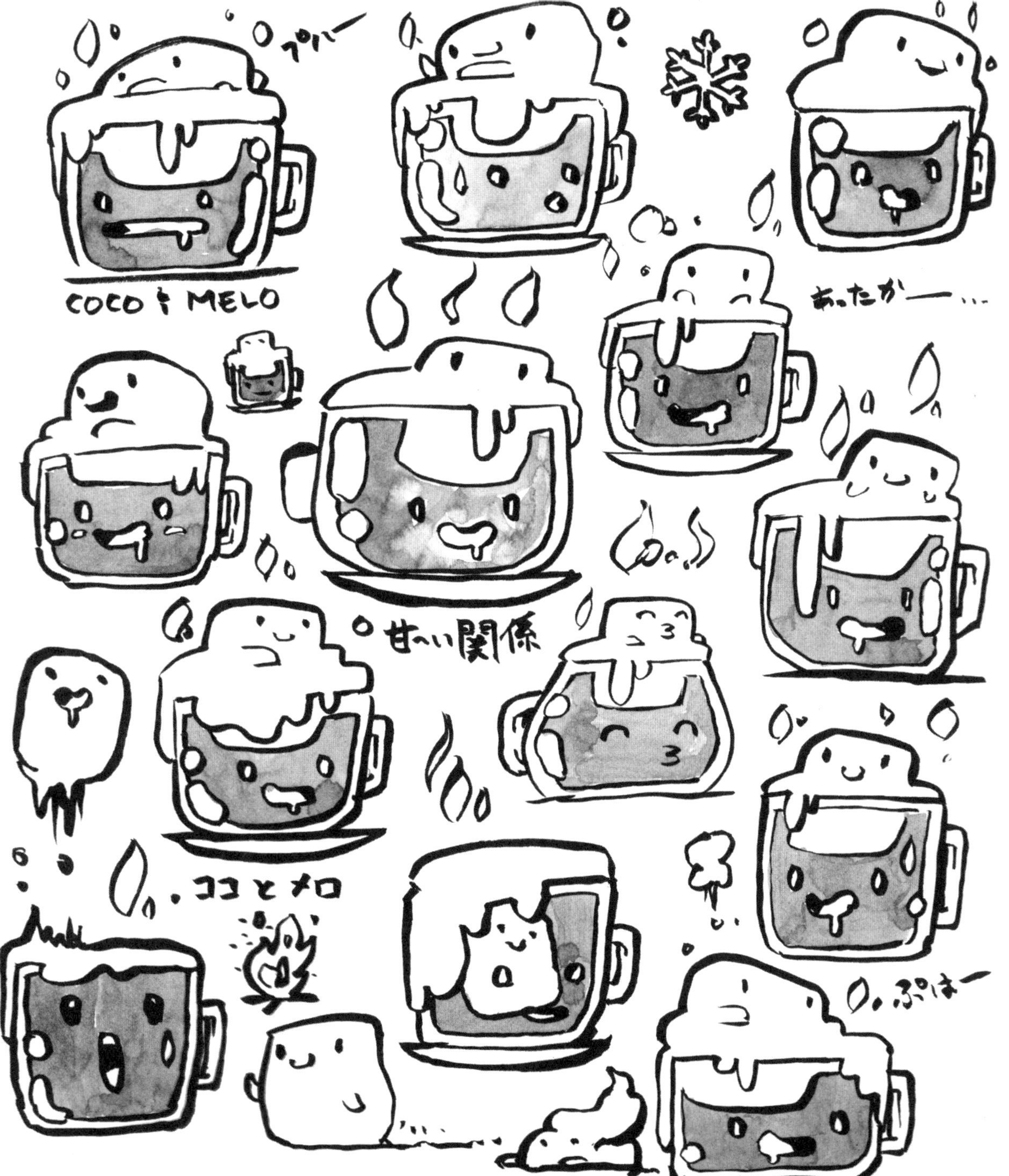
プハー
COCO & MELO
あったかー…
甘〜い関係
ココとメロ
ぷはー

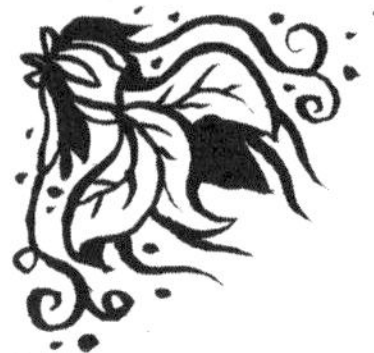

Hey boi pokes around
and inserts itself
into conversations.

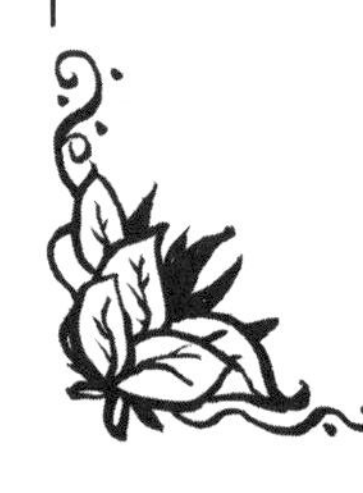

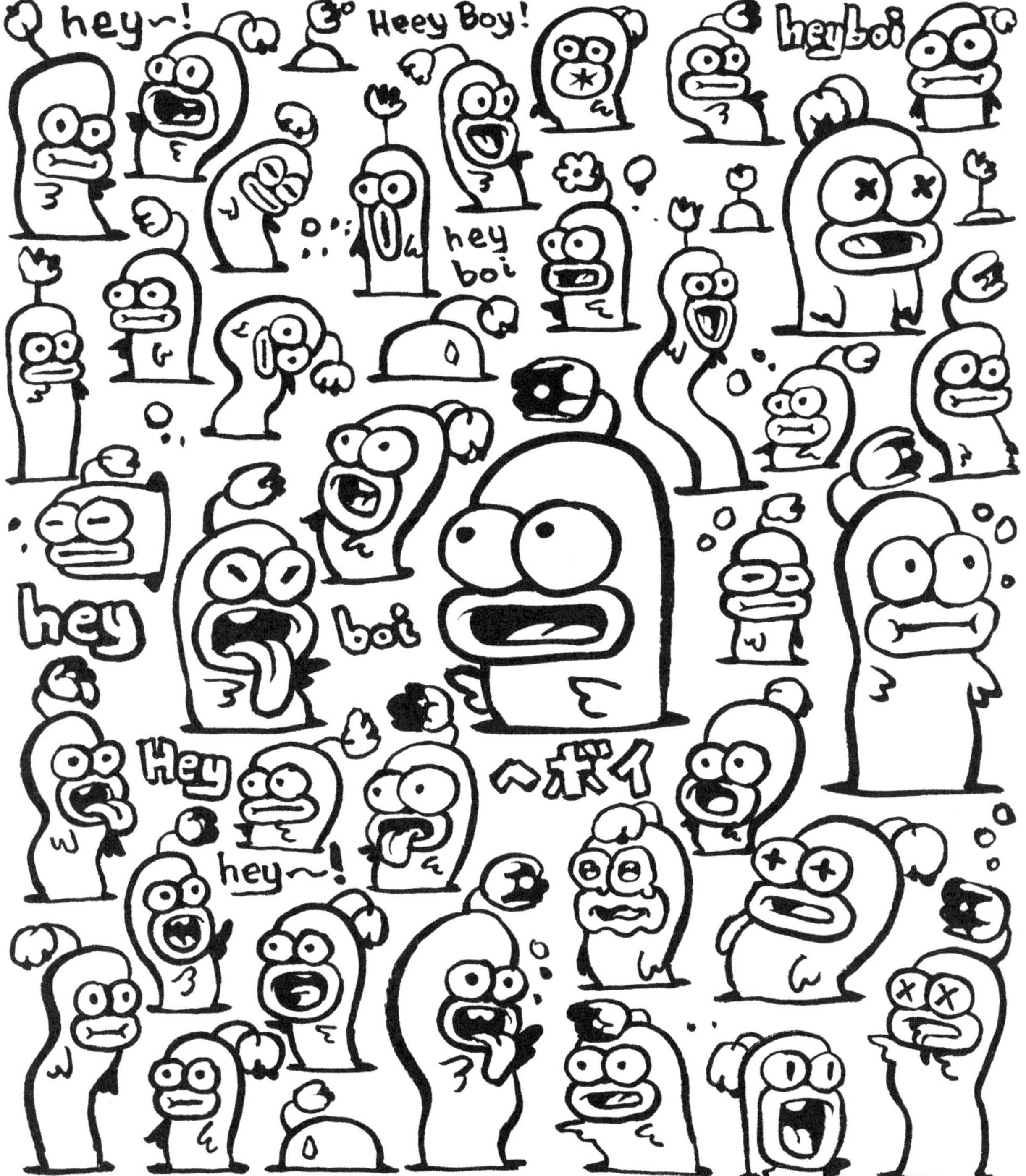

hey~!
Heey Boy!
heyboi
hey
boi
hey
boi
Hey
ヘボイ
hey~!

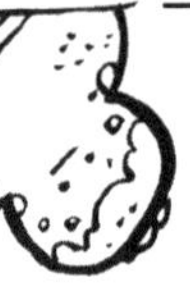

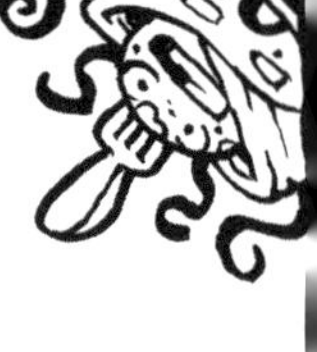

Self propelled.

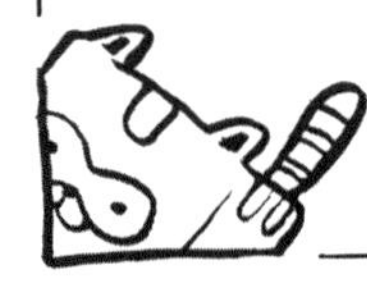

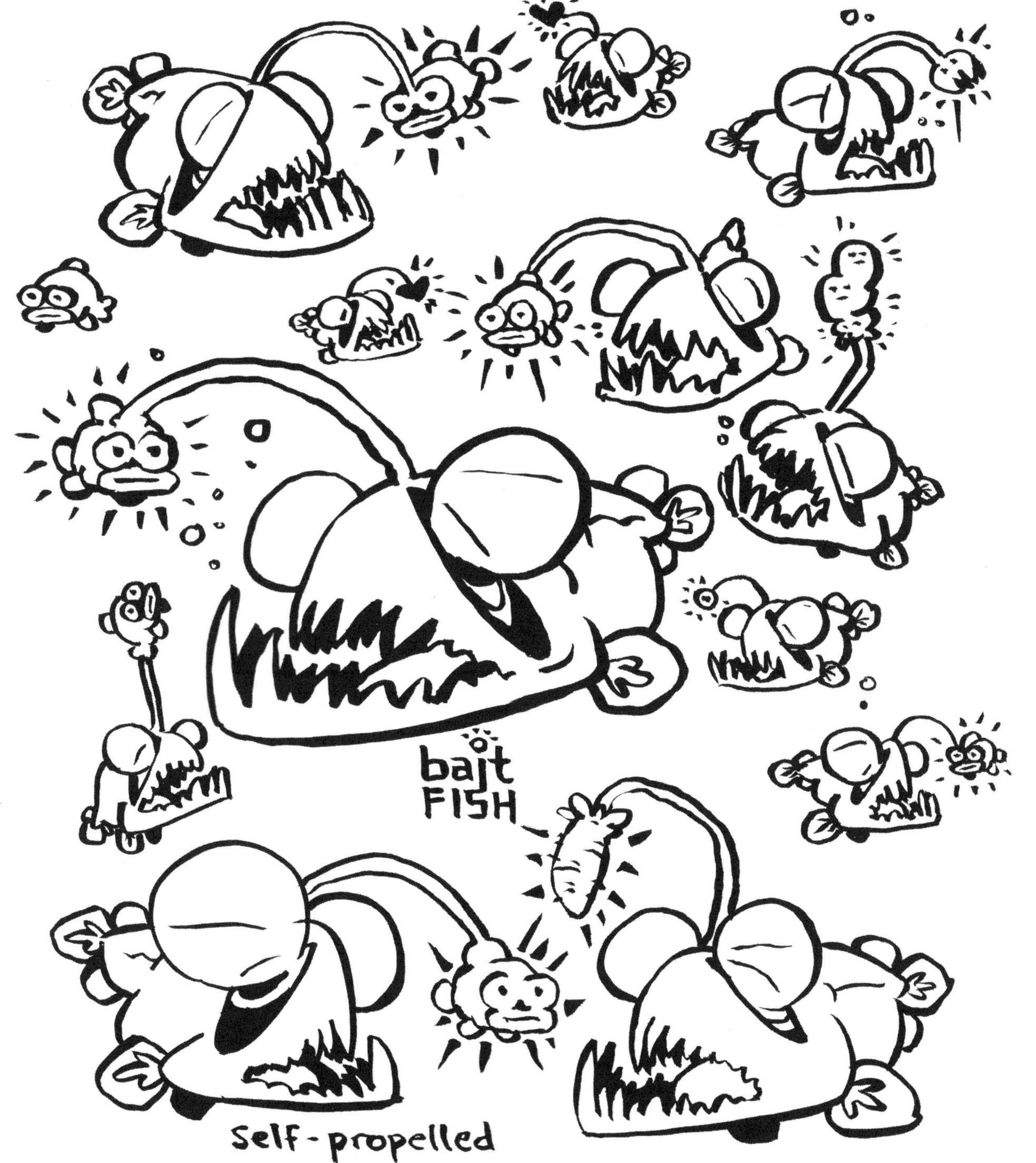
bait
FISH
self-propelled

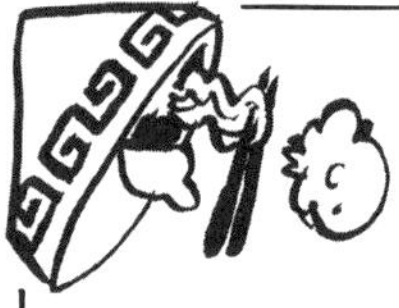

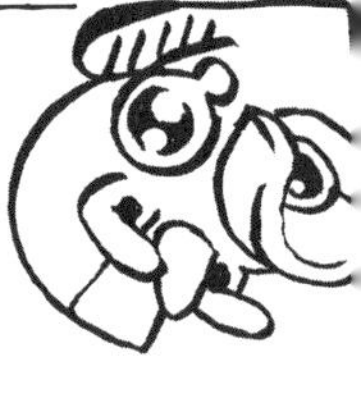

Don has many friends.

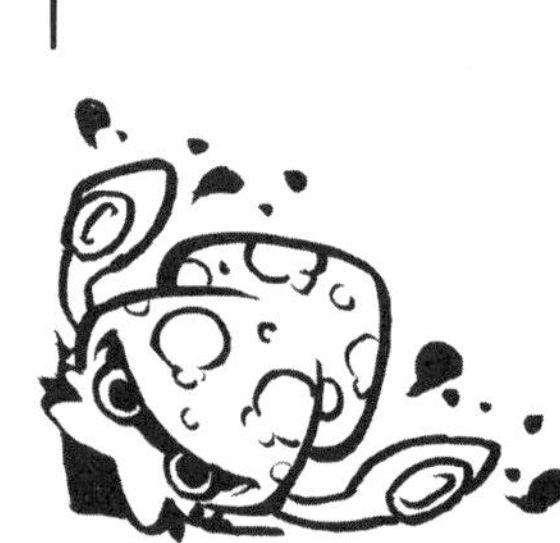

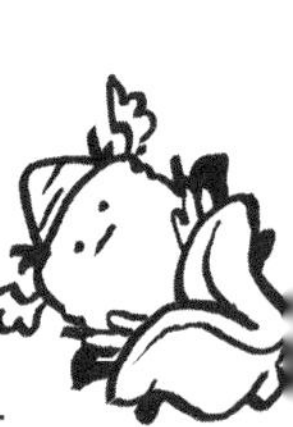

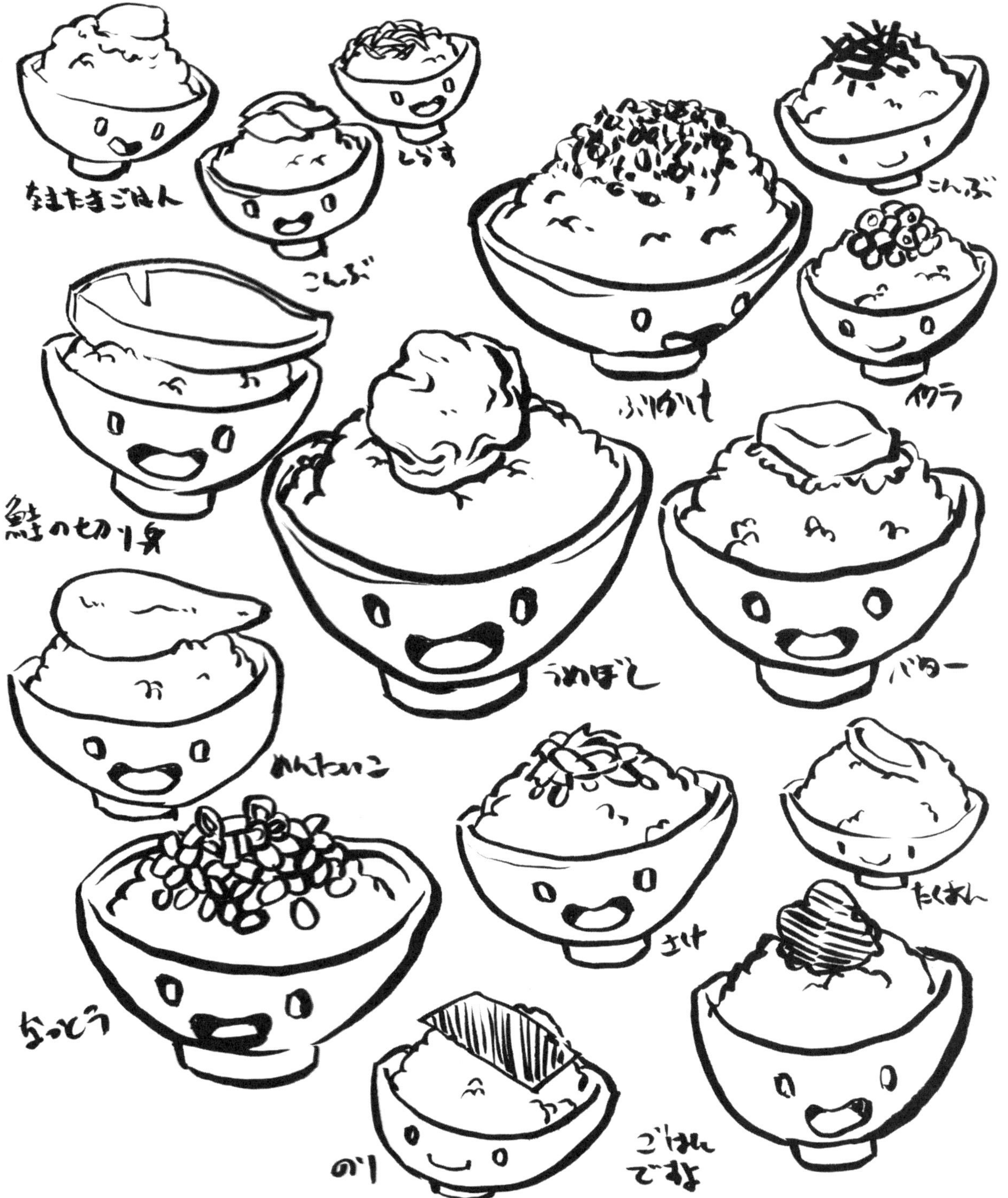
なまたまごはん
しらす
こんぶ
こんぶ
ふりかけ
イクラ
鮭の切り身
うめぼし
バター
めんたいこ
さけ
たくあん
なっとう
のり
ごはんですよ

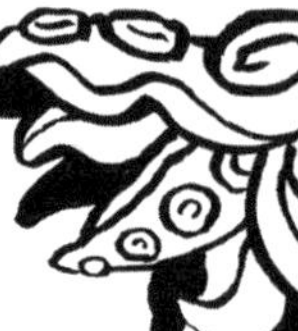

woke.

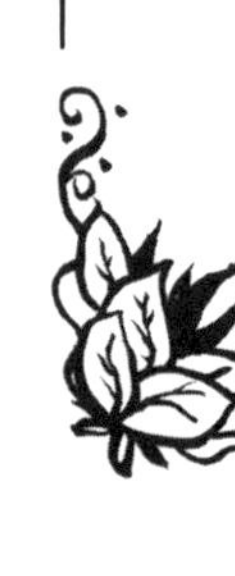

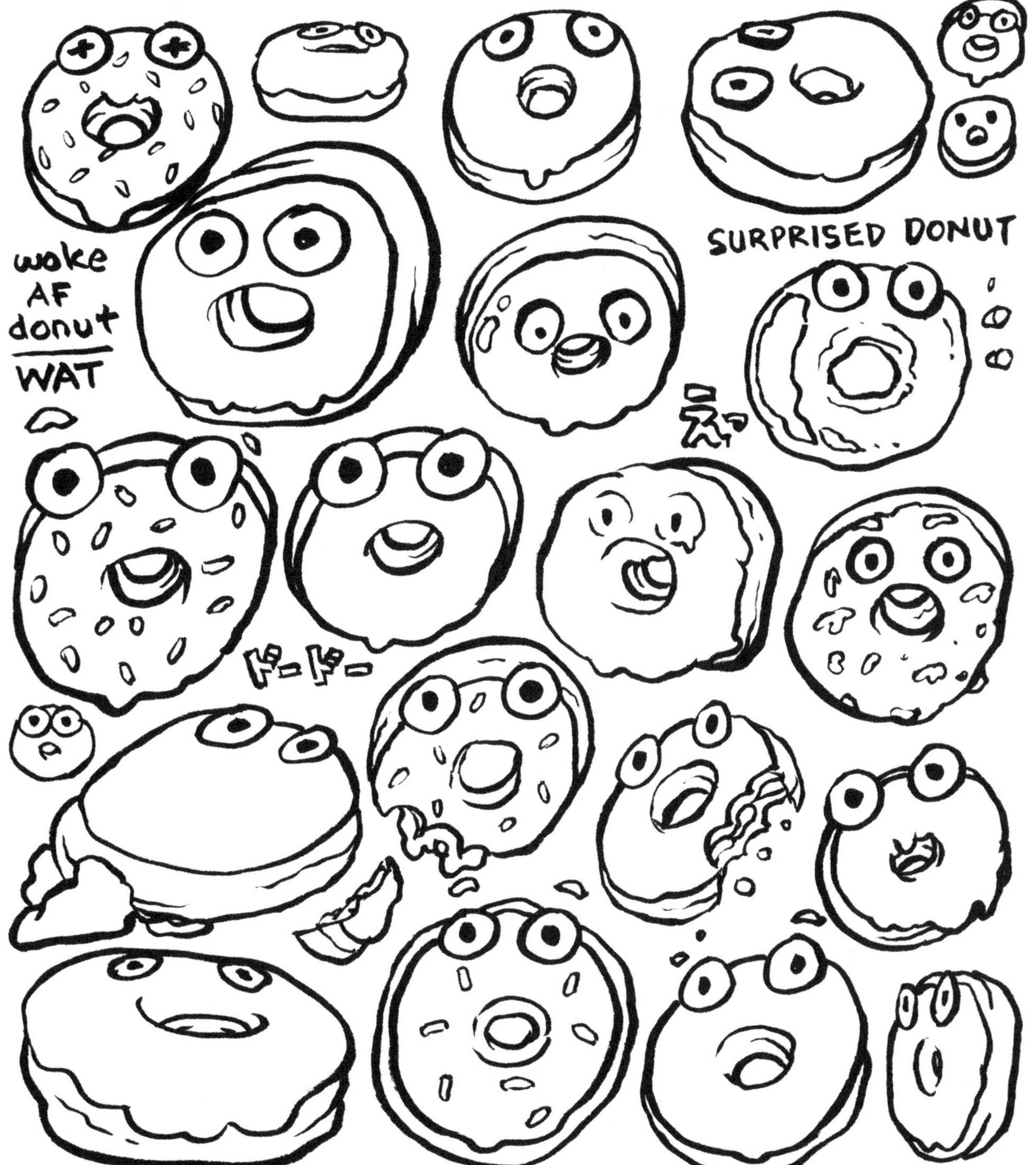
woke AF donut
WAT
SURPRISED DONUT
えっ
ドードー

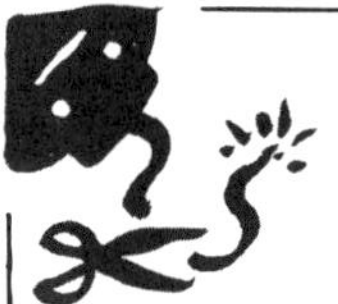

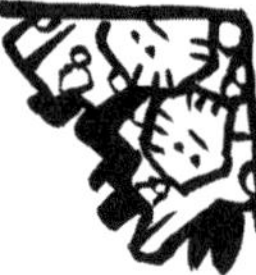

Hidden maintenance.

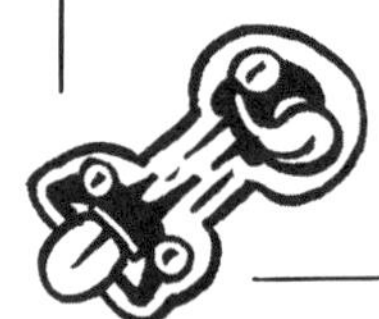

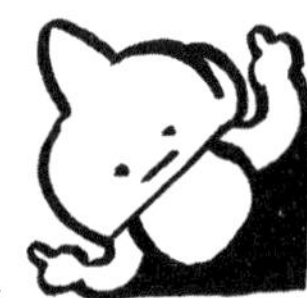

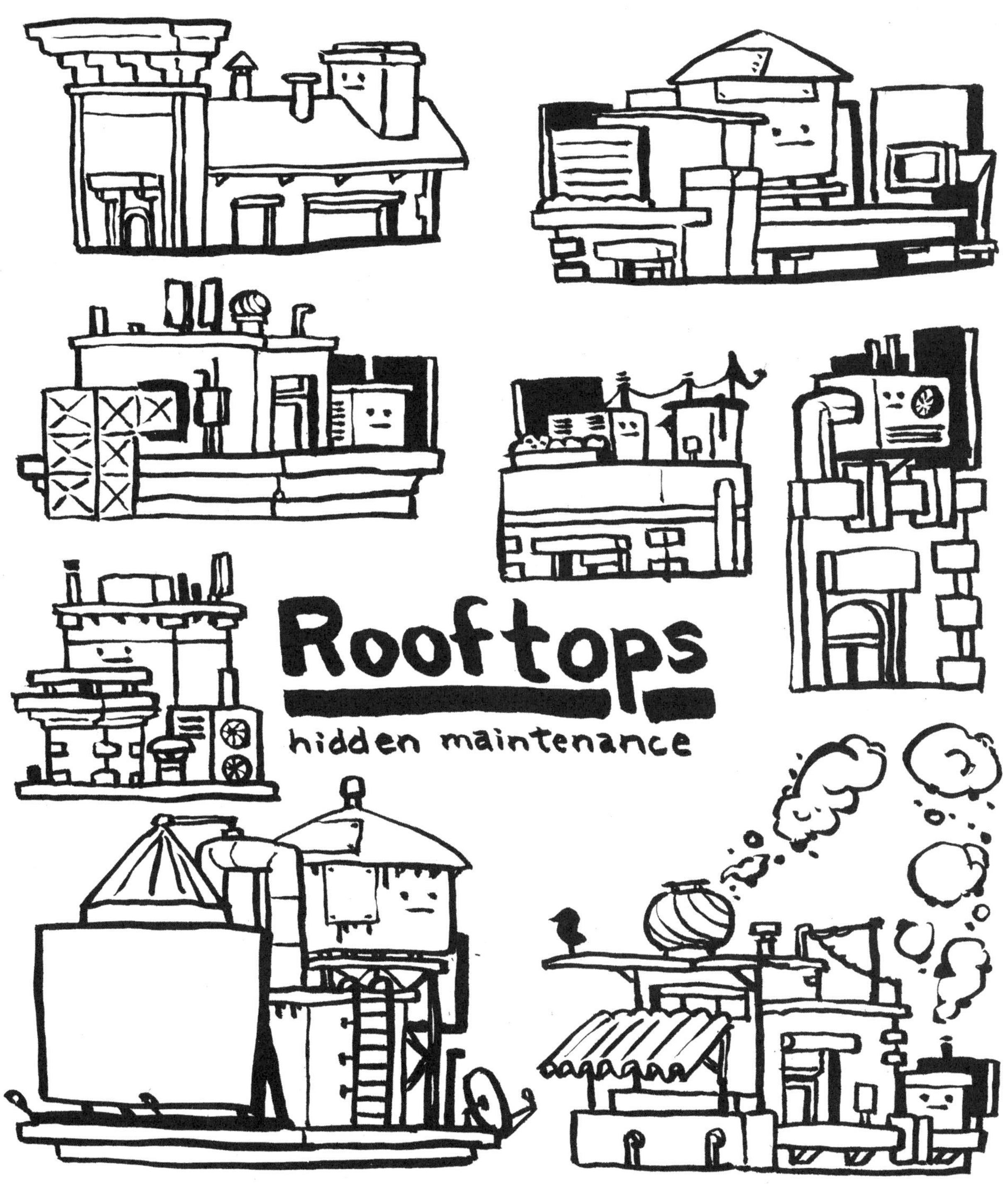
Rooftops
hidden maintenance

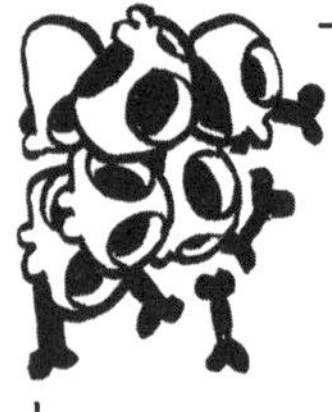

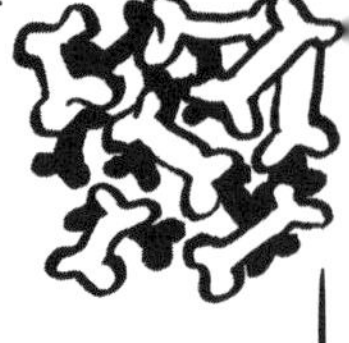

A comic about imposter syndrome.

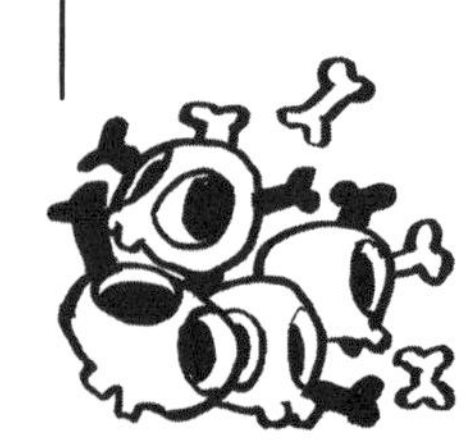

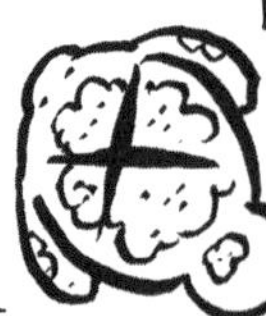

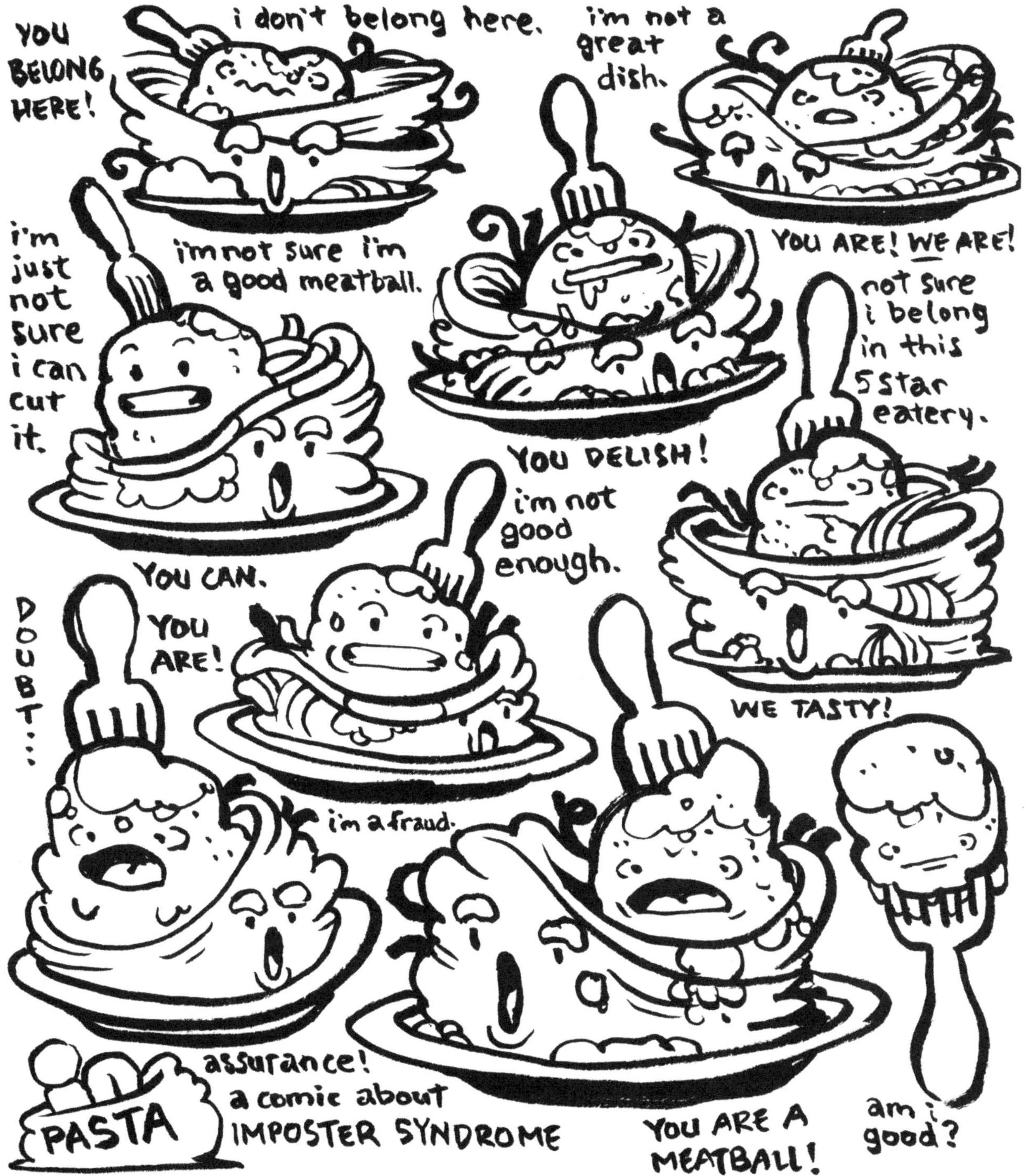

YOU BELONG HERE!
i don't belong here.
i'm not a great dish.
YOU ARE! WE ARE!
i'm just not sure i can cut it.
i'm not sure i'm a good meatball.
not sure i belong in this 5 star eatery.
YOU DELISH!
i'm not good enough.
YOU CAN.
YOU ARE!
WE TASTY!
DOUBT...
i'm a fraud.
PASTA
assurance!
a comic about
IMPOSTER SYNDROME
YOU ARE A MEATBALL!
am i good?

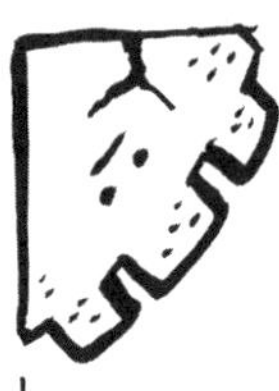

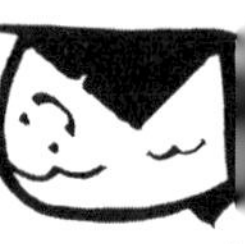

Protecting hearts.

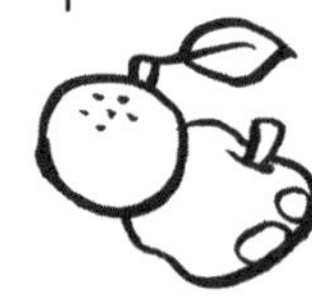

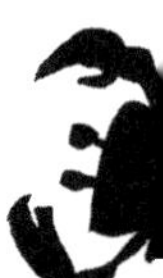

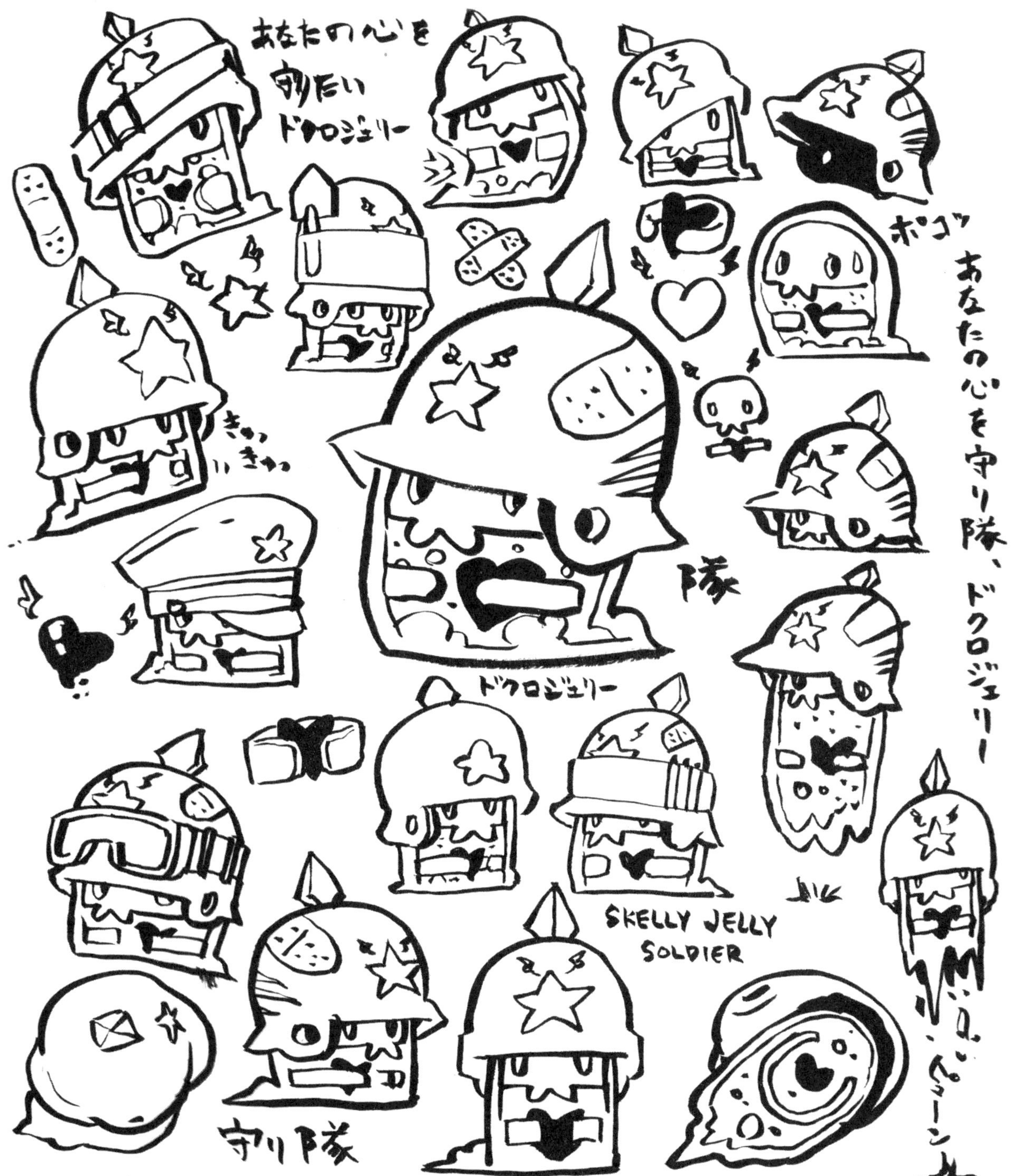

あなたの心を
守りたい
ドクロジェリー
ボコッ
あなたの心を守り隊、ドクロジェリー
きゅっ
きゅっ
隊
ドクロジェリー
SKELLY JELLY
SOLDIER
守り隊
ぴょーン

Grilled and wrapped in nori and ready to burst! It's all about the timing.

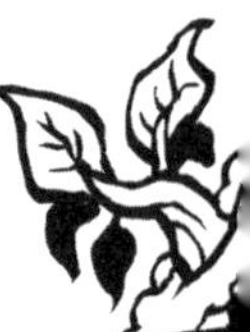

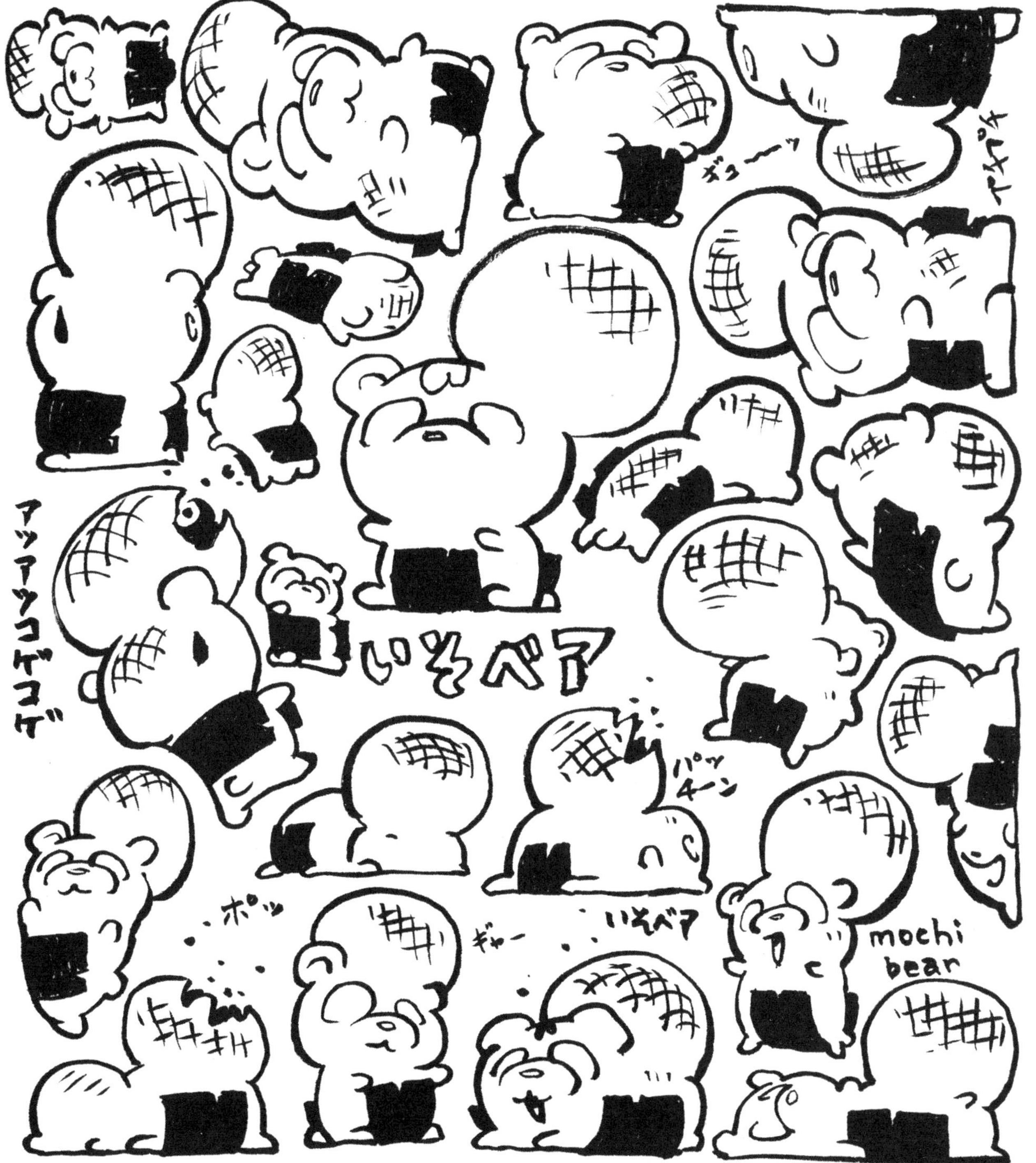
ギュ〜〜ッ
アッアッコゲコゲ
いそベア
パッ
クーン
ポッ
ギャー
いそベア
mochi
bear

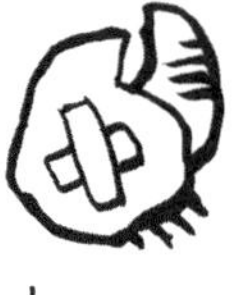

Extravagantly cheap.

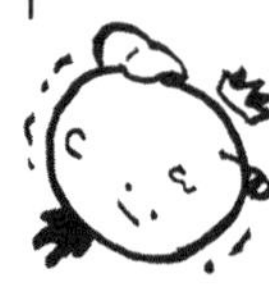

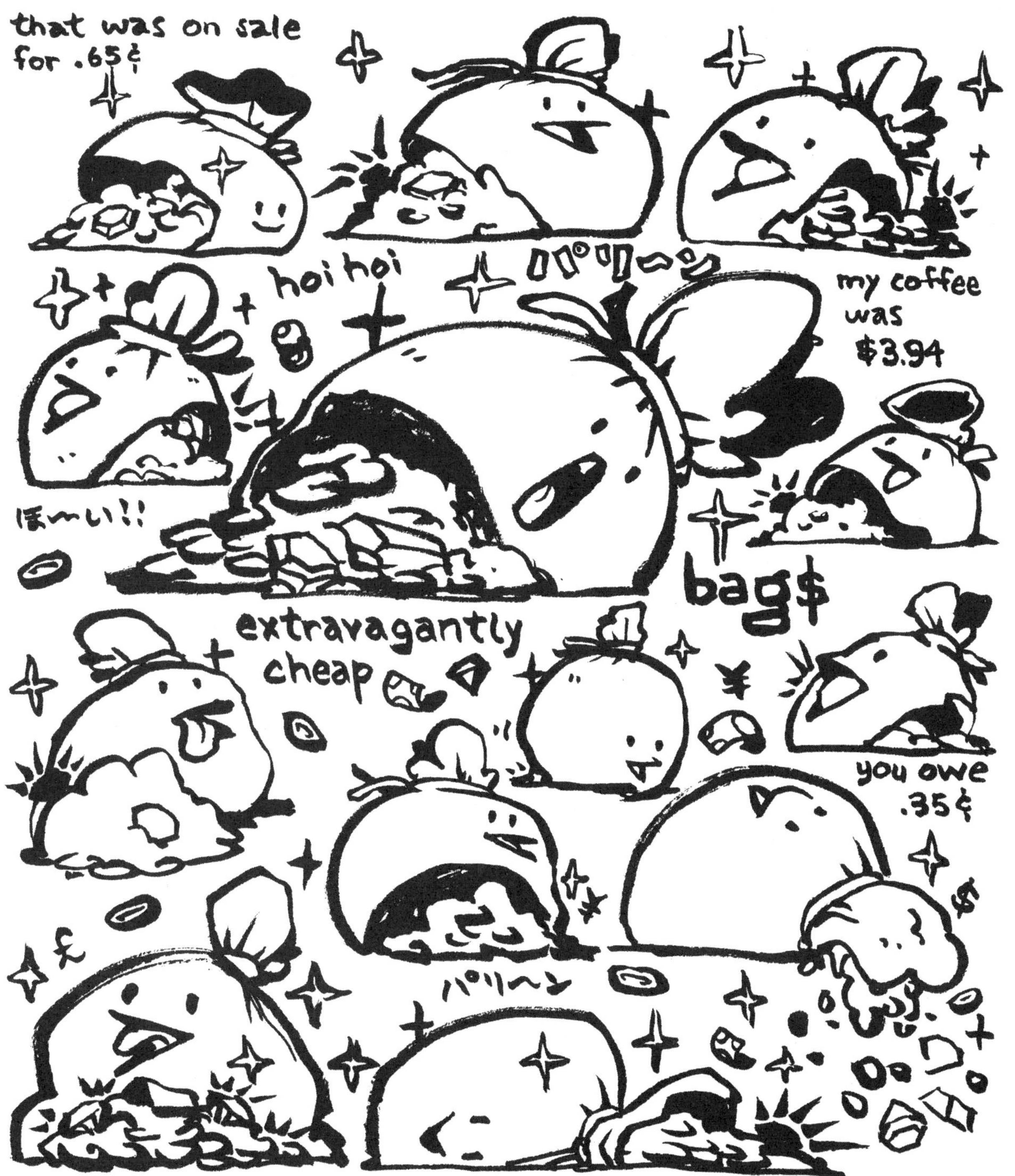
that was on sale
for .65¢
hoi hoi
パパパーン
my coffee
was
$3.94
ほしい!!
bag$
extravagantly
cheap
you owe
.35¢
£
$
¥
パリーン

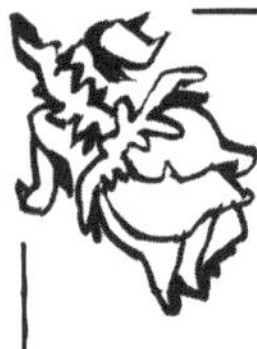

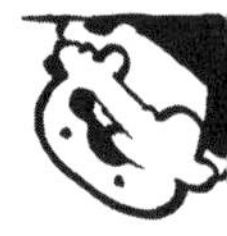

Judgement fish is judging you.

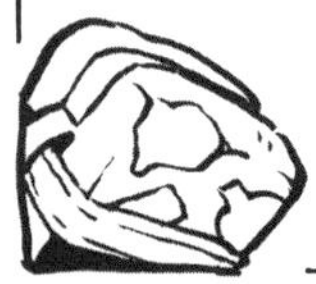

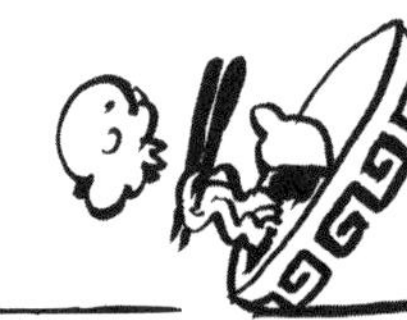

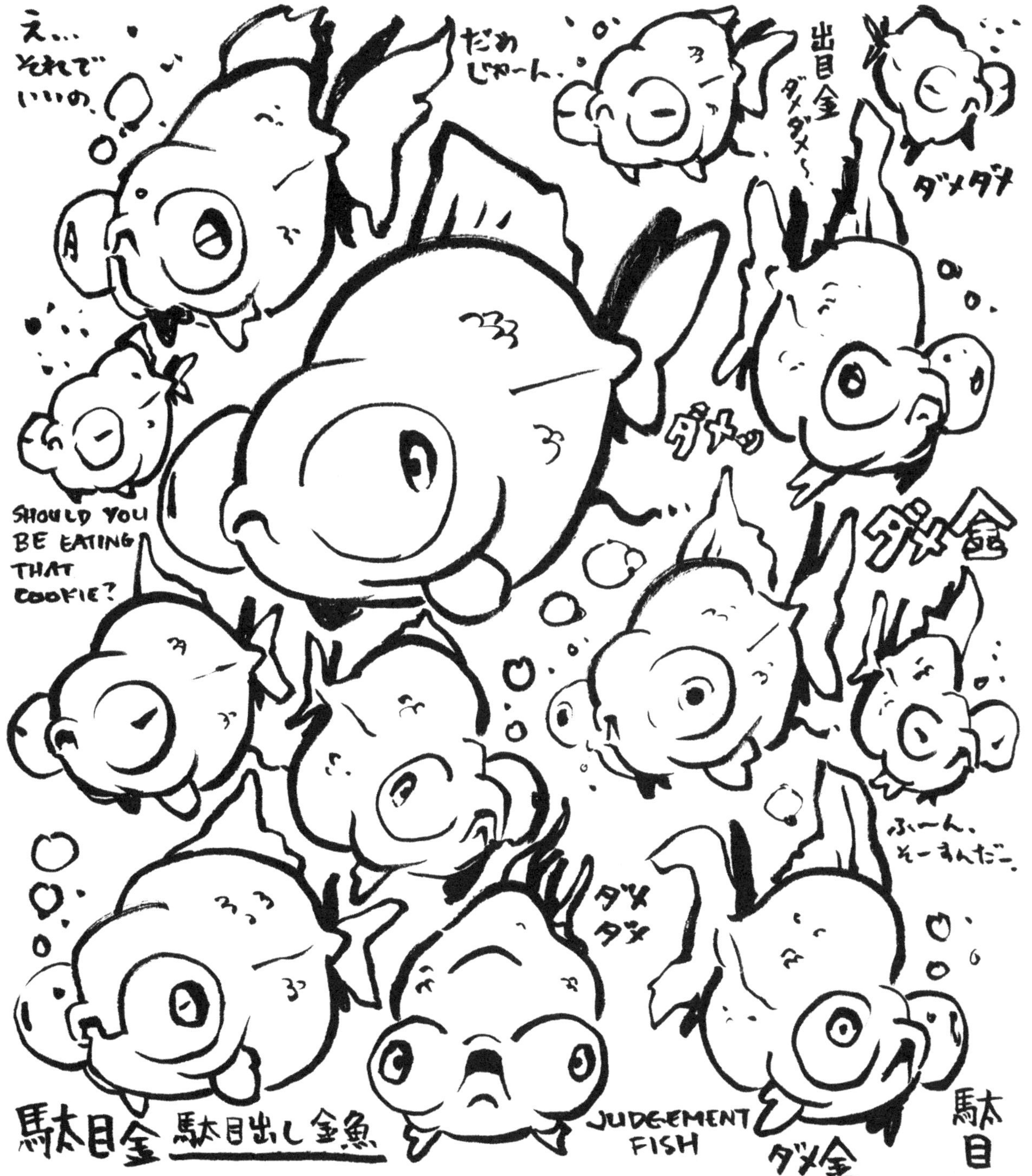

え…
それでいいの。
だめじゃーん。
出目金
ダメダメ～。
ダメダメ
ダメッ
SHOULD YOU BE EATING THAT COOKIE?
ダメ金
ふーん。そーなんだー。
ダメダメ
馬太目金
駄目出し金魚
JUDGEMENT FISH
ダメ金
馬太目

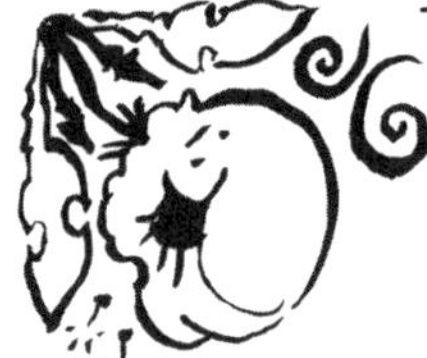

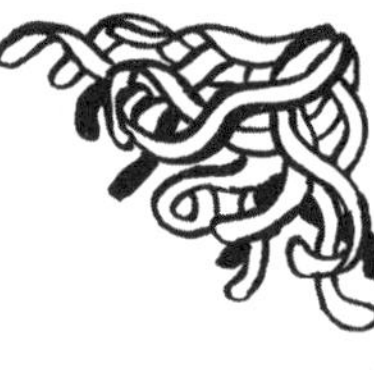

Spread shot.

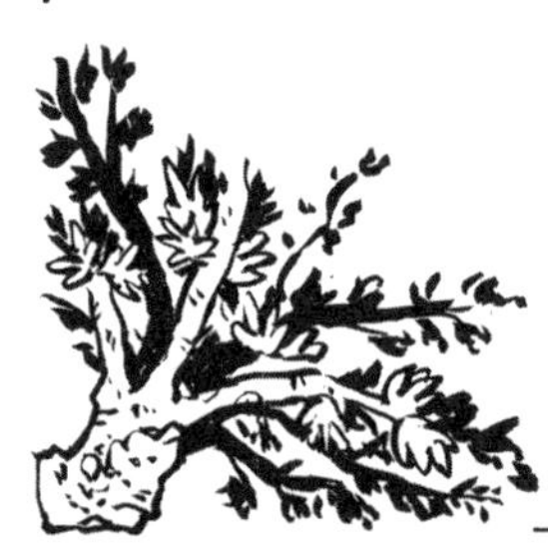

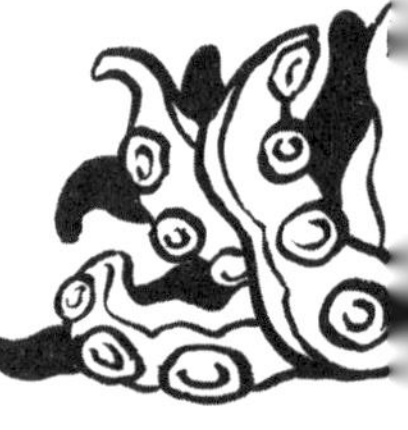

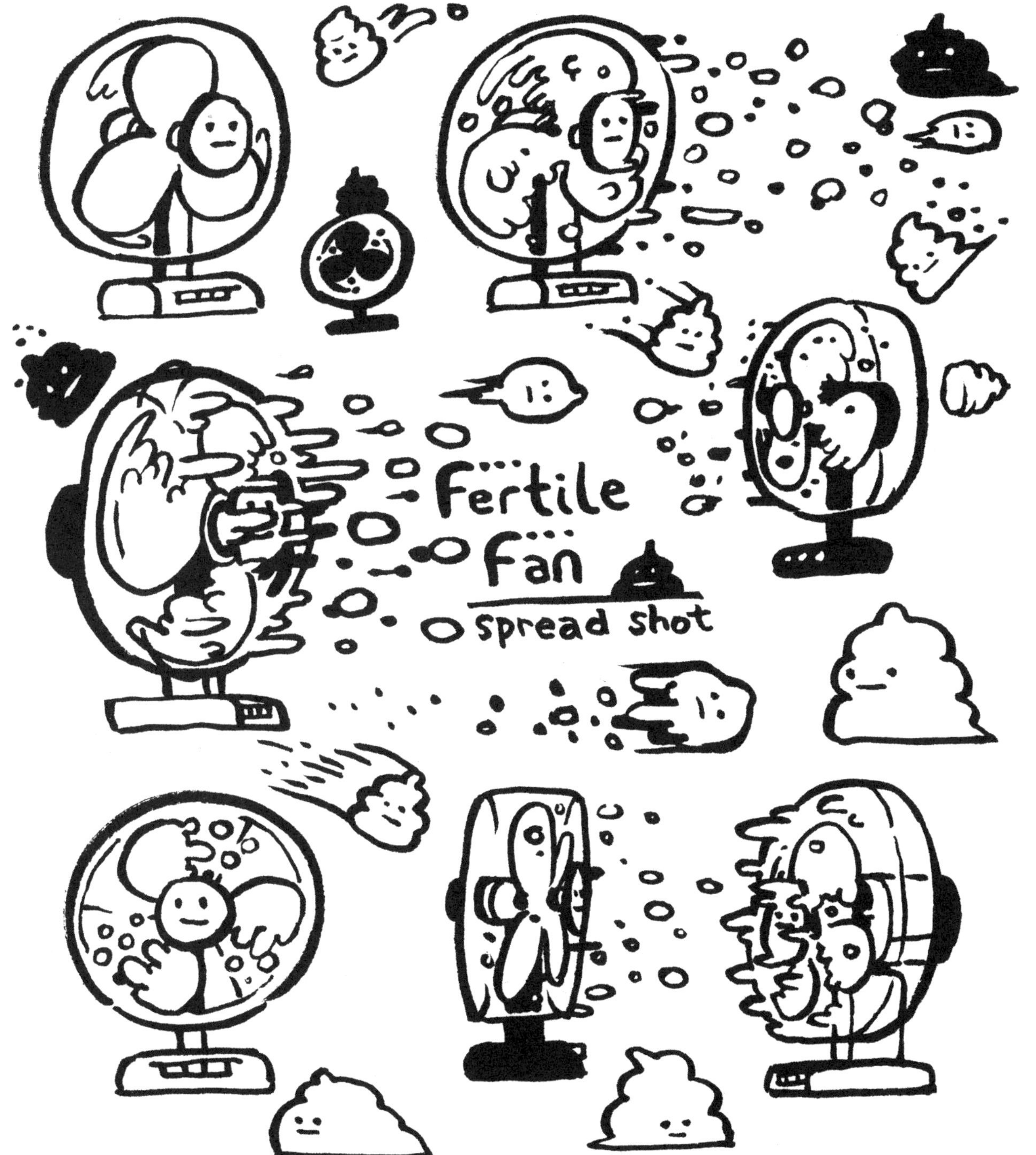
Fertile Fan
spread shot

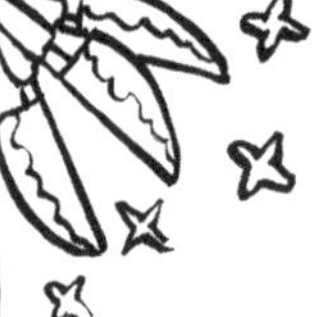

Kewl Baby's got it.

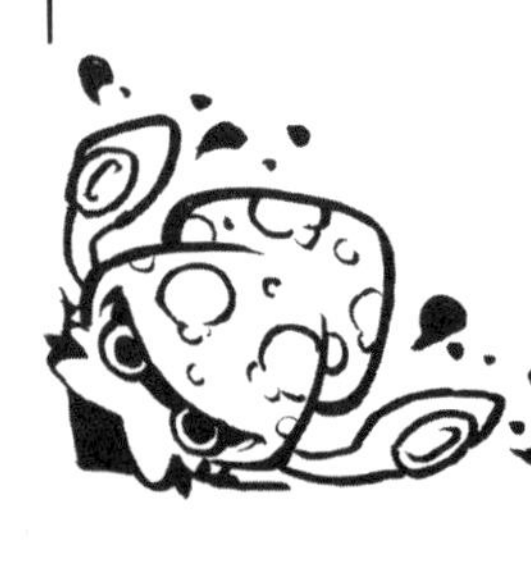

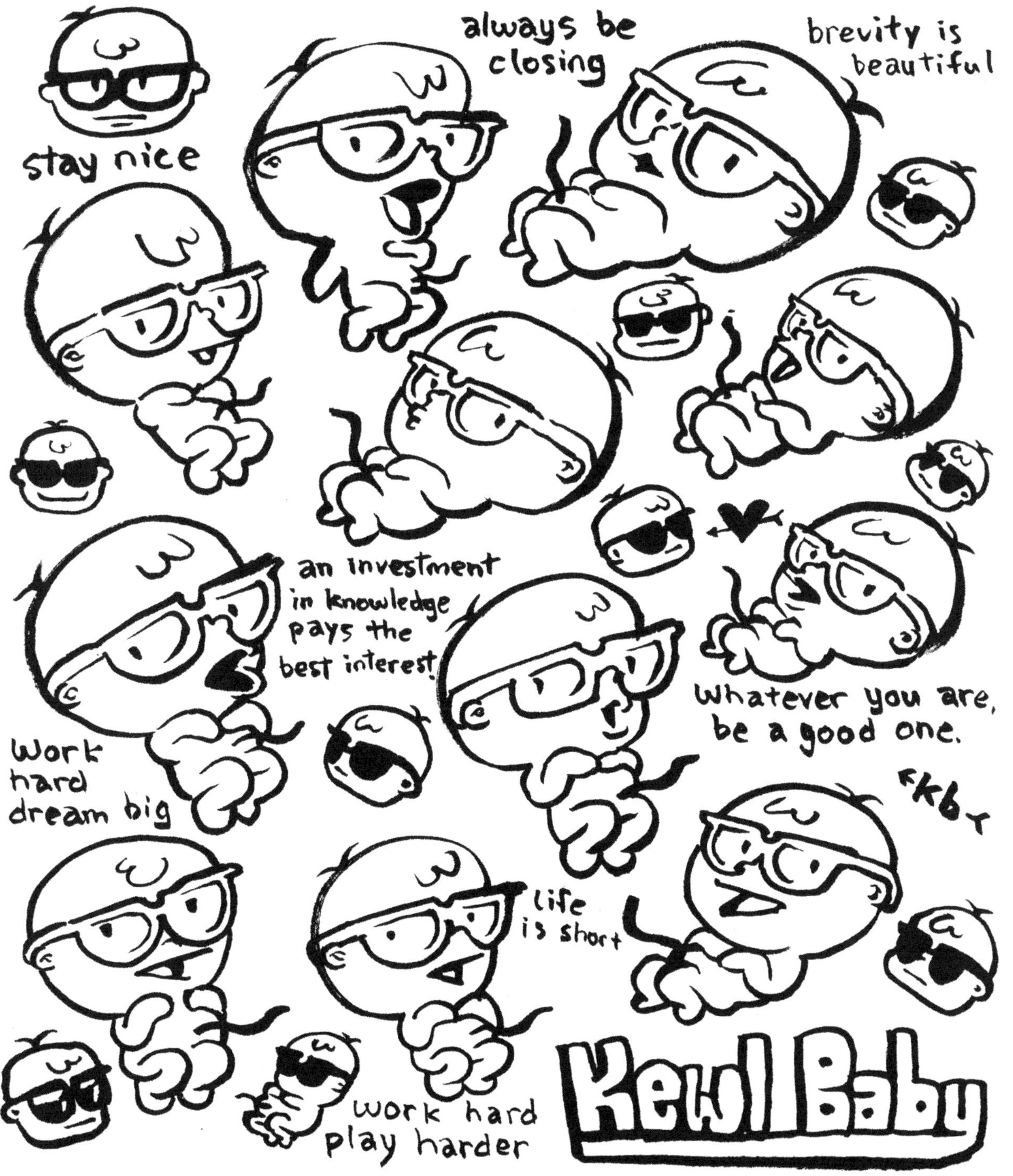
stay nice
always be closing
brevity is beautiful
an investment in knowledge pays the best interest!
whatever you are, be a good one.
work hard dream big
life is short
work hard play harder
Kewl Baby

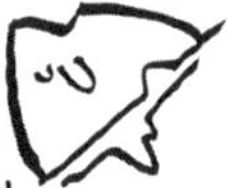

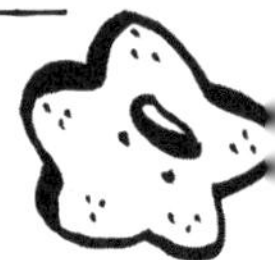

Prickly but poppable.

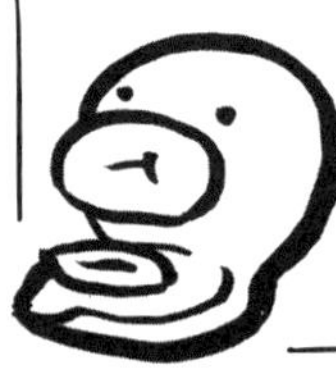

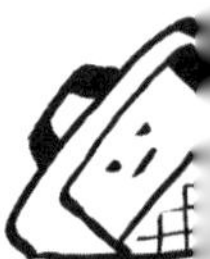

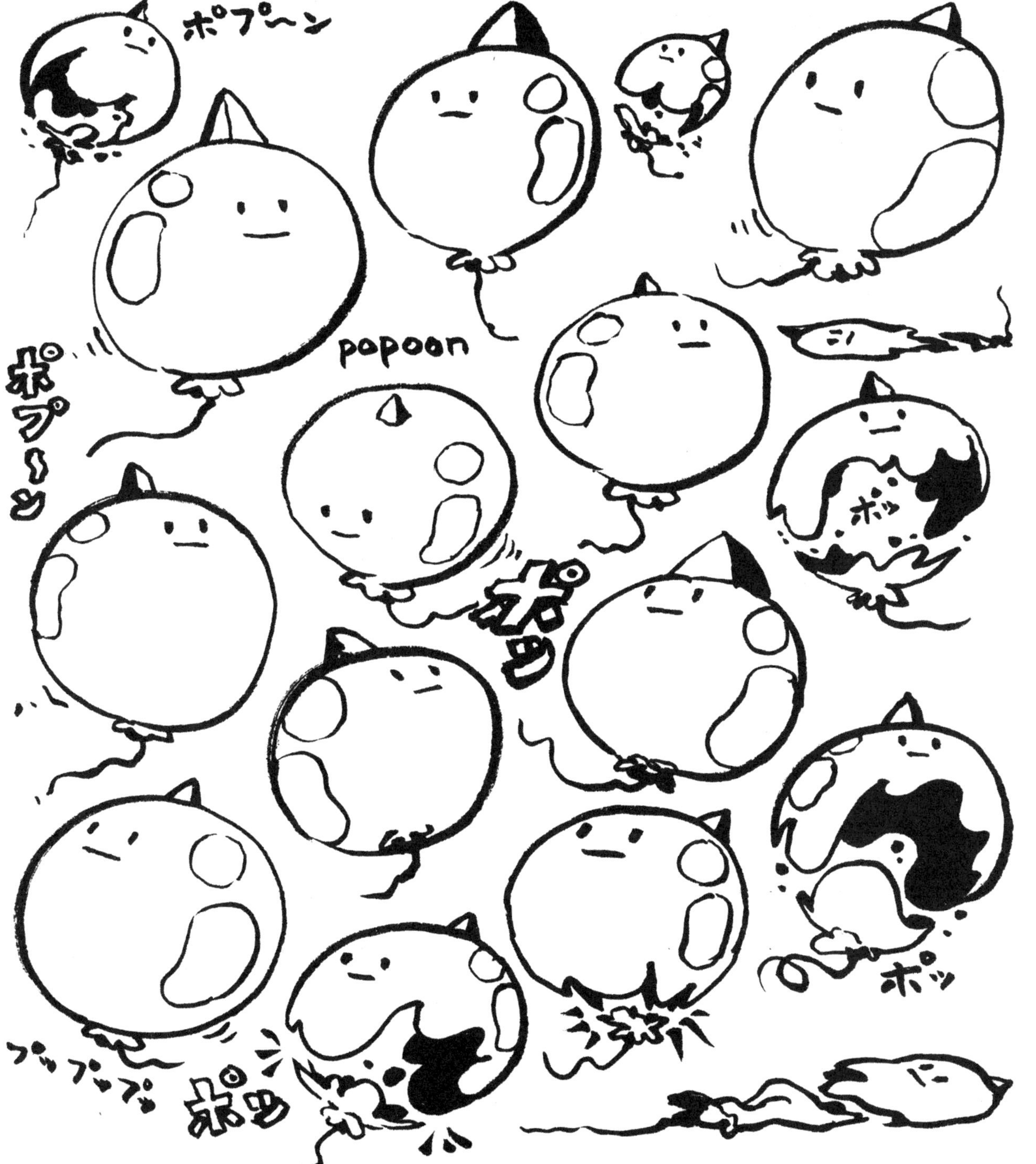
ポプ〜ン
popoon
ポプ〜ン
ポッ
ポッ
ポッ
プップップッ
ポッ

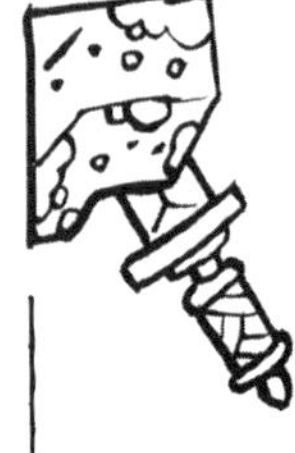

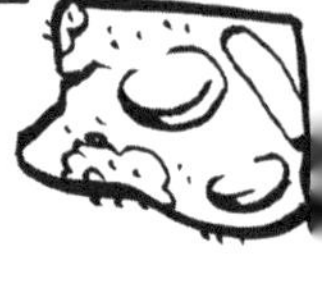

You complete me.

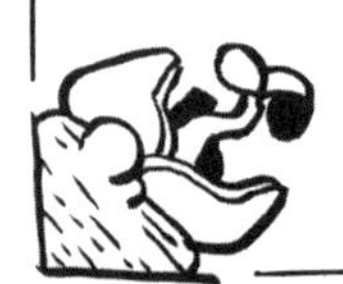

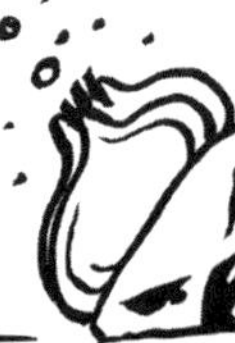

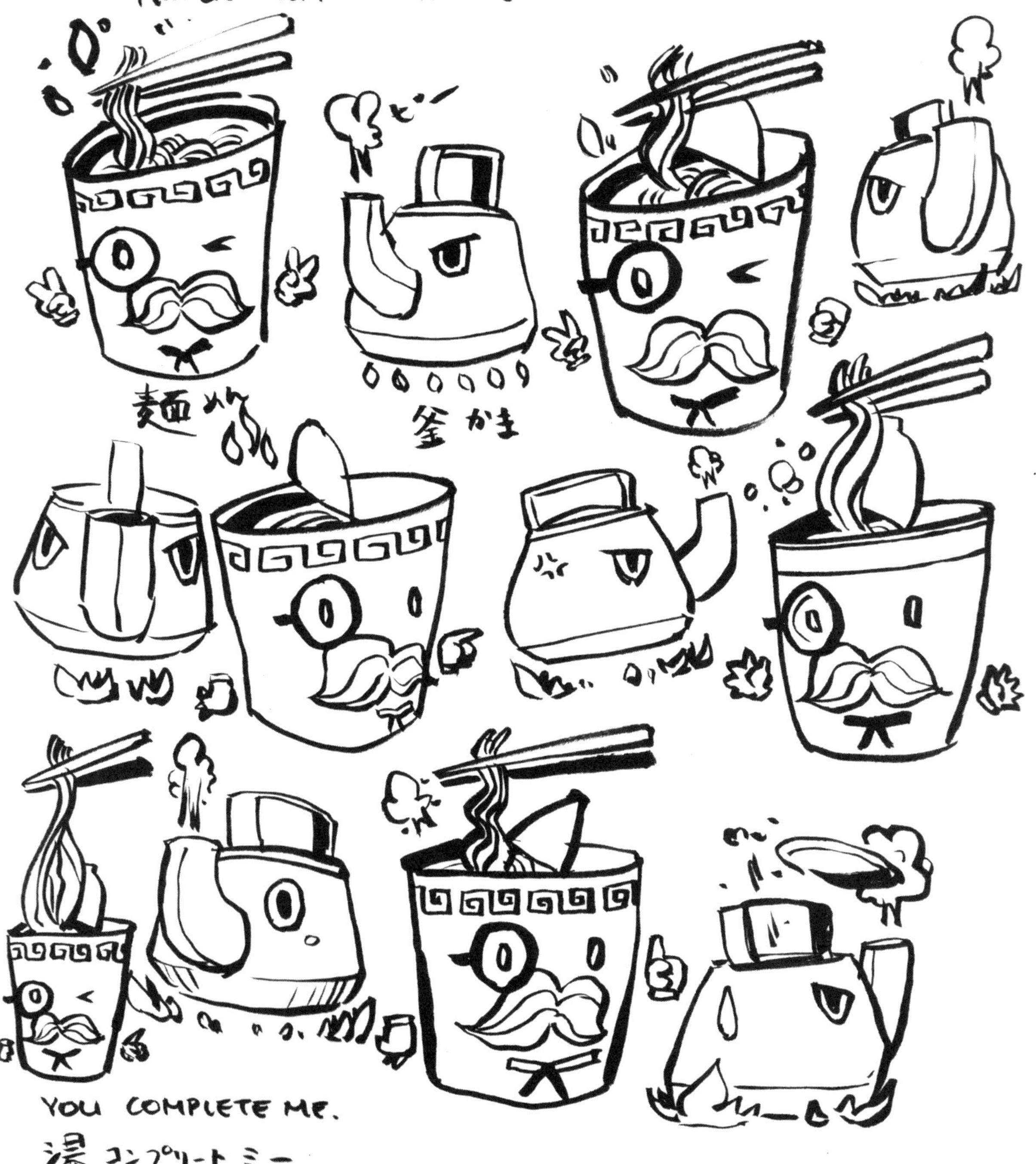
MR. GENTLEMAN & HOTTIE
麺 めん
釜 かま
YOU COMPLETE ME.
湯 コンプリート ミー。

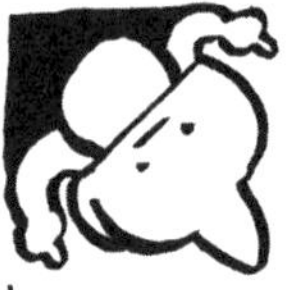

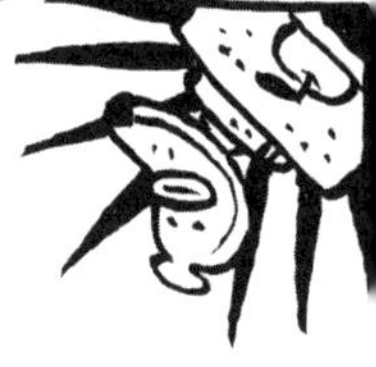

Unattended yet fine.

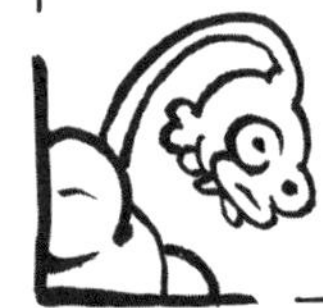

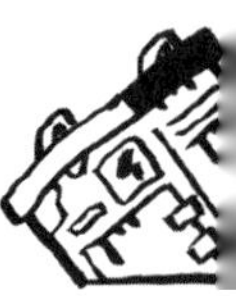

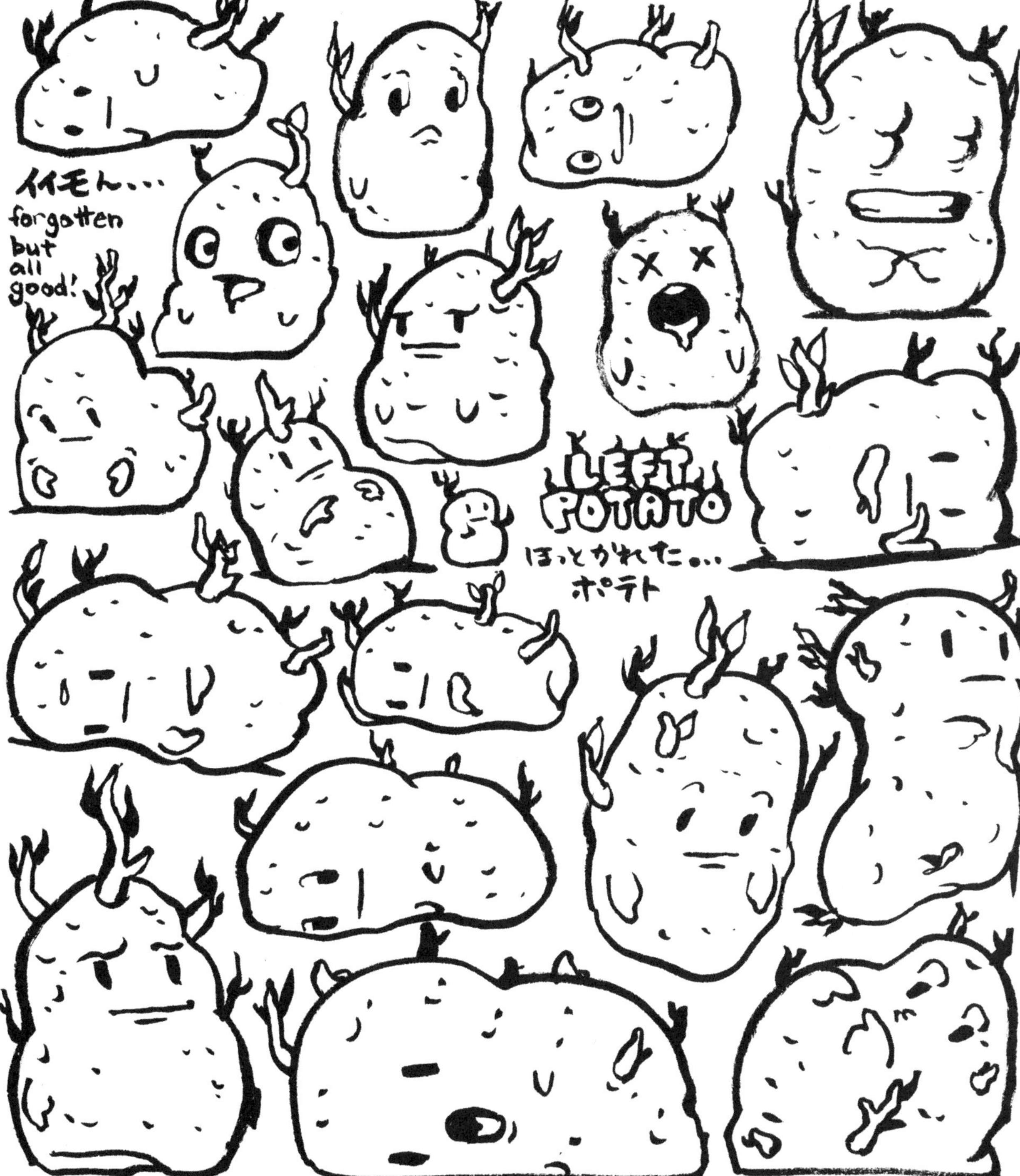
イイモん…
forgotten
but
all
good!
LEFT
POTATO
ほっとかれた…
ポテト

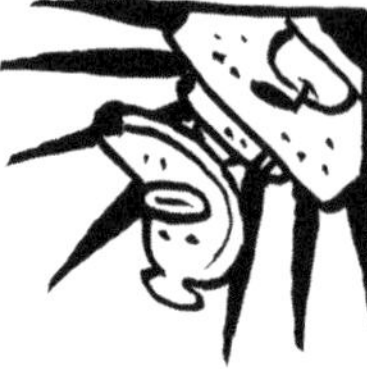

Rehash rehearse.

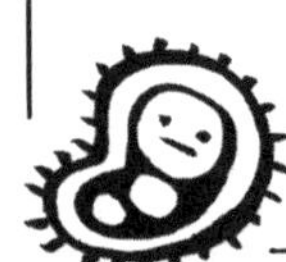

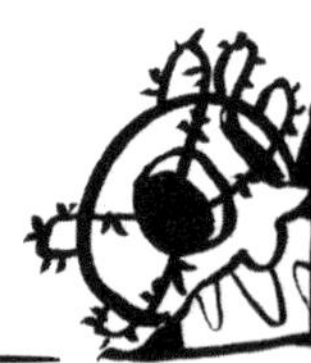

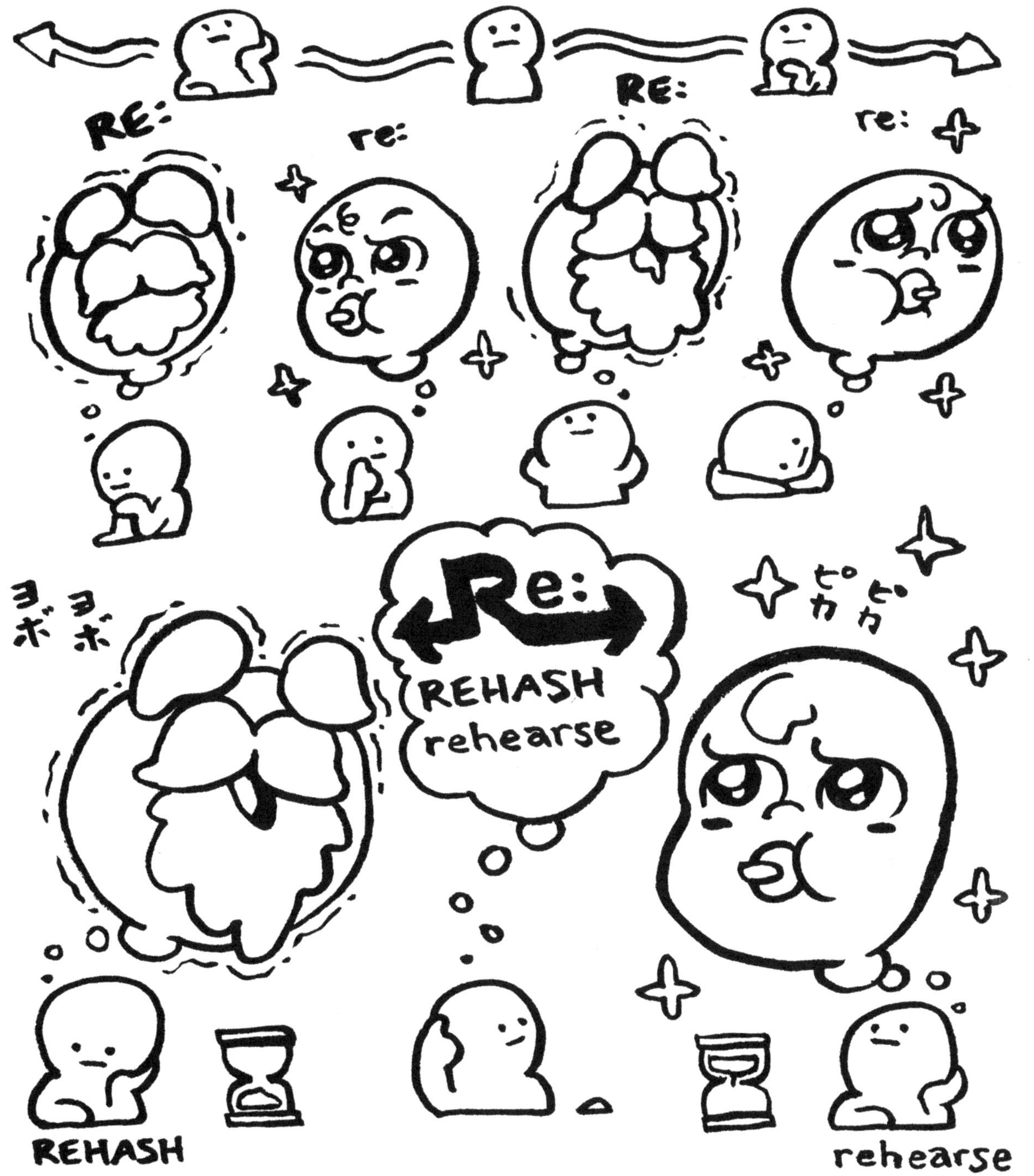
RE:
re:
RE:
re:
ヨボヨボ
Re:
REHASH
rehearse
ピカピカ
REHASH
rehearse

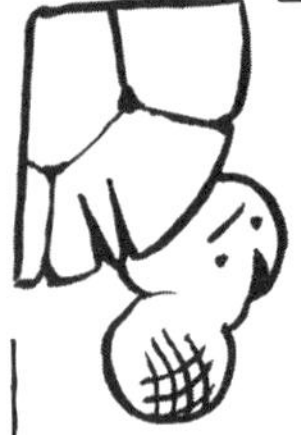

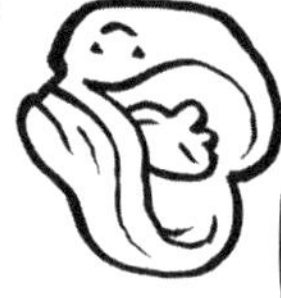

Bill isn't the fastest so
he's always in last place...
yet he still runs.
Go Billy!

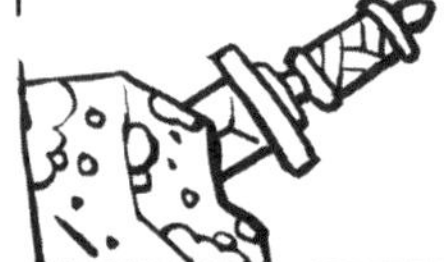

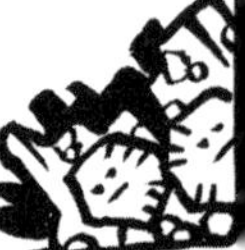

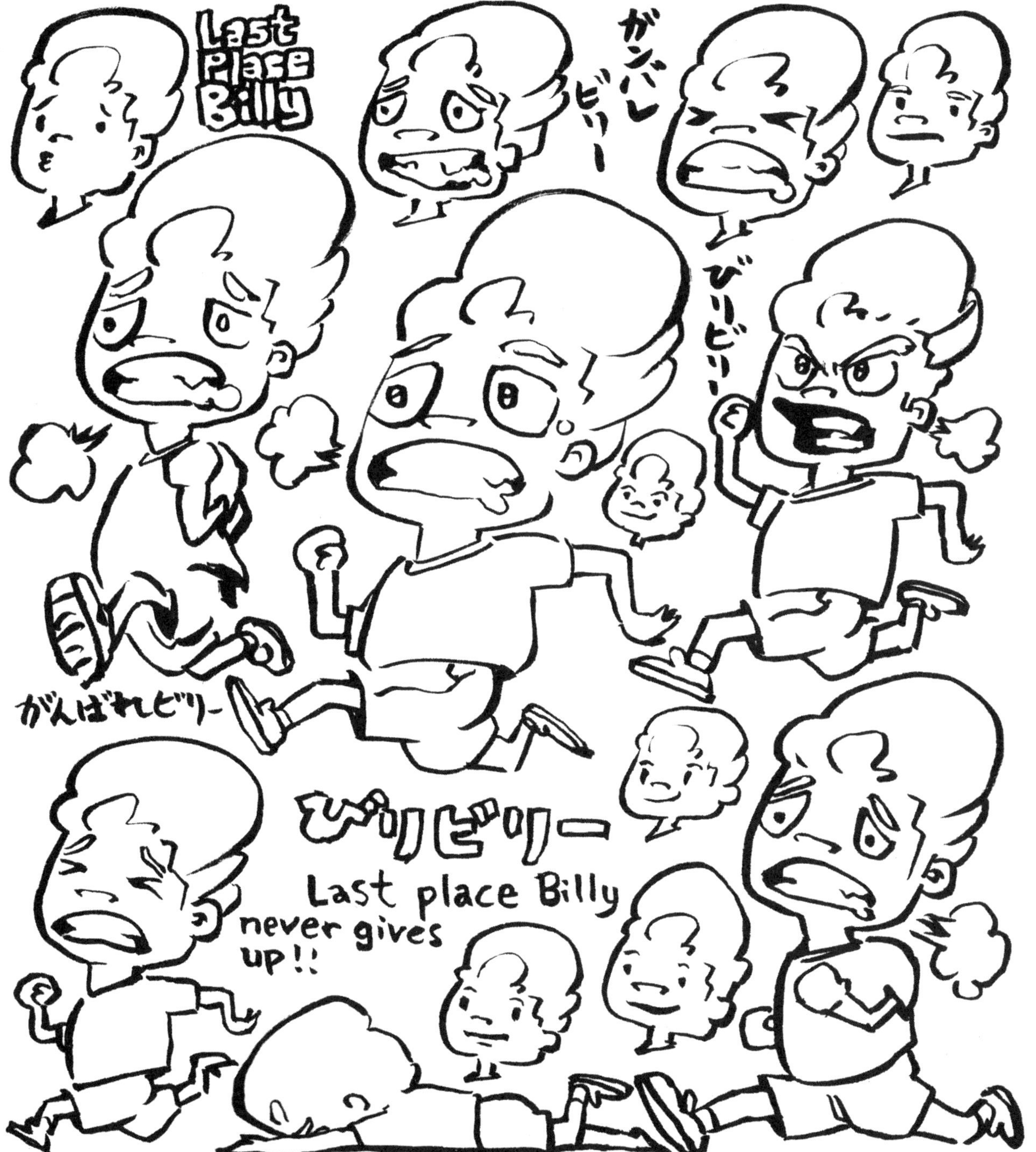

Last place Billy
ガンバレ
ビリー
びりビリー
がんばれビリー
びりビリー
Last place Billy
never gives up!!

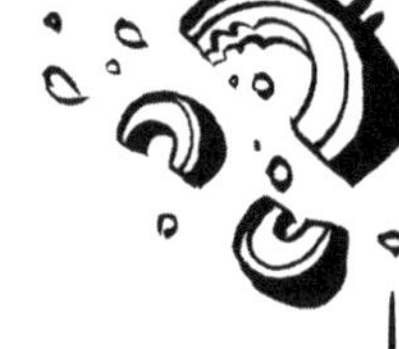

Huebert may grant
you your wish.

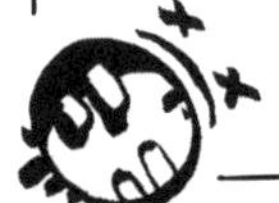

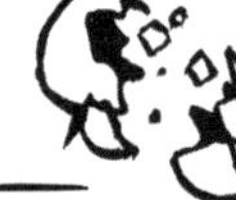

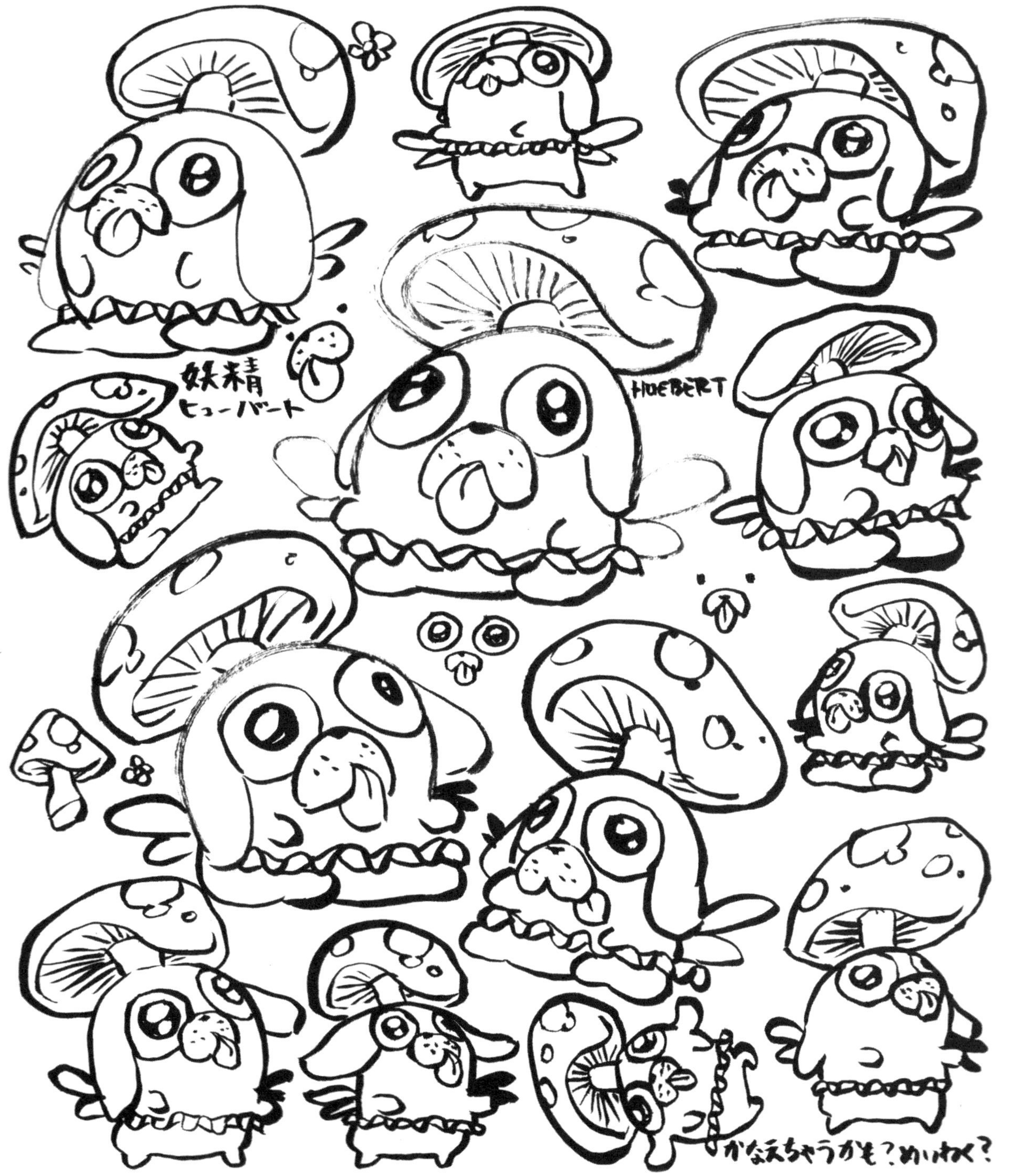
妖精
ヒューバート
HUEBERT
かなえちゃうかも？めいわく？

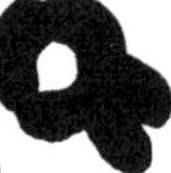

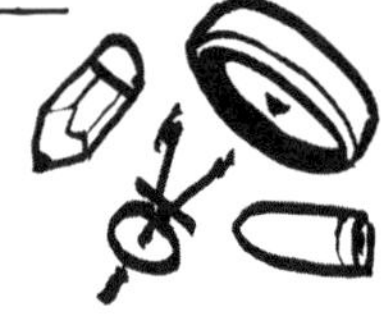

Simple solution,
complex problem.

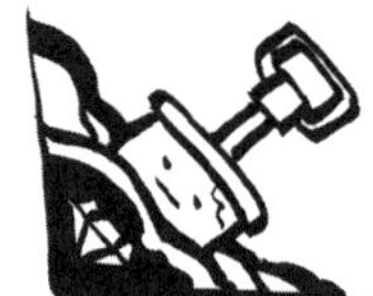

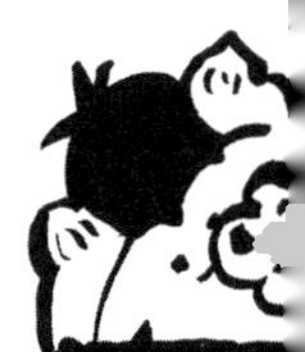

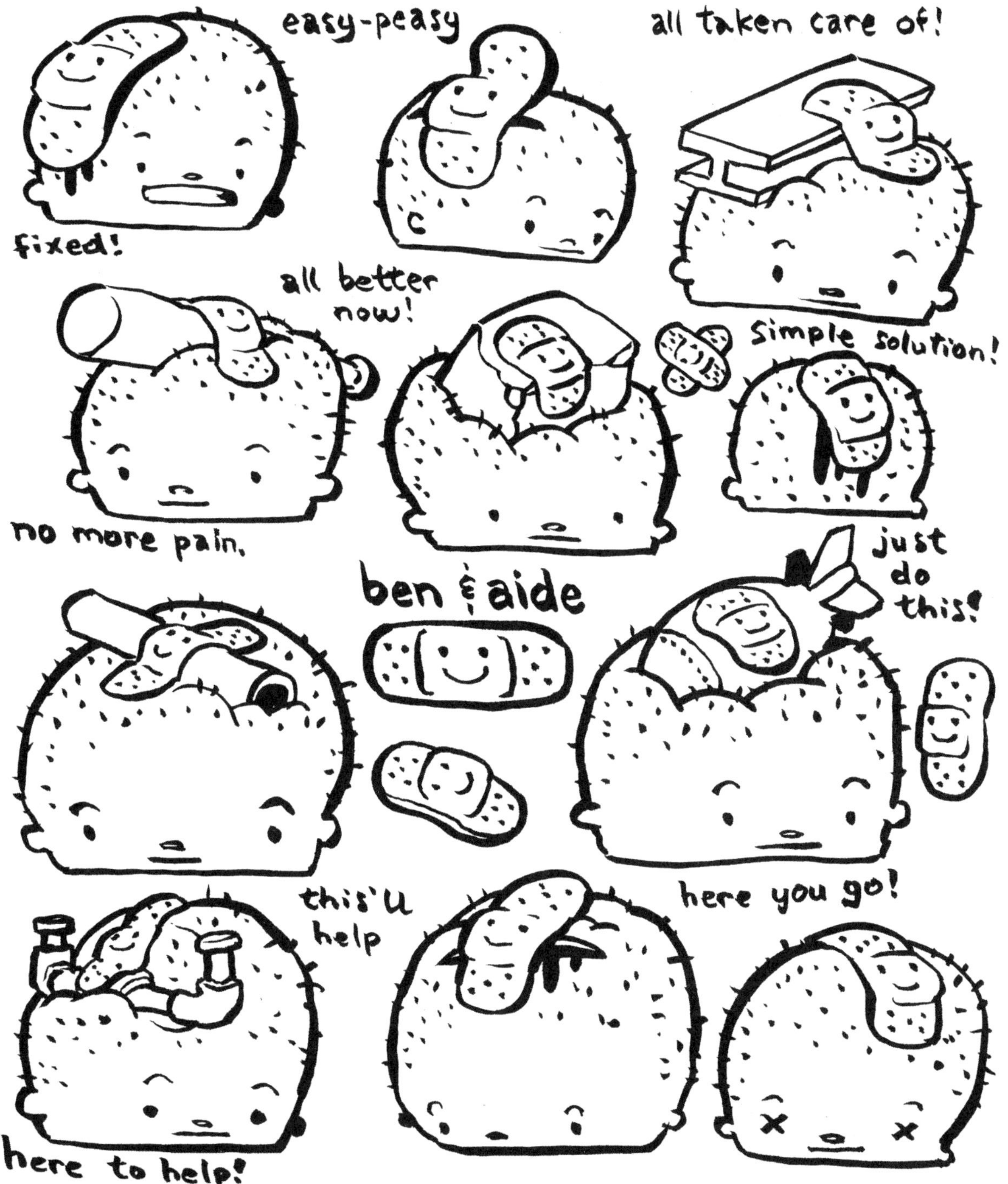

easy-peasy
all taken care of!
fixed!
all better now!
simple solution!
no more pain.
ben & aide
just do this!
this'll help
here you go!
here to help!

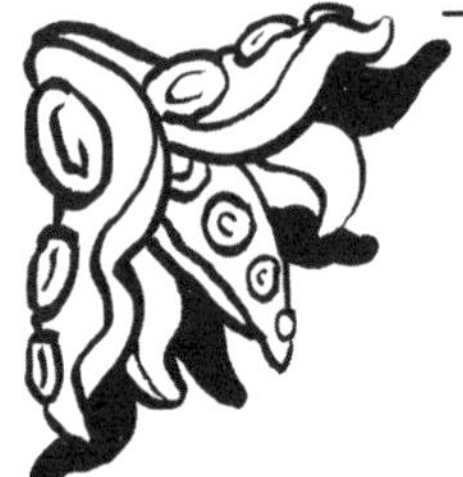

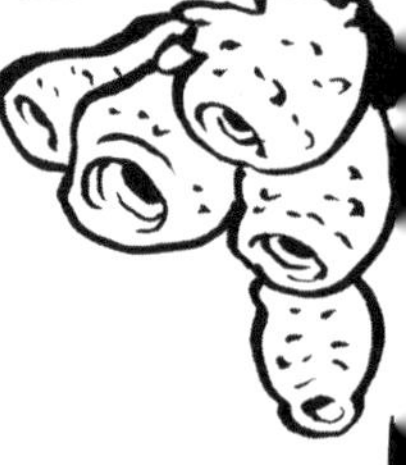

Bramble brier.

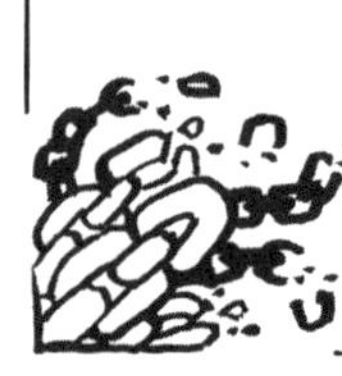

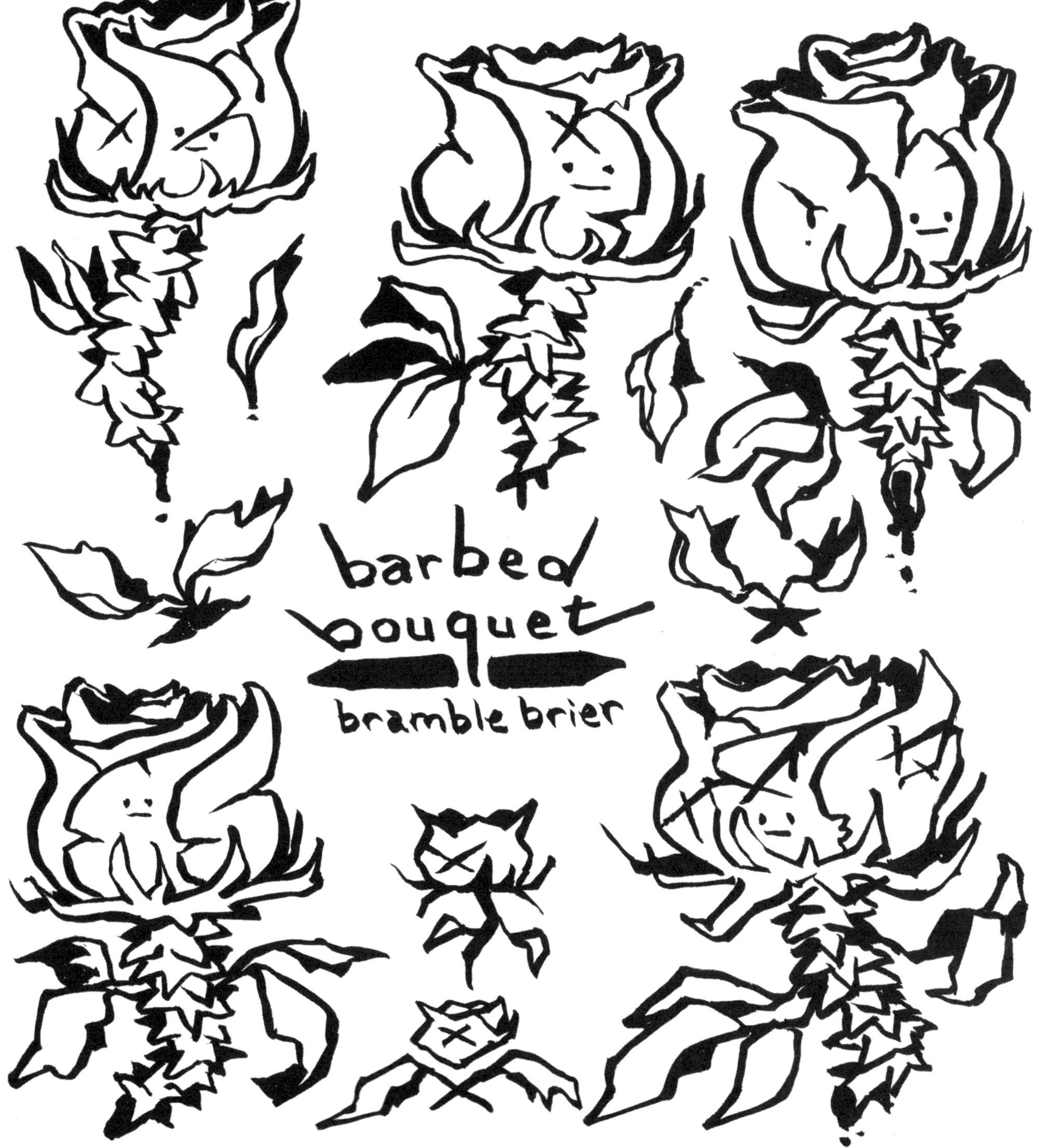
barbed
bouquet
bramble brier

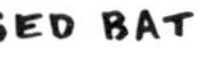

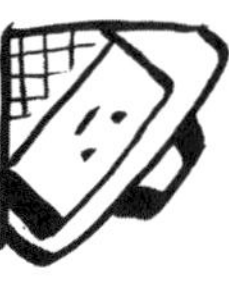

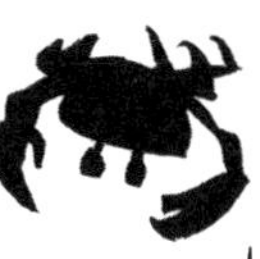

Carrot failure.

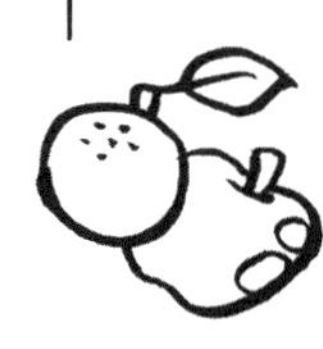

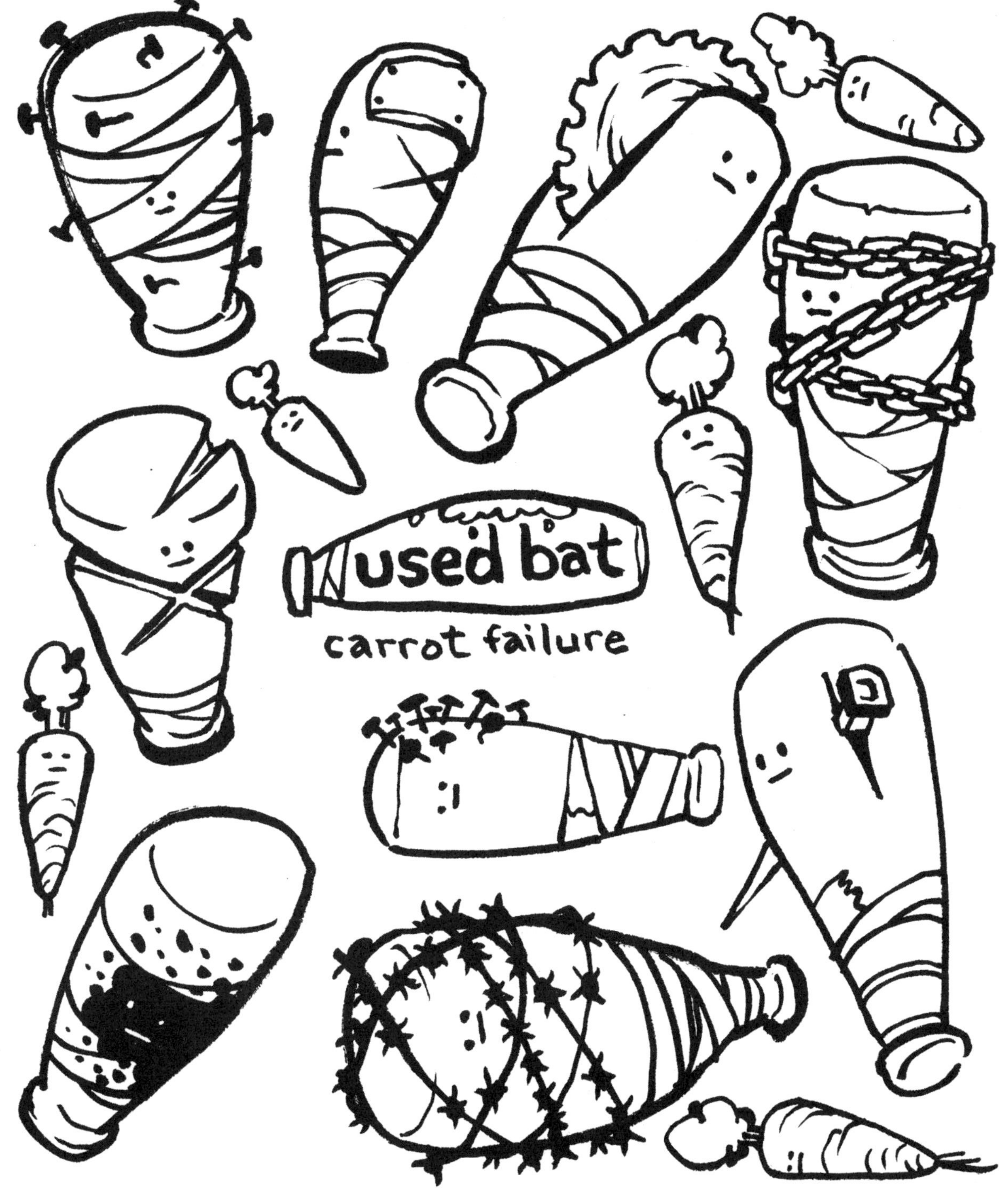
used bat
carrot failure

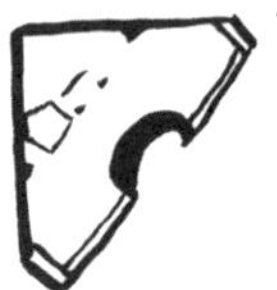

The tenacious chef Sammy and apprentices Lofa & Pisuke run the island's only 3 starfish joint.

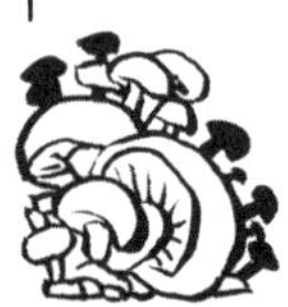

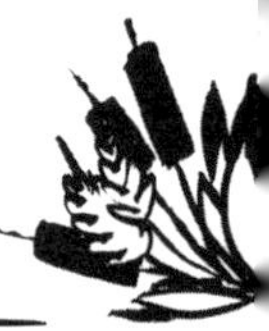

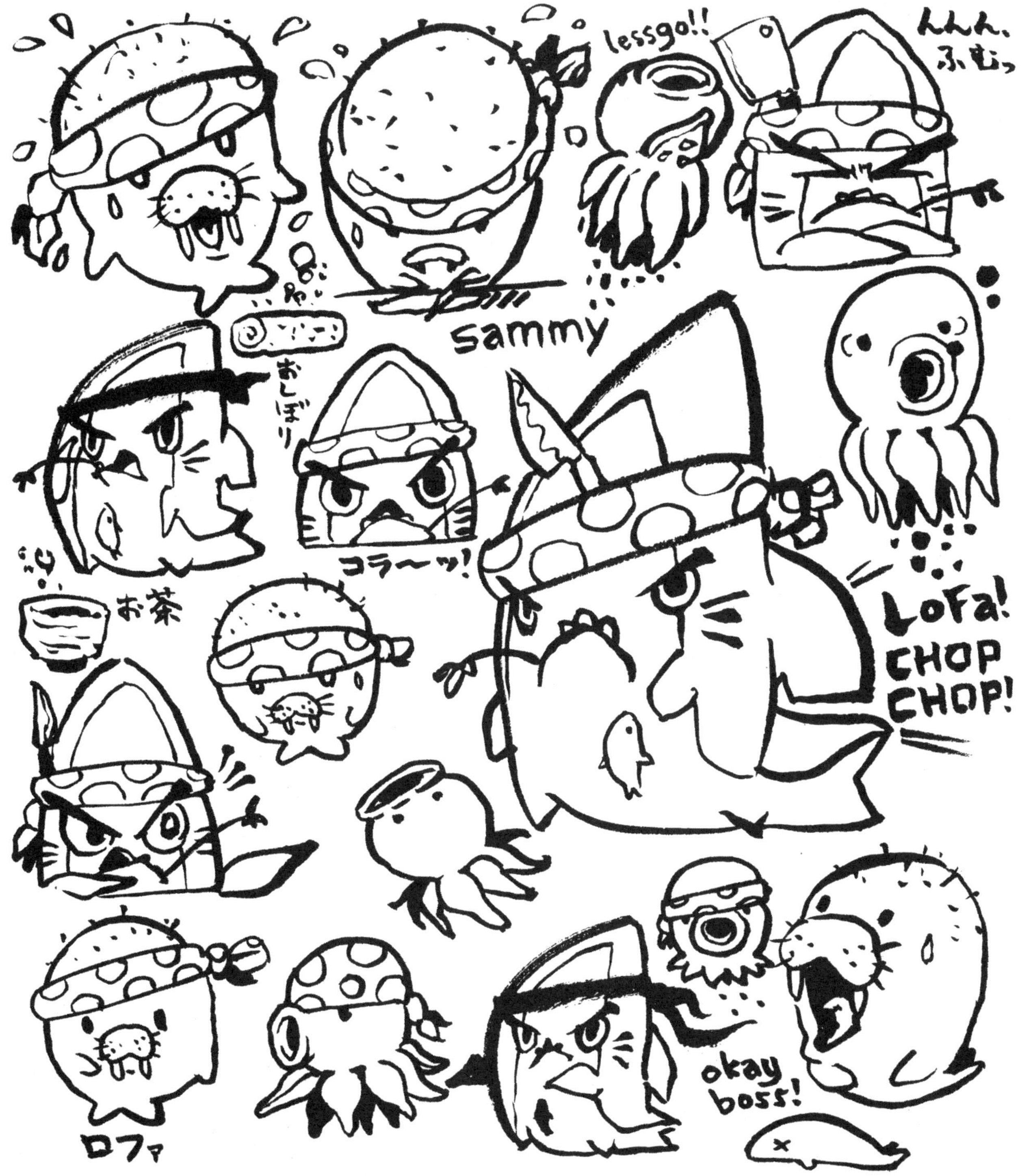
lessgo!!
んんん、
ふむっ
sammy
おしぼり
コラ〜ッ!
お茶
LoFa!
CHOP
CHOP!
okay
boss!
ロファ

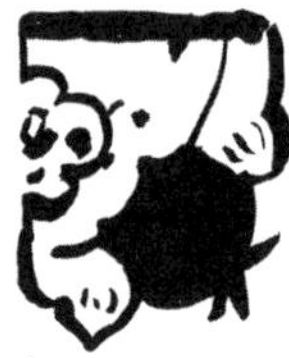

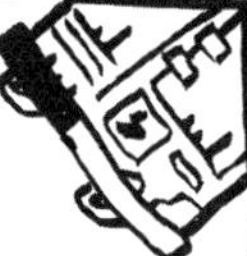

Blown opportunity.

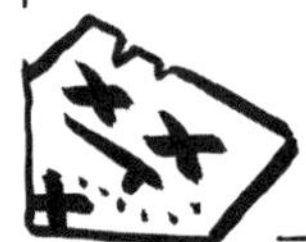

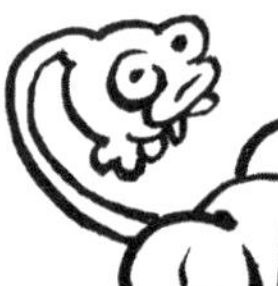

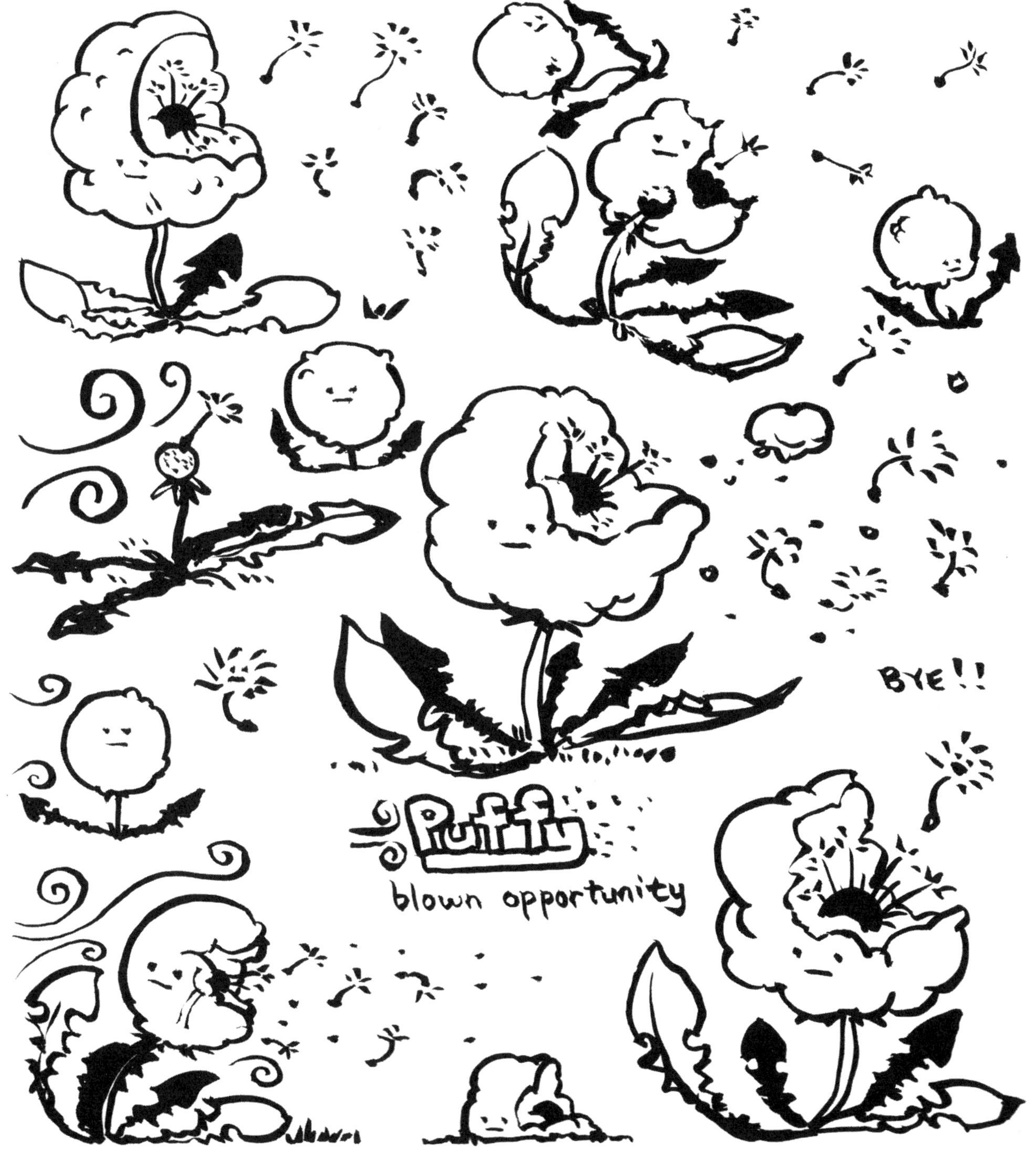
BYE!!
Puffy
blown opportunity

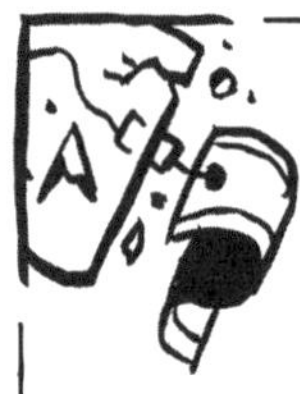

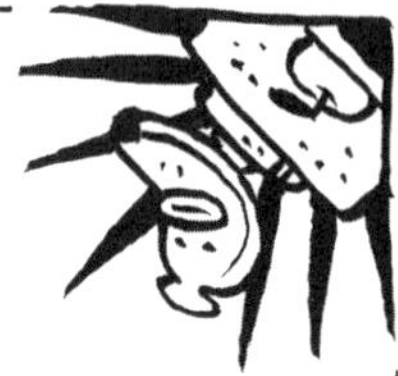

Self inflicted.

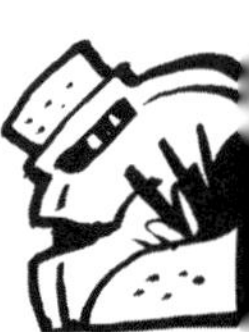

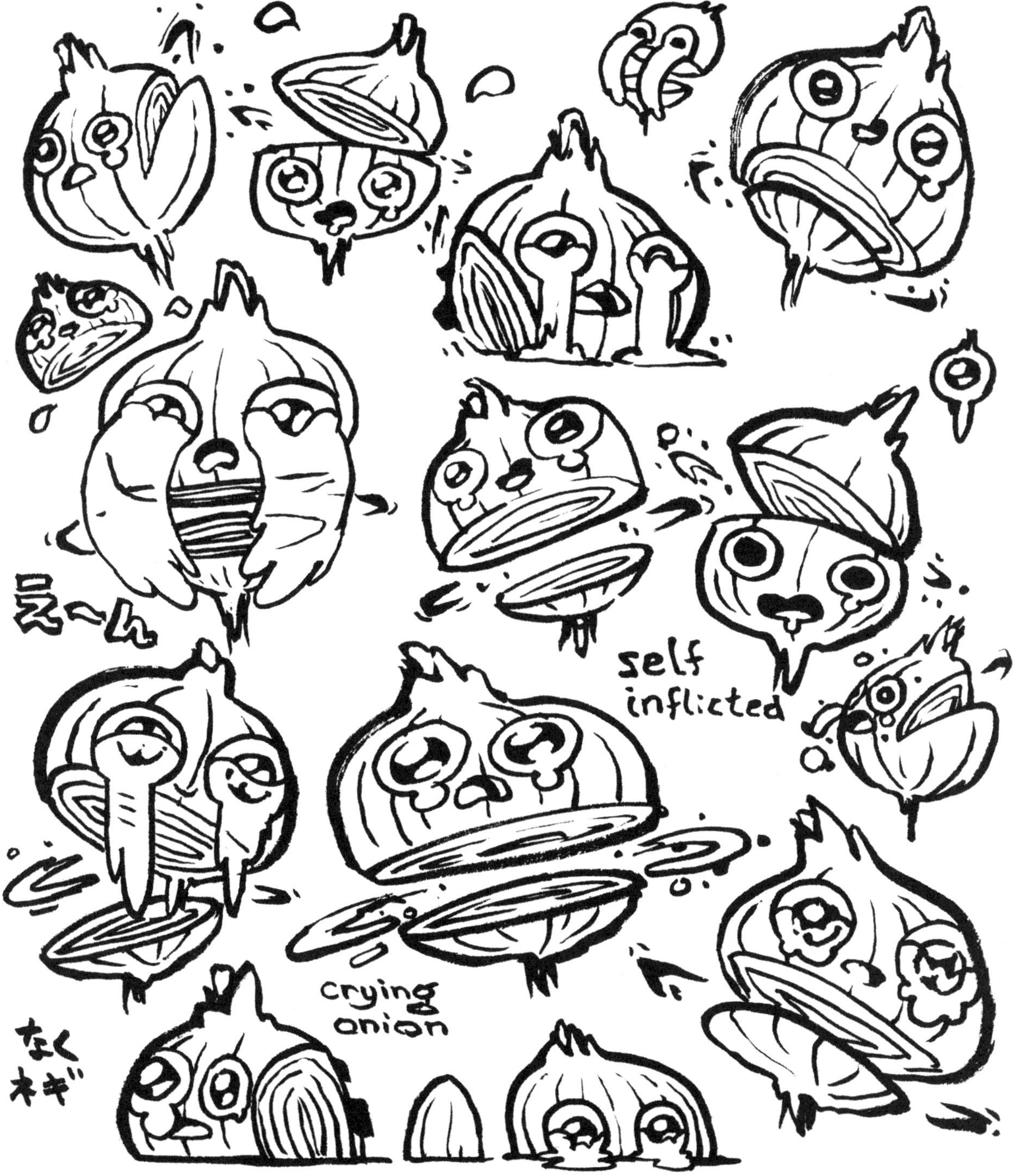

えーん
self inflicted
crying onion
なく
ネギ

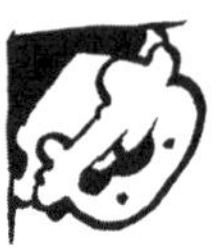

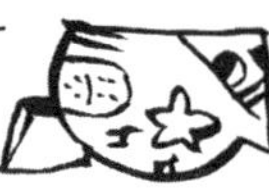

He reacts
for nobody.

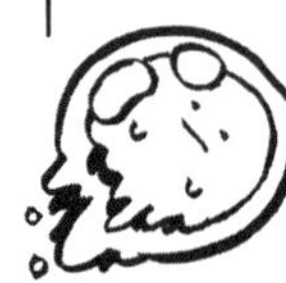

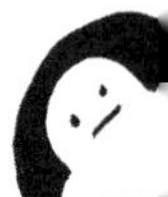

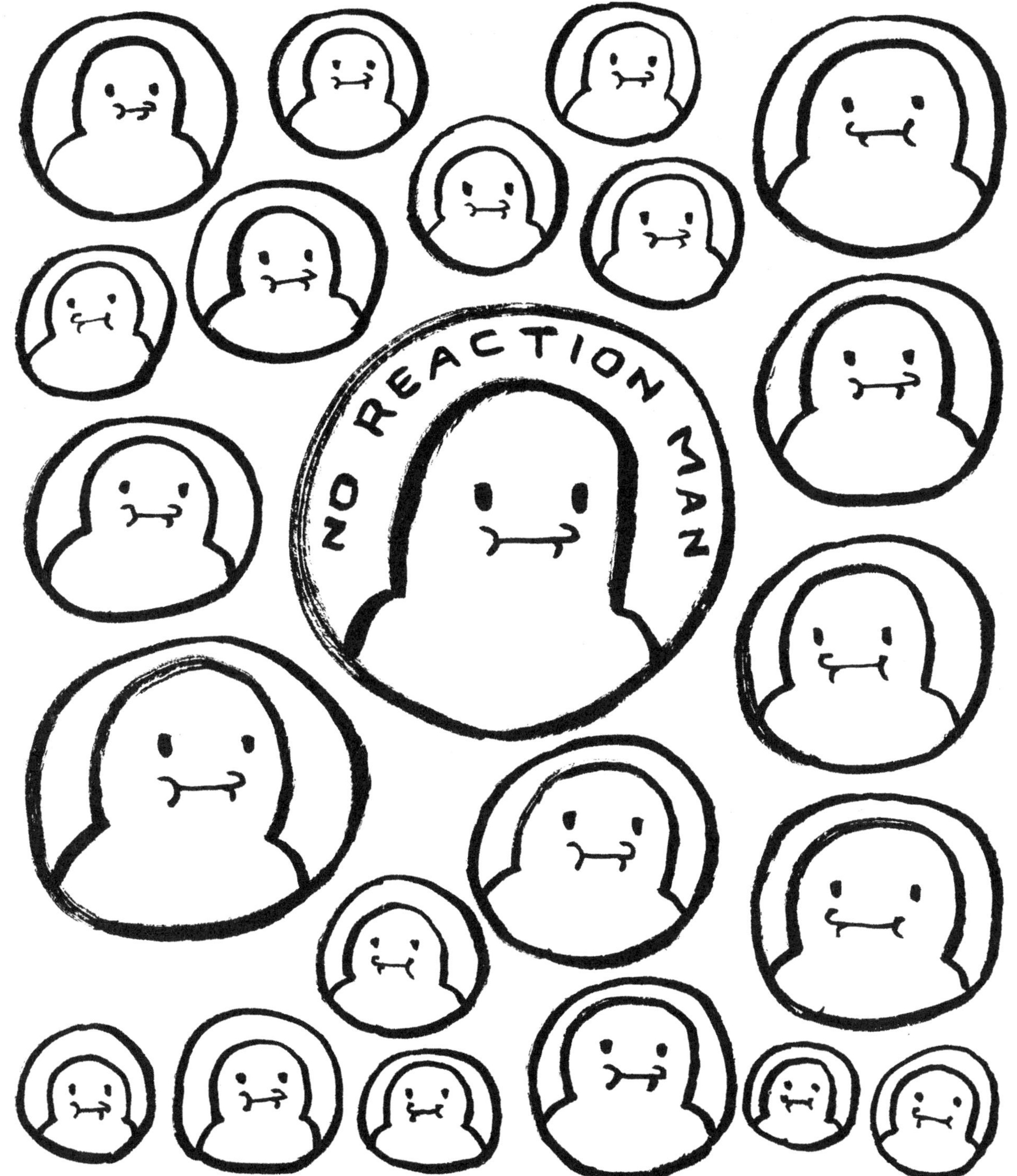
NO REACTION MAN

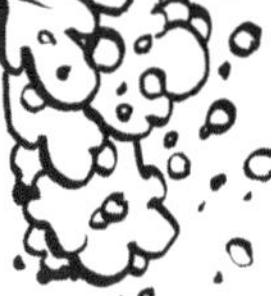

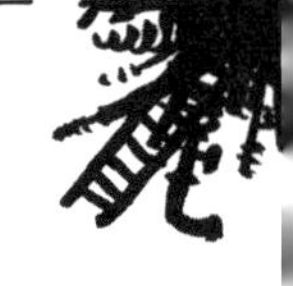

I'm going to grow!

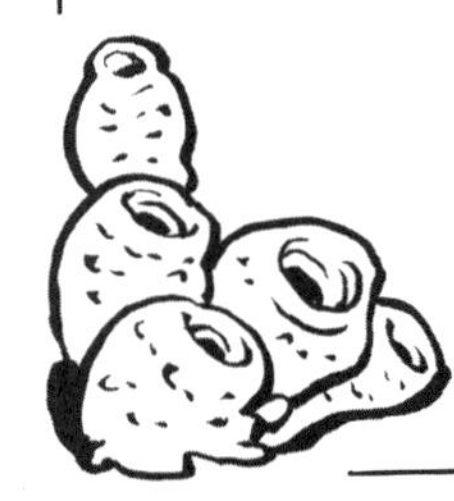

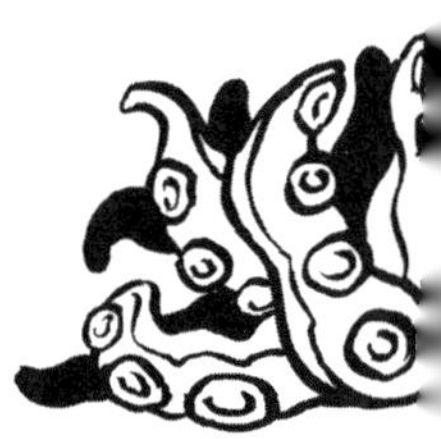

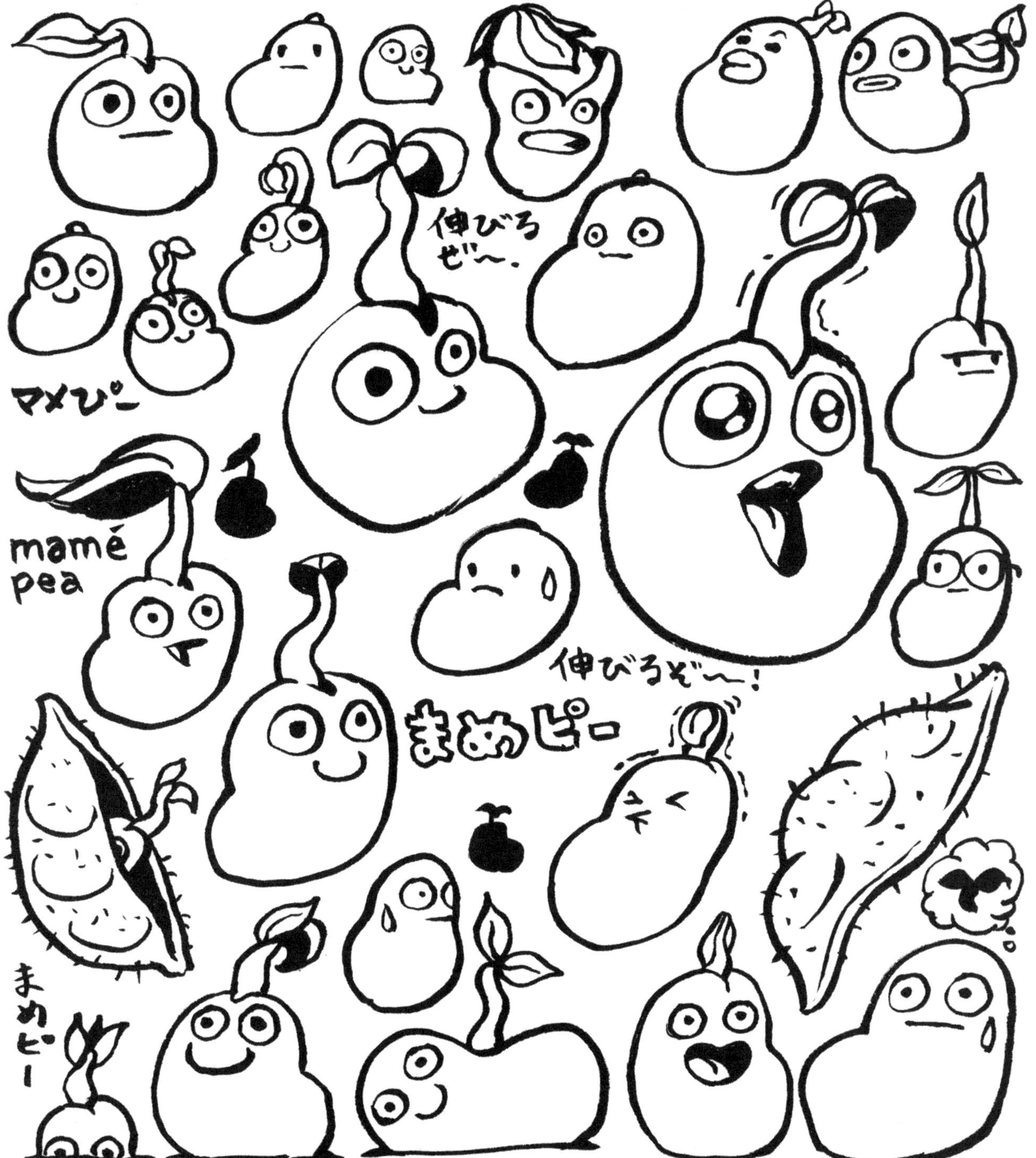
伸びろ
ぜ〜.
マメぴー
mamé
pea
伸びろぞ〜!
まめピー
まめピー

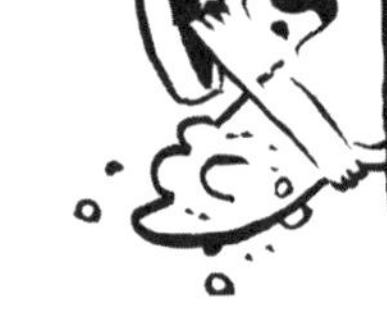

Kewp.

Following you around!

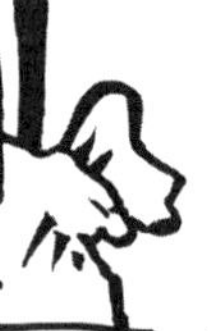

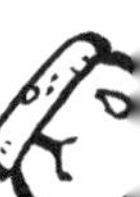

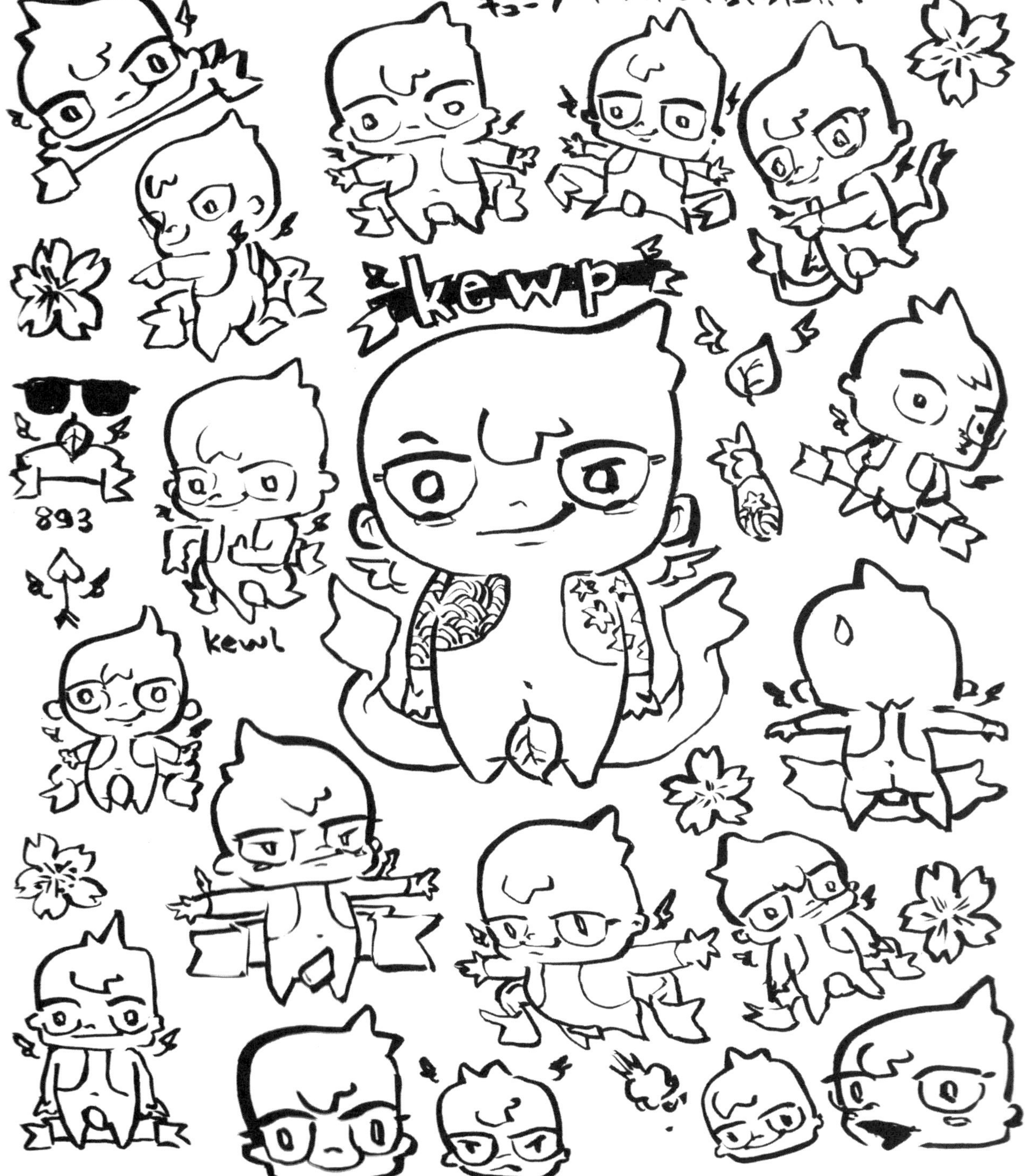
キューピーついてきちゃった!!♥
kewp
893
kewl

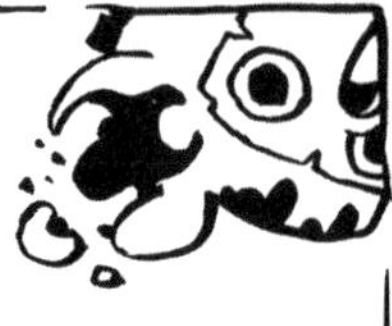

I'd had lunch.

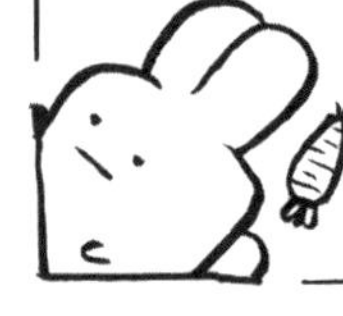

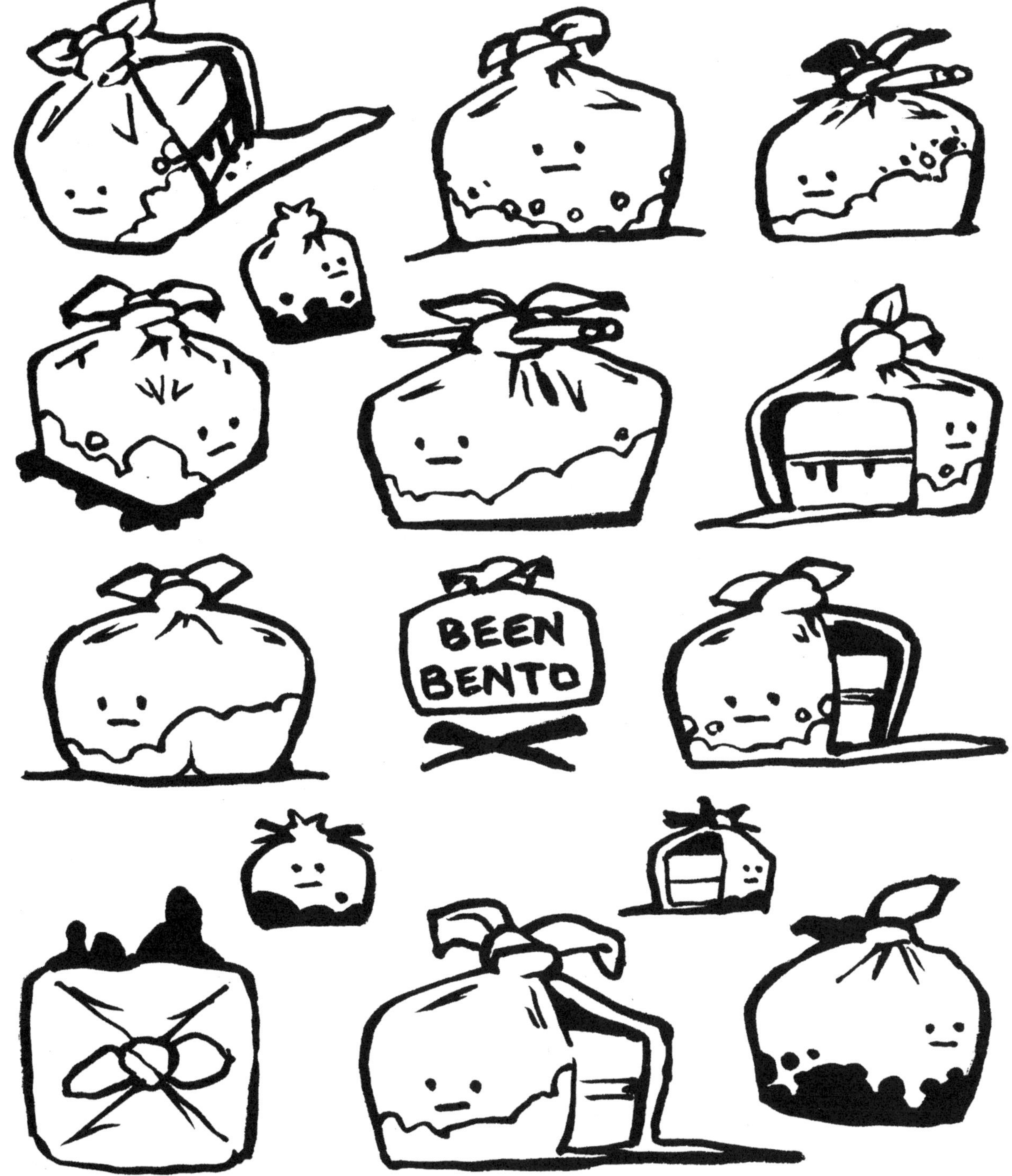
BEEN
BENTO

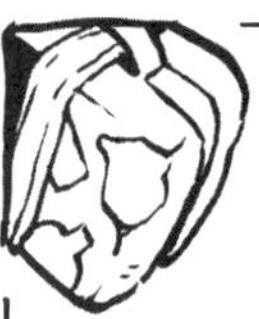

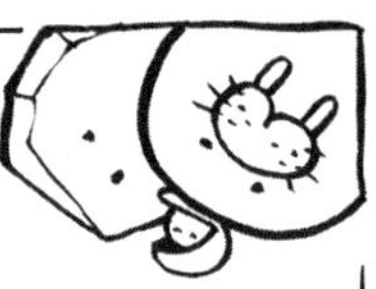

DJ Ink drops
mics not beats.
Check it.

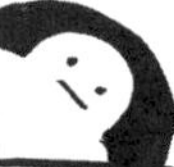

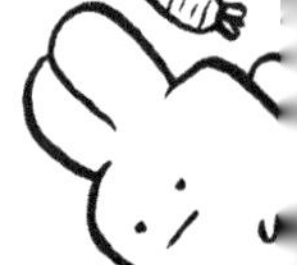

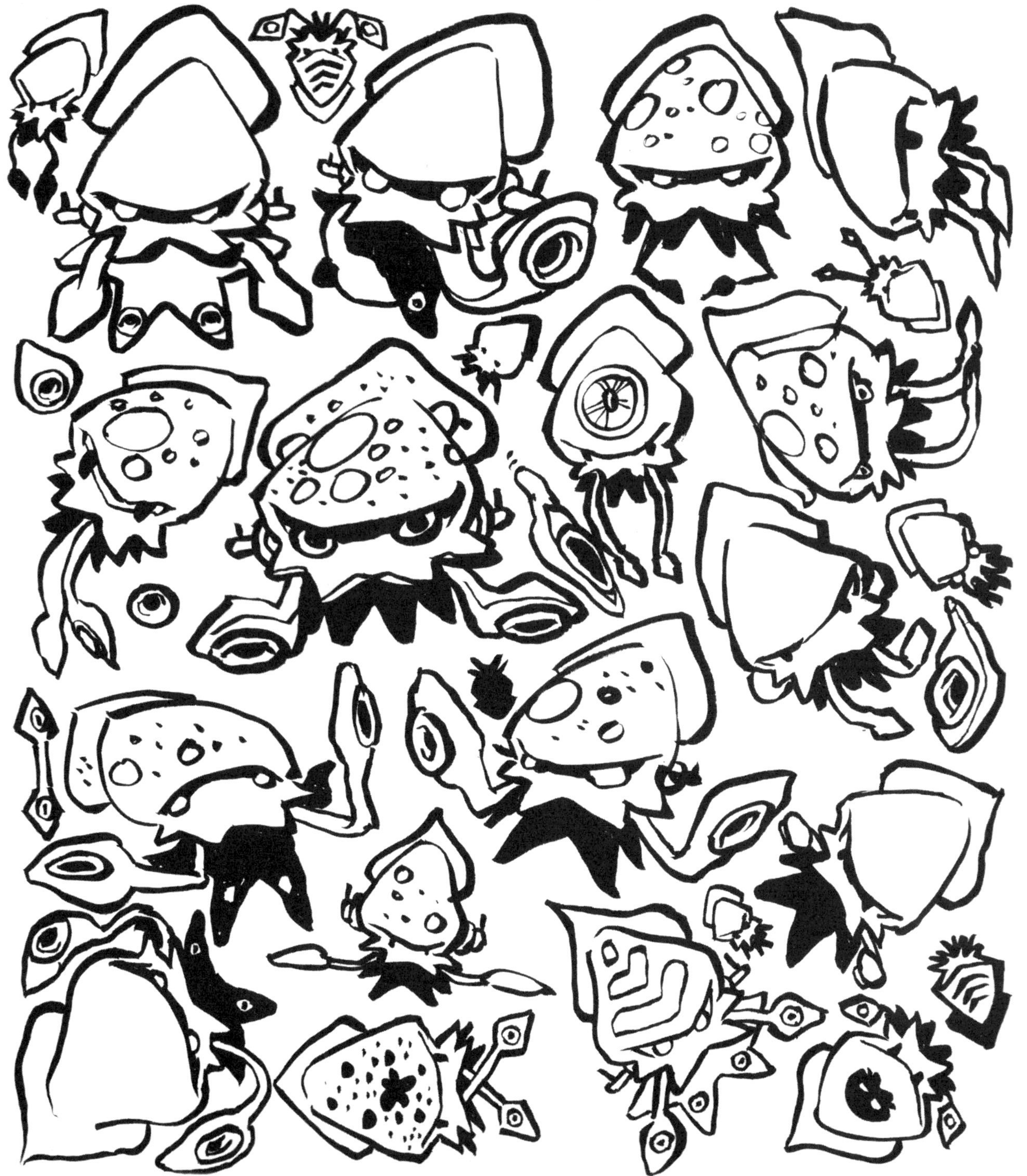

Play with prey.

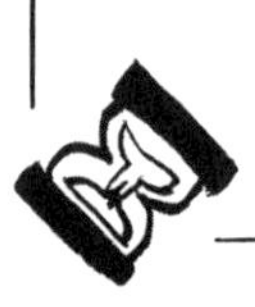

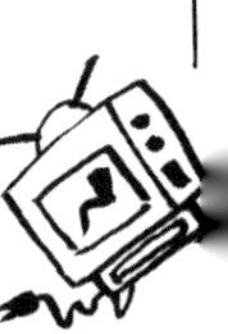

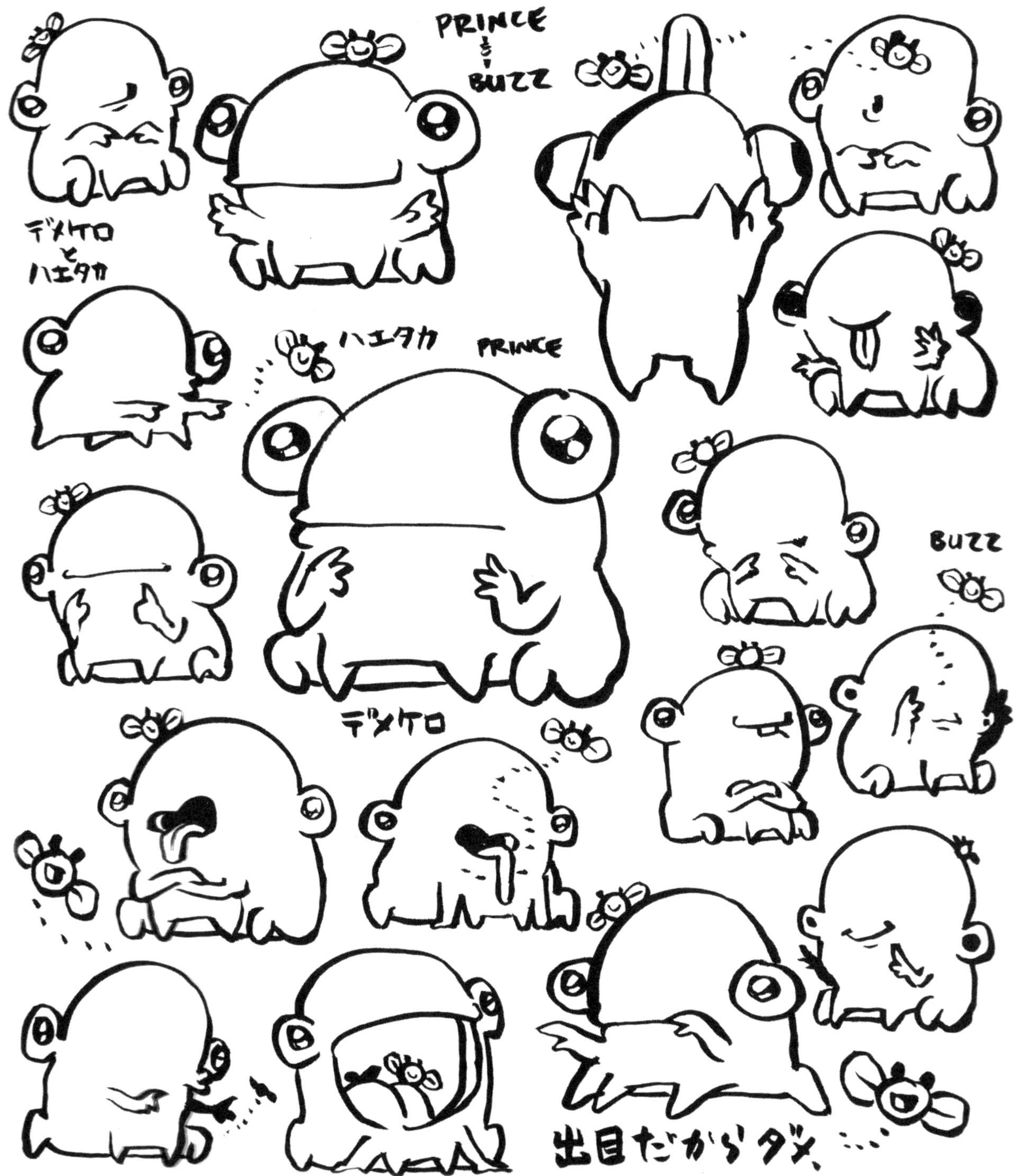
PRINCE
と
BUZZ
デメケロ
と
ハエタカ
ハエタカ
PRINCE
BUZZ
デメケロ
出目だからダメ。

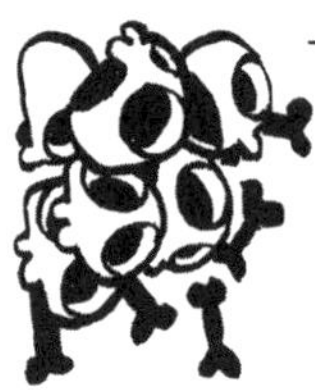

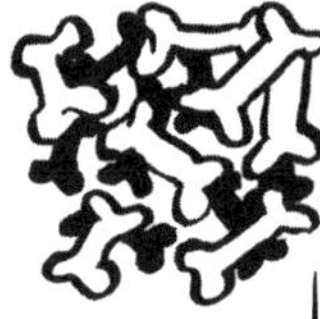

Neko Bako Chan
finds her box
the perfect fit.

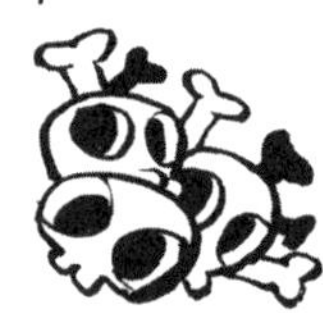

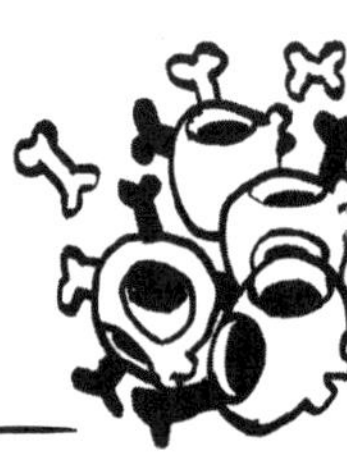

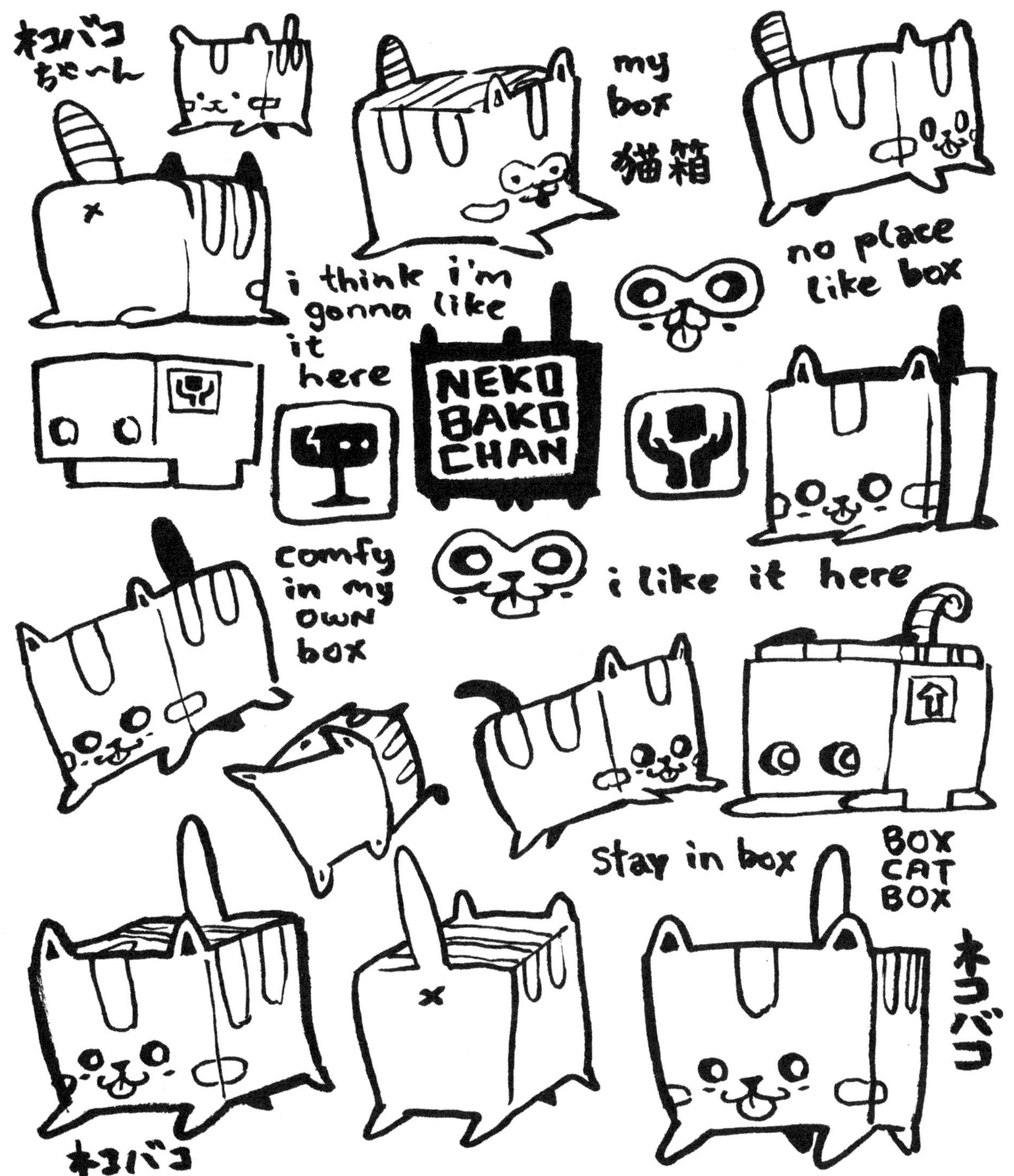
ネコバコ
ちゃ~ん
my
box
猫箱
no place
like box
i think i'm
gonna like
it
here
NEKO
BAKO
CHAN
comfy
in my
OWN
box
i like it here
Stay in box
BOX
CAT
BOX
ネコバコ
ネコバコ

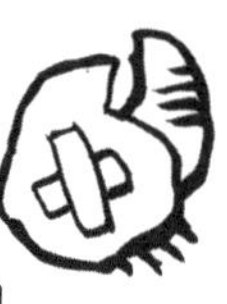

Inaccurate.

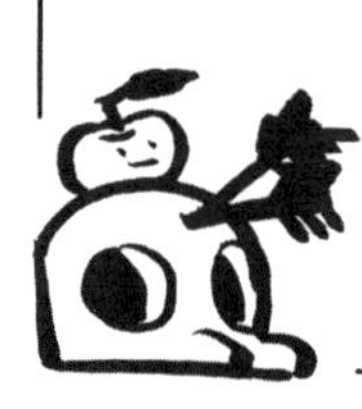

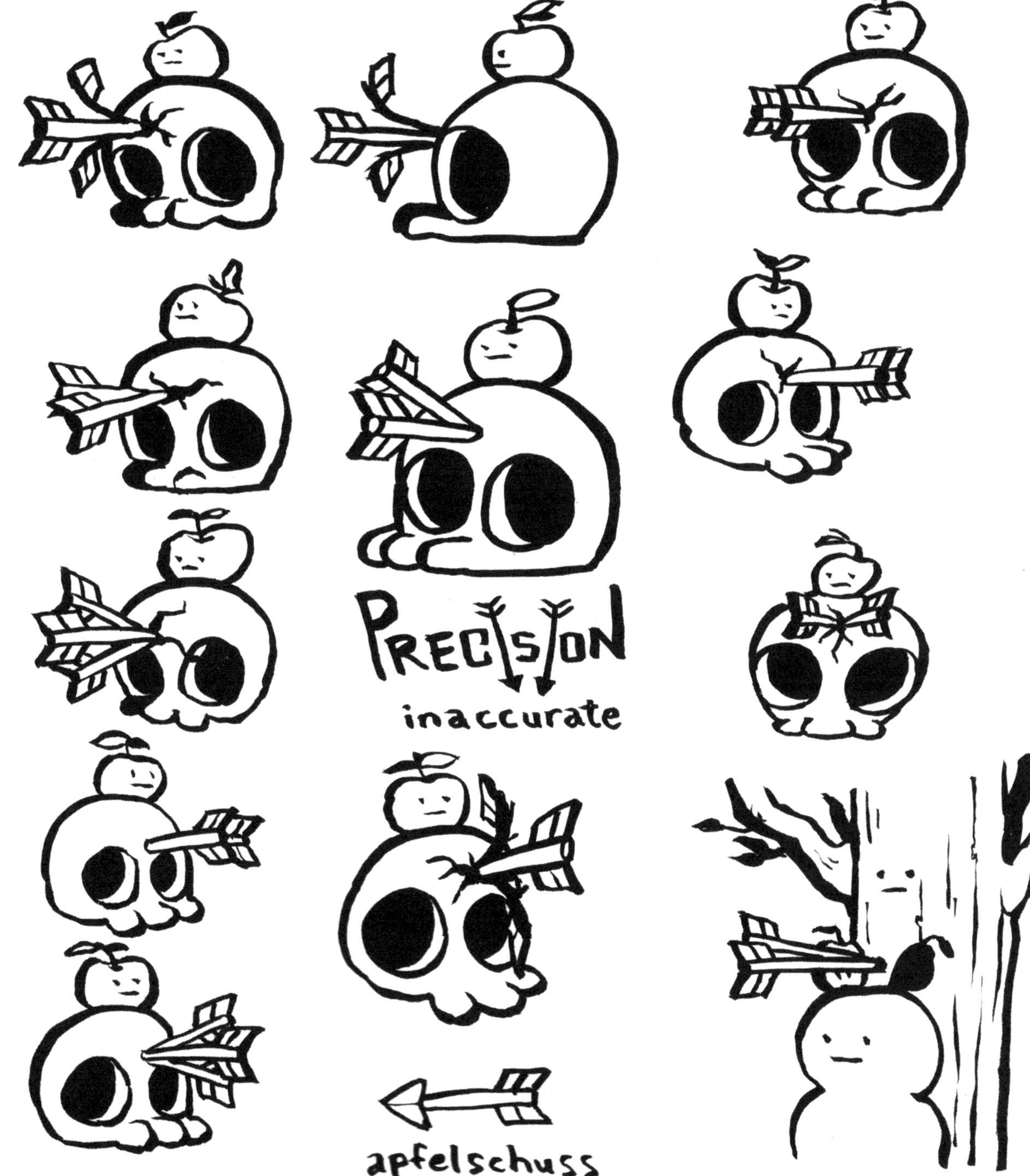
PRECISION
inaccurate
apfelschuss

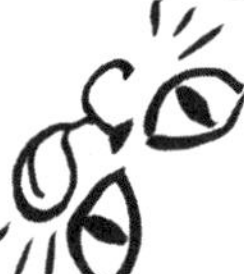
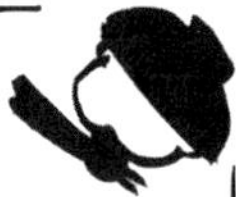

They think
they're better.

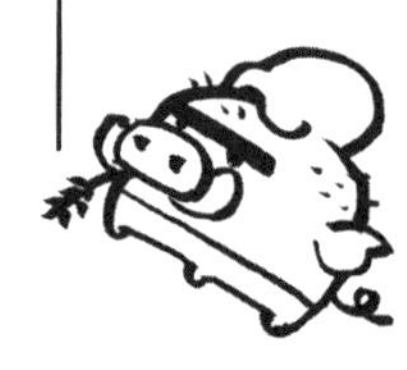
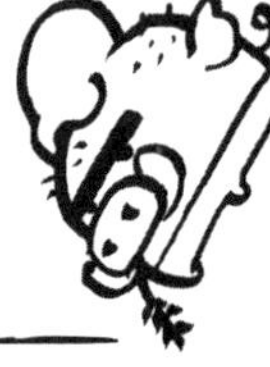

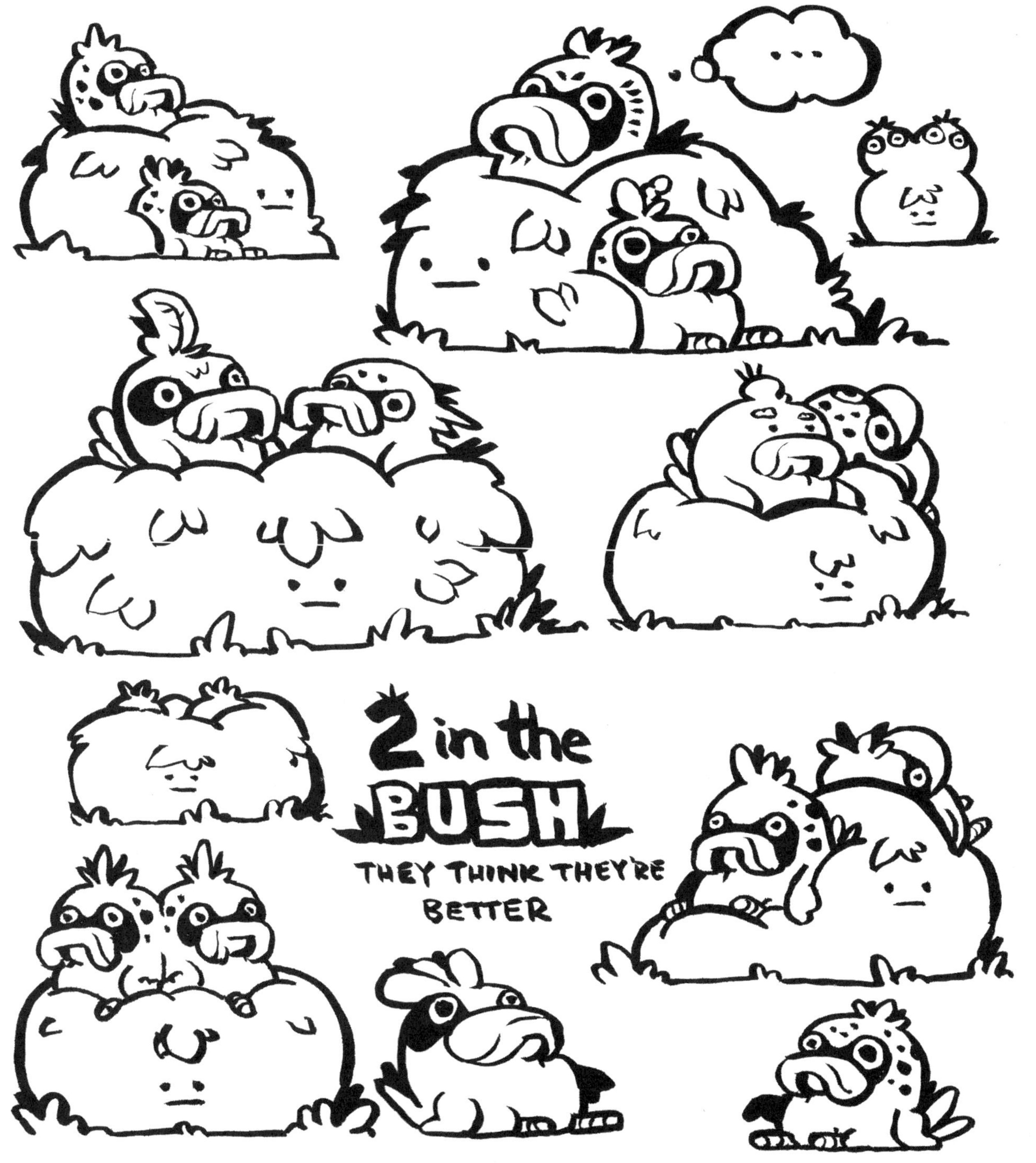
...
2 in the
BUSH
THEY THINK THEY'RE
BETTER

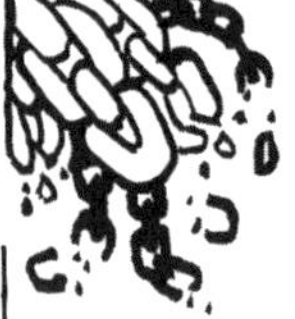

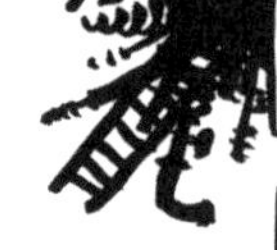

Destructive,
yet meant well.

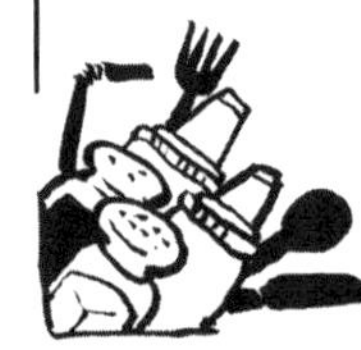

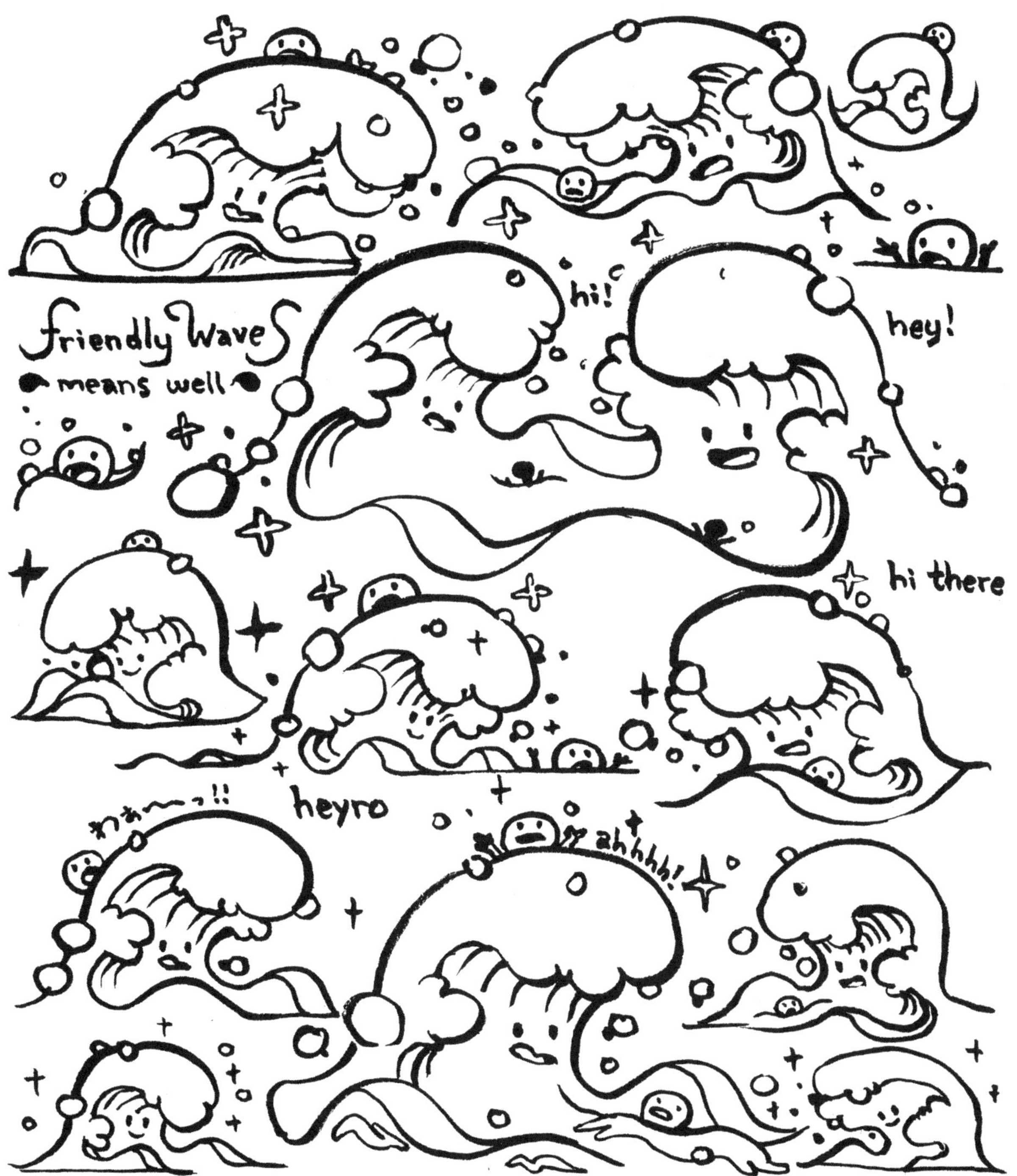
friendly waves
means well
hi!
hey!
hi there
heyro
わあ〜っ!!
ahhhh!

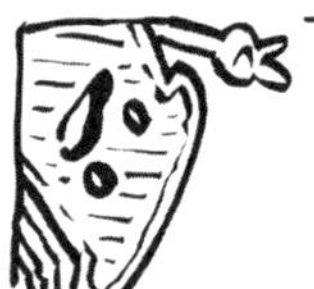

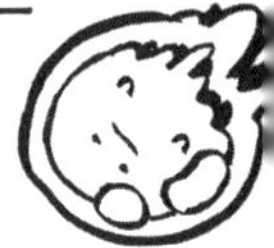

Fluffy, friendly,
and appetizing.

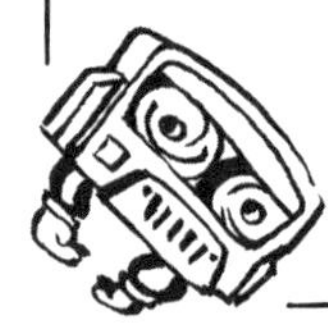

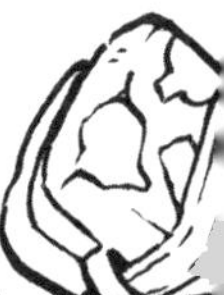

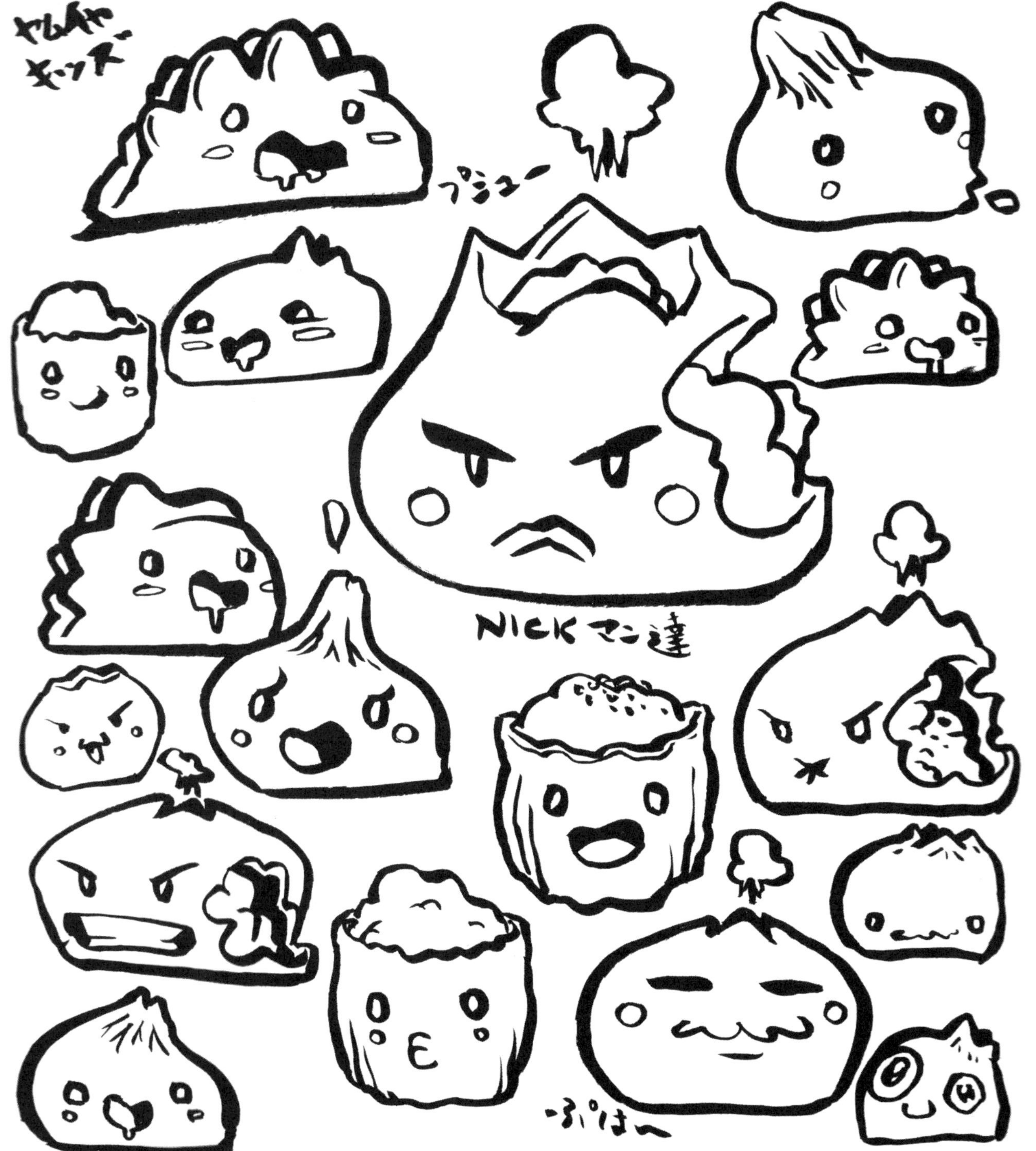
ヤムチャー
キッズー
プシュー
NICKマン達
ーぷはへ

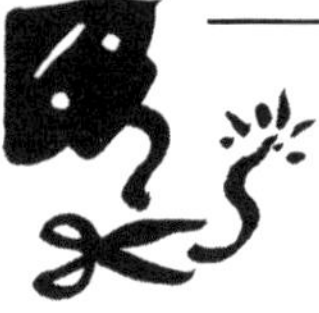

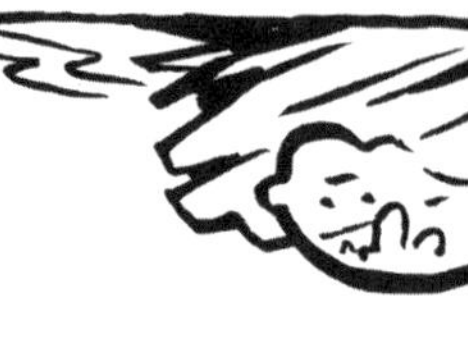

Hope you are all okay.

Stay safe.

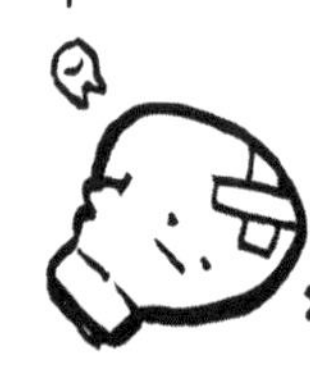

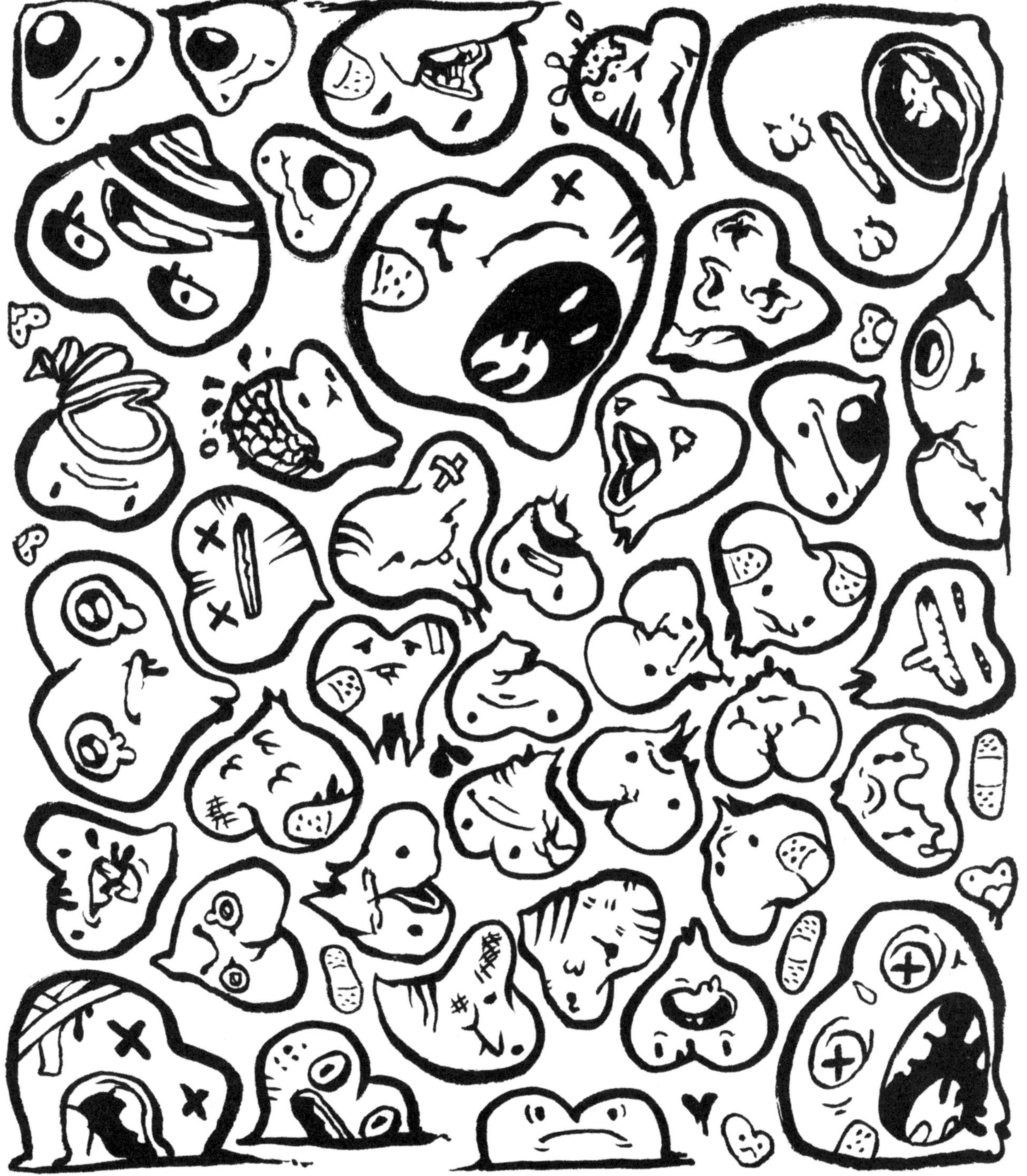

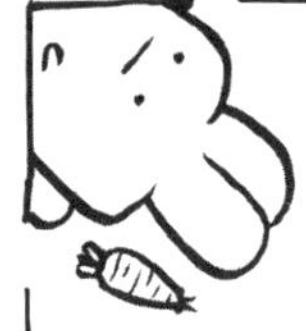

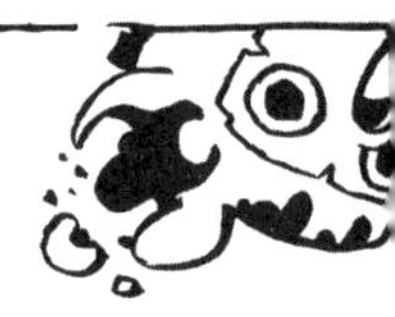

Panki stacks.
Fluffy sticky buttery
stacks of pancakes.

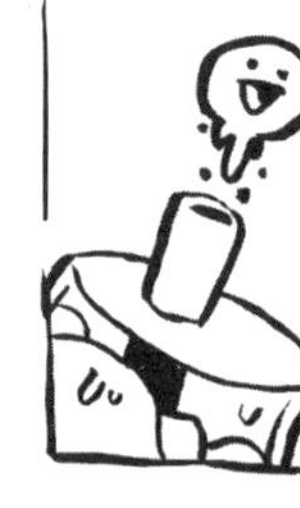

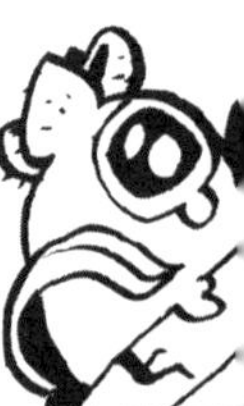

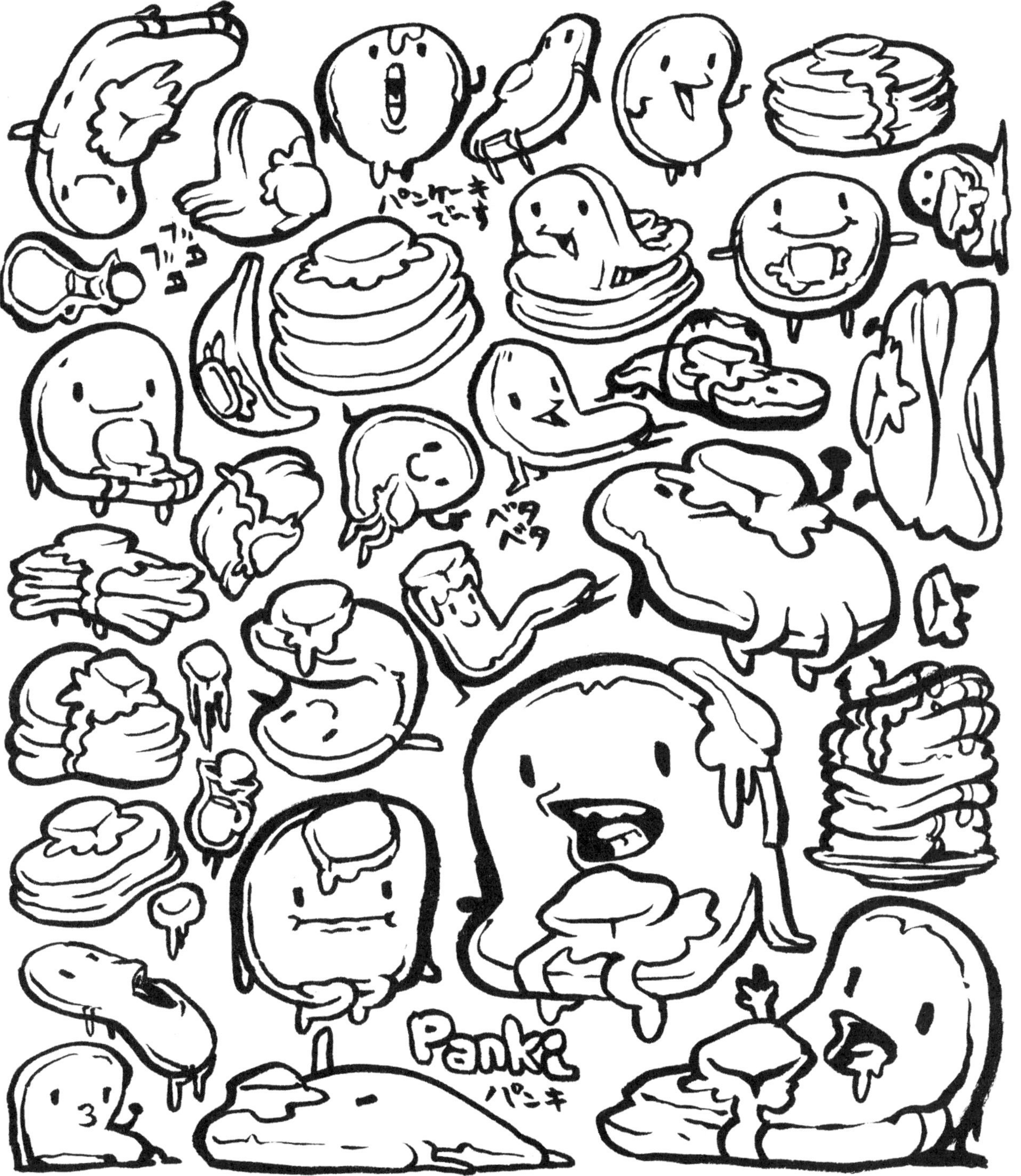
ブタ
ブタ
パンケーキ
でーす
ベタ
ベタ
Panki
パンキ

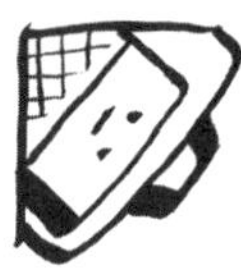

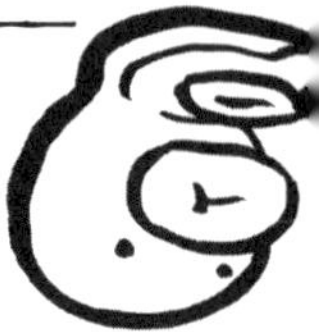

Draw, erase,

and draw again.

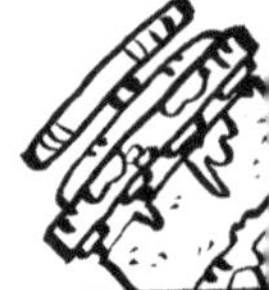

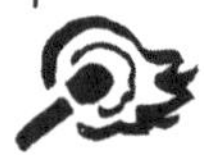

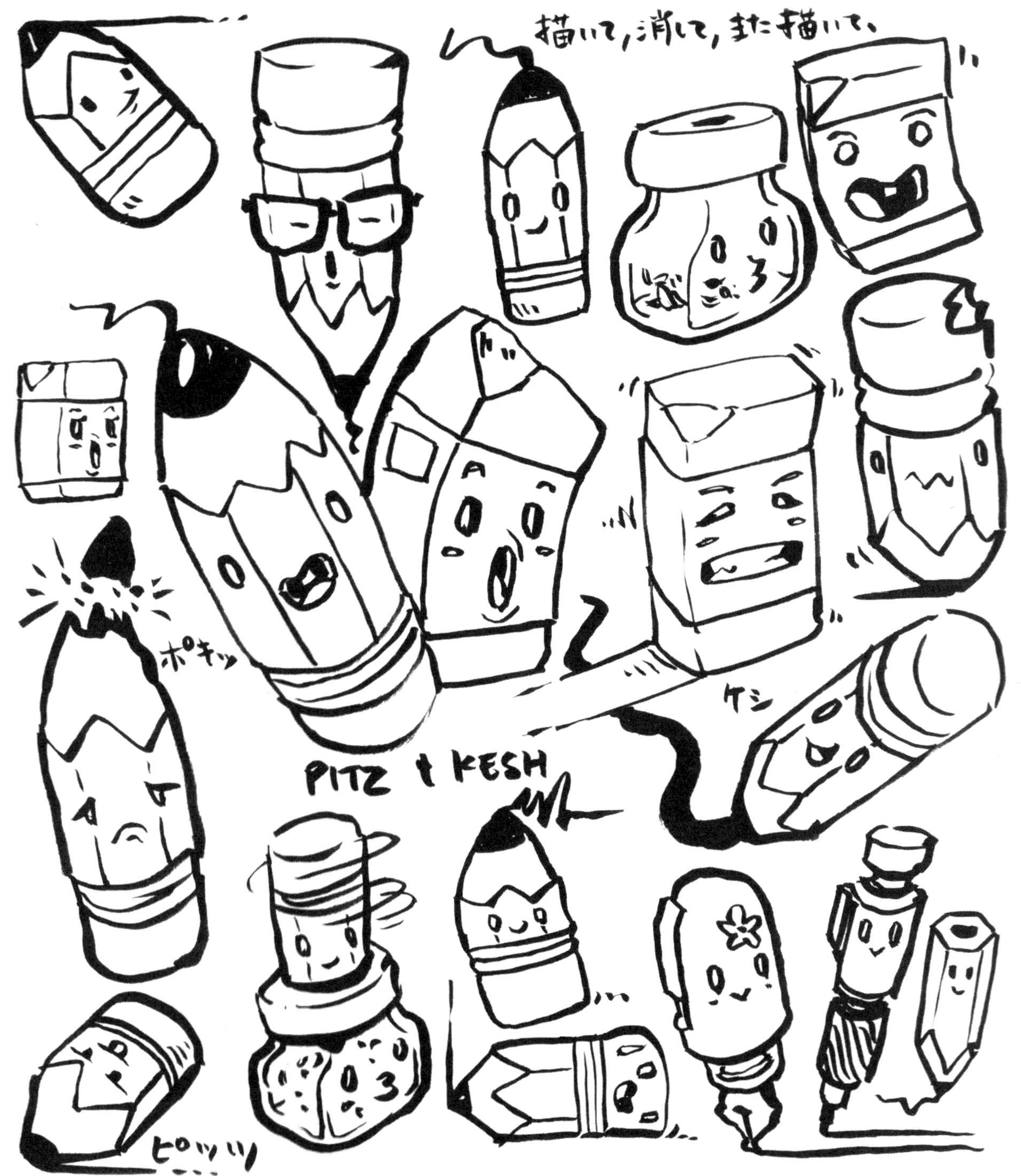
描いて，消して，また描いて、
ポキッ
ケシ
PITZ & KESH
ピロッツ

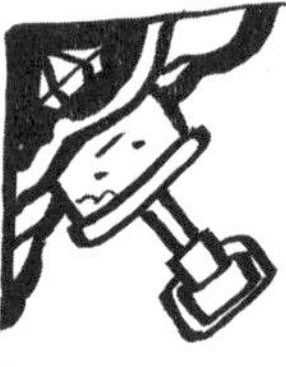

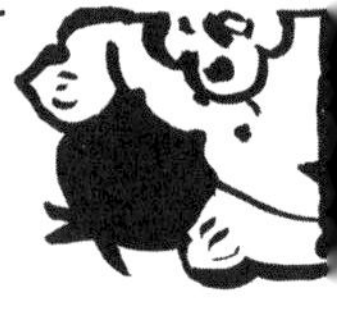

Sticky handprints
all over.

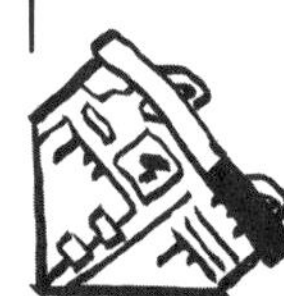

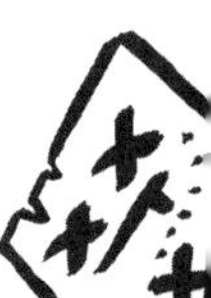

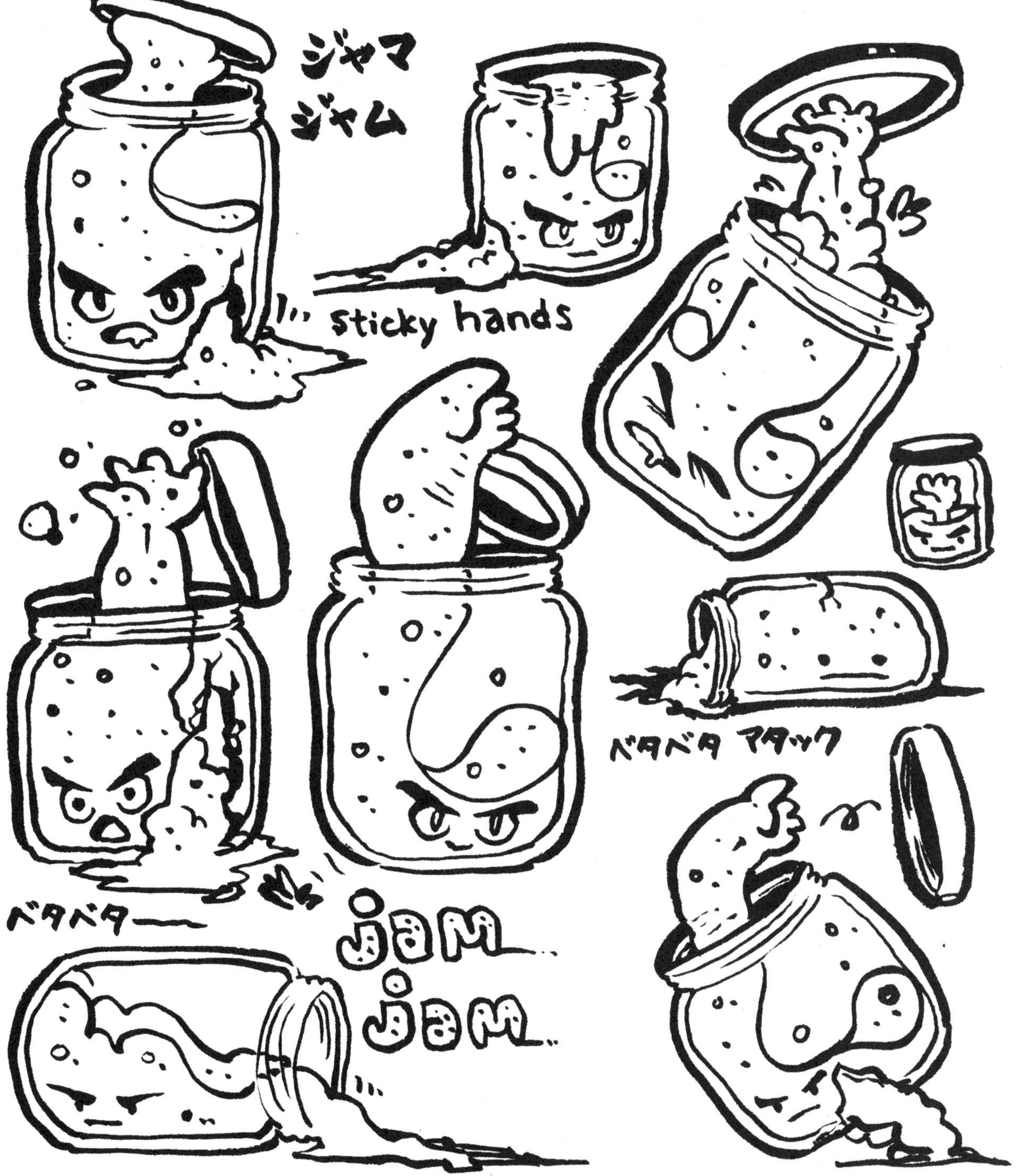
ジャマ
ジャム
sticky hands
ベタベタ アタック
ベタベター
jam
jam

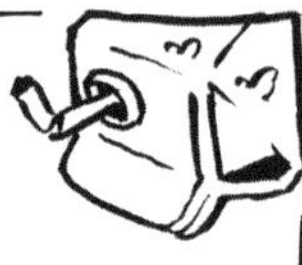

Single use friend.

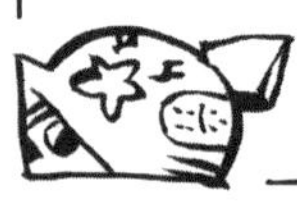

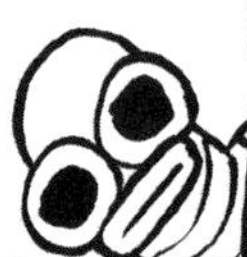

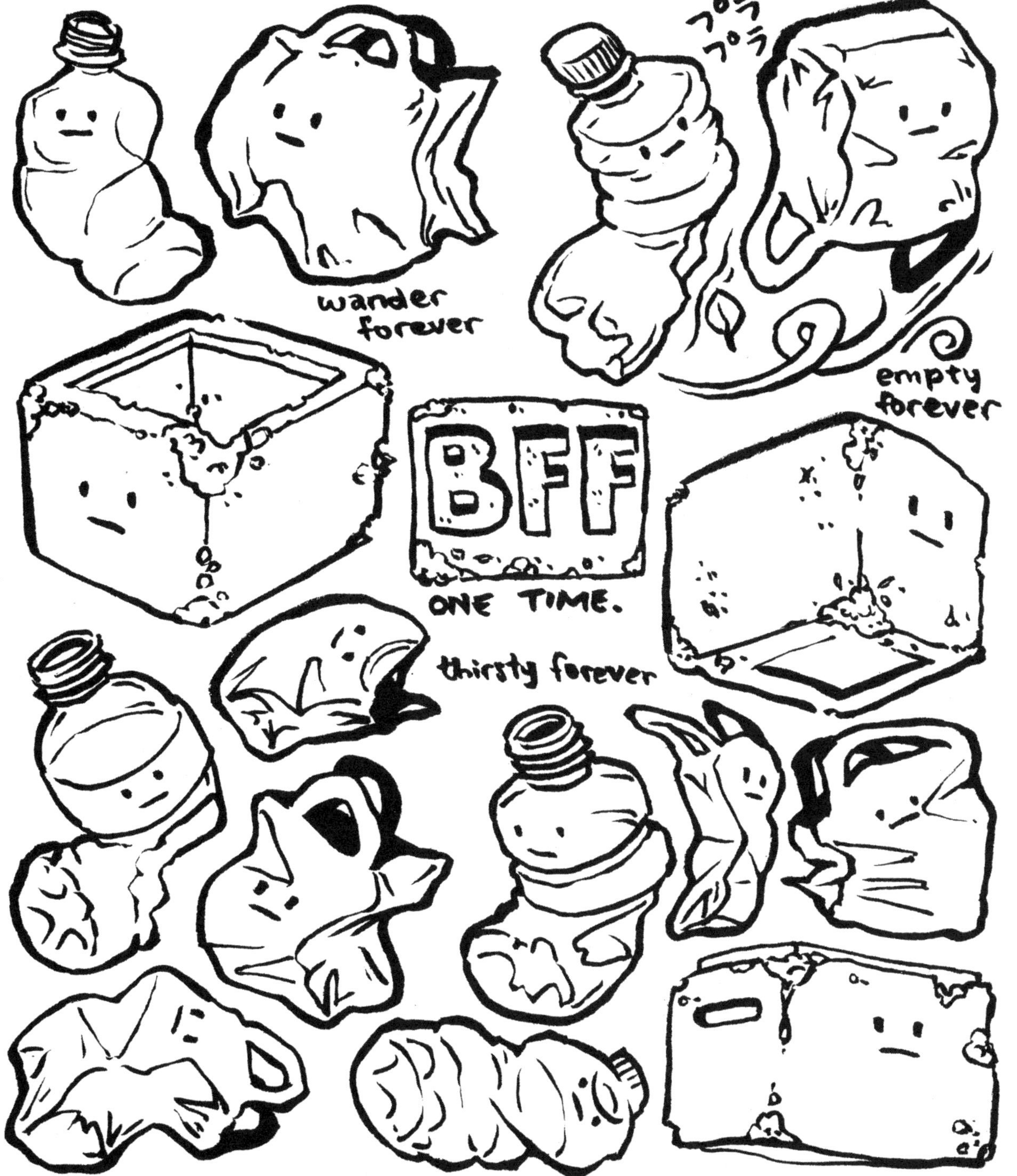

wander forever
プラ
プラ
empty forever
BFF
ONE TIME.
thirsty forever

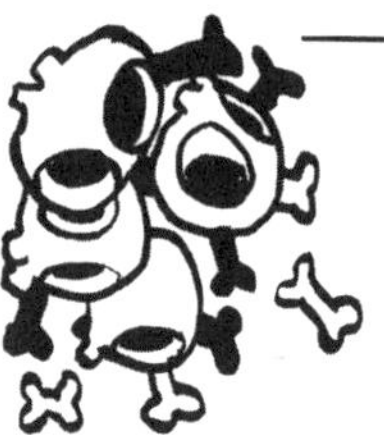

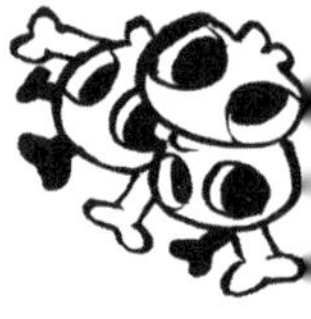

Ready to eat.

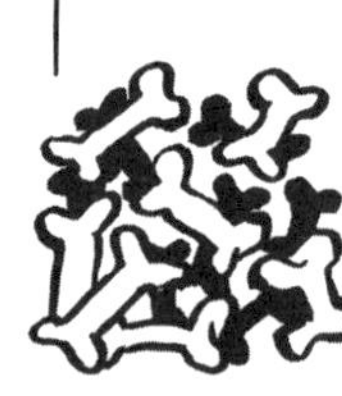

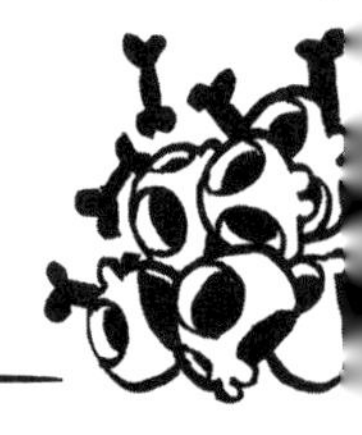

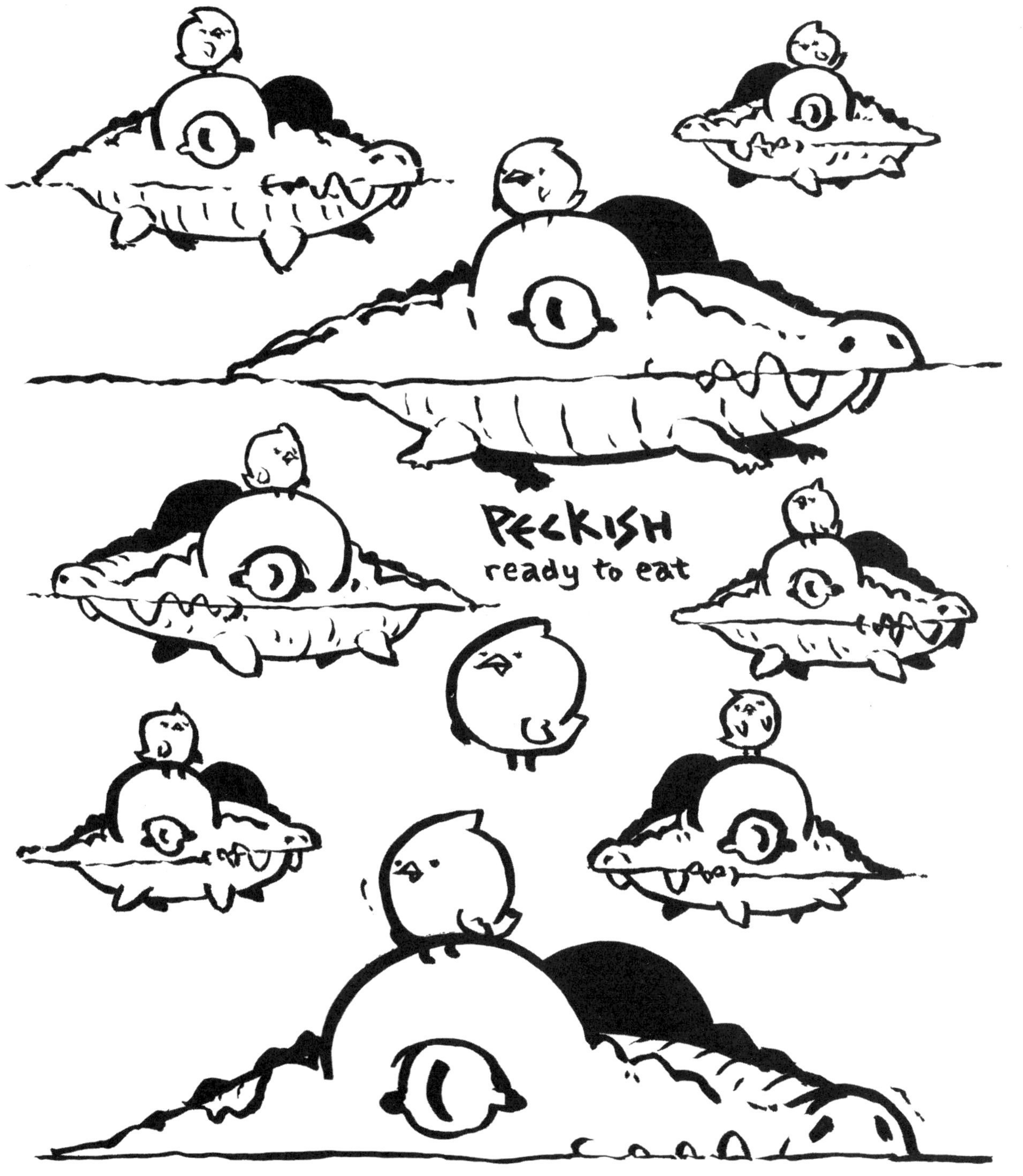
PECKISH
ready to eat

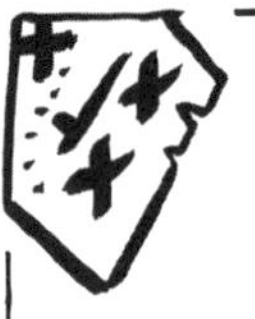

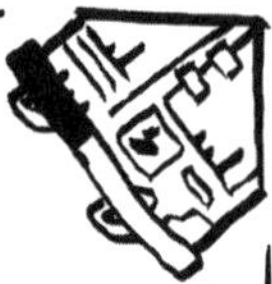

Not pretty,

but cute.

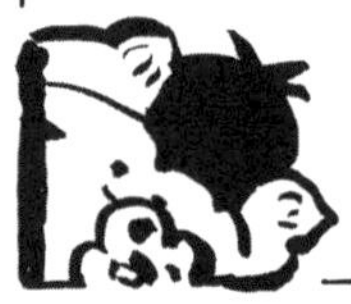

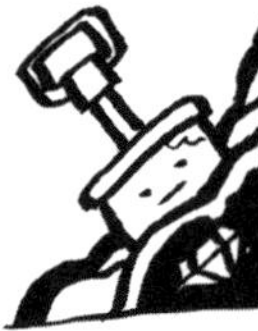

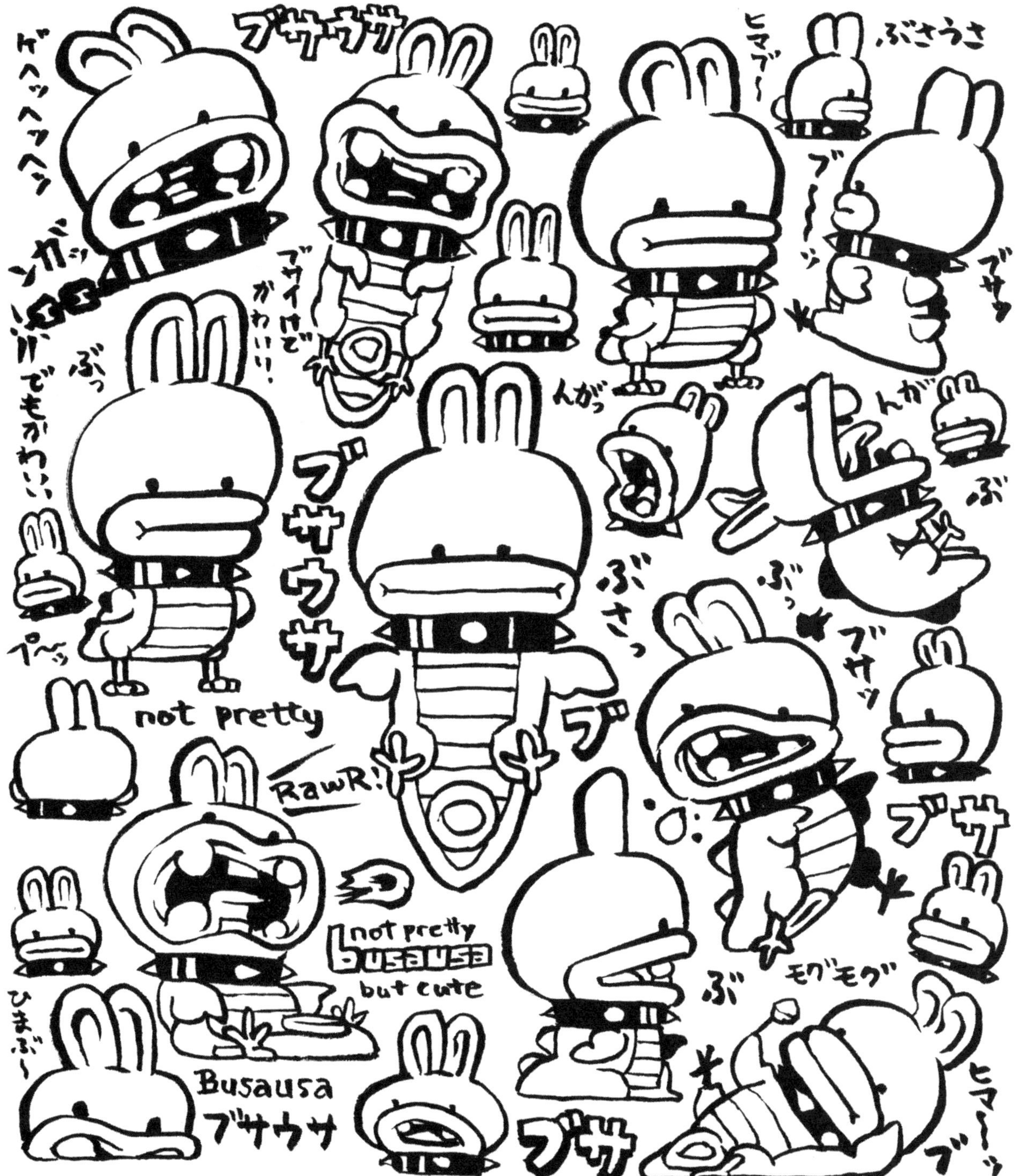

ブサウサ
ぶさうさ
ヒマブー~
ゲヘッヘッヘッヘッ
ンガッ
ブサイけでかわい!!
ブ~~ッ
ブサッ
んがっ
んが
ブサウサ
ぶさっ
ぶっ
ブサッ
ブ
ぶ
ぷ~ッ
not pretty
RawR!
not pretty
busausa
but cute
ブサ
モグモグ
ぶ
Busausa
ブサウサ
ブサ
ひまぶ~
ヒマ~~ブ~ッ

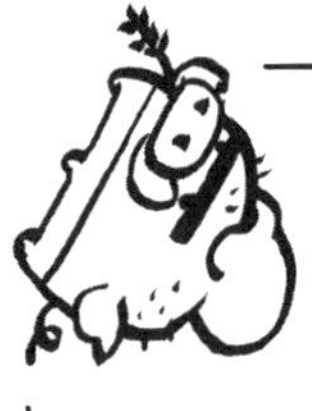

Life is all side quests.

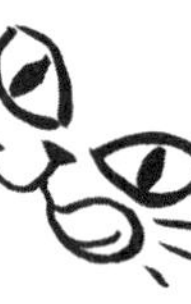

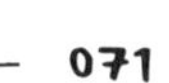

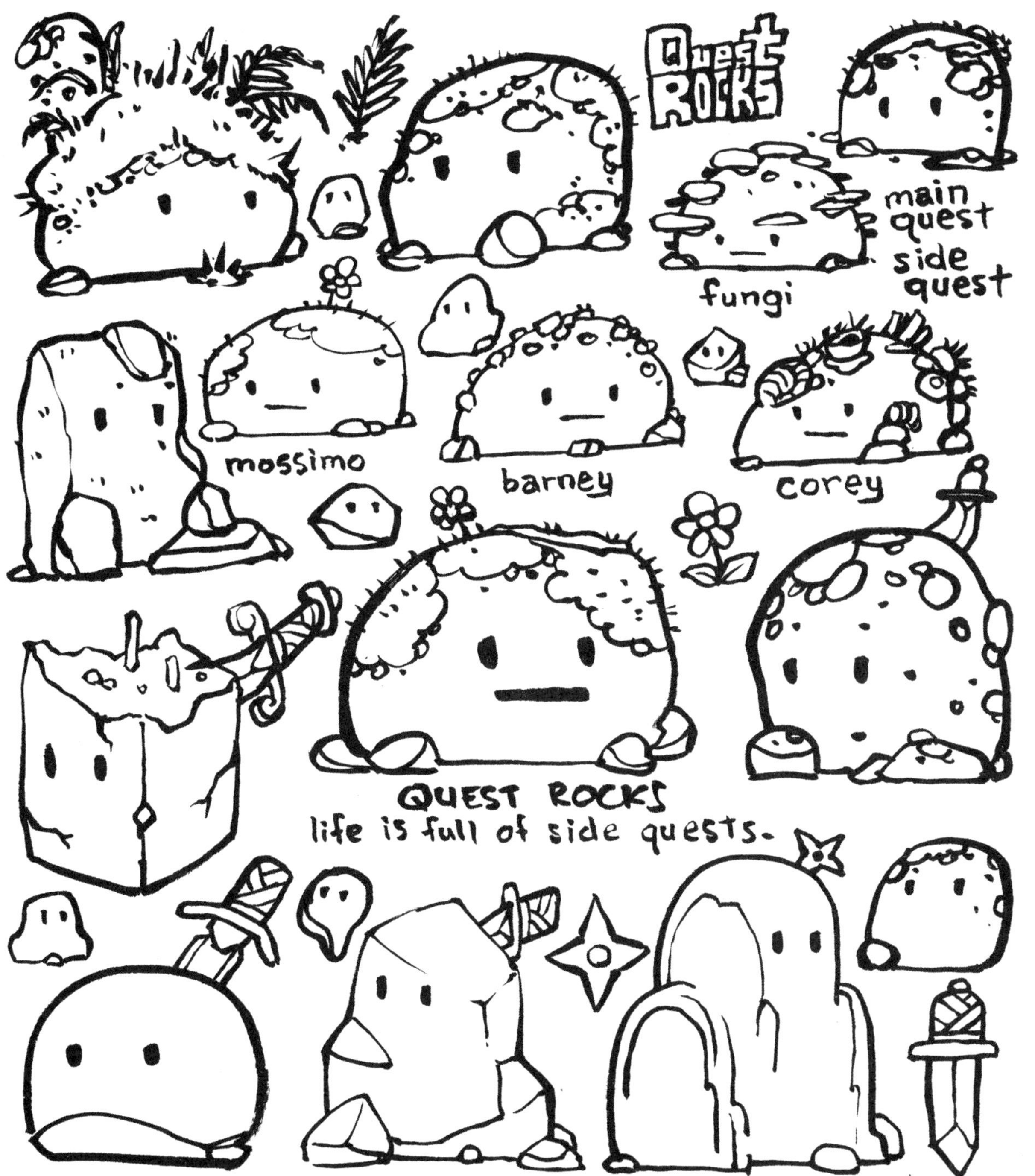
Quest ROCKS
main quest
side quest
fungi
mossimo
barney
corey
QUEST ROCKS
life is full of side quests.

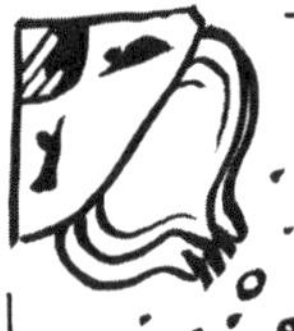

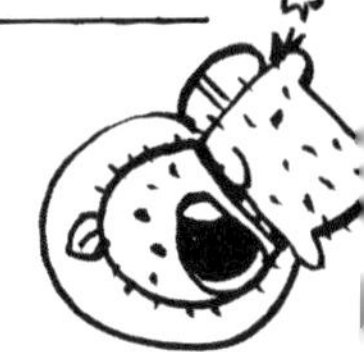

Pig 'n pants.

Flaps around papapapa.

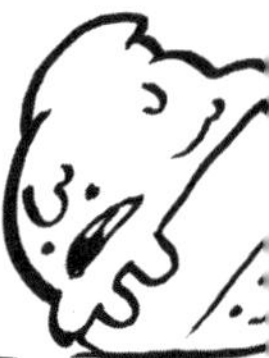

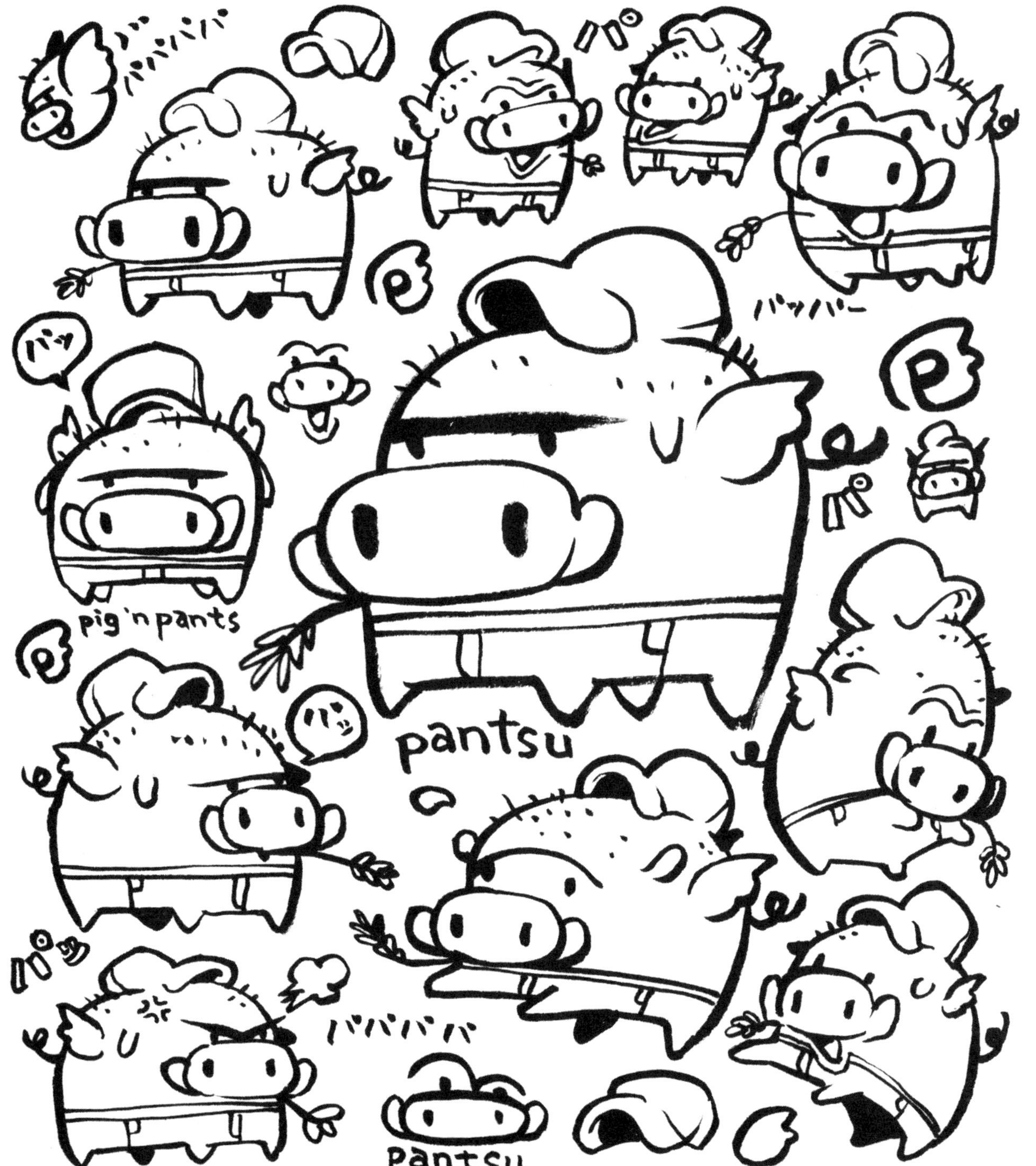

バババババ
パ
バッバー
バッ
pig'n pants
パ
バッ
pantsu
パッ
バババ
pantsu

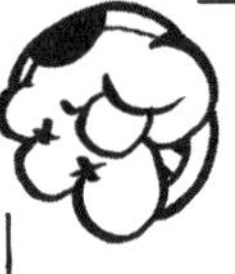

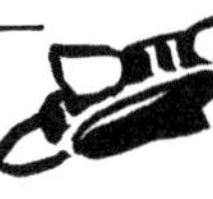

Hot and melty.

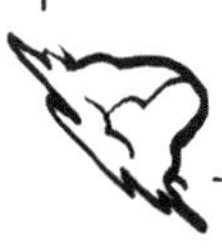

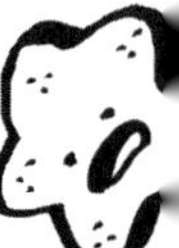

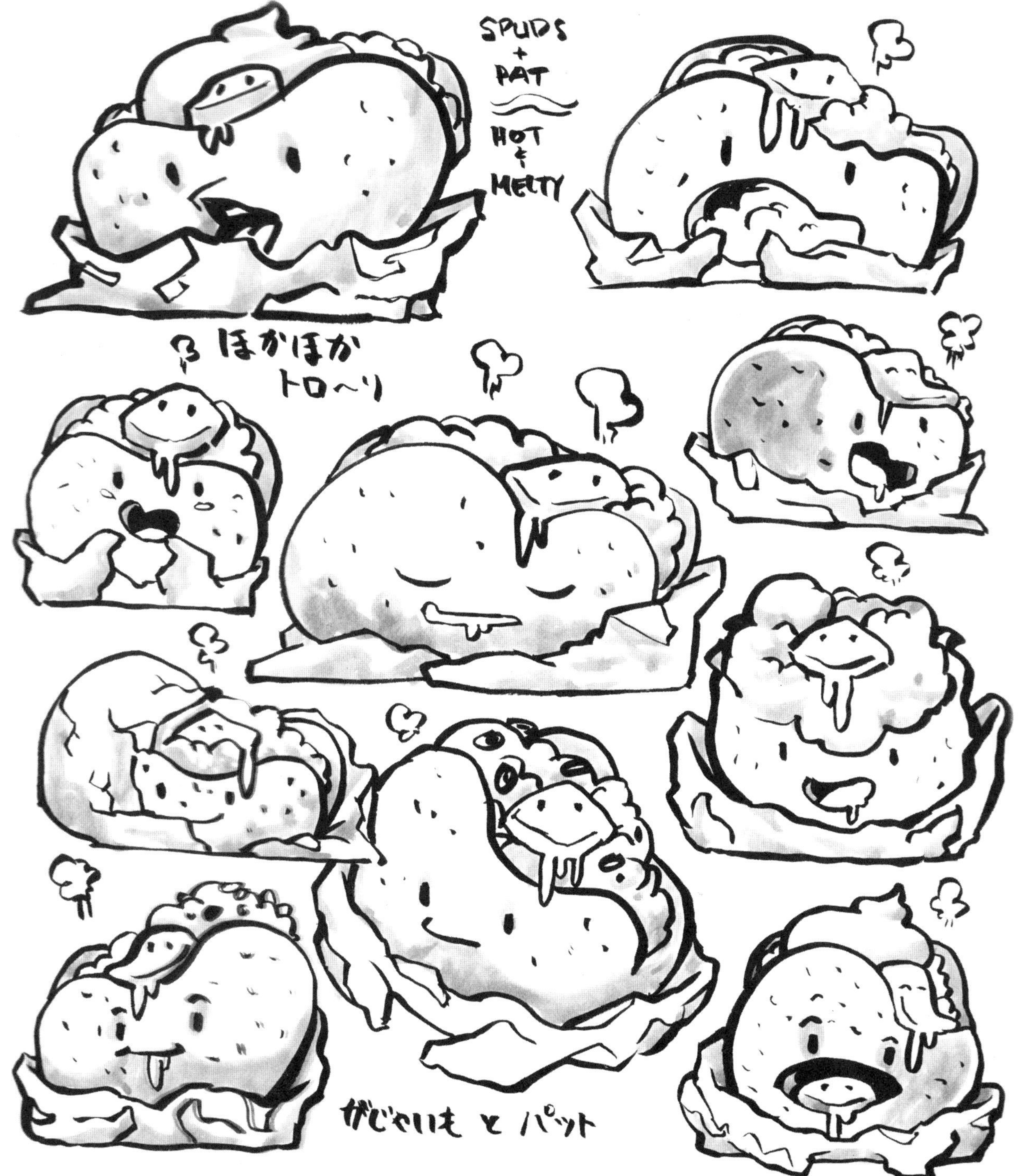
SPUDS + PAT
HOT & MELTY
ほかほか
トロ〜り
がじゃいも と パット

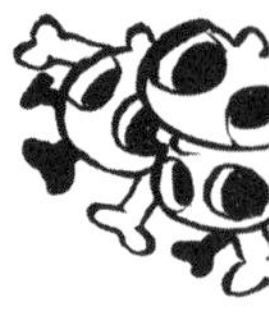

I can't bite well
wiv dis toof.

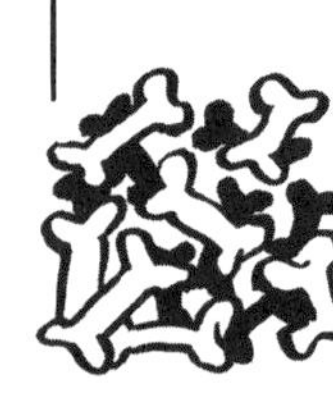

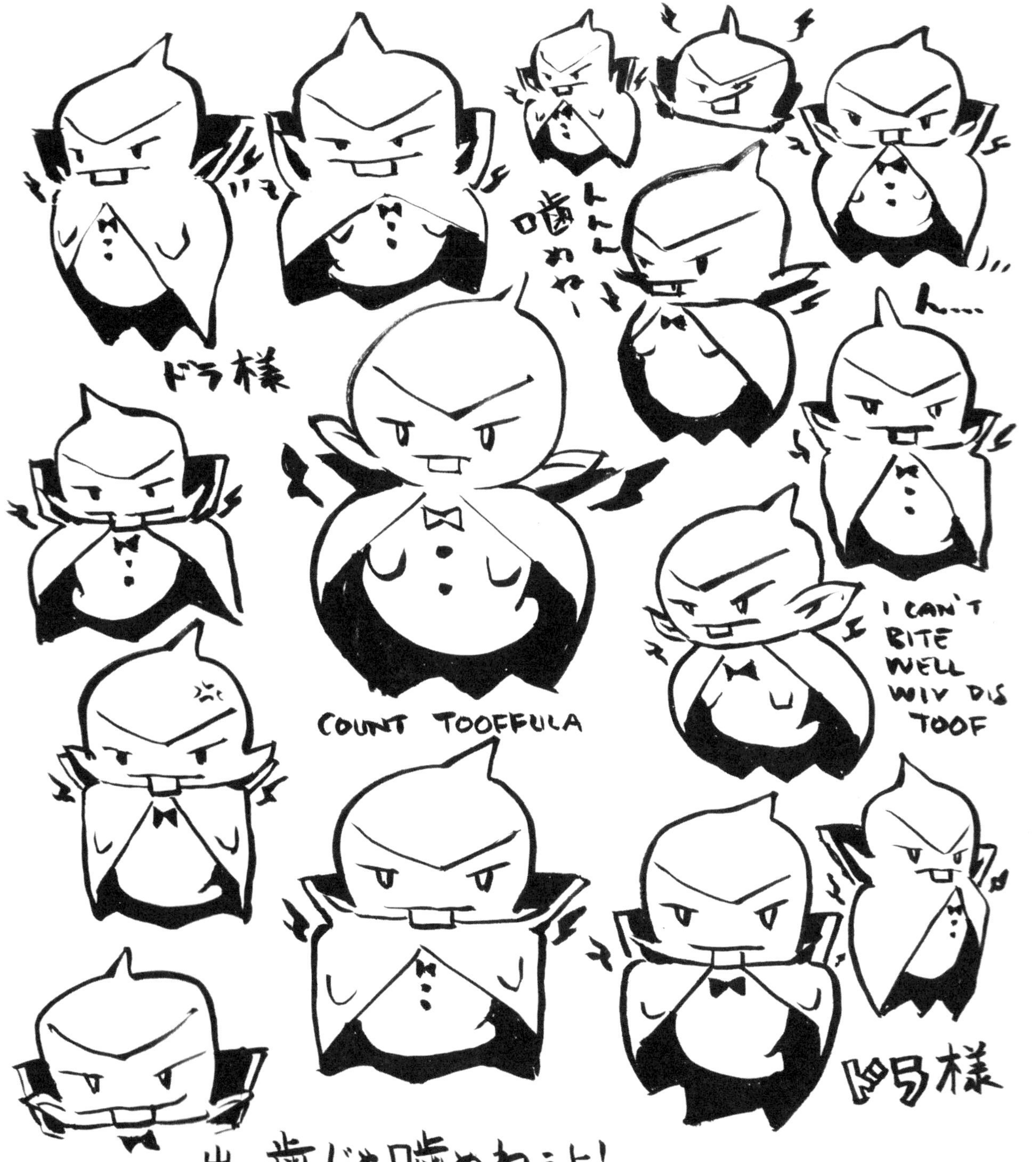
ドラ様
んんん
噛めねー
ん….
COUNT TOOFFULA
I CAN'T BITE WELL WIV DIS TOOF
ドラ様
出っ歯じゃ噛めねぇよ!

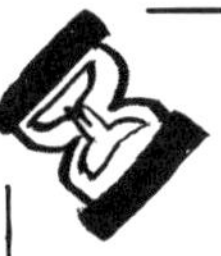

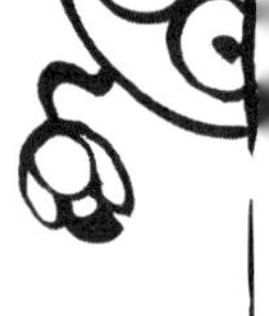

Unnecessary memorial.

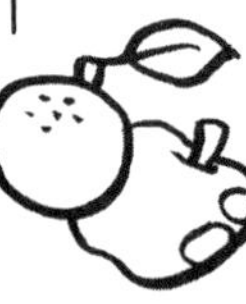

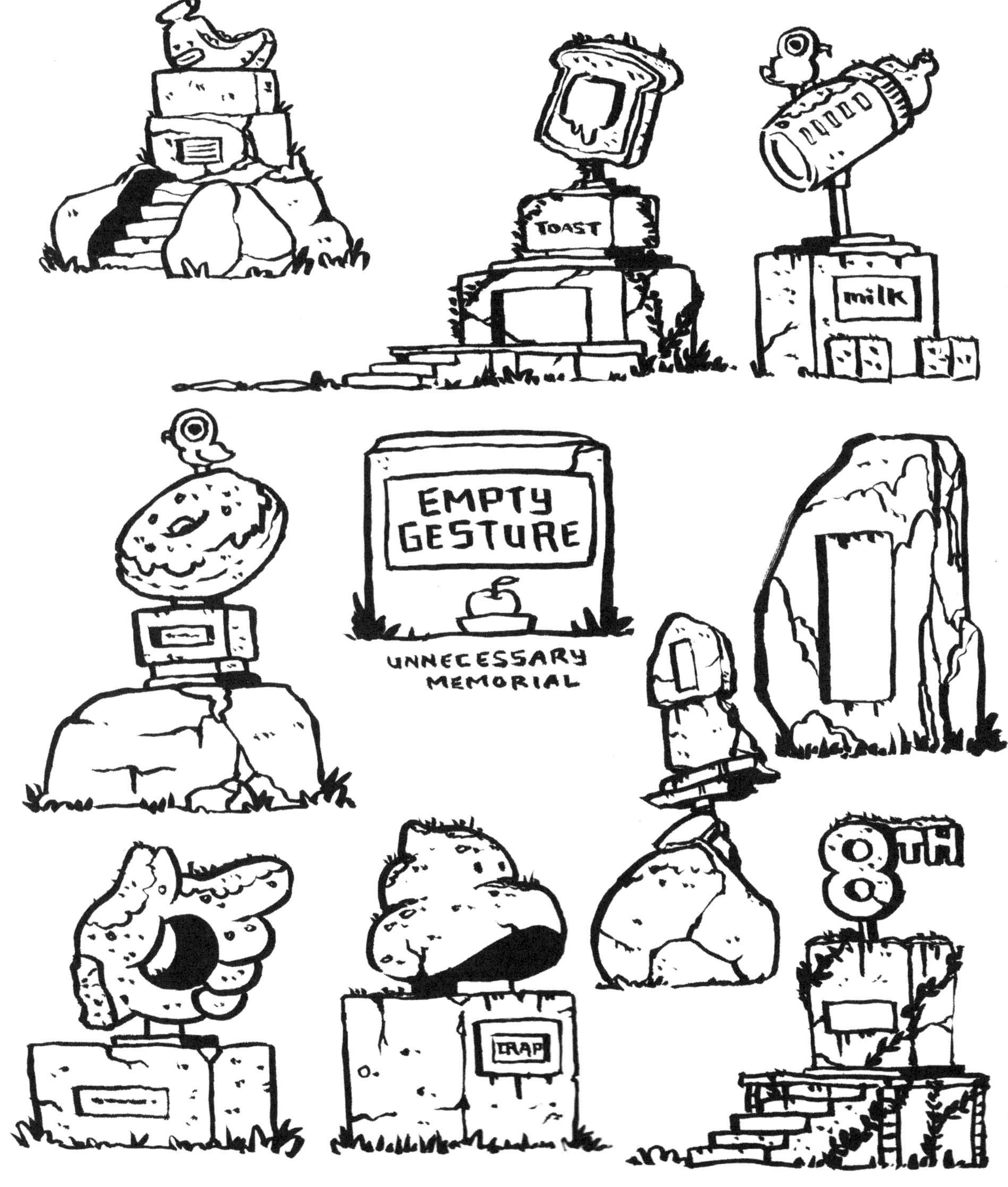
TOAST
milk
EMPTY GESTURE
UNNECESSARY MEMORIAL
TRAP
8TH

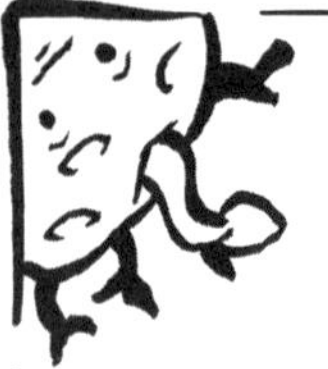

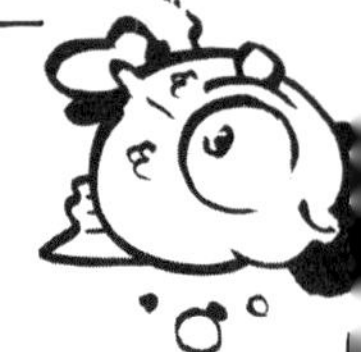

Tina Tuna telling Minnie Minnows a bit of her mind at Predator Defense School.

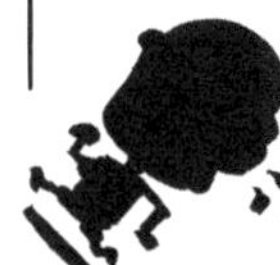

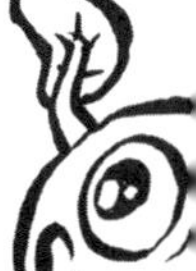

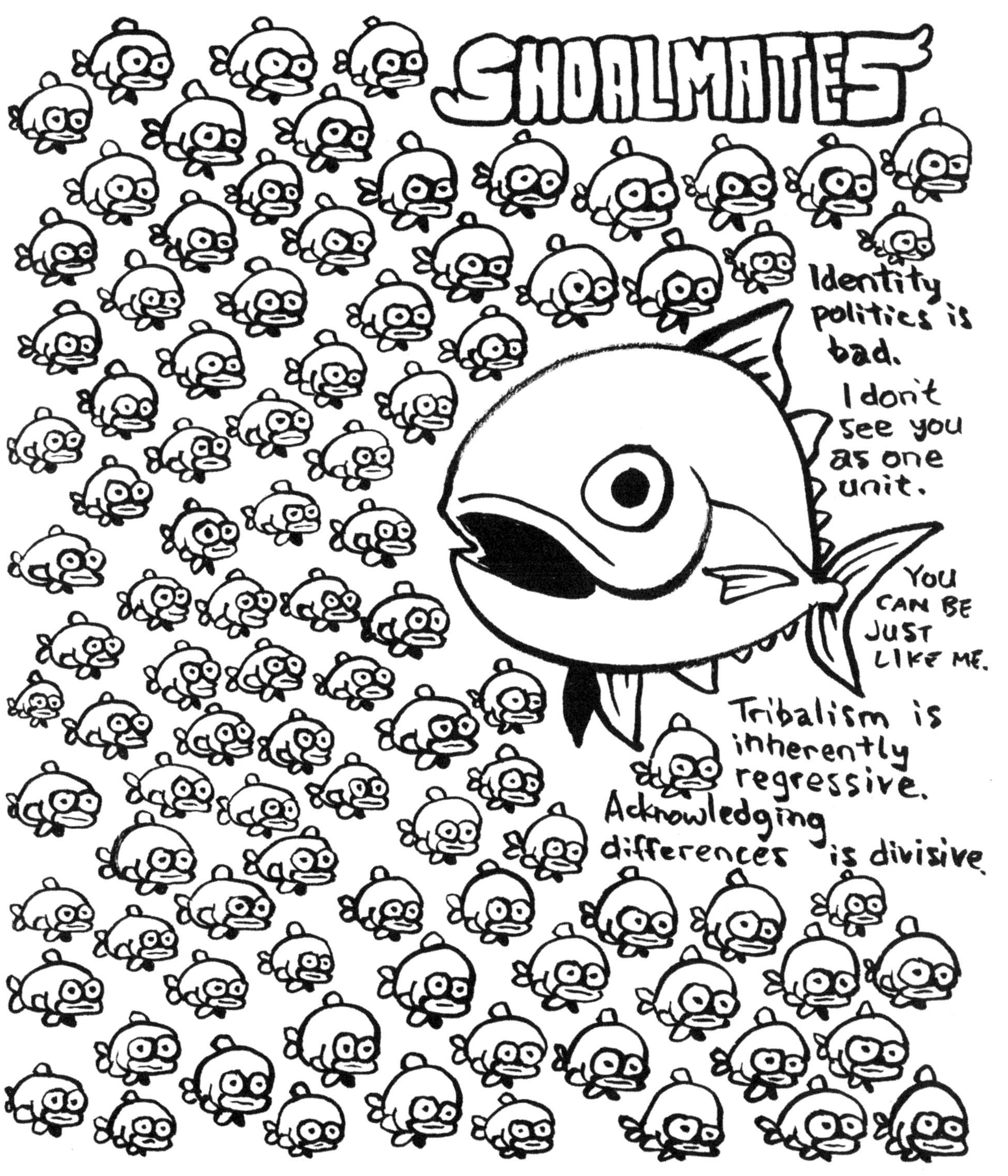
SHOALMATES
Identity politics is bad.
I don't see you as one unit.
YOU CAN BE JUST LIKE ME.
Tribalism is inherently regressive.
Acknowledging differences is divisive.

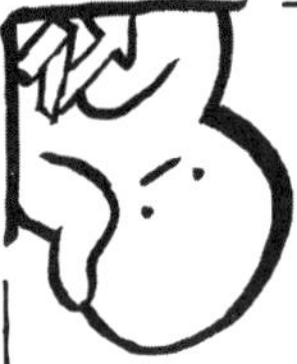

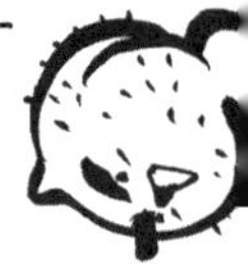

Everything is
a threat.

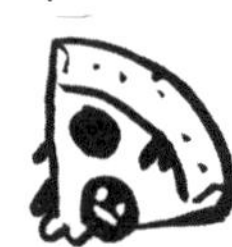

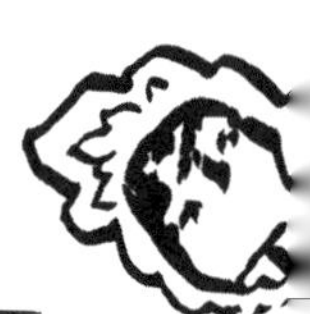

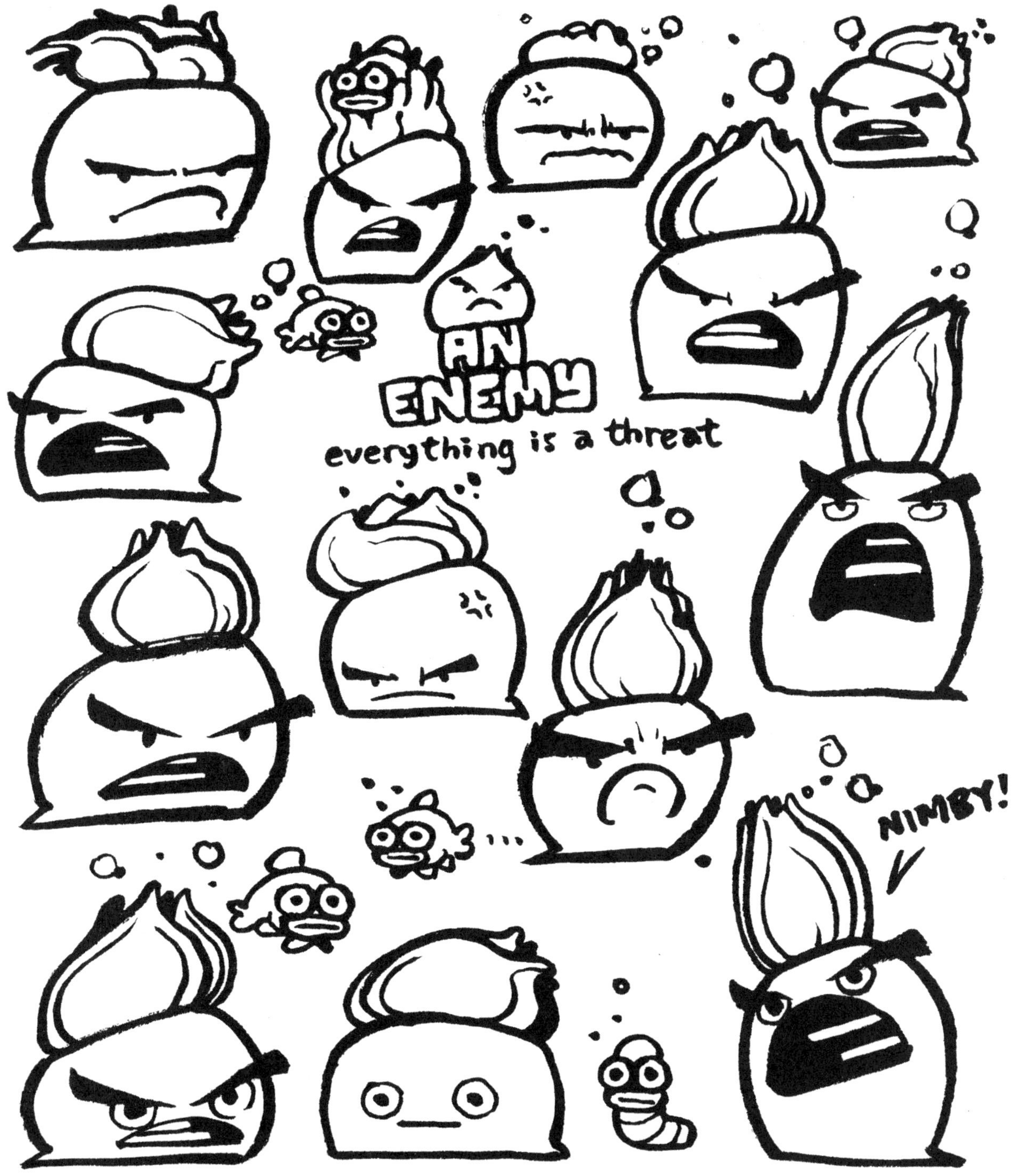
AN
ENEMY
everything is a threat
NIMBY!

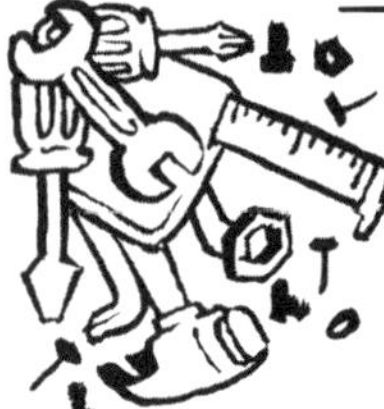

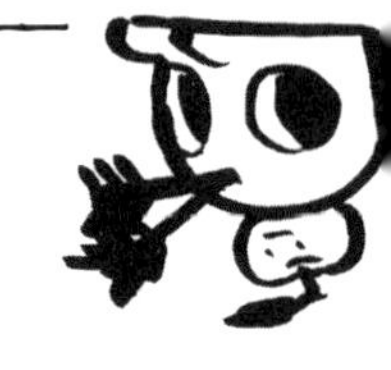

Overthink king.

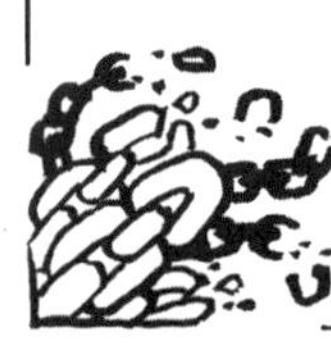

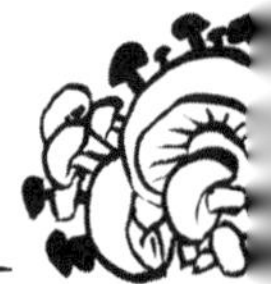

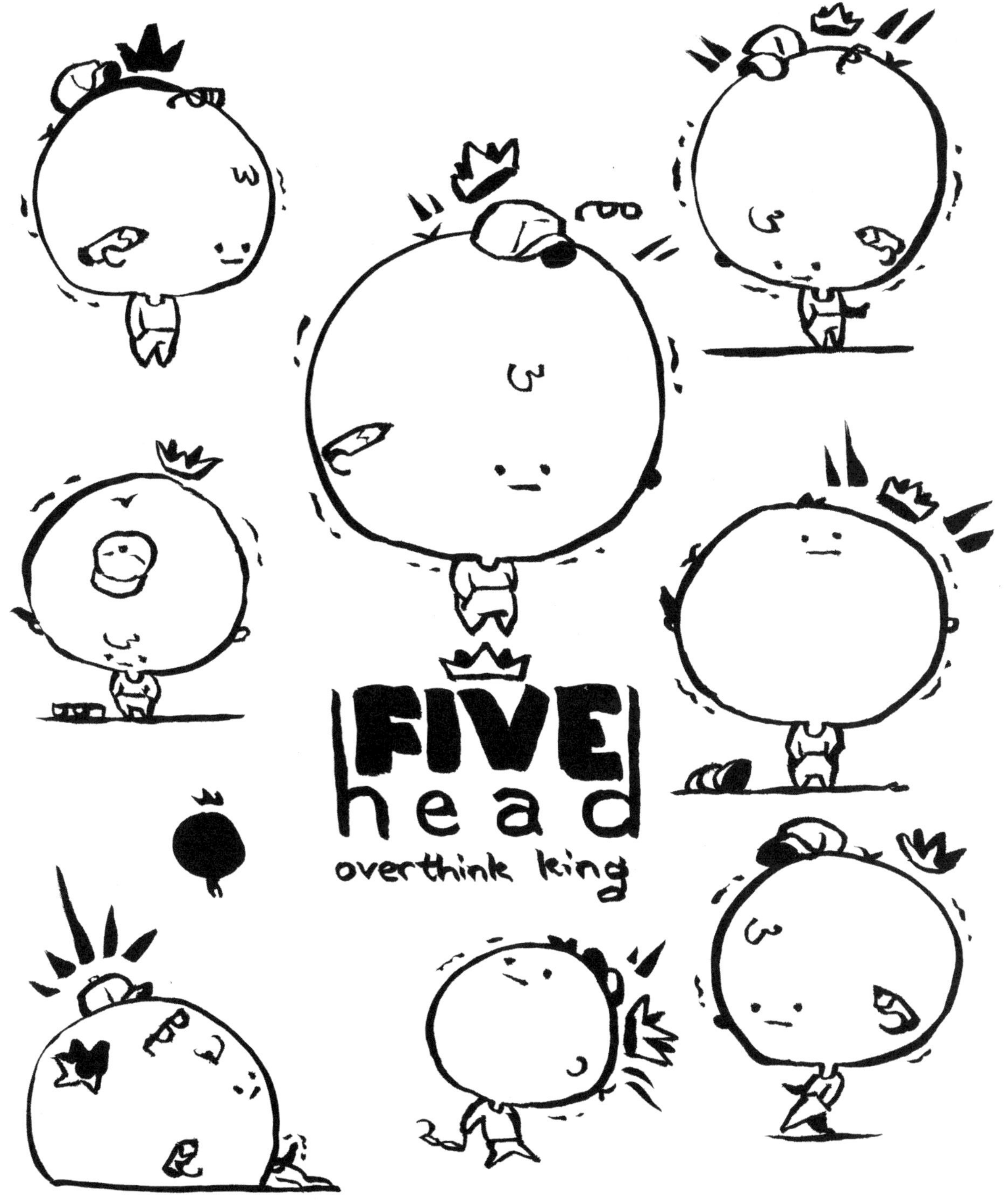
FIVE
head
overthink king

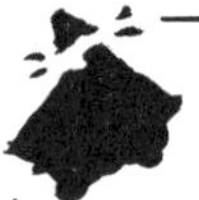

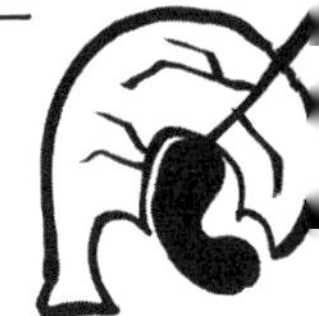

watch, read,

and enjoy.

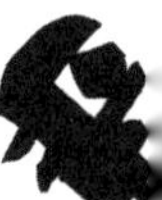

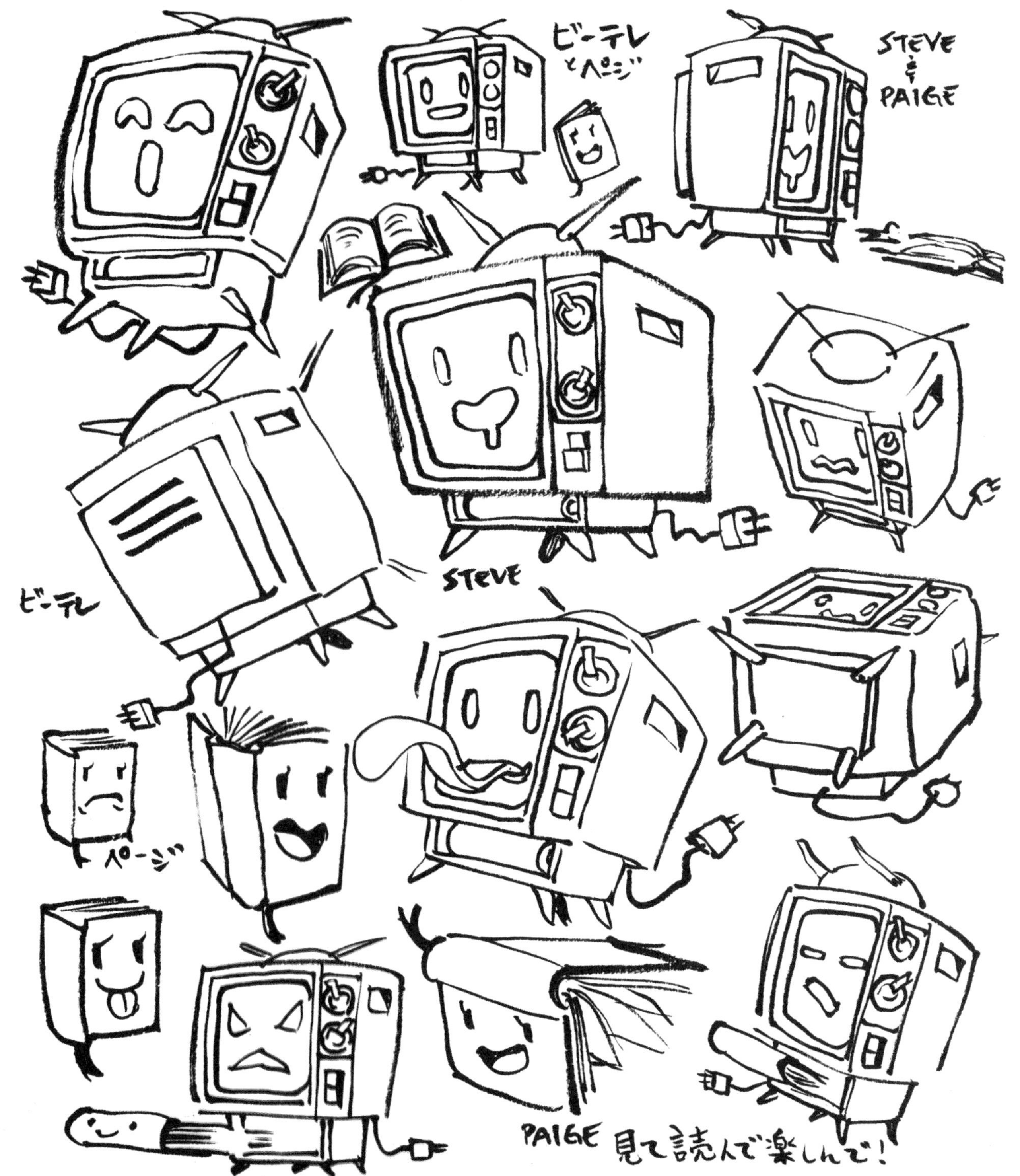
ビーテレとページ
STEVE & PAIGE
ビーテレ
STEVE
ページ
PAIGE
見て読んで楽しんで!

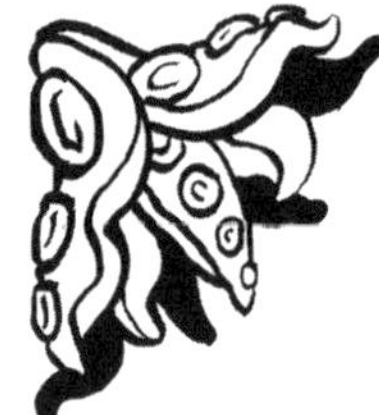

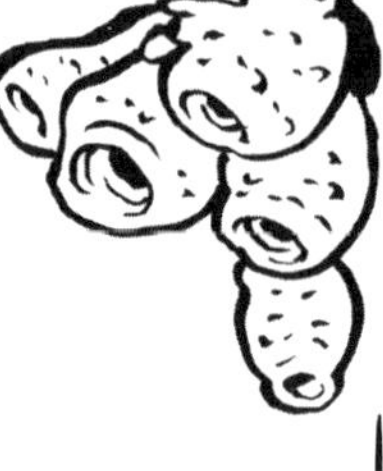

who was that?

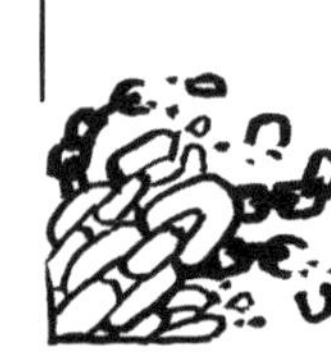

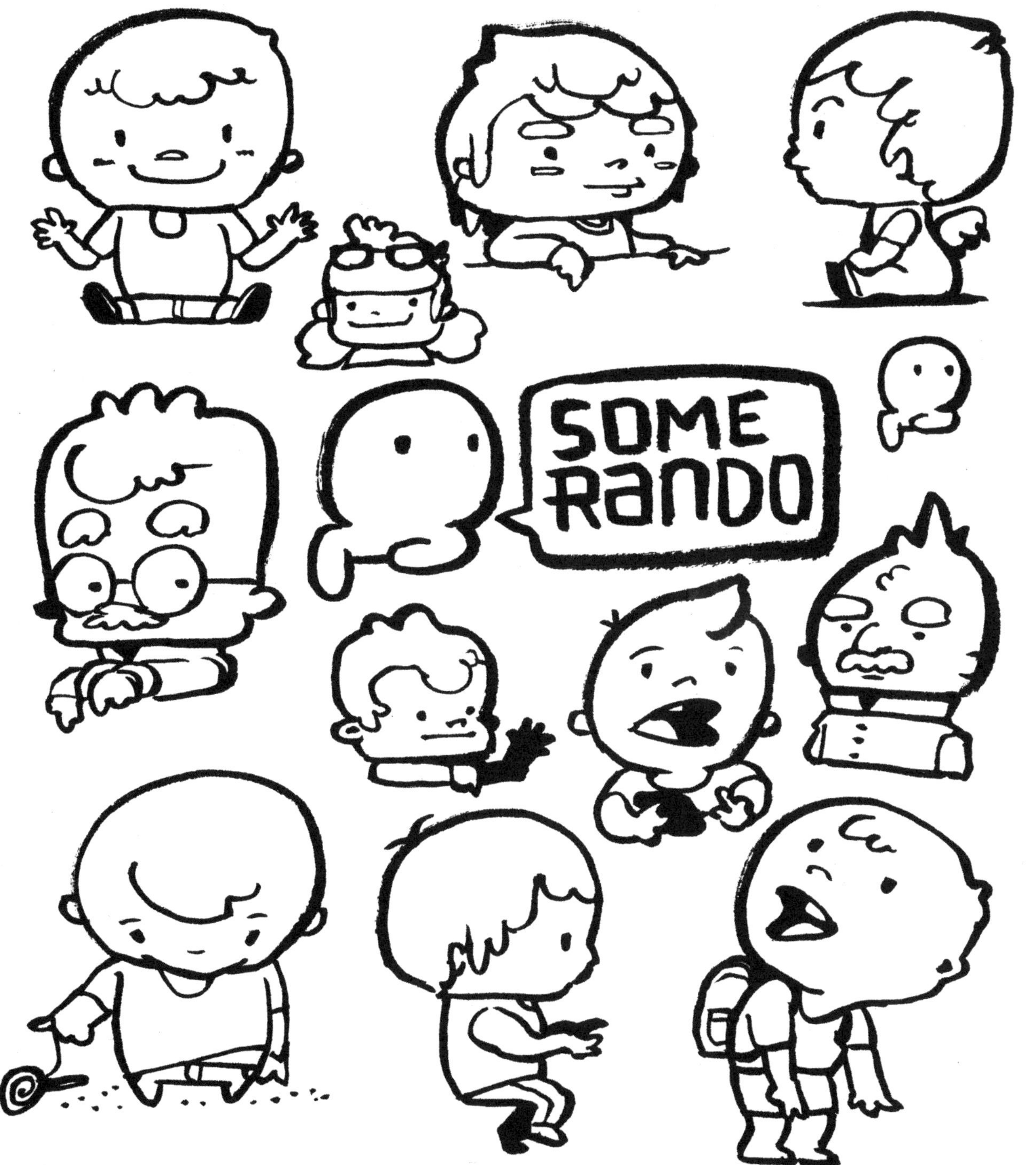
SOME
RANDO

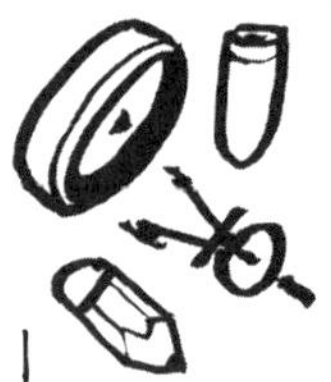

Bob the astronaut
just got his lifeline cut.

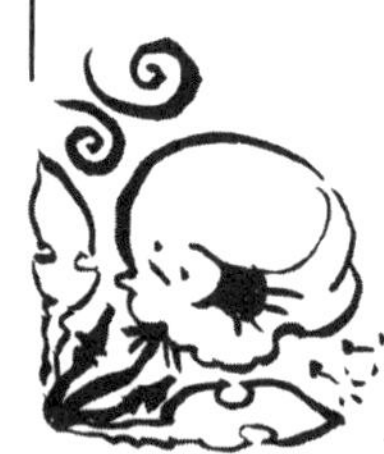

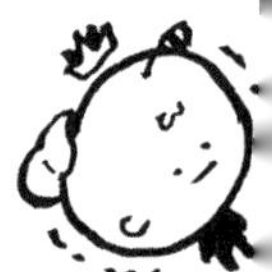

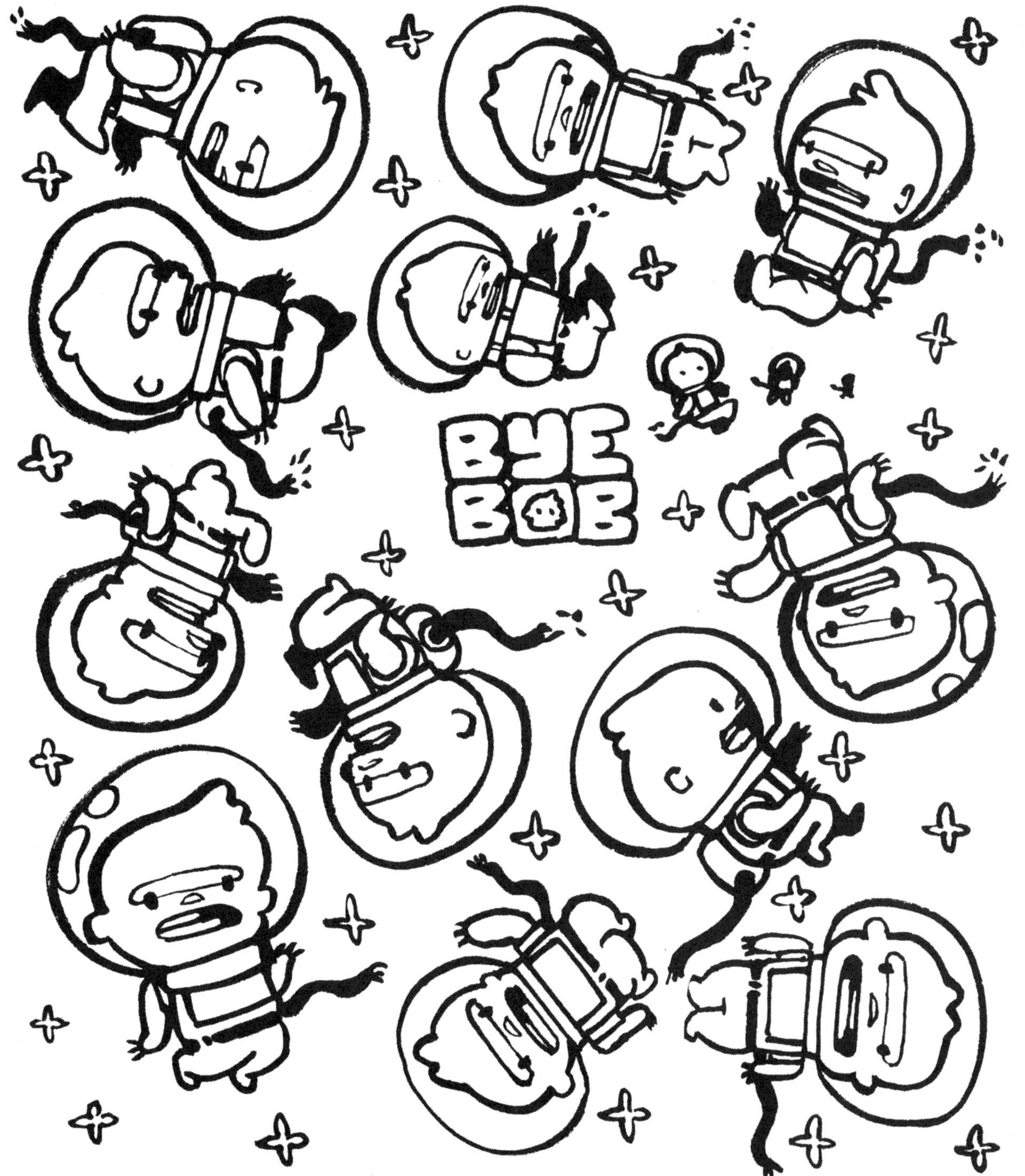
BYE BOB

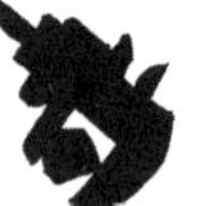

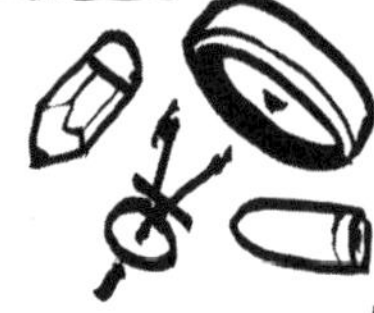

The breaks.

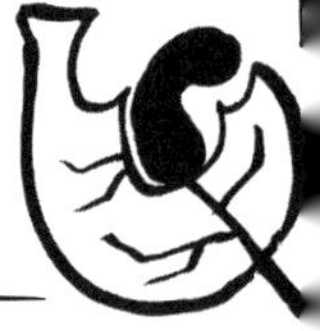

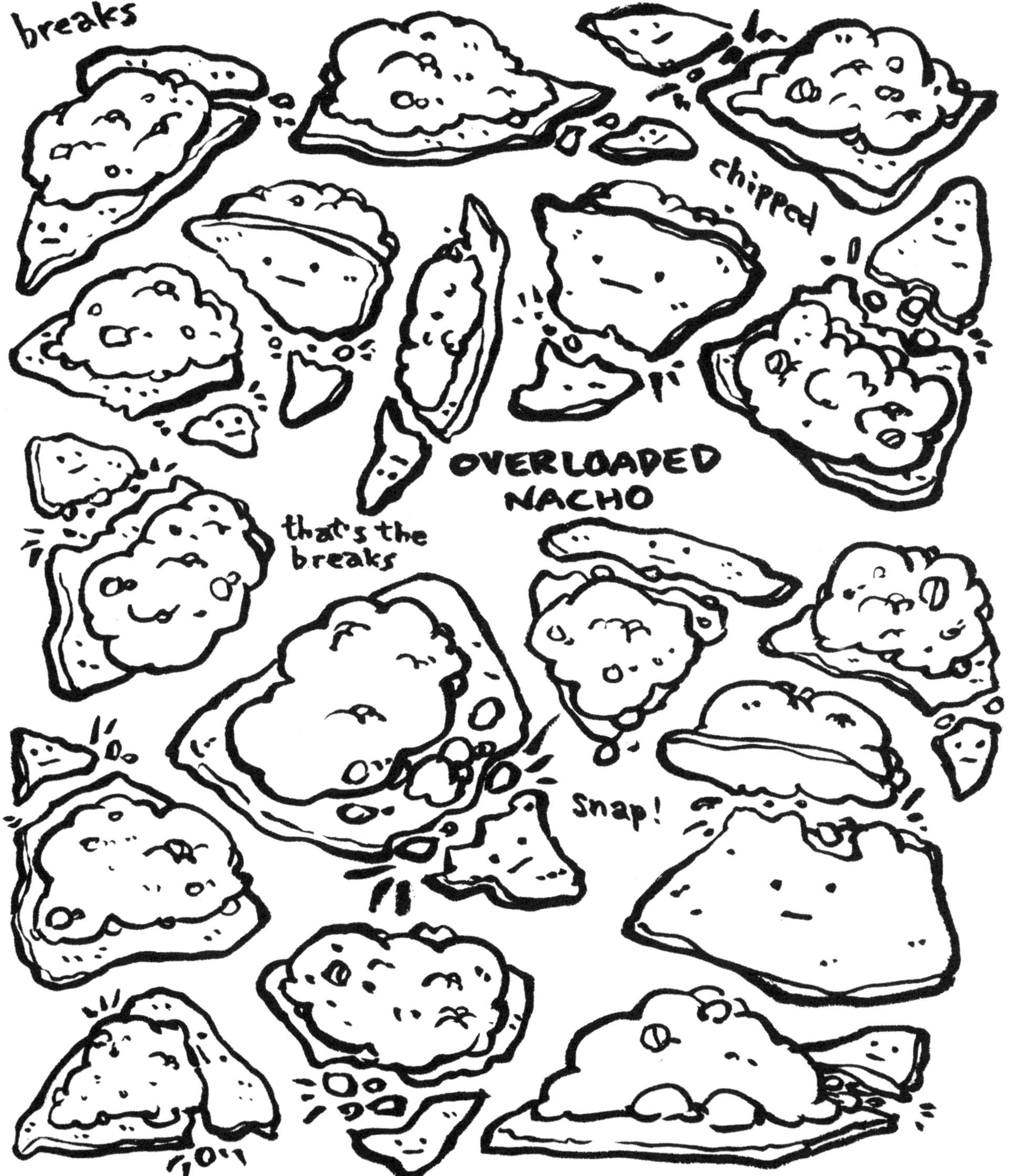
breaks
chipped
OVERLOADED NACHO
that's the breaks
Snap!

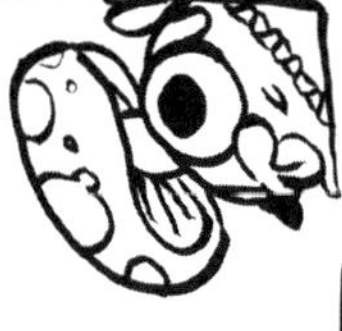

Nnnn... so soft.

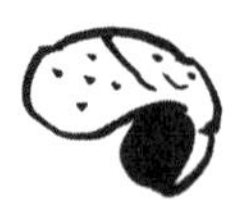

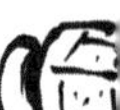

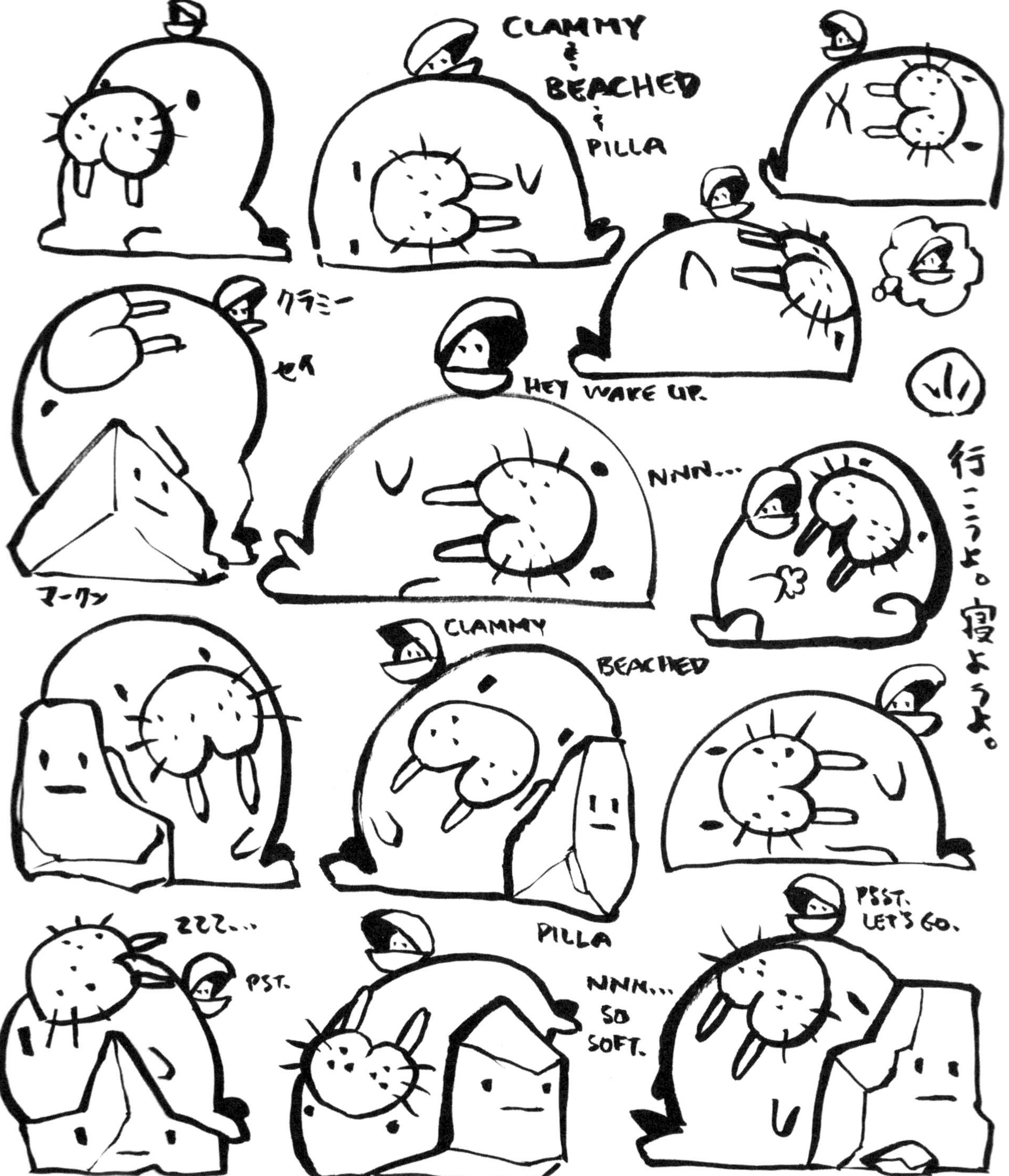
CLAMMY
&
BEACHED
&
PILLA
クラミー
セイ
HEY WAKE UP.
NNN...
行こうよ。寝ようよ。
マークン
CLAMMY
BEACHED
PILLA
ZZZ...
PST.
NNN...
SO
SOFT.
PSST.
LET'S GO.

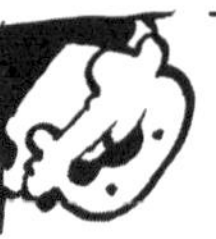

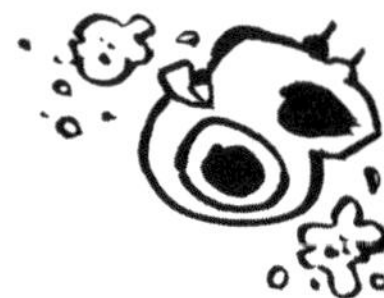

Well pruned nest.

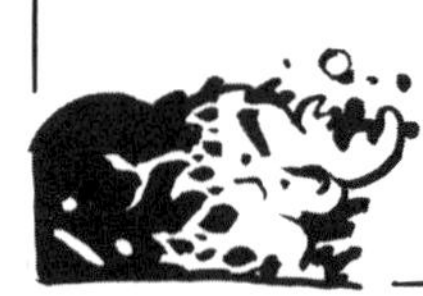

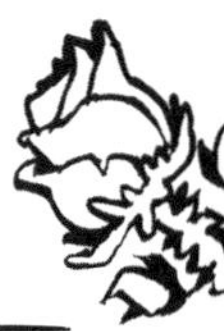

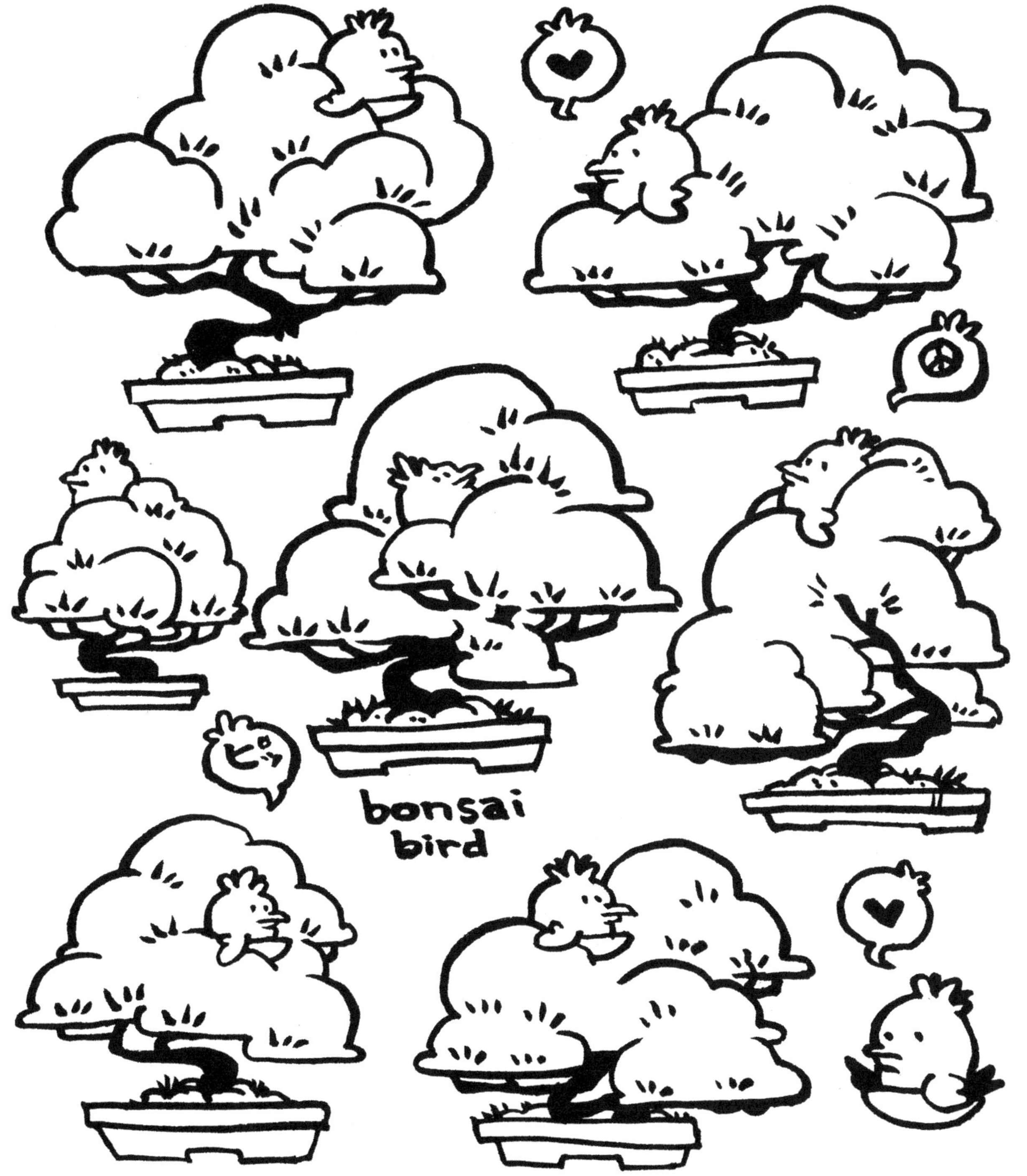
ピッ
bonsai
bird

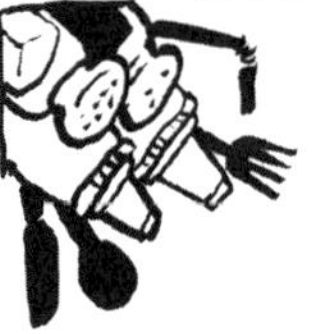

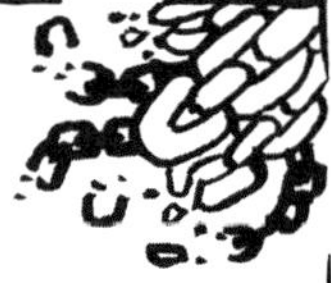

Coming in hot!

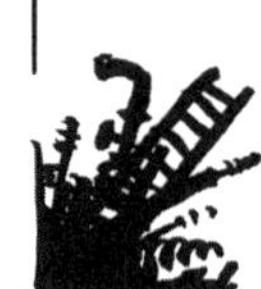

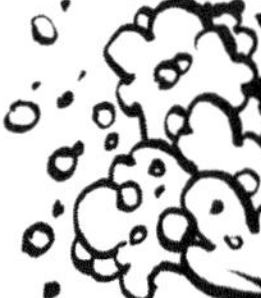

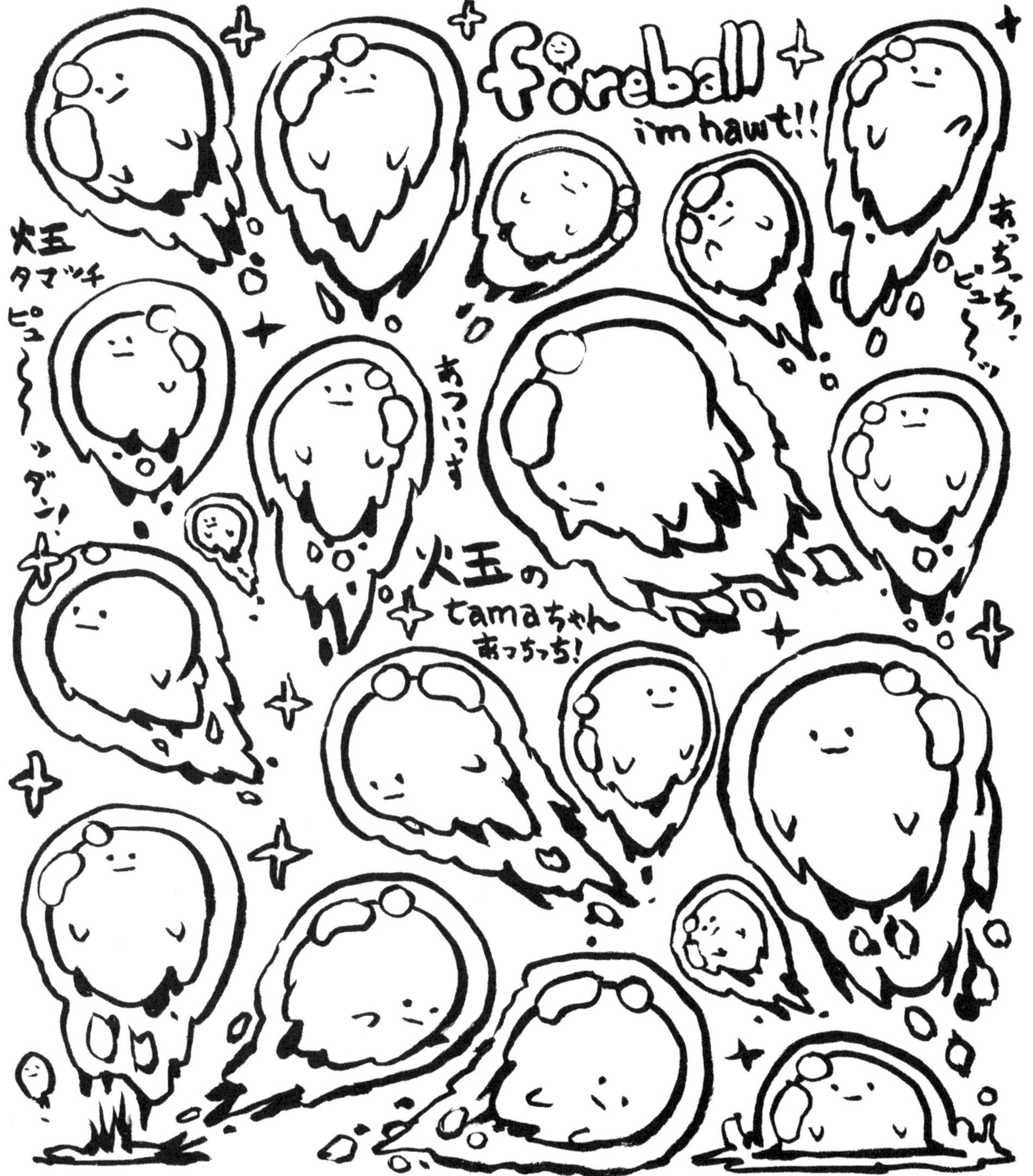
fireball
i'm hawt!!
火玉
タマッチ
ピュ〜〜ッダン!
あついっす
あっちっち!
ピュ〜〜ッ
火玉の
tamaちゃん
あっちっち!

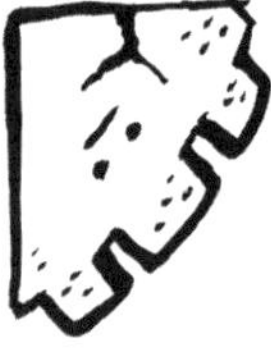

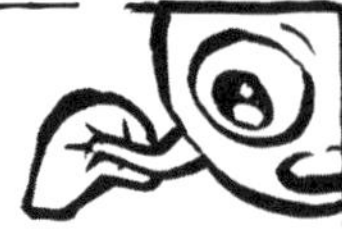

You are what
you think.

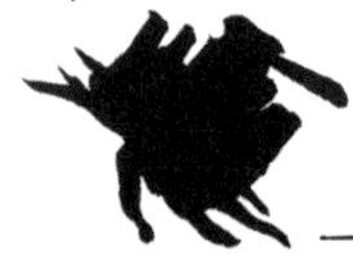

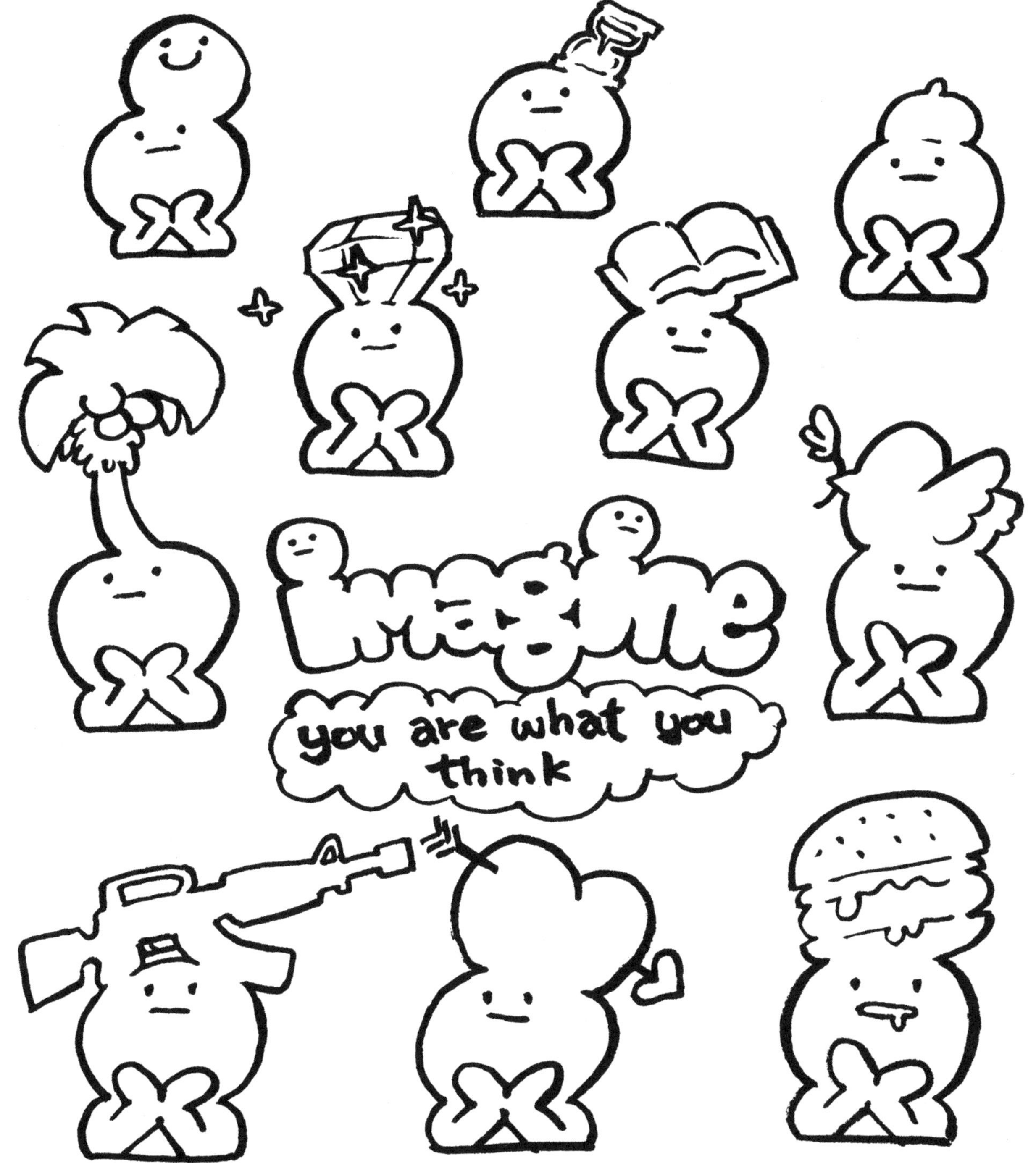
imagine
you are what you think

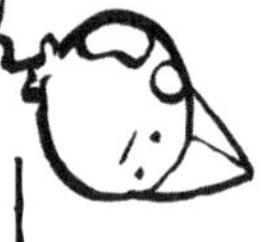

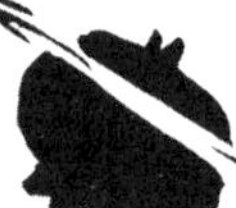

MINE.

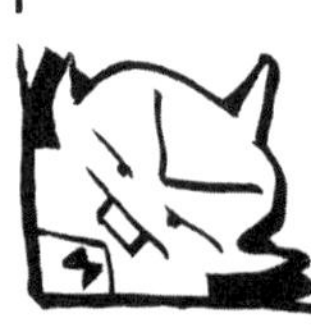

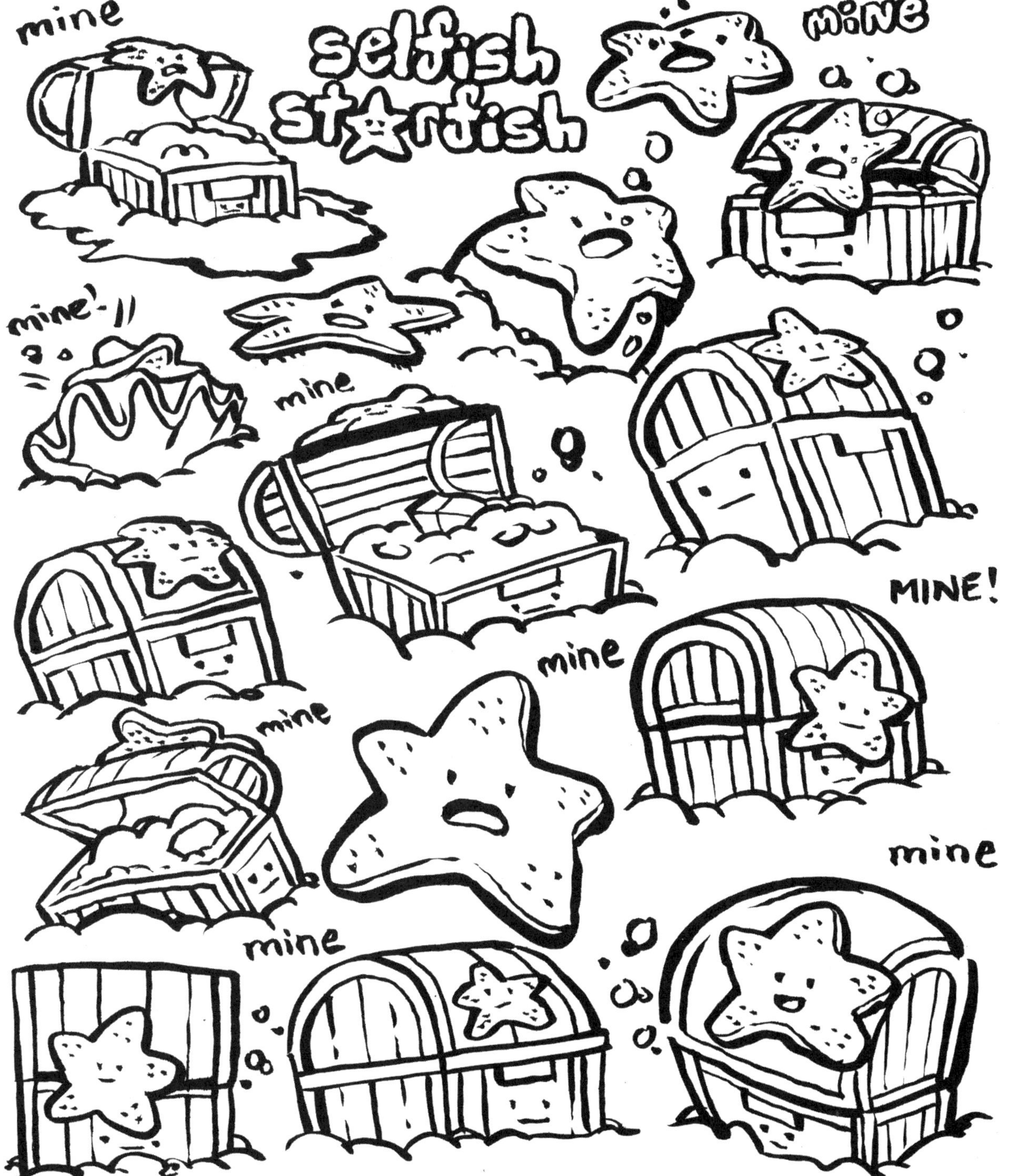
mine
selfish starfish
mine
mine!
mine
MINE!
mine
mine
mine
mine

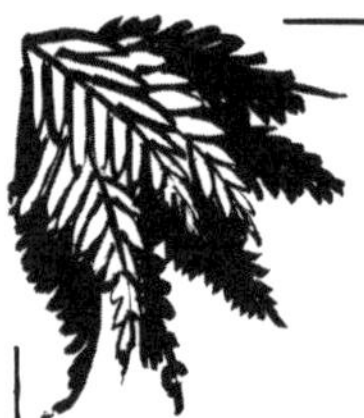

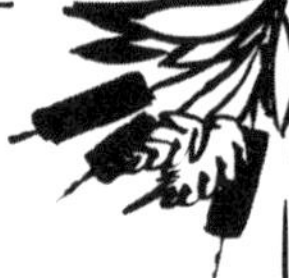

Made with leftovers.

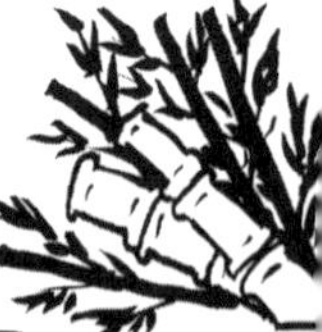

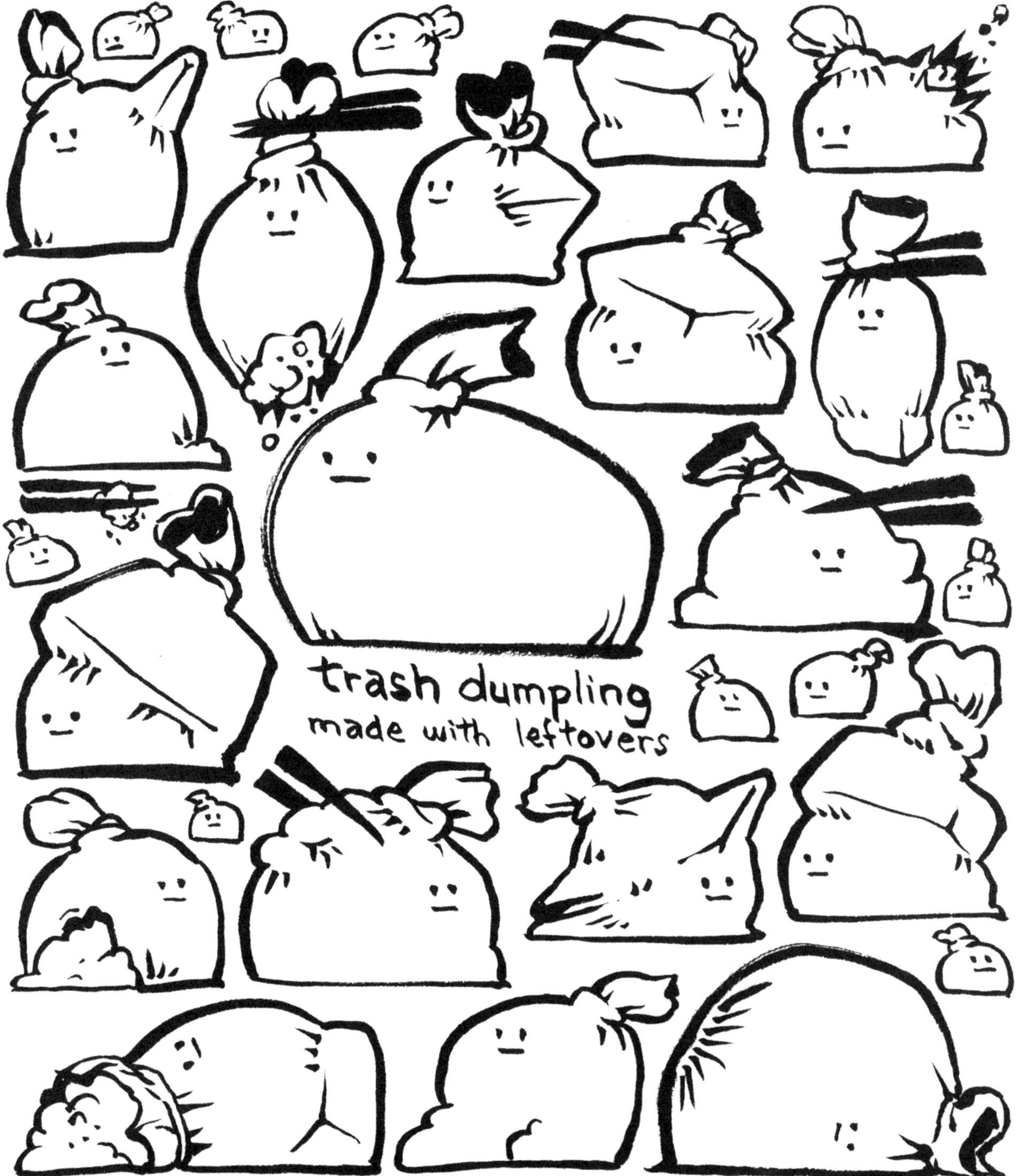
trash dumpling
made with leftovers

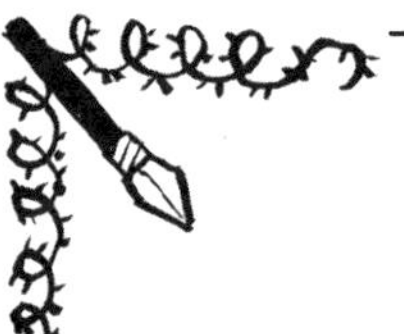

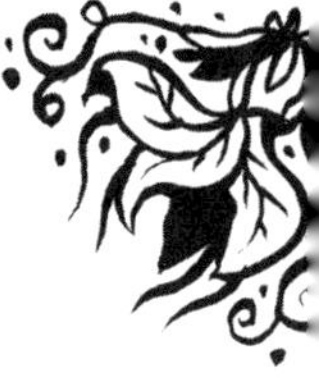

I am this.

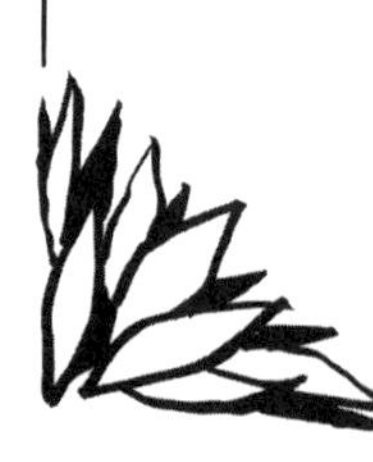

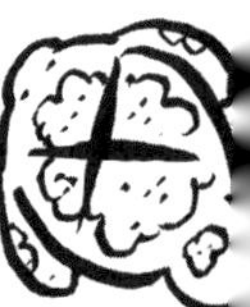

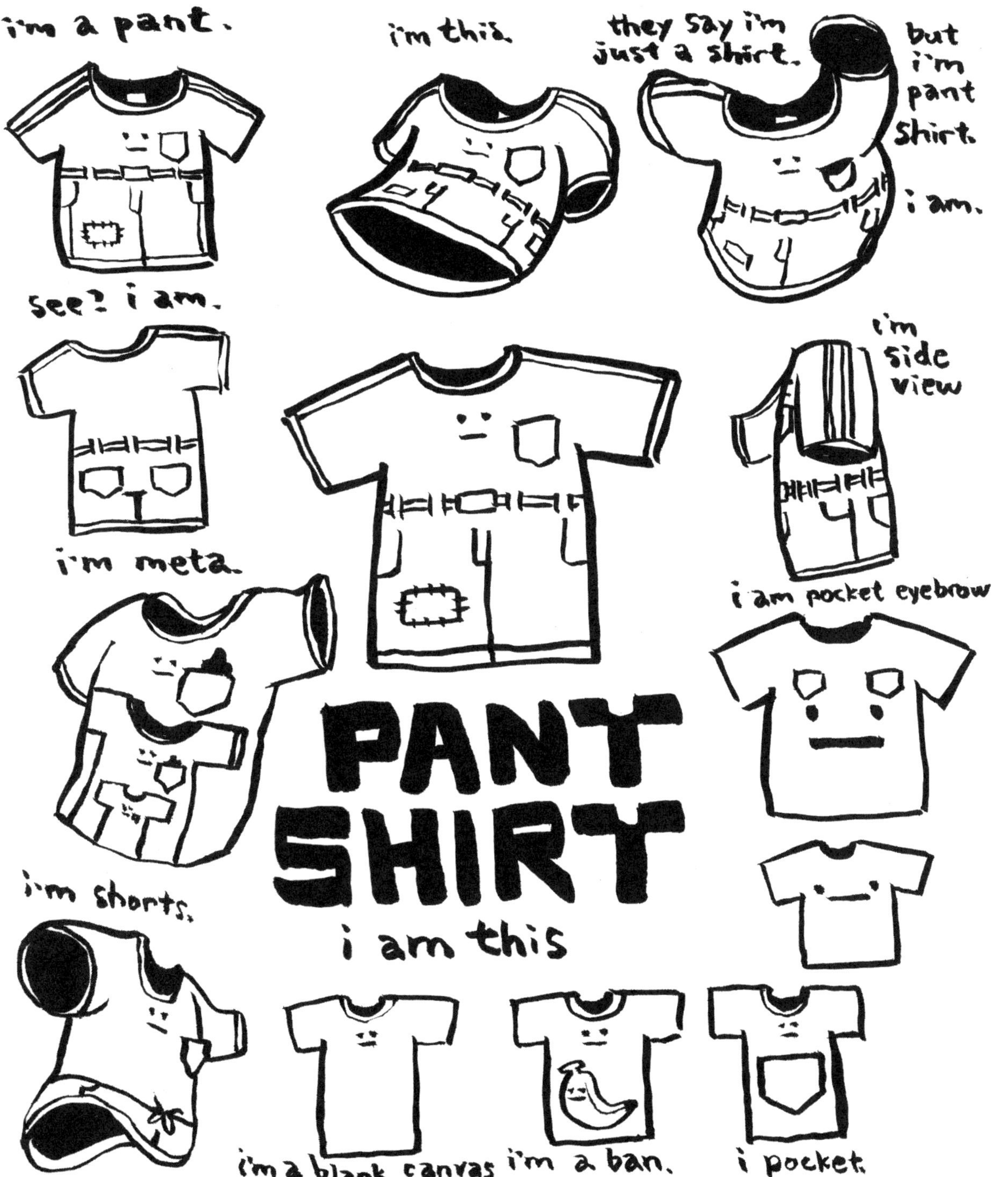

i'm a pant.
i'm this.
they say i'm just a shirt.
but i'm pant shirt.
i am.
see? i am.
i'm side view
i'm meta.
i am pocket eyebrow
PANT SHIRT
i am this
i'm shorts.
i'm a blank canvas
i'm a ban.
i pocket.

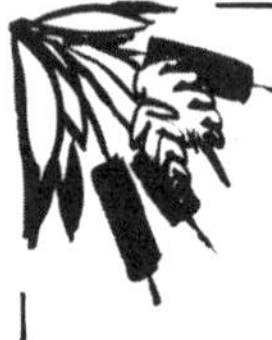

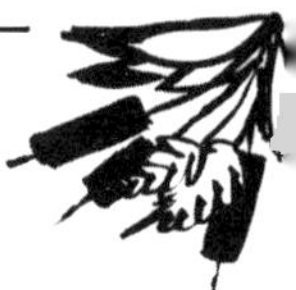

Bad advice
bookworm.

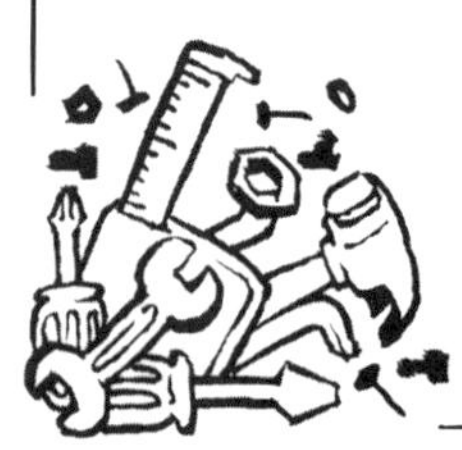

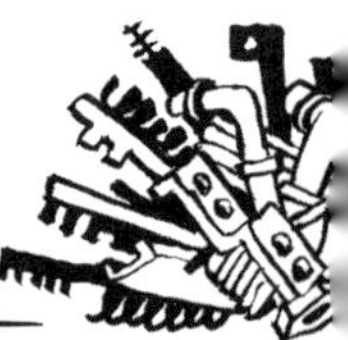

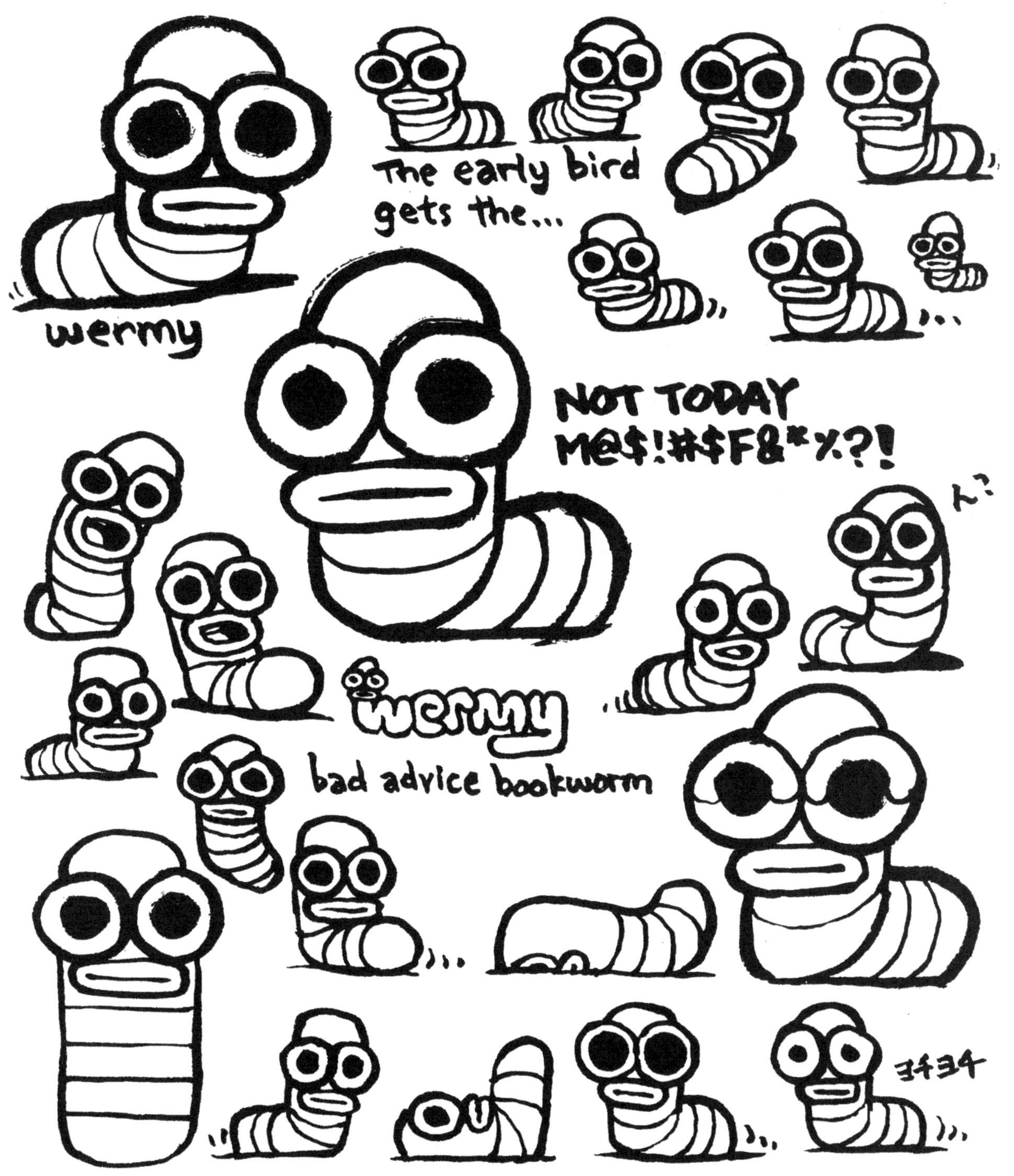
wermy
The early bird
gets the...
NOT TODAY
M@$!#$F&*%?!
ん?
wermy
bad advice bookworm
ヨチヨチ

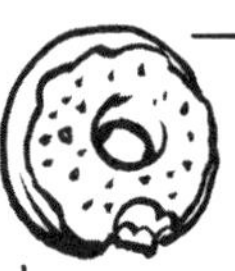

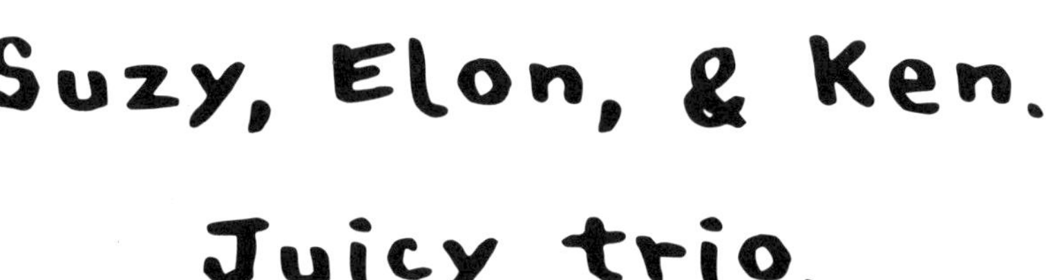
Suzy, Elon, & Ken.
Juicy trio.

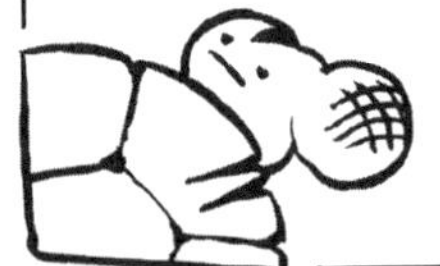

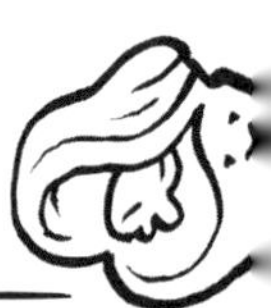

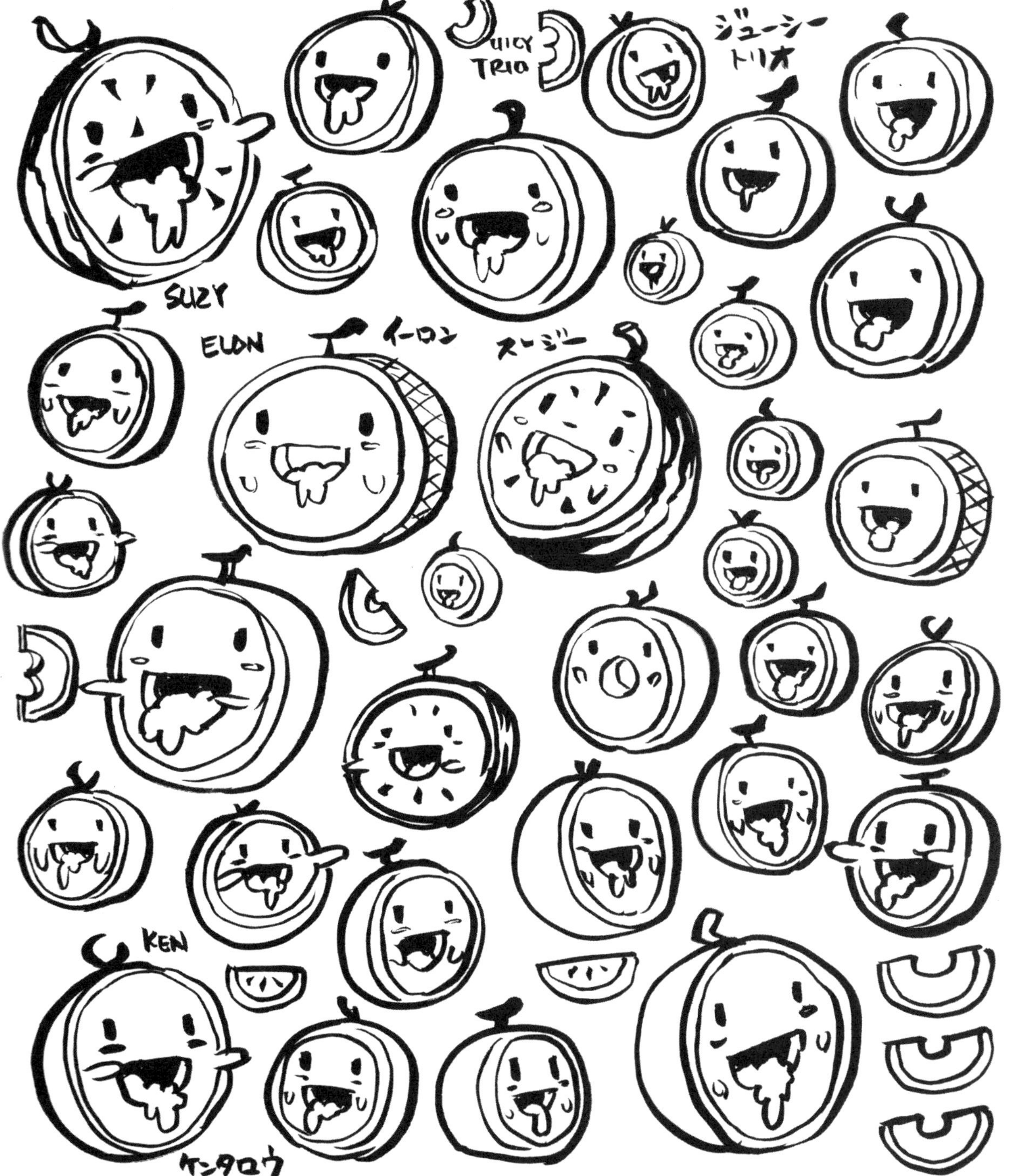

JUICY TRIO
ジューシートリオ
SUZY
ELON
イーロン
スージー
KEN
ケンタロウ

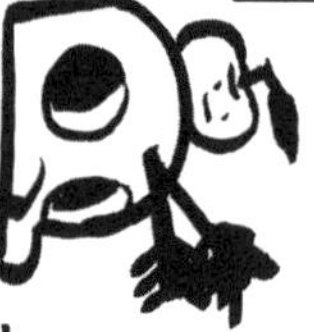

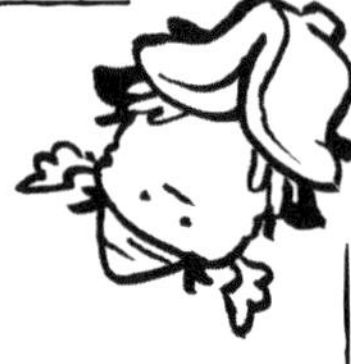

Savior sausage.

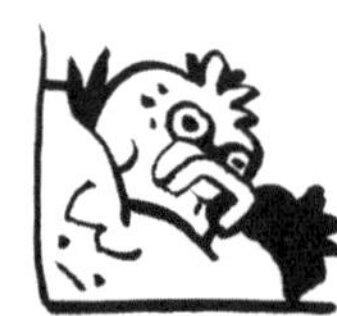

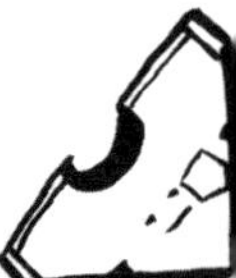

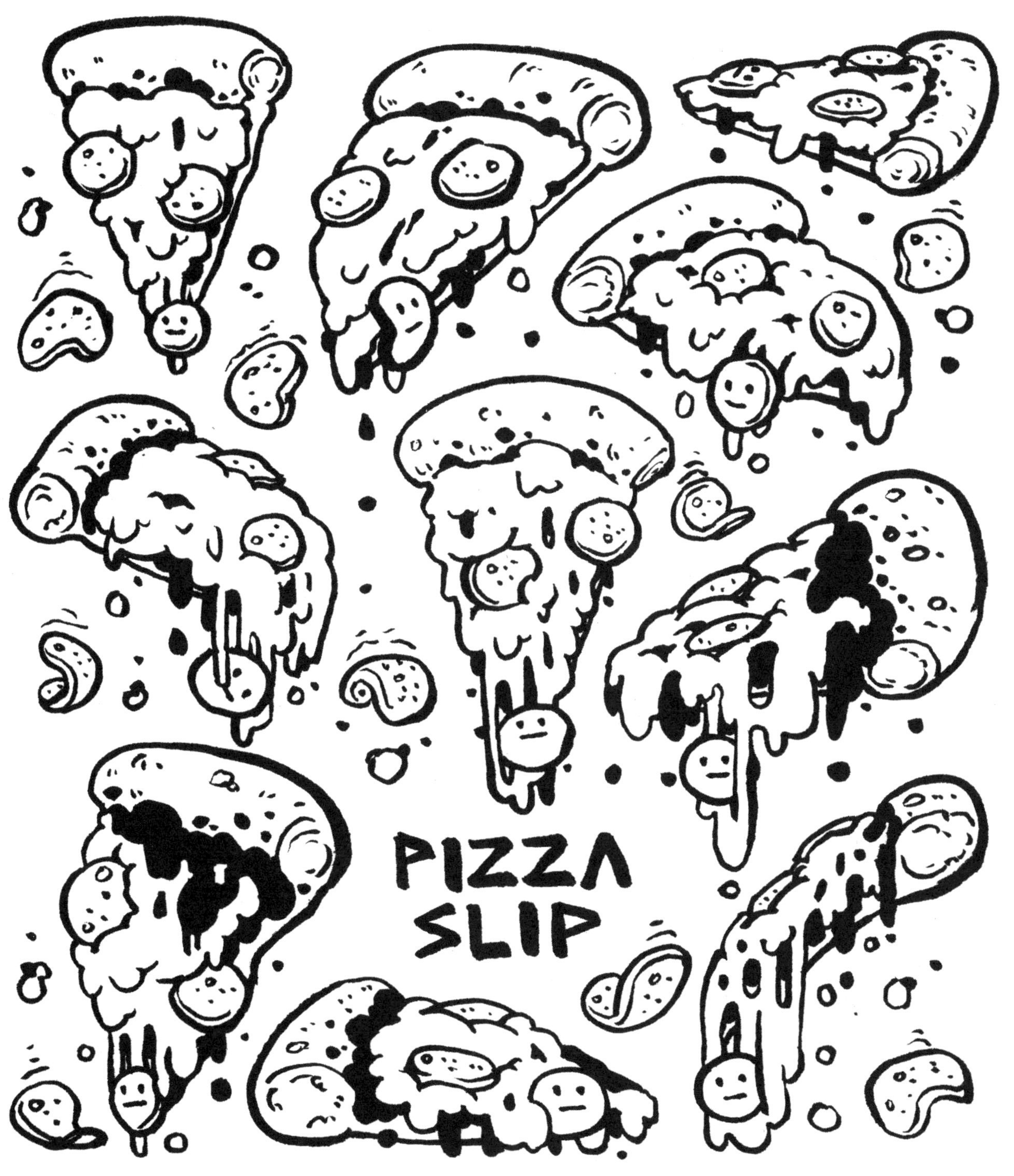
PIZZA
SLIP

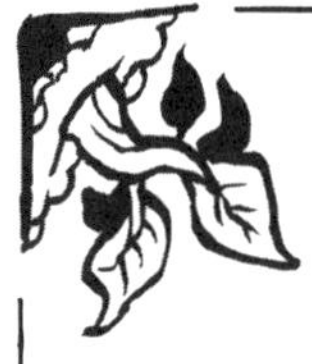

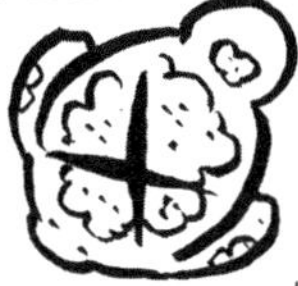

Confidence as a proxy
for competence.

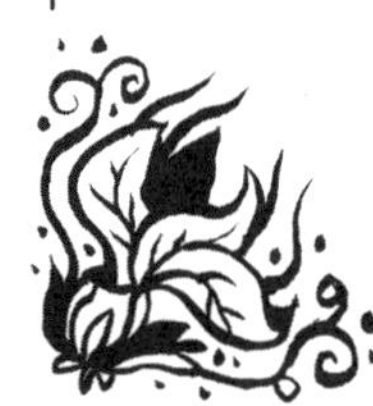

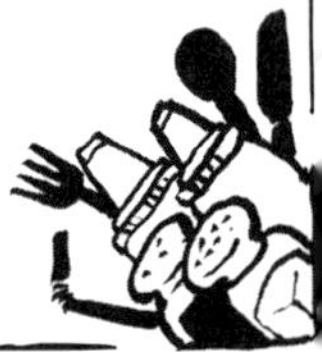

confidence as a proxy for competence

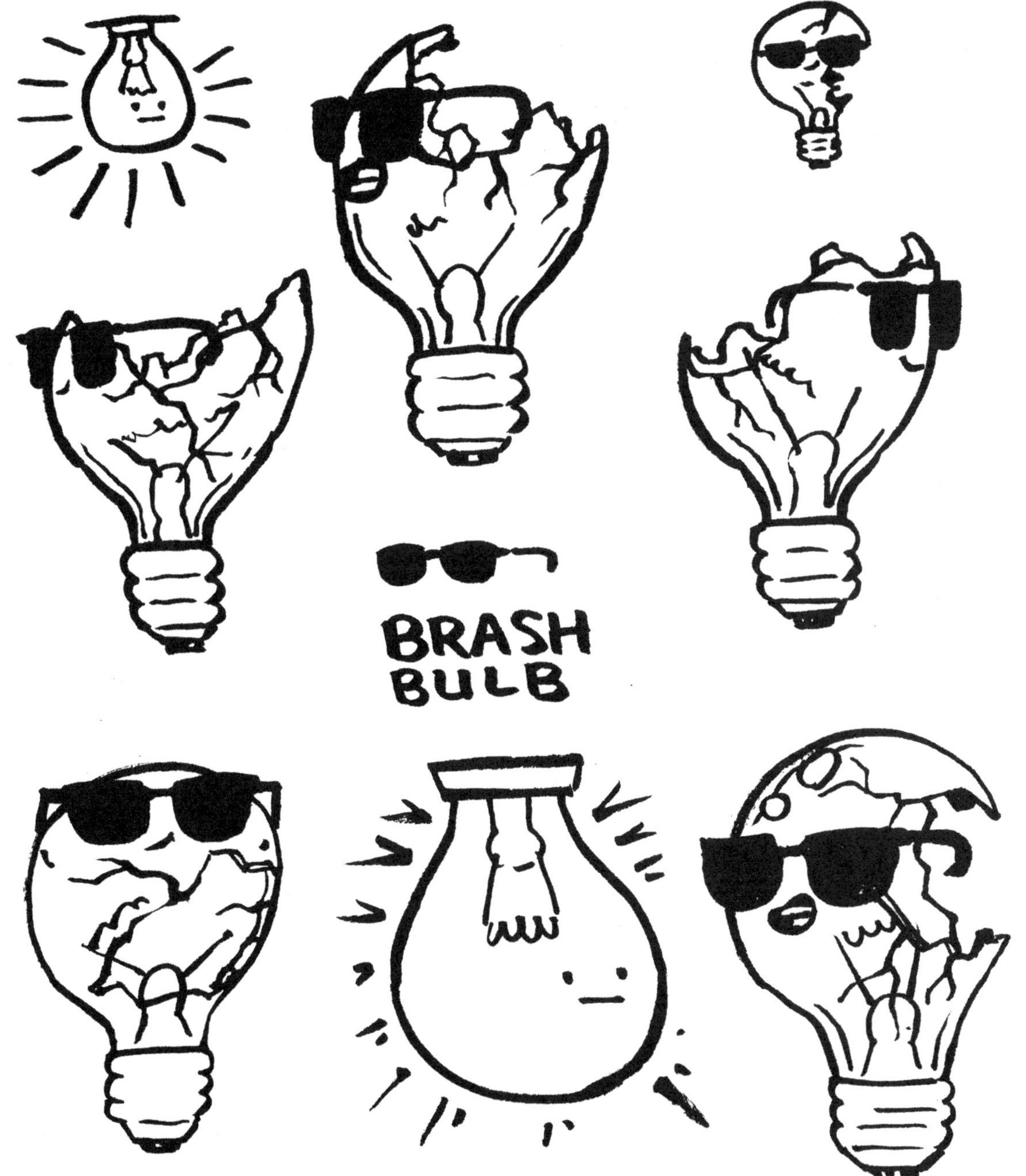

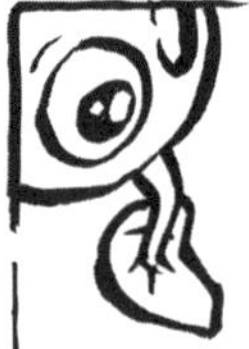

Don't yuck

my yum.

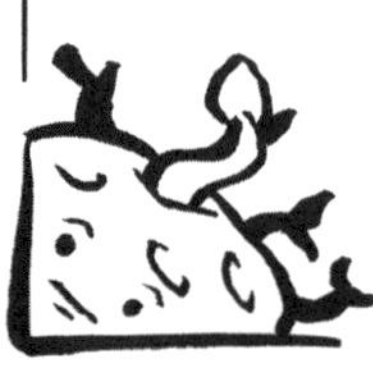

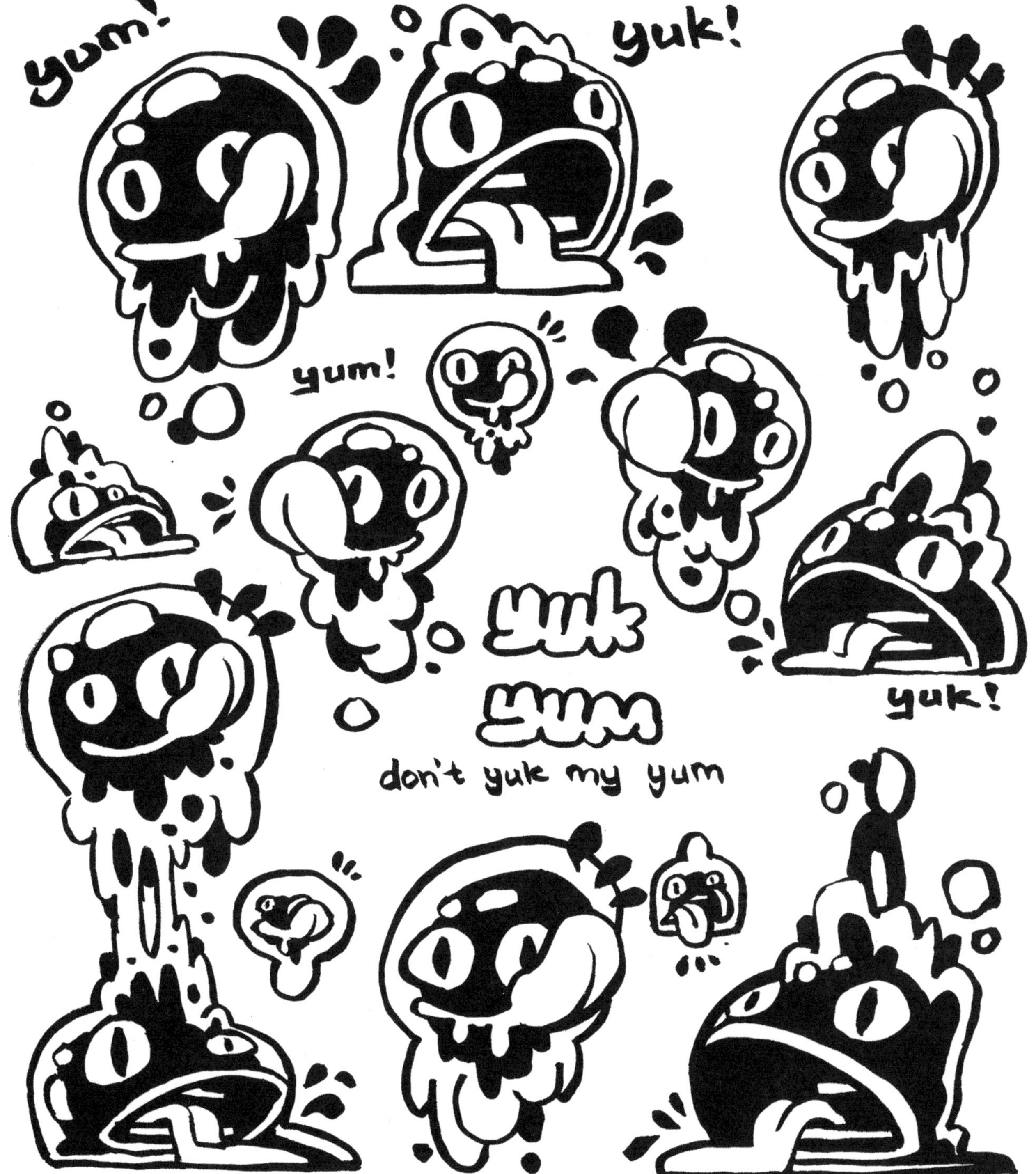
yum!
yuk!
yum!
yuk
yum
don't yuk my yum
yuk!

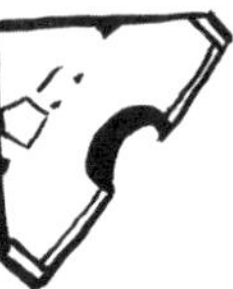

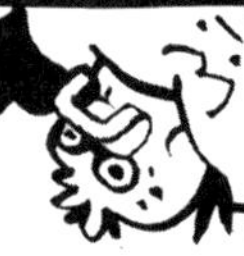

Always something
to prove.

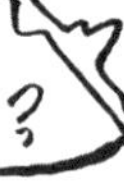

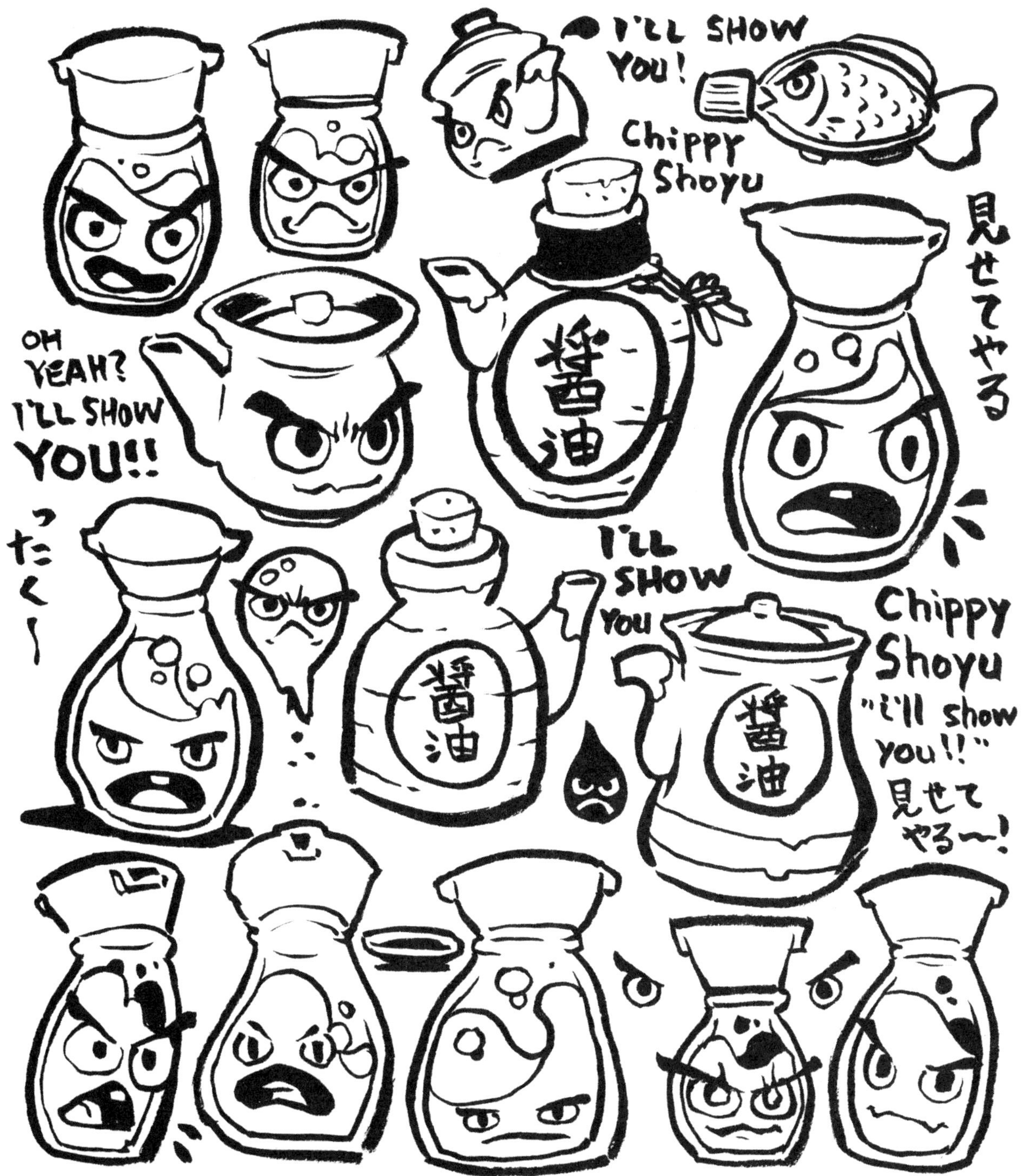

I'LL SHOW YOU!
Chippy Shoyu
見せてやる
OH YEAH? I'LL SHOW YOU!!
醤油
ったく～
I'LL SHOW YOU
醤油
醤油
Chippy Shoyu
"I'll show you!!"
見せてやる～!

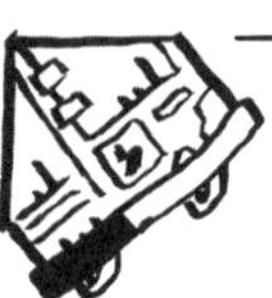

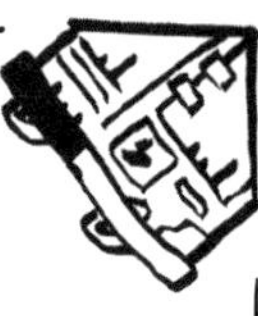

Traveled.

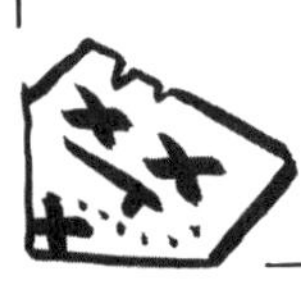

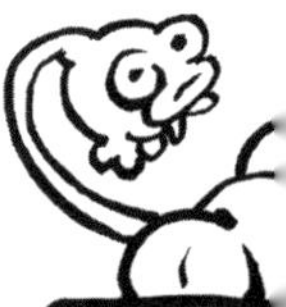

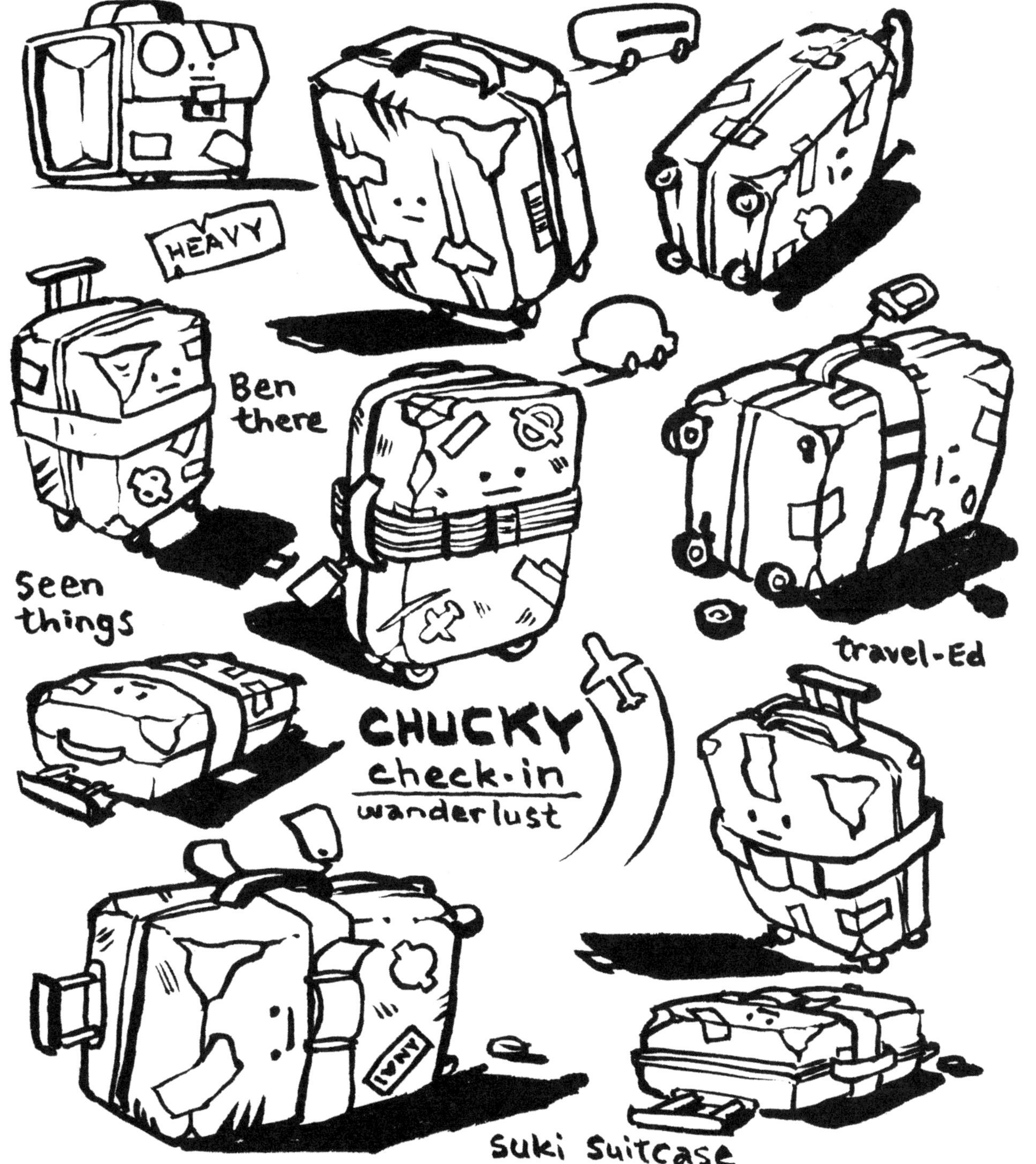
HEAVY
Ben there
seen things
travel-Ed
CHUCKY
check-in
wanderlust
I♥NY
Suki Suitcase

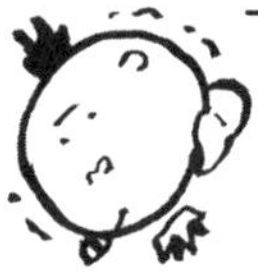

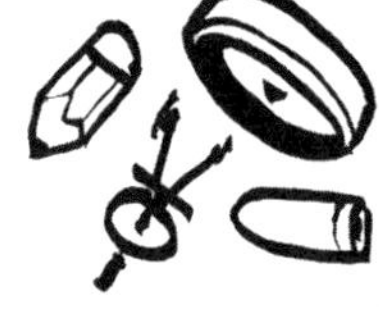

Puny pathogen.

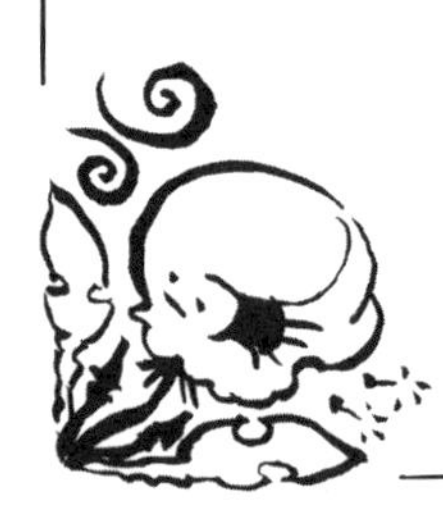

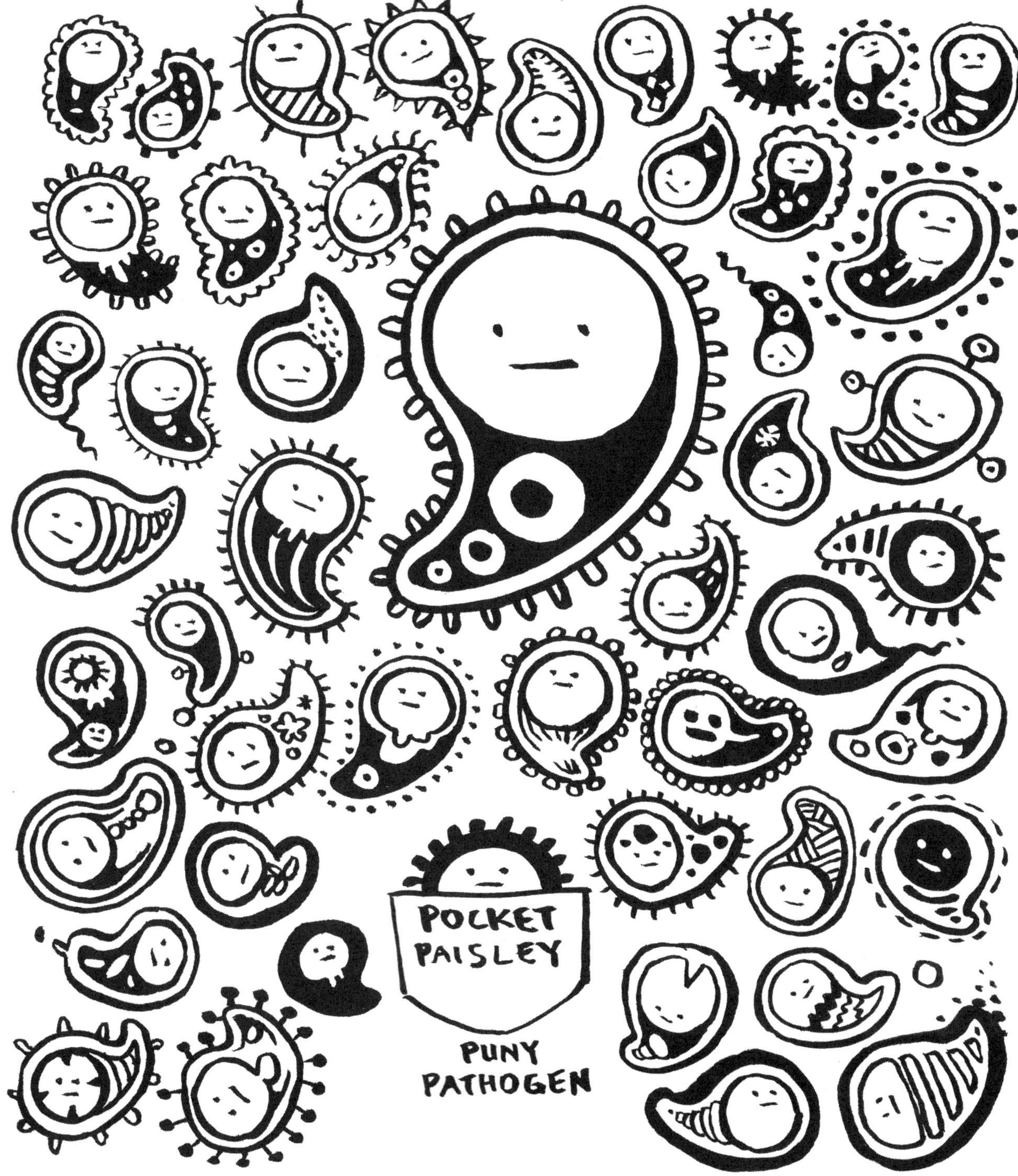
POCKET PAISLEY
PUNY PATHOGEN

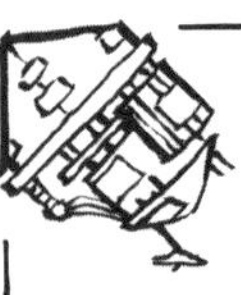

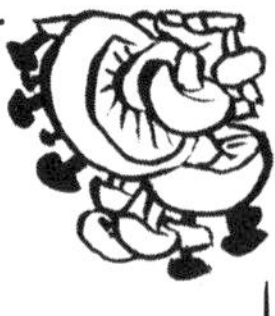

Get bored easily.

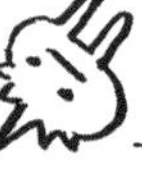

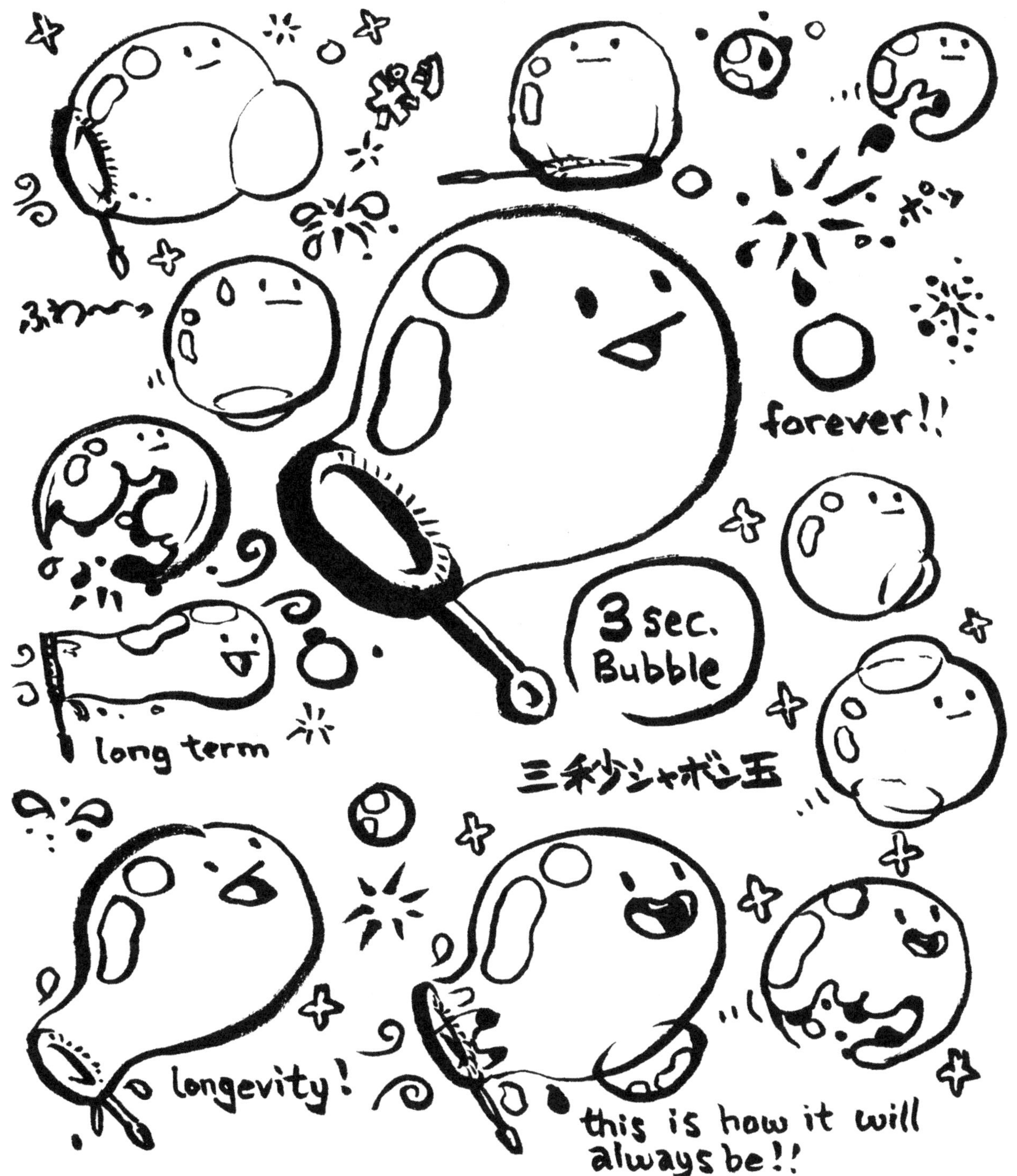
ふわ〜っ
ポッ
forever!!
3 sec.
Bubble
long term
三秒シャボン玉
longevity!
this is how it will
always be!!

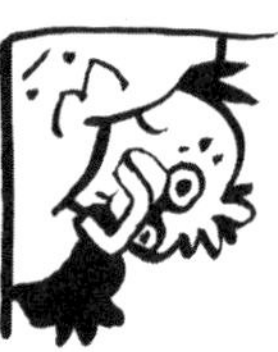

It'll get worse
before it gets better.

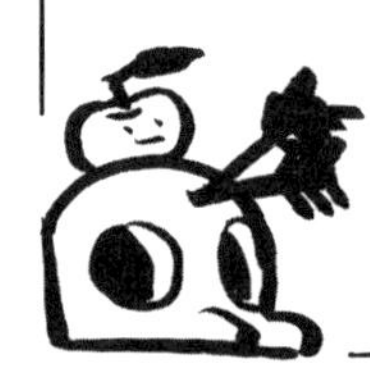

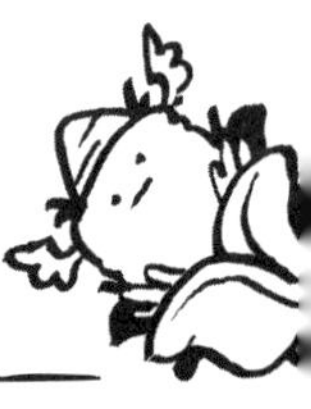

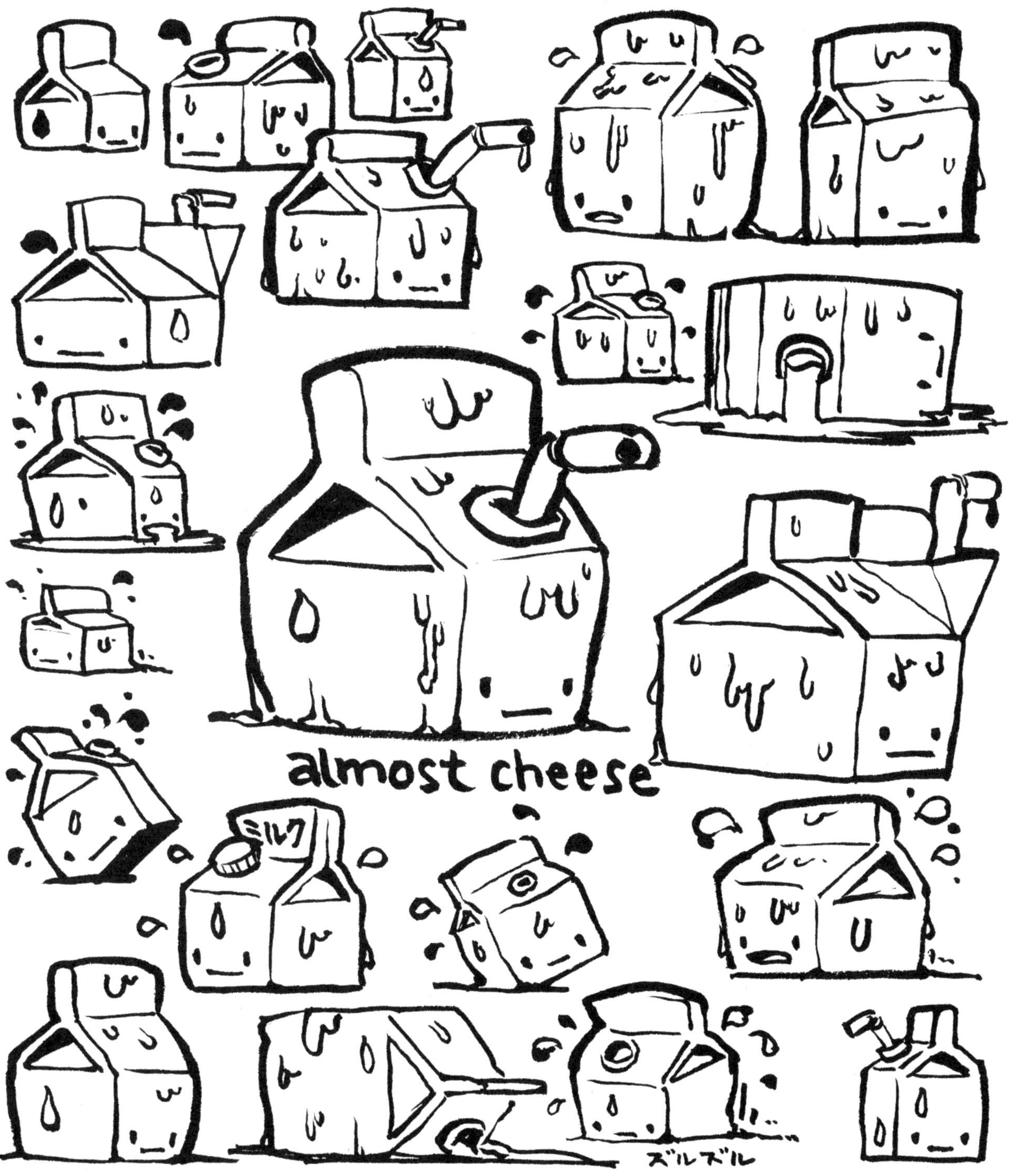
almost cheese
ミルク
ズルズル

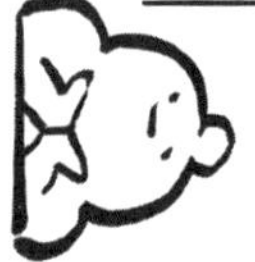

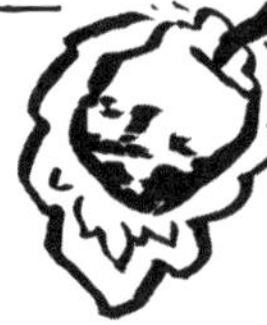

Close shave.

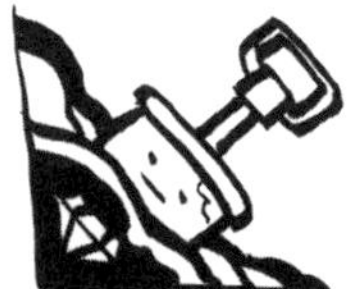

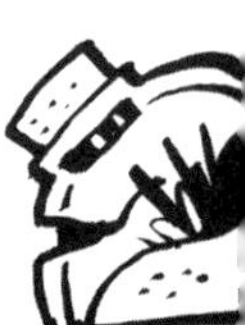

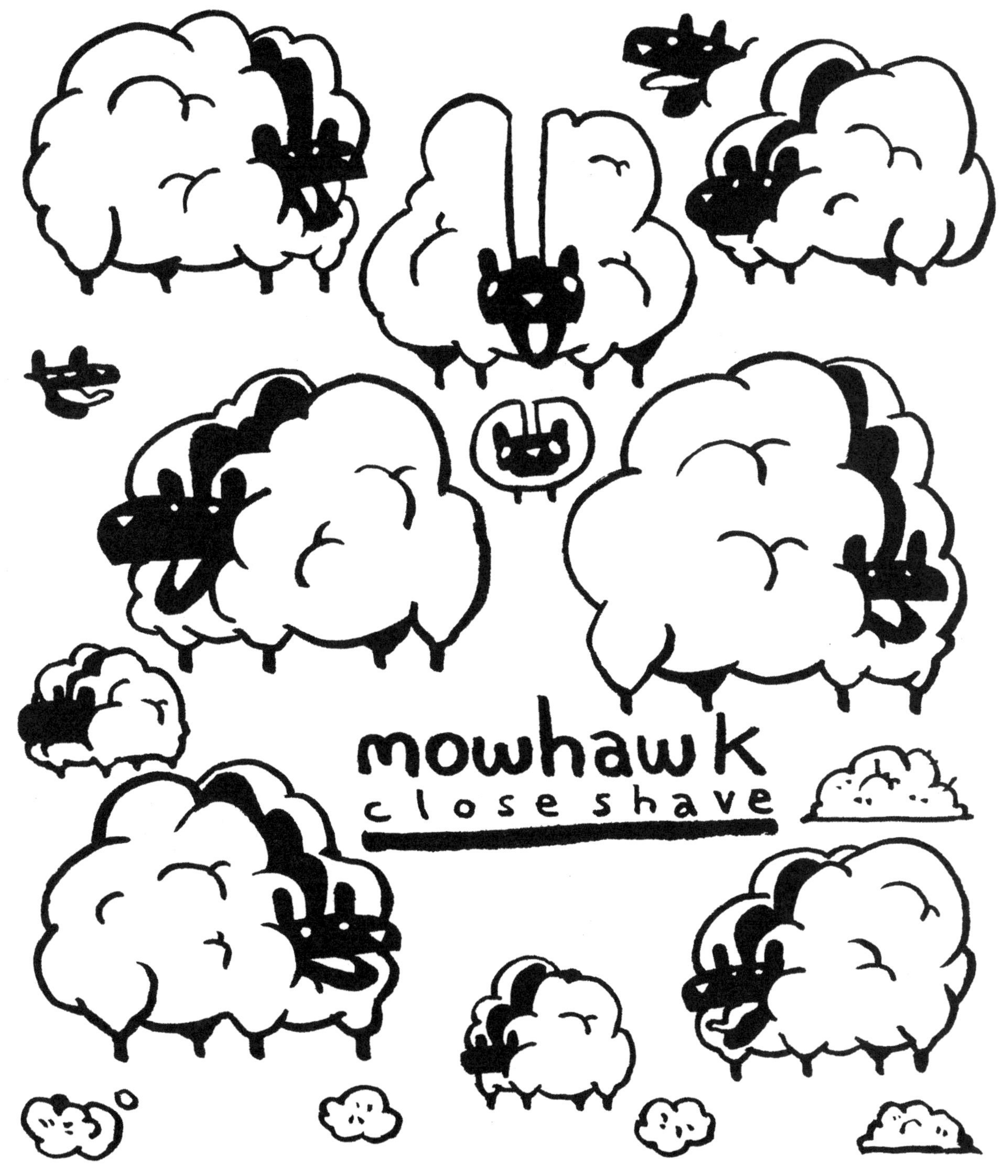
mowhawk
close shave

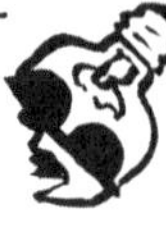

B! L! T!
...and bread.
What am I...?

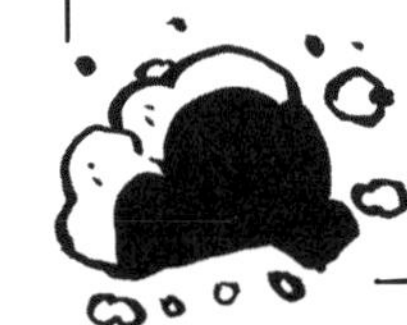

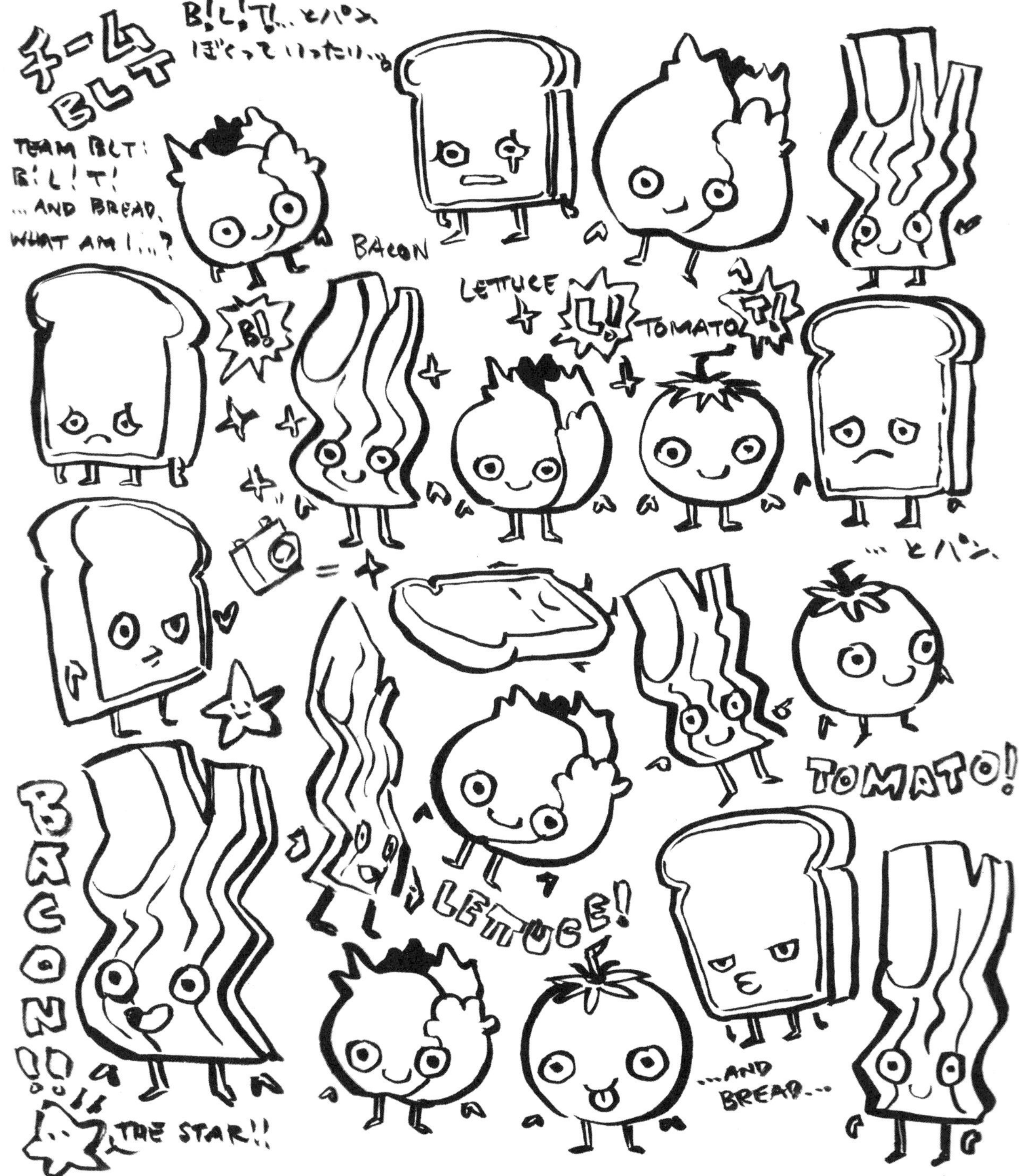

チーム BLT
B!L!T!…とパン。
ぼくっていったい…。
TEAM BLT:
B! L! T!
…AND BREAD.
WHAT AM I…?
BACON
LETTUCE
TOMATO
B!
L!
T!
…とパン。
TOMATO!
LETTUCE!
BACON!!
THE STAR!!
…AND BREAD…

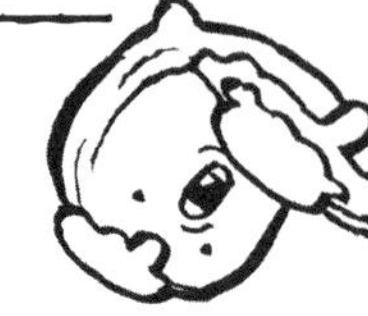

Eyes on
the prize.

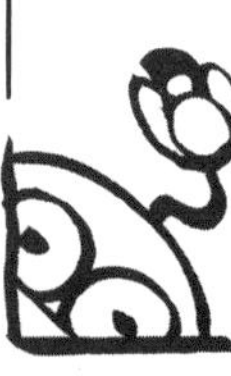

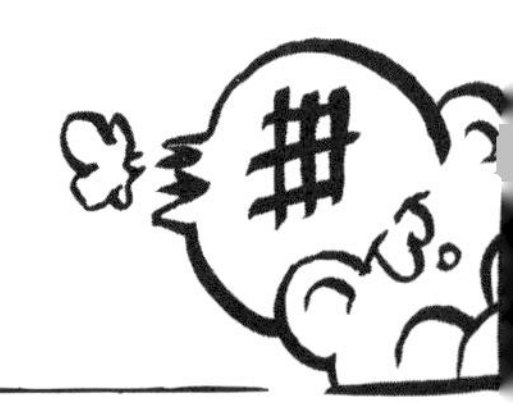

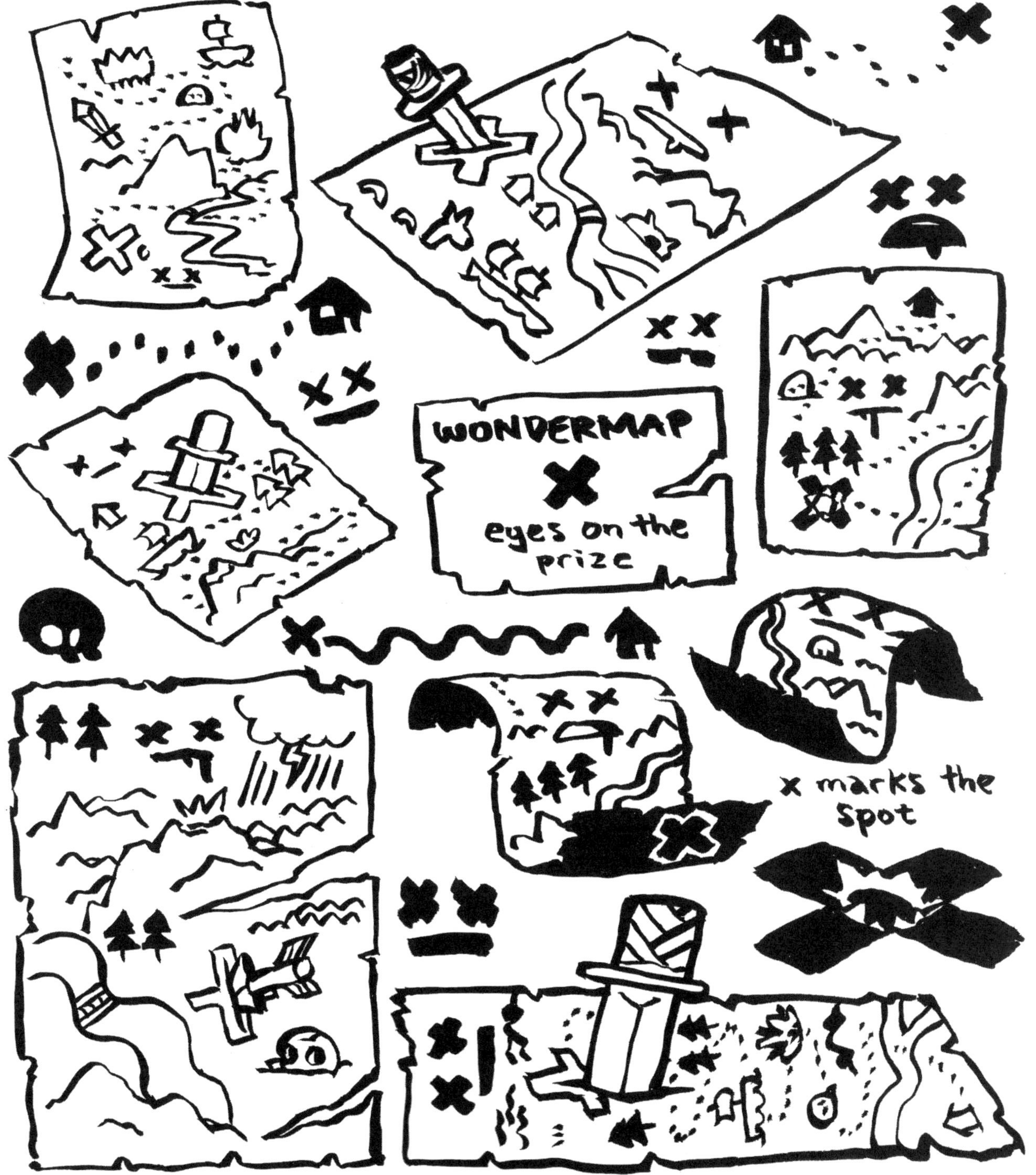
WONDERMAP
eyes on the prize
x marks the spot

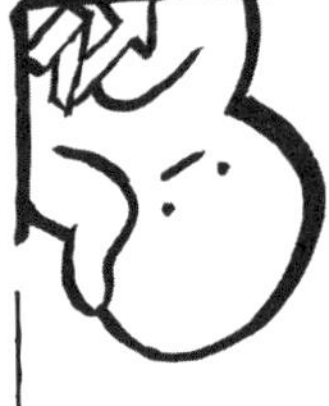

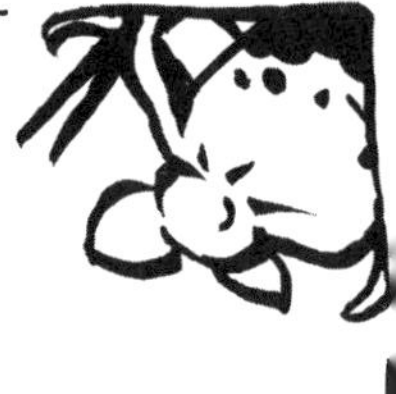

Is it though?

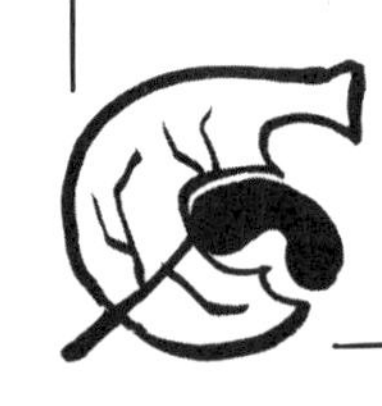

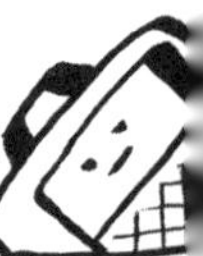

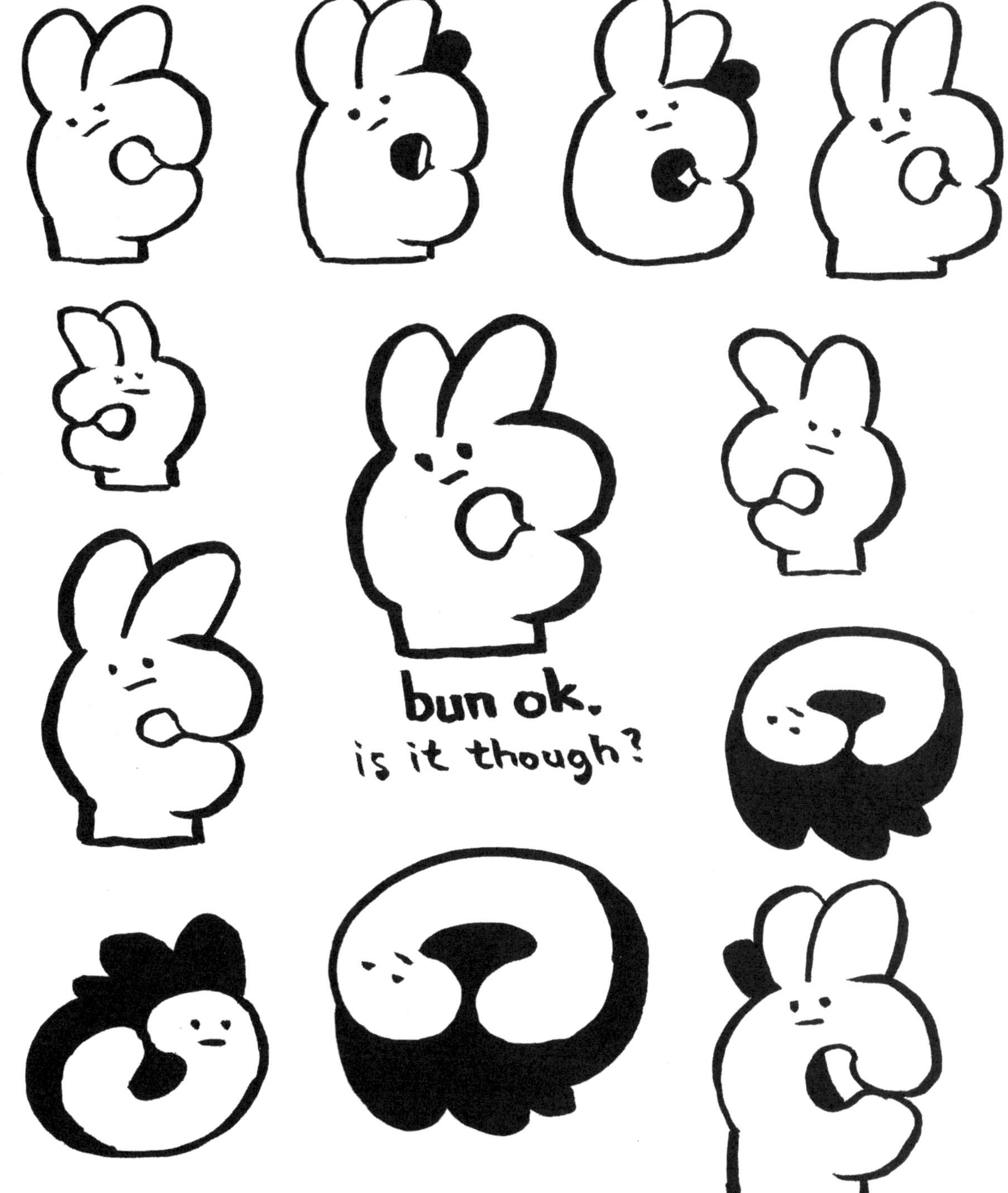
bun ok.
is it though?

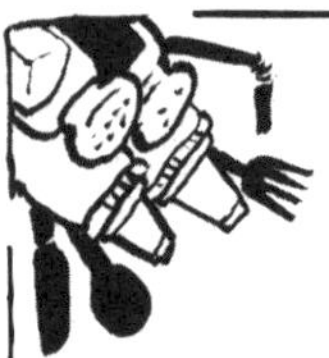

Fsh has trouble focusing but is still hungry.

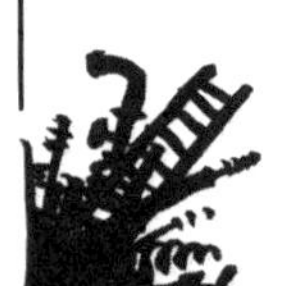

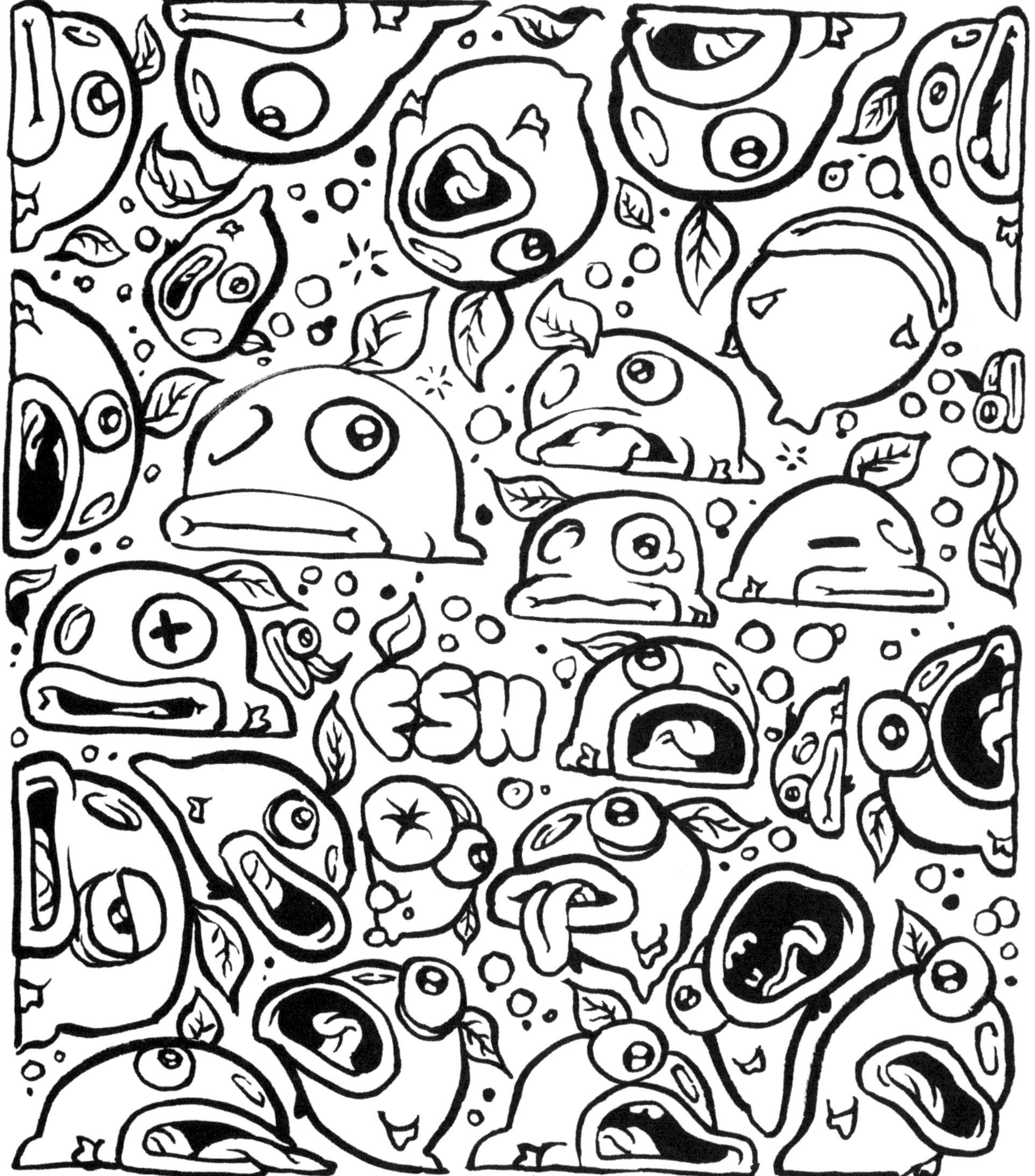
ESH

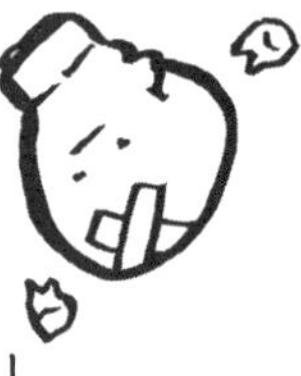

Let's play!

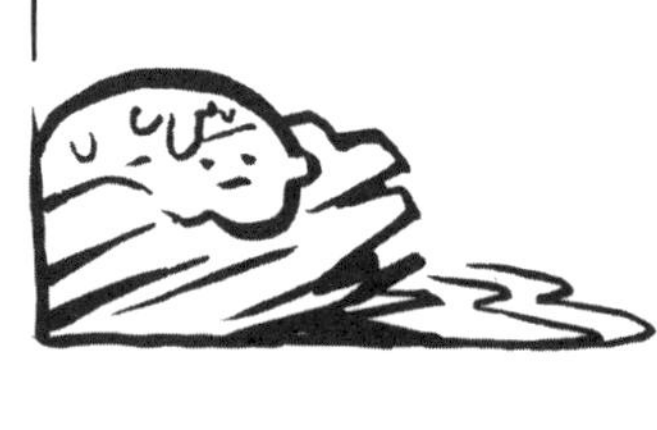

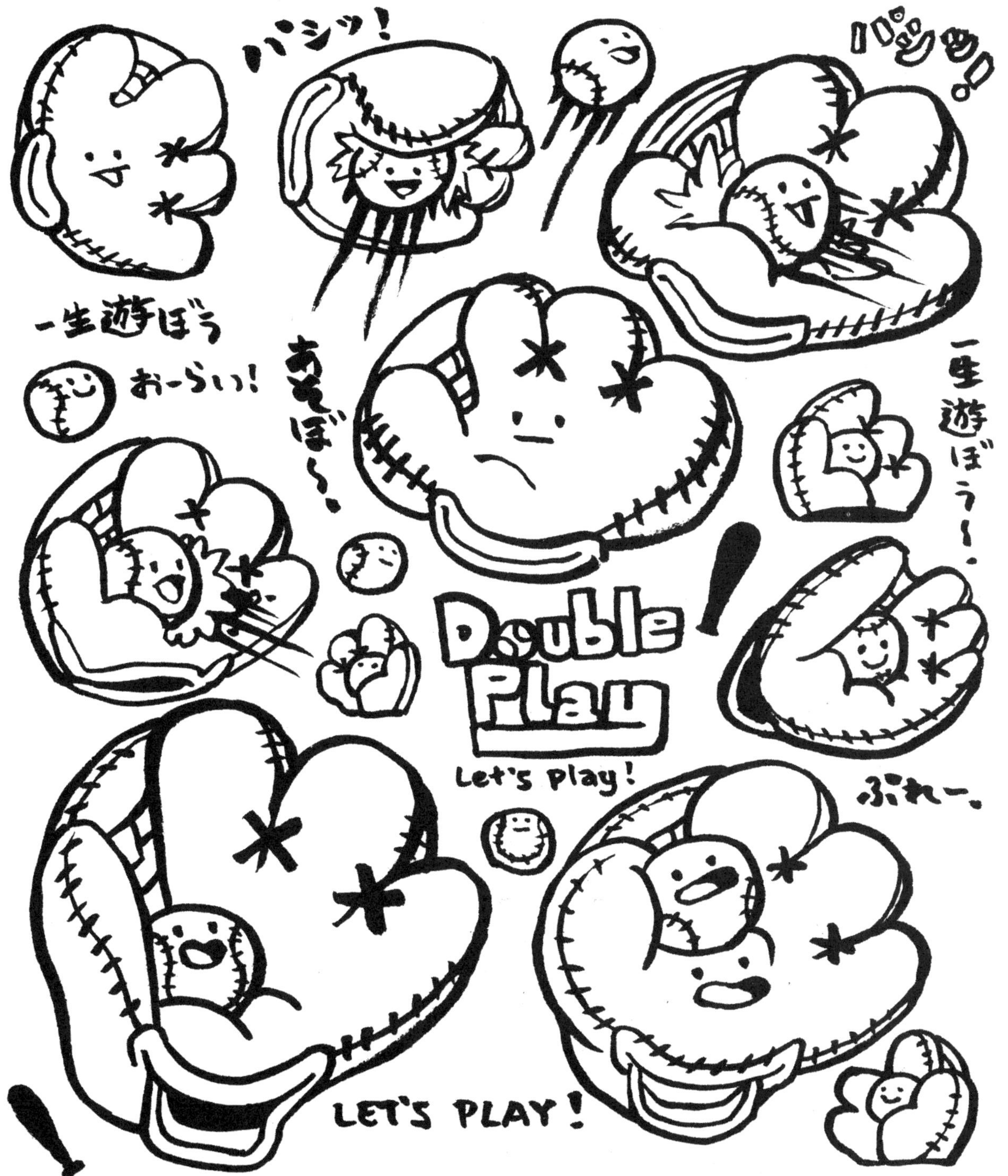

パシッ！
パシッ！
一生遊ぼう
おーらいっ！
あそぼ〜。
一生遊ぼう〜。
Double Play
Let's play!
ぷれー。
LET'S PLAY!

To die on.

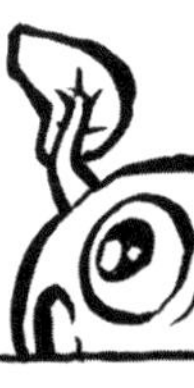

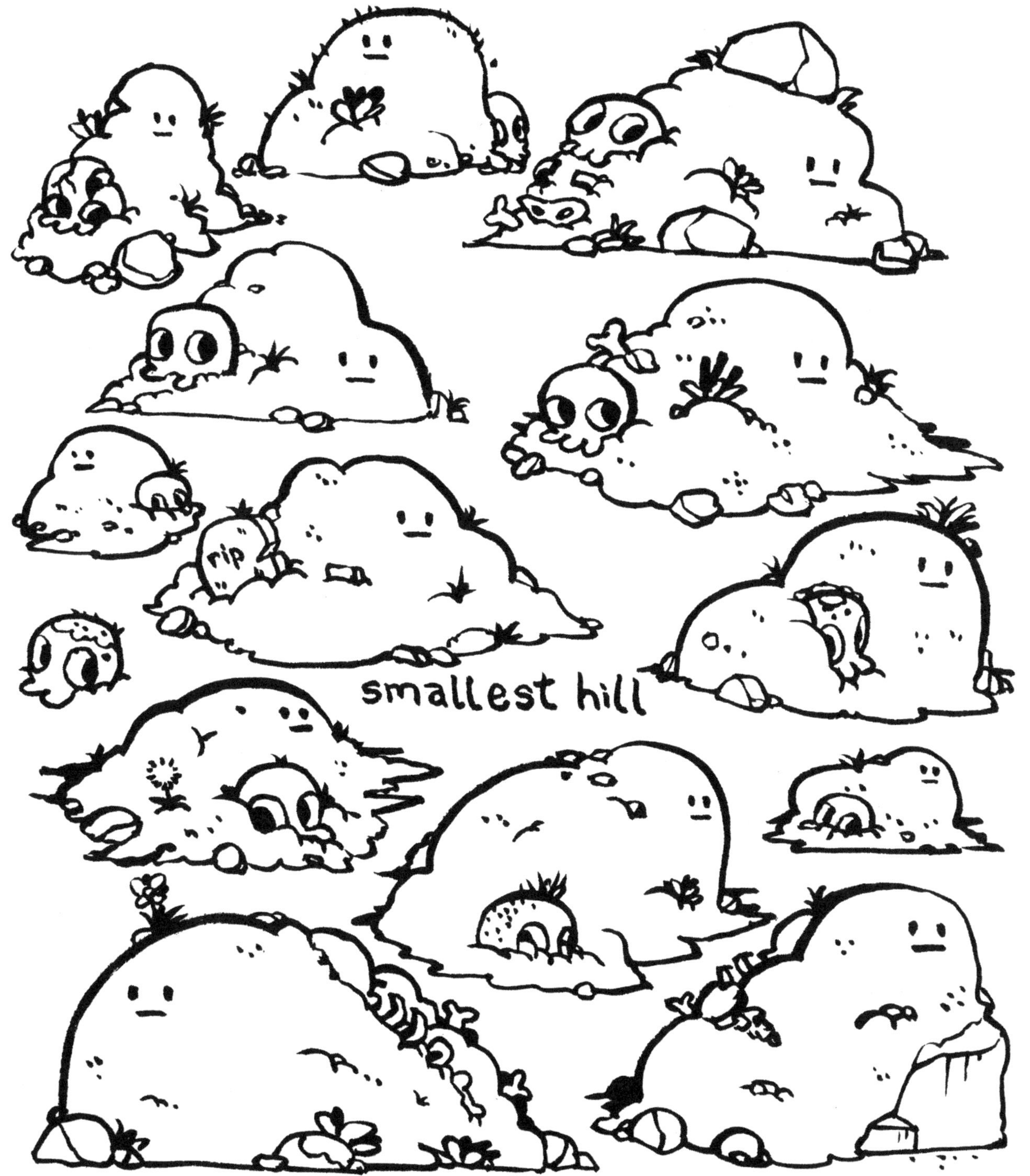
rip
smallest hill

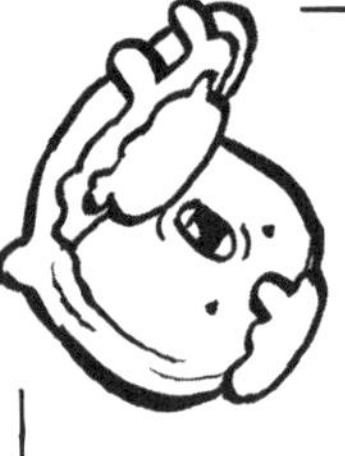

Accidental goodness.

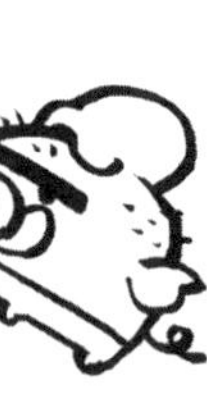

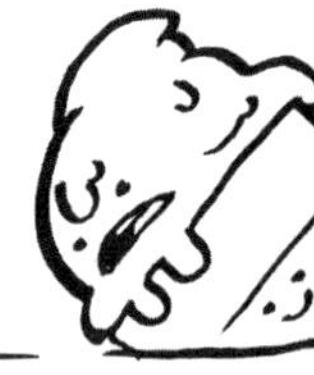

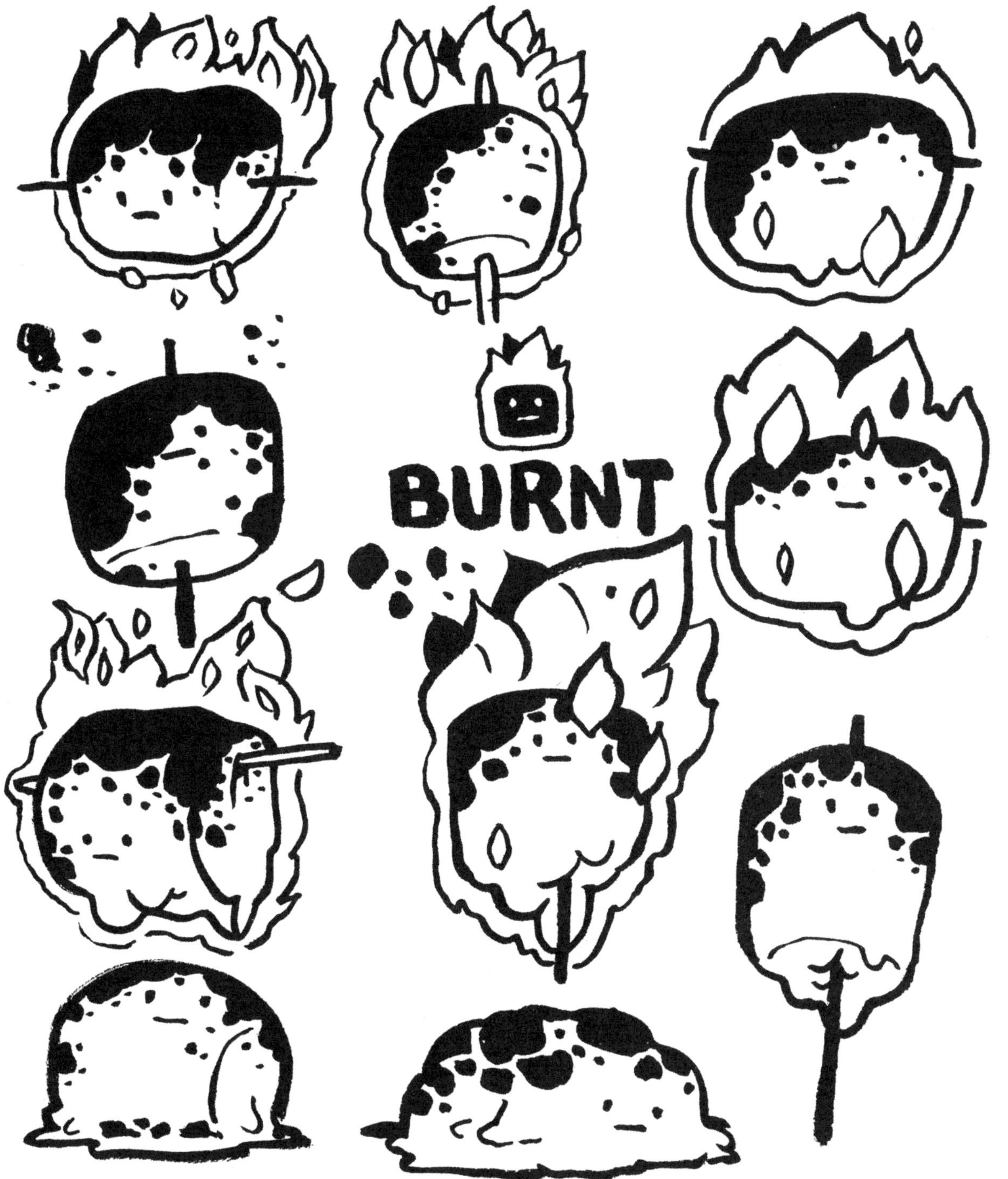
BURNT

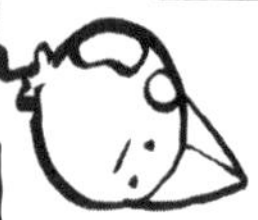

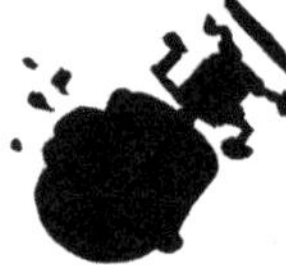

Check!

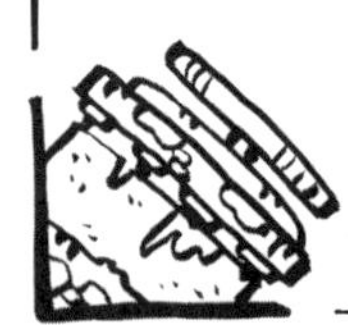

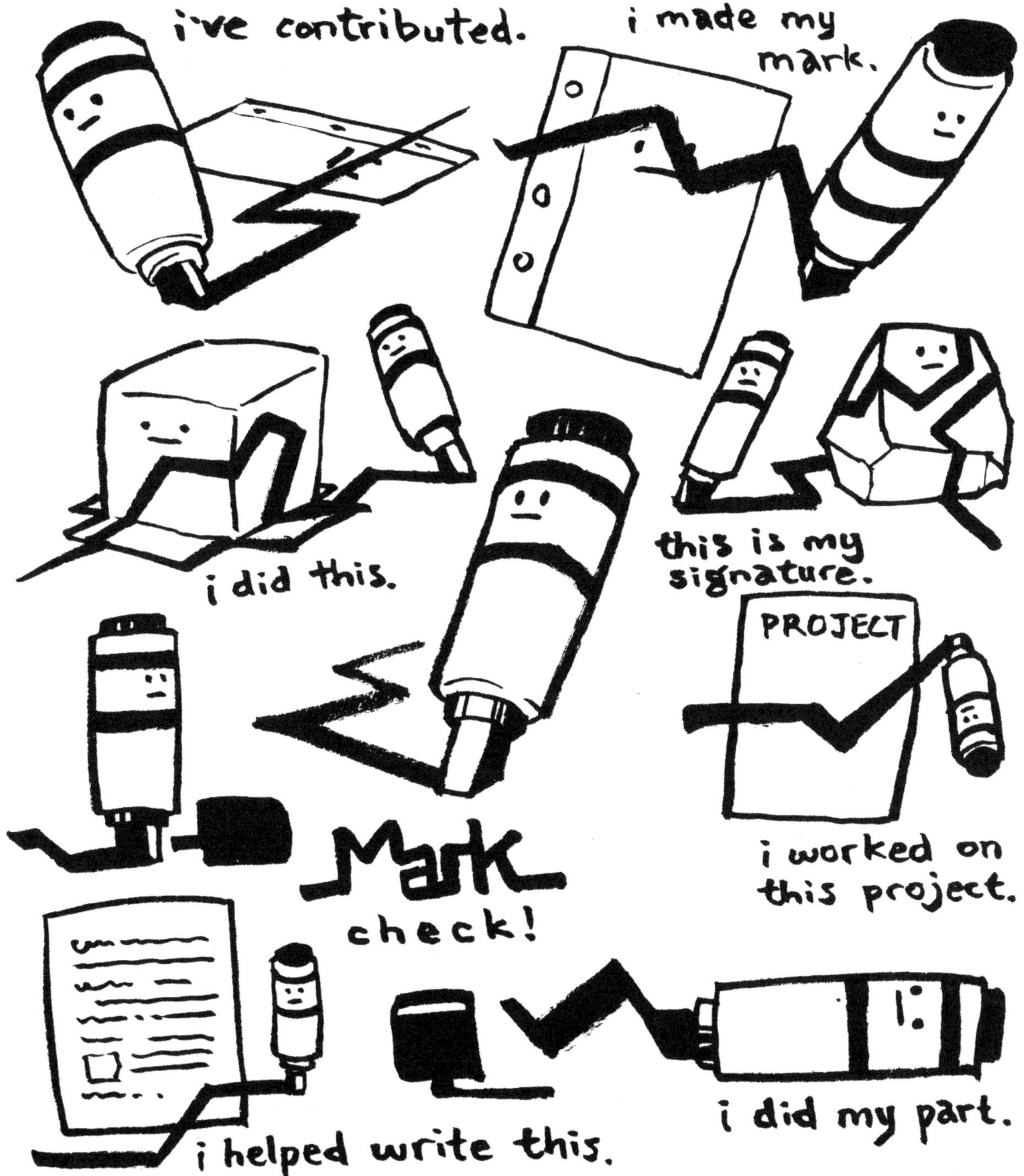

i've contributed.
i made my mark.
i did this.
this is my signature.
PROJECT
Mark
check!
i worked on this project.
i did my part.
i helped write this.

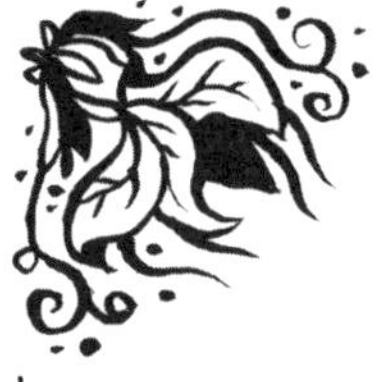

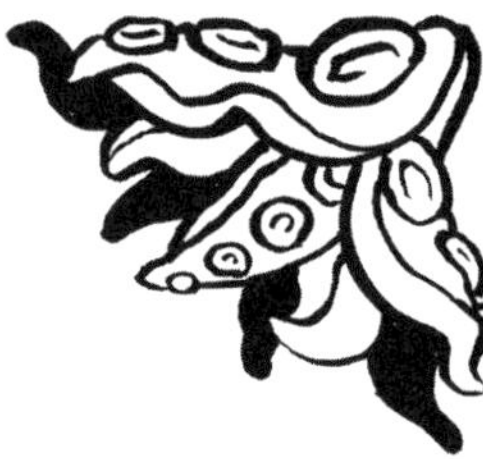

Overconsumption.

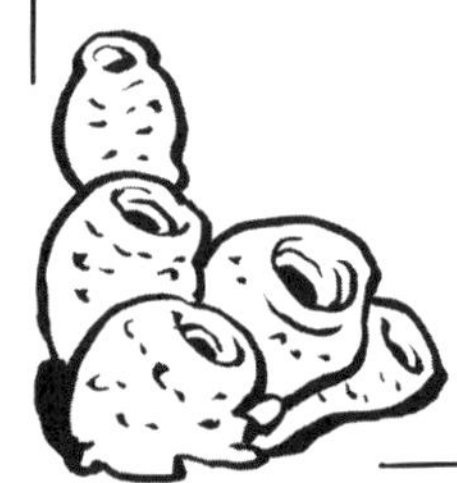

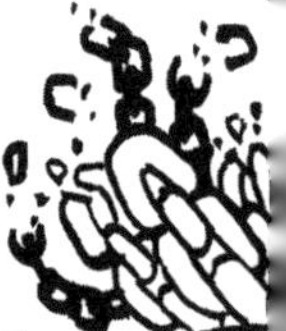

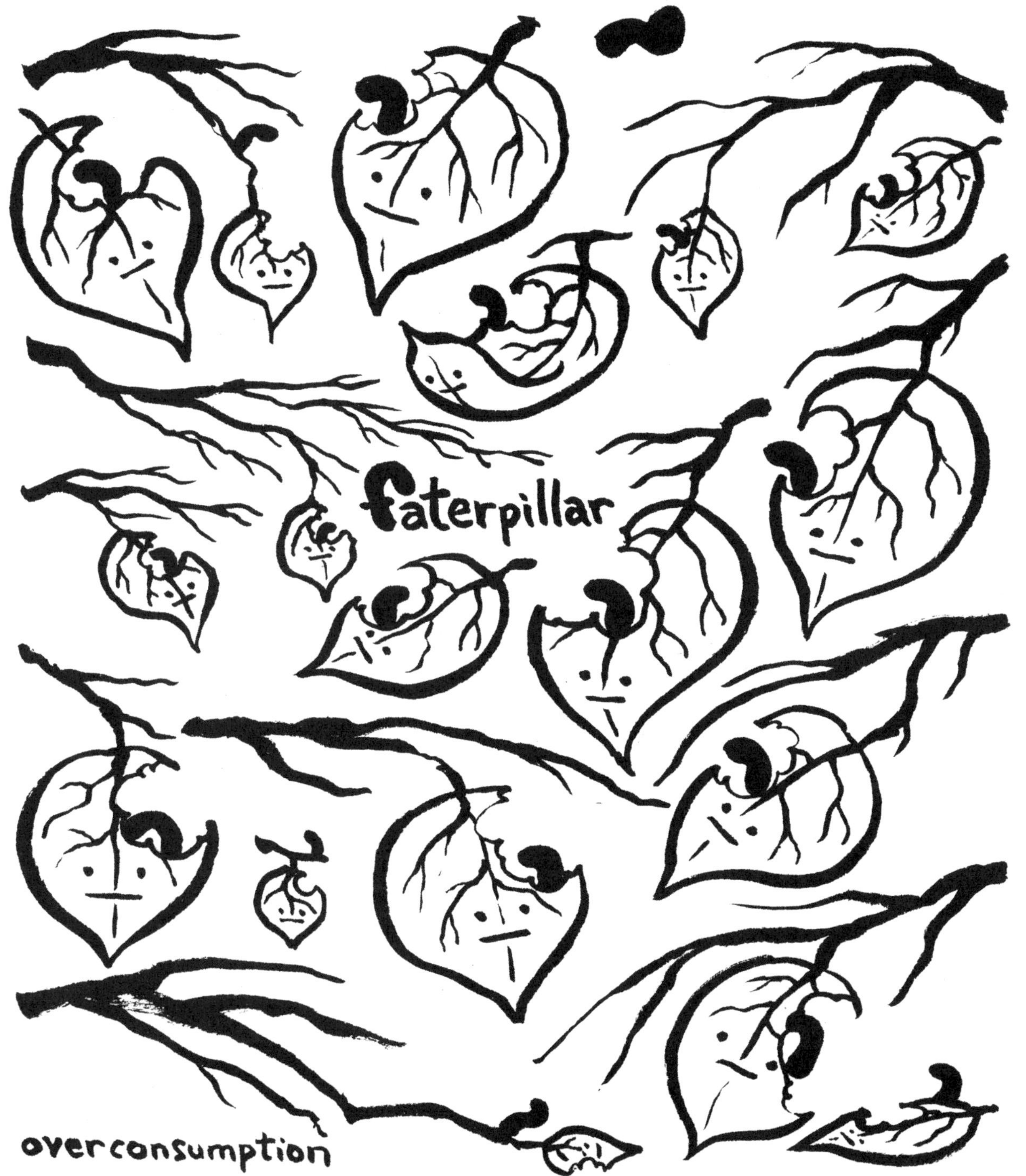
faterpillar
overconsumption

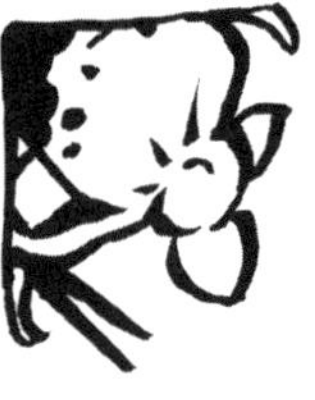

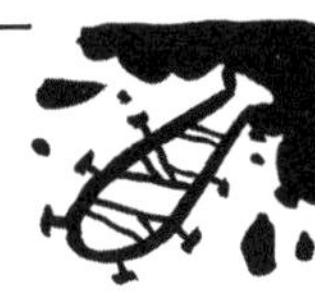

I'm better!

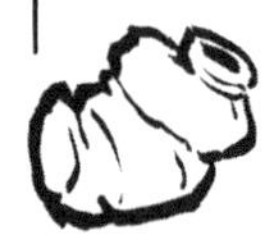

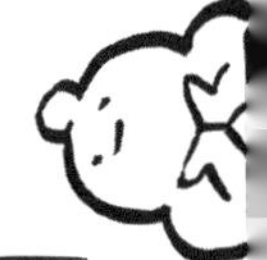

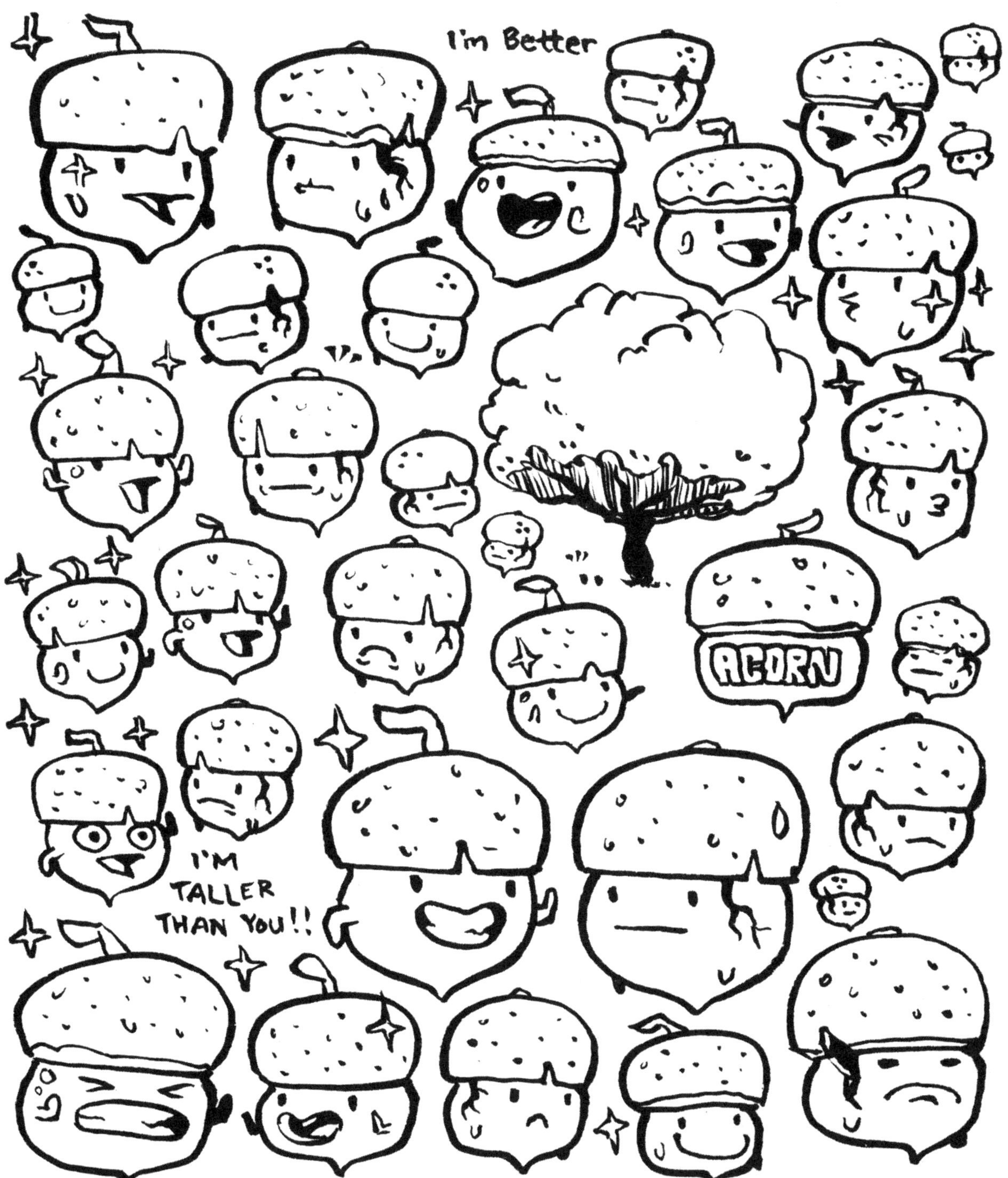
I'm Better
ACORN
I'M TALLER THAN YOU!!

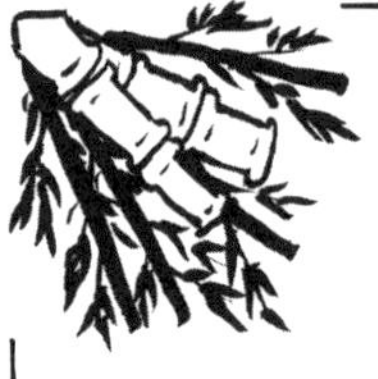

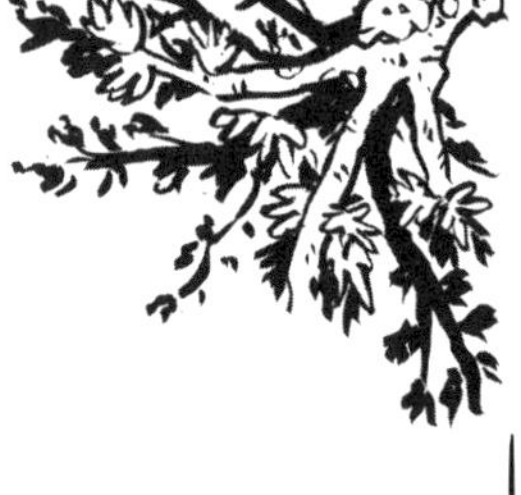

Unknowingly
irreverent.

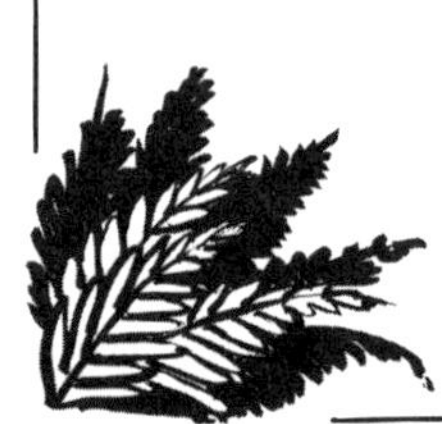

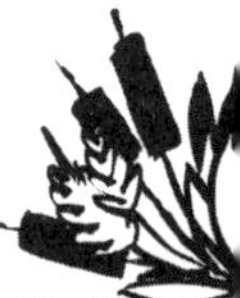

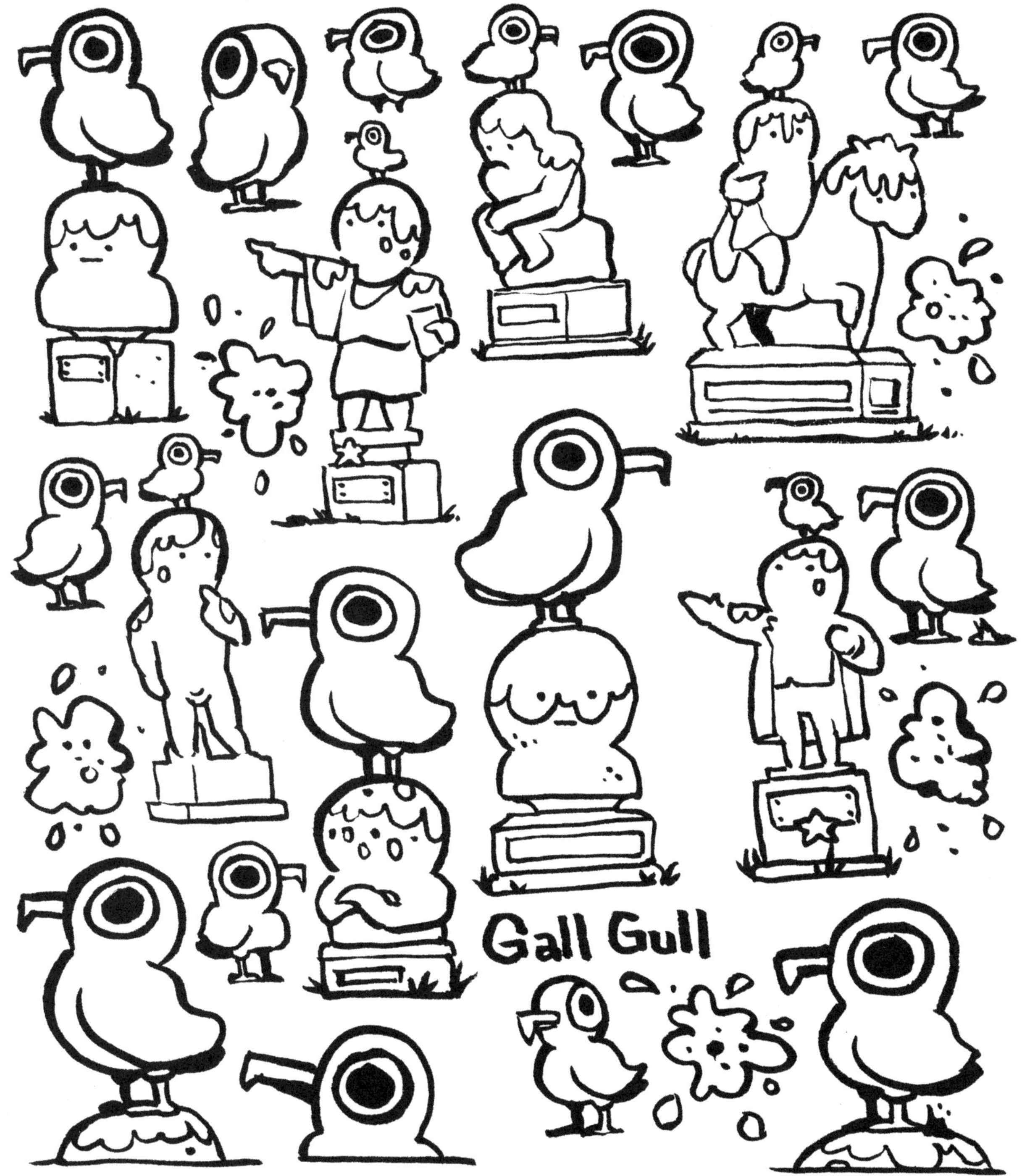
Gall Gull

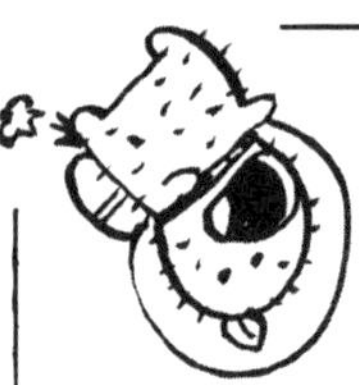

Grill it to Pow!

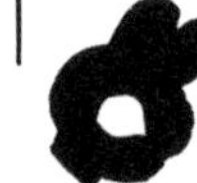

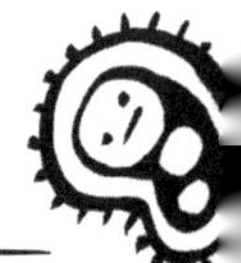

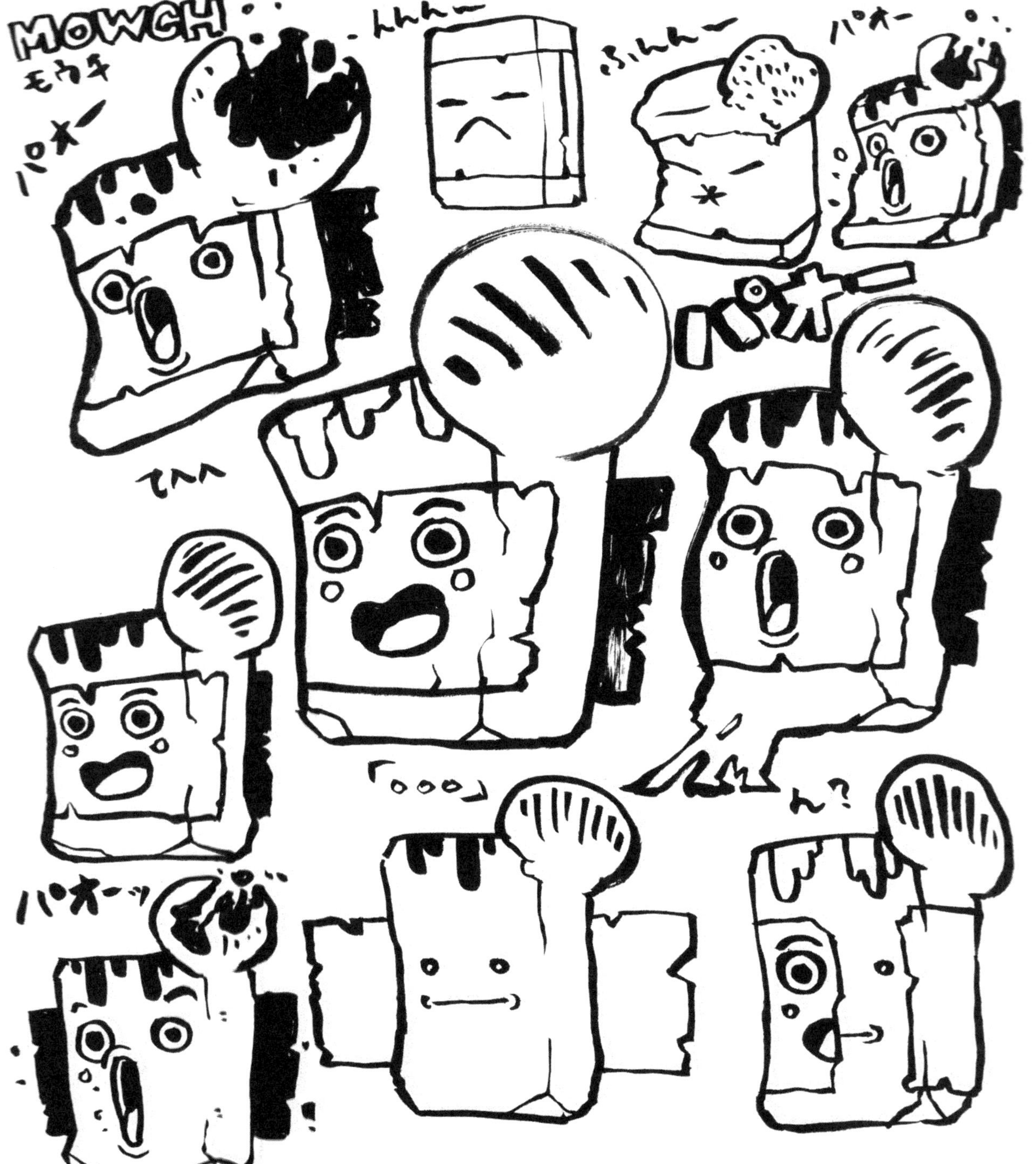
MOWCH
モウチ
パオー
んんん〜
ふんんー
パオー
パオ
てへへ
「ooo」
ん?
パオーッ

Neko Purin's sweetness will jiggle its way to your heart.

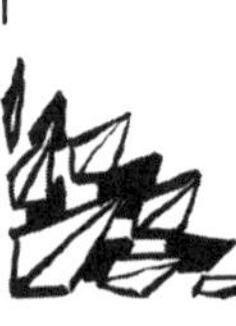

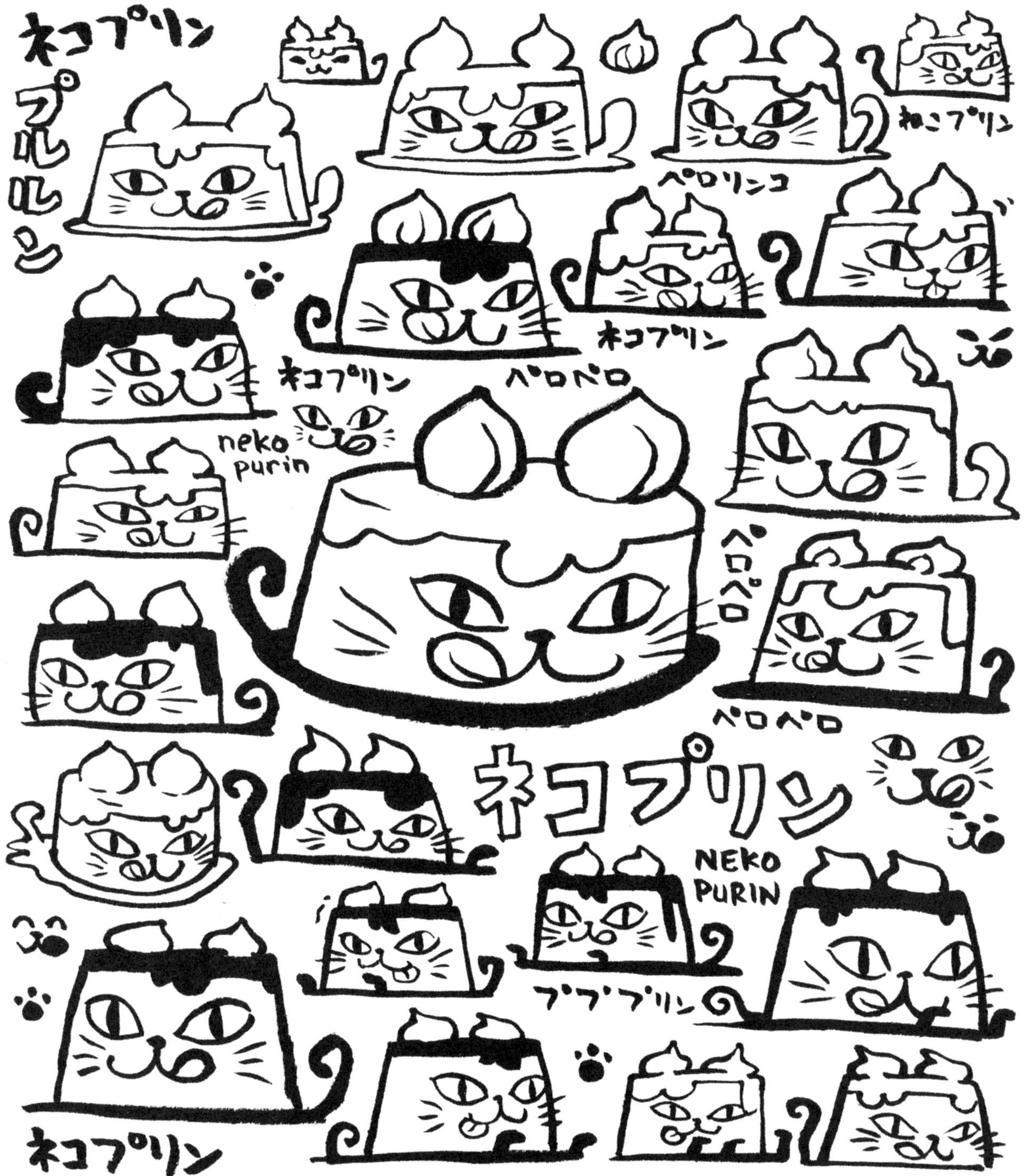
ネコプリン
プルルルン
ねこプリン
ペロリンコ
ネコプリン
ネコプリン
ペロペロ
neko
purin
ペロペロ
ペロペロ
ネコプリン
NEKO
PURIN
プププリン
ネコプリン

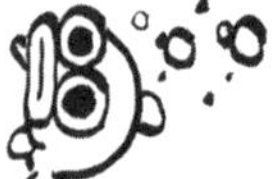

Had cake ate two.

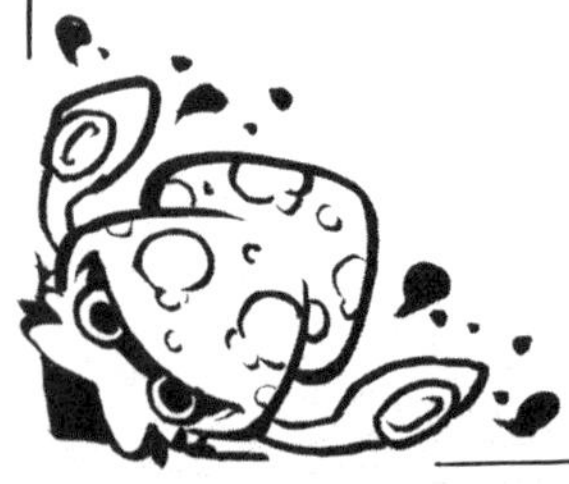

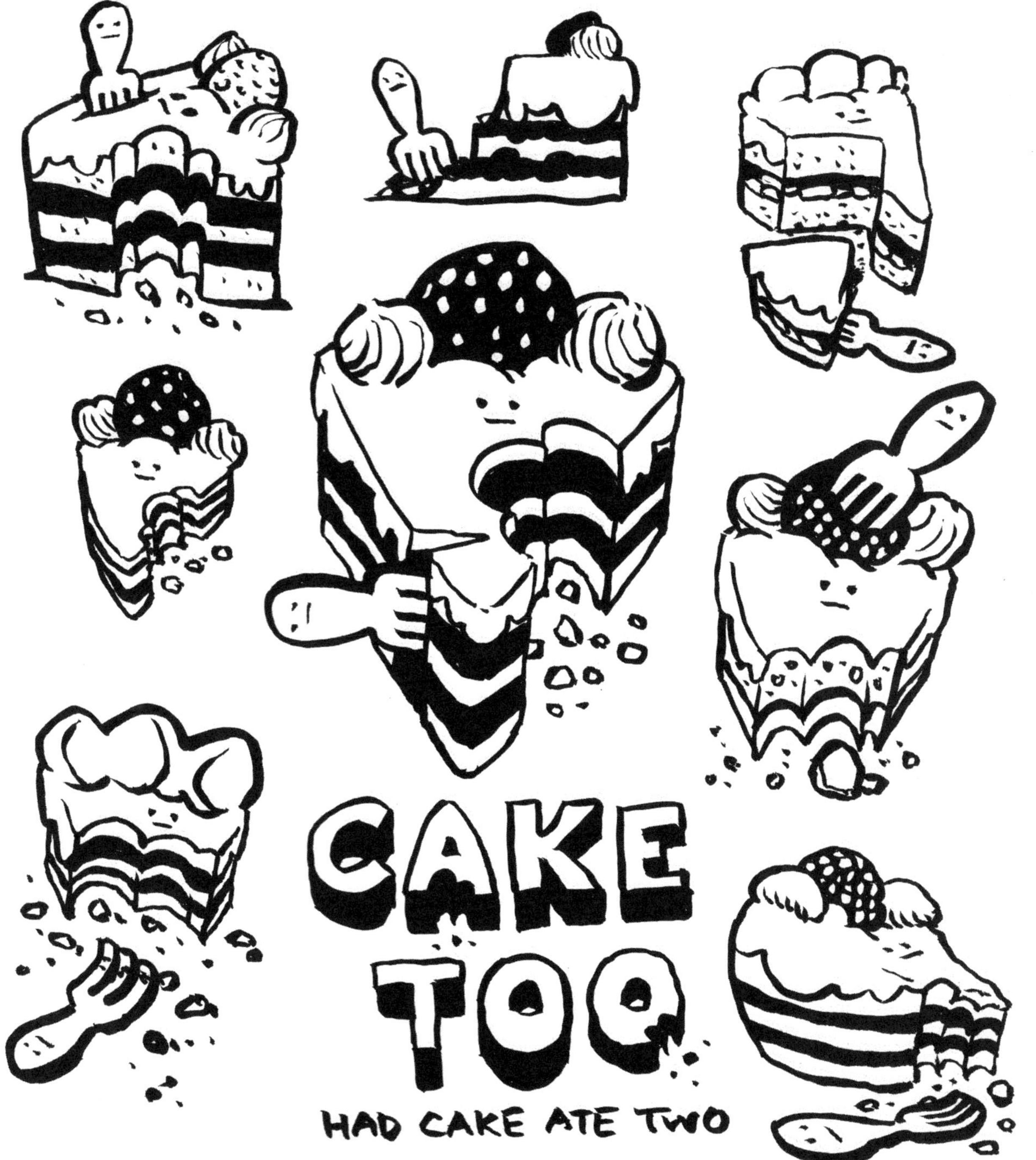
CAKE
TOO
HAD CAKE ATE TWO

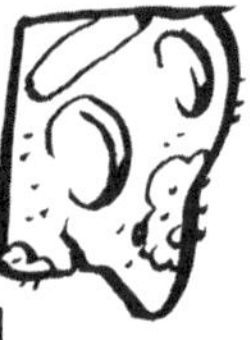

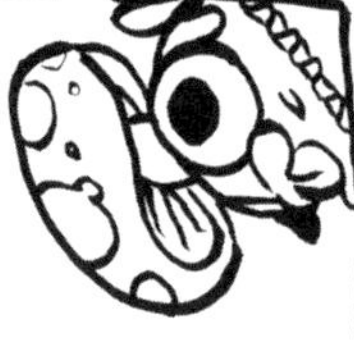

Relaxing hard at work.

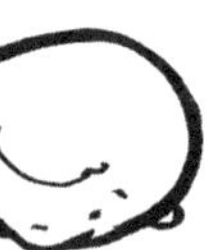

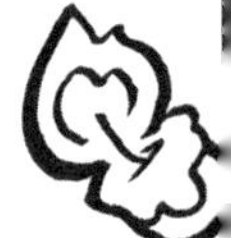

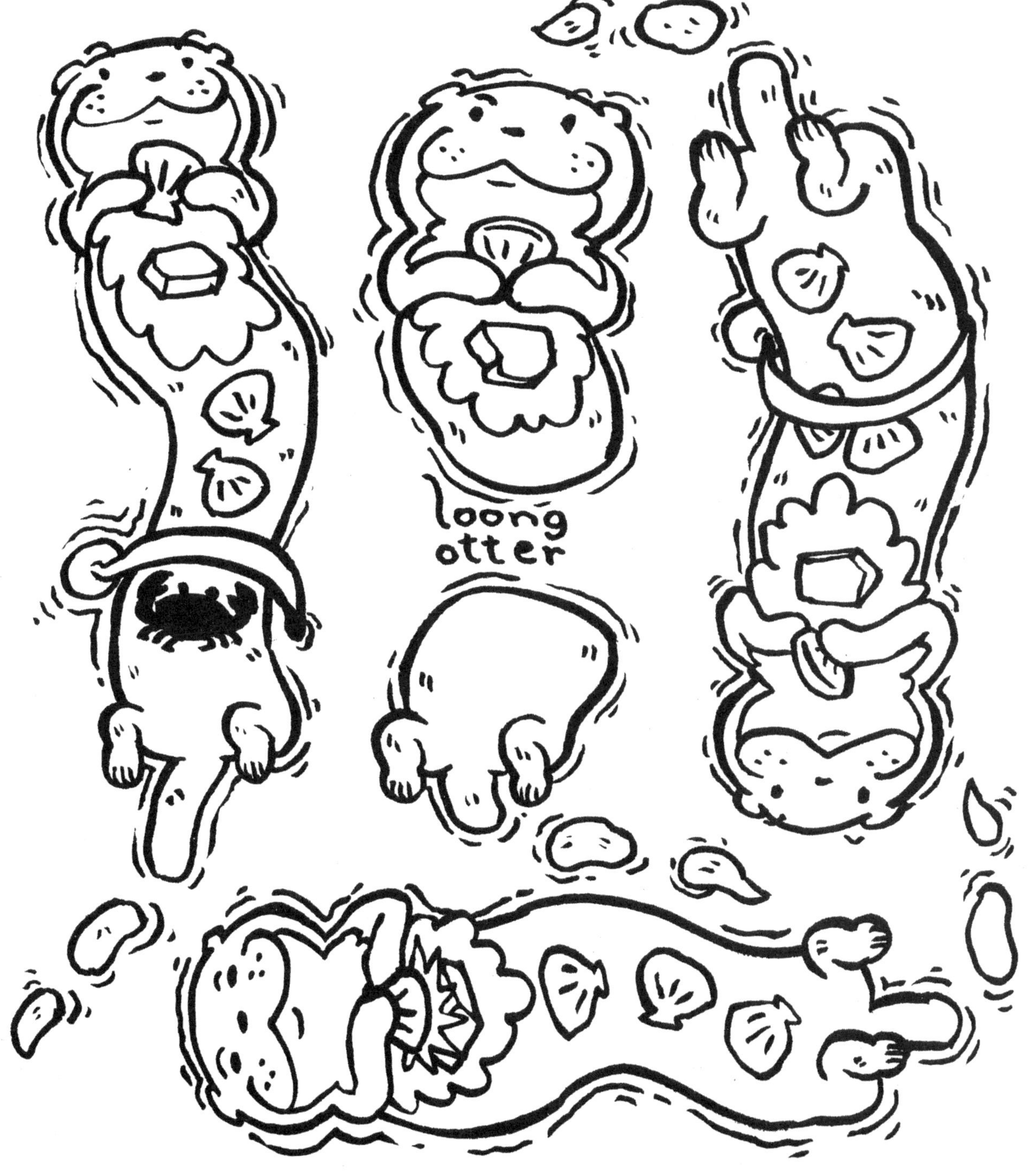
loong
otter

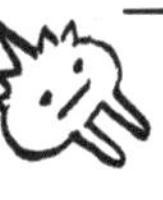

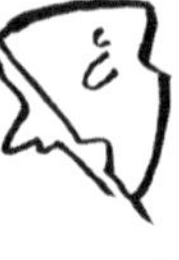

Advice ignored.

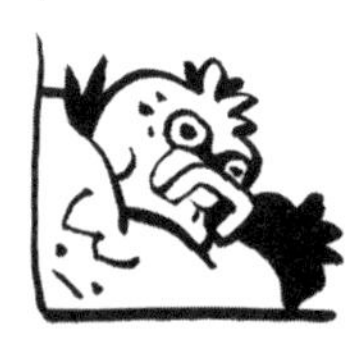

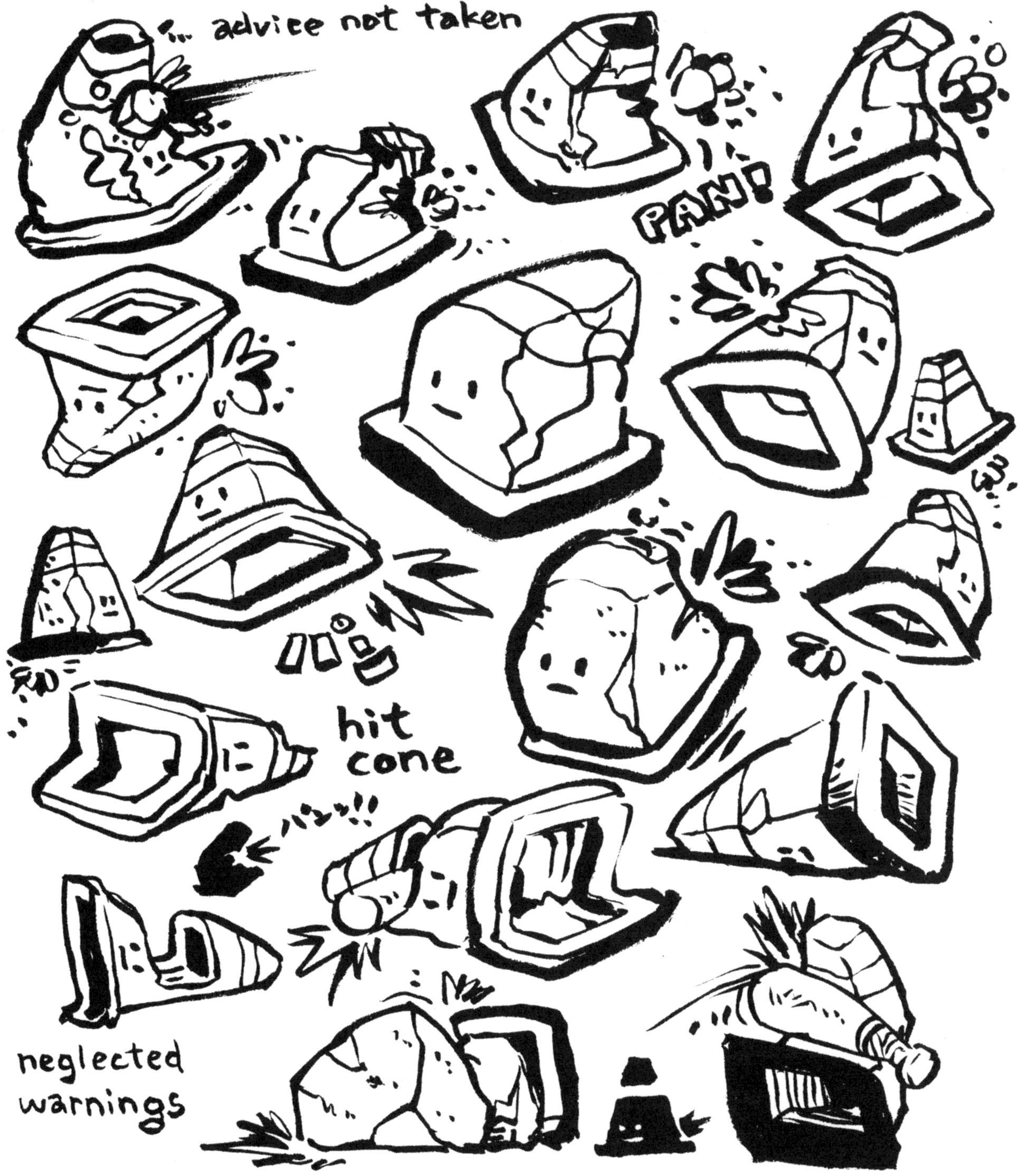
advice not taken
PAN!
hit cone
パンッ!!
neglected warnings

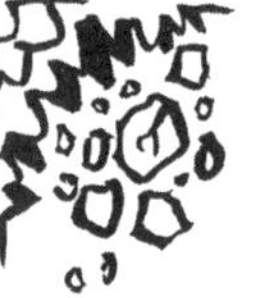
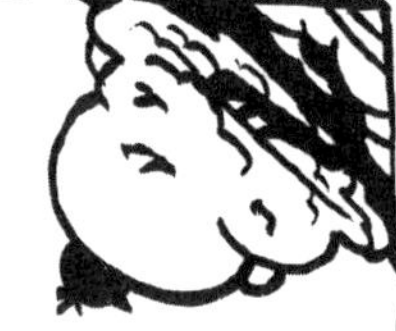

Baby believes its accomplishments were achieved solely by its own efforts.

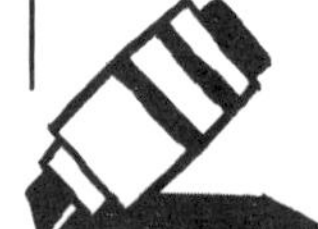
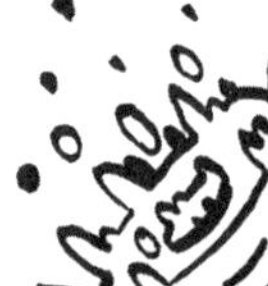

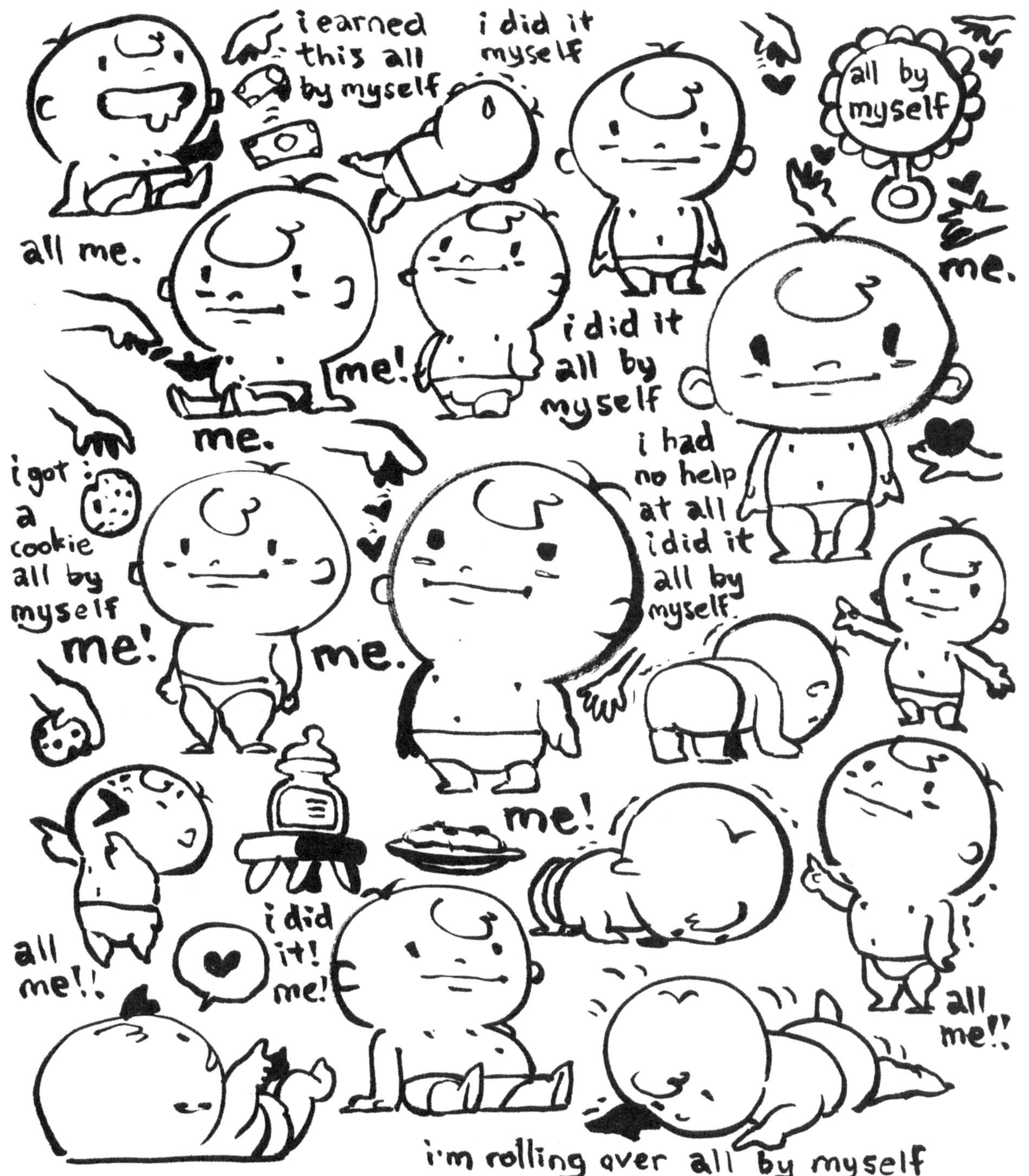
i earned this all by myself
i did it myself
all by myself
all me.
me.
me!
i did it all by myself
me.
i had no help at all i did it all by myself
i got a cookie all by myself
me!
me.
me!
i did it! me!
all me!!
all me!!
i'm rolling over all by myself

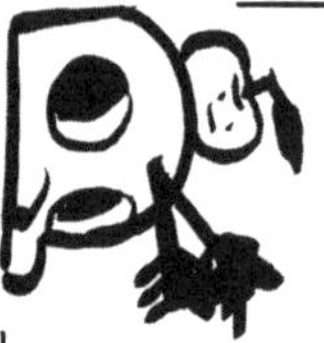

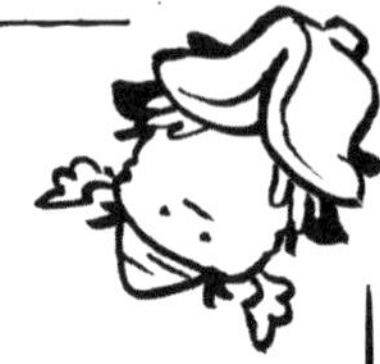

Fast forgiver.

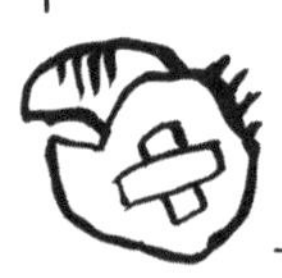

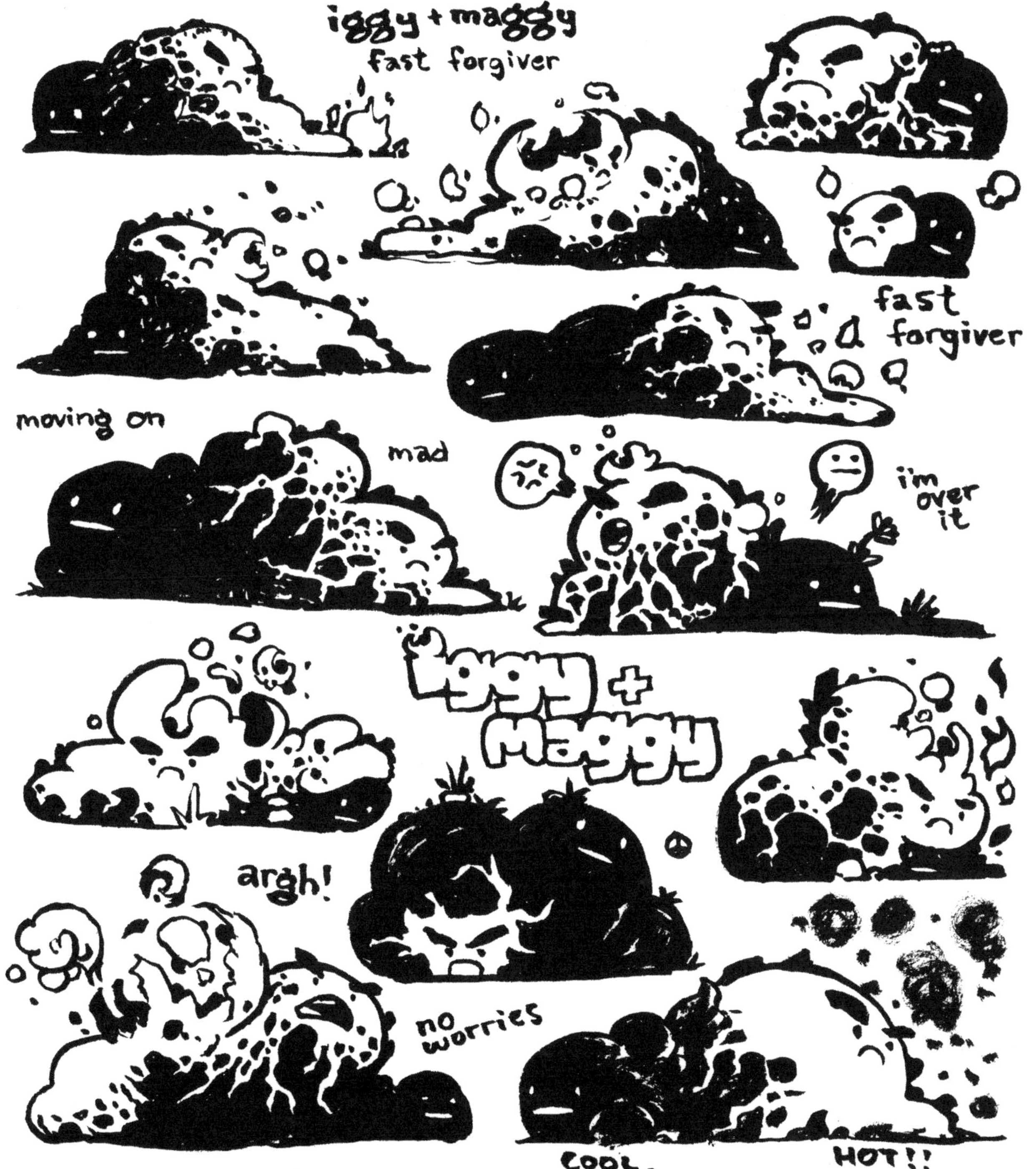

iggy + maggy
fast forgiver
fast forgiver
moving on
mad
i'm over it
iggy + maggy
argh!
no worries
COOL.
HOT!!

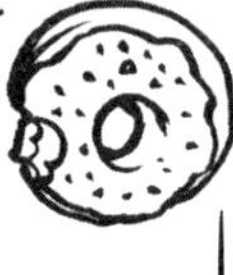

Street cred.

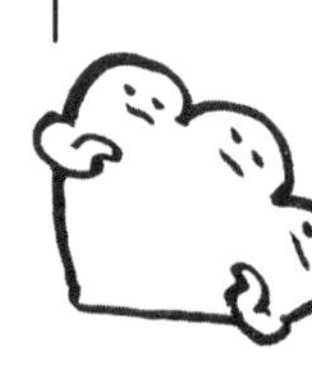

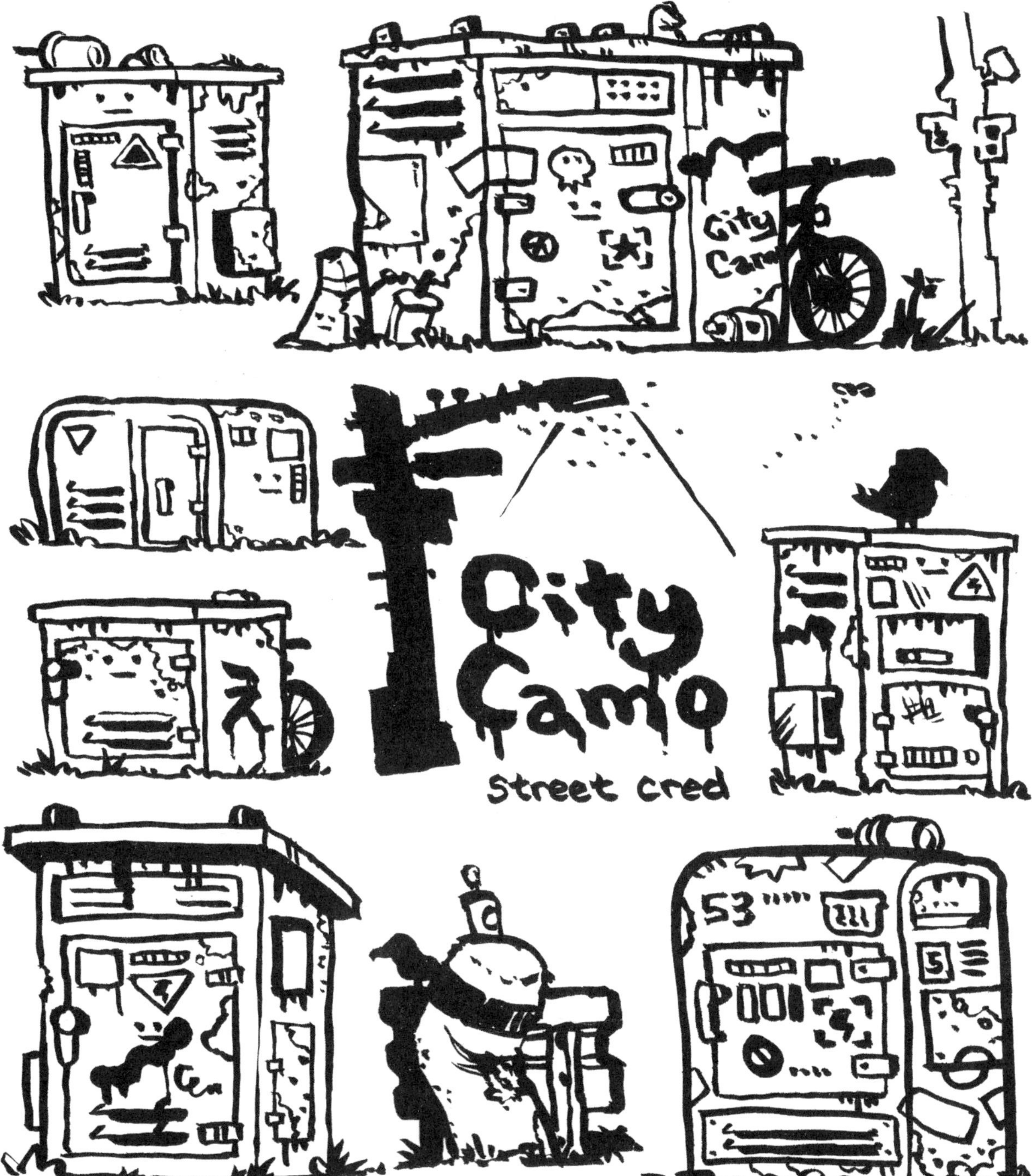
City Camo
Street cred
53

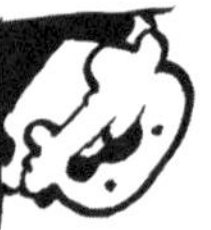

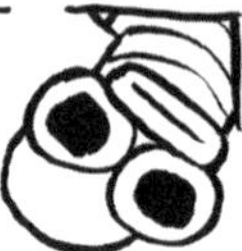

Death Junya

aka

Reaps the 2nd.

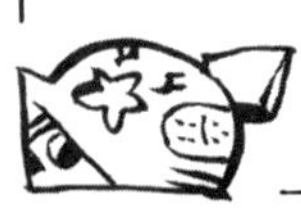

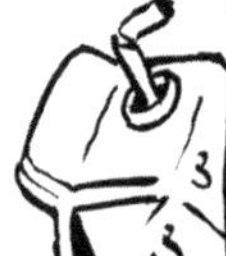

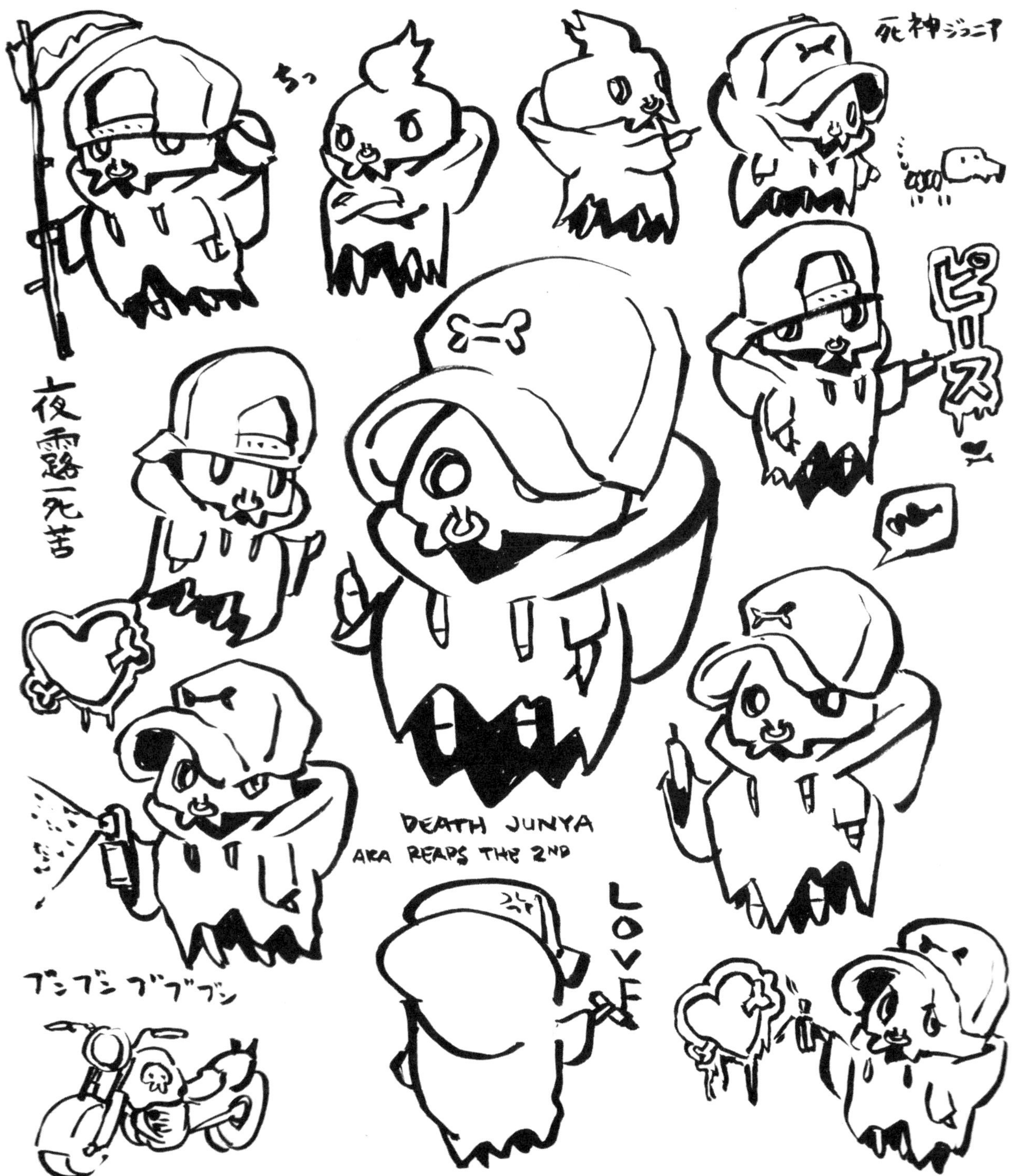

死神ジュニア
ちっ
ピース
夜露路一死苦
DEATH JUNYA
AKA REAPS THE 2ND
LOVE
ブンブン ブブブン

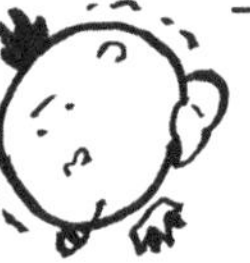

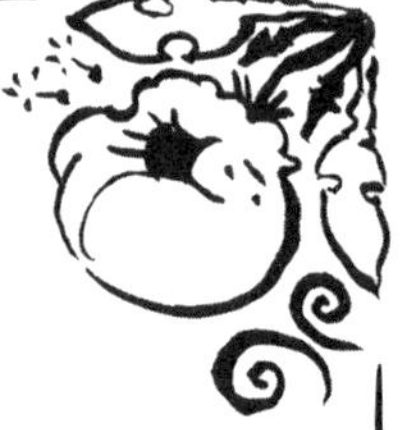

Solitary...

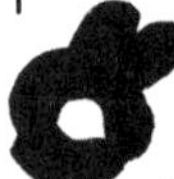

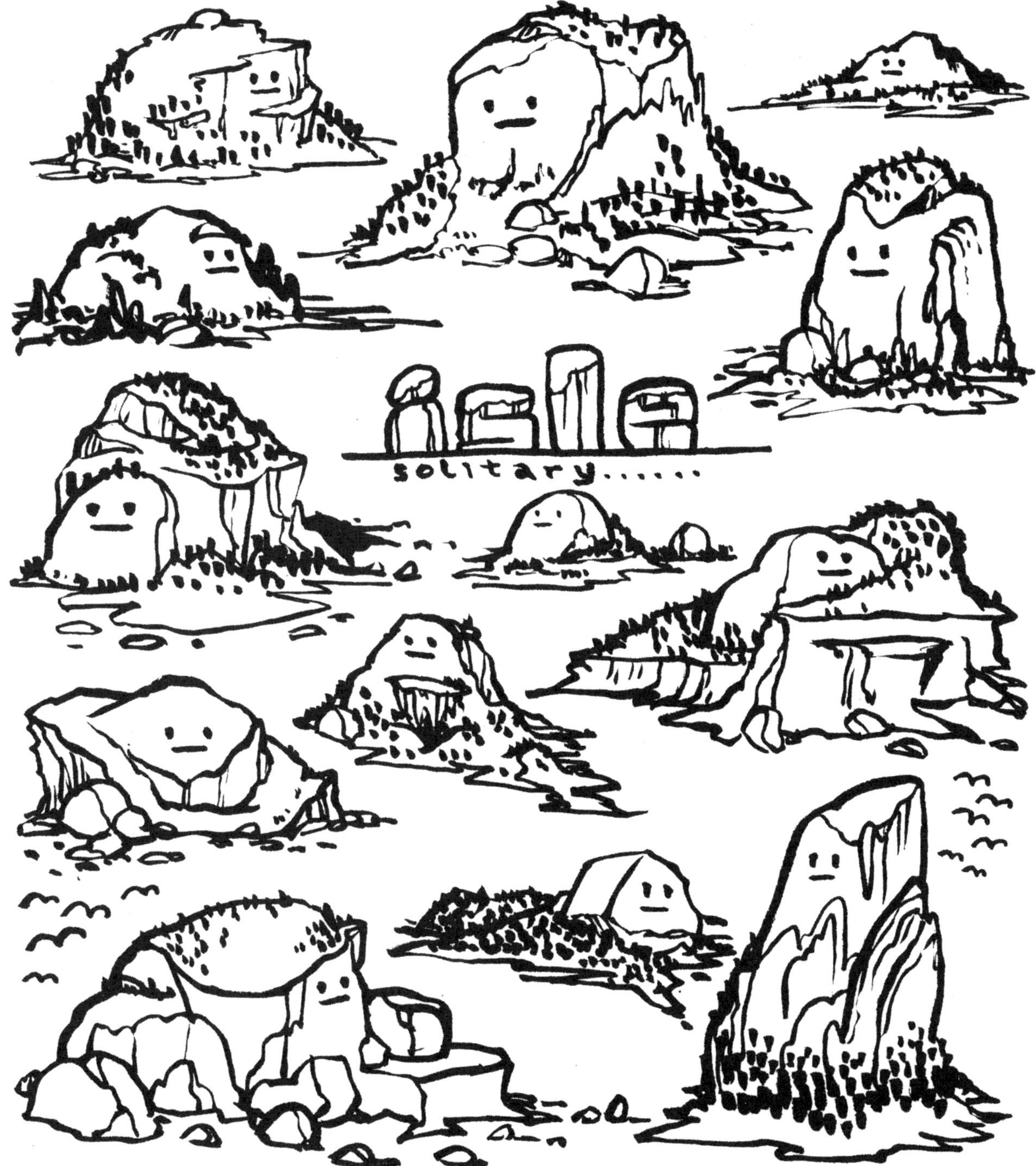
solitary......

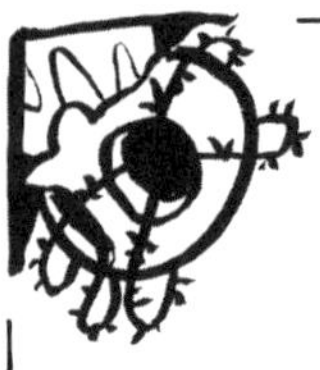

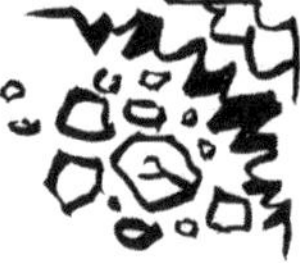

Unless escaping
captivity.

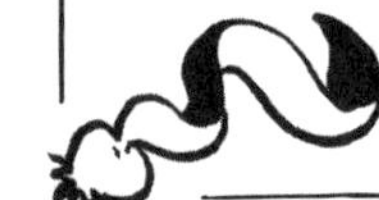

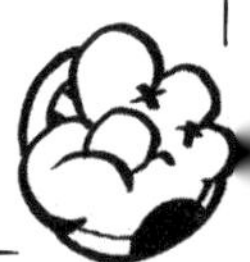

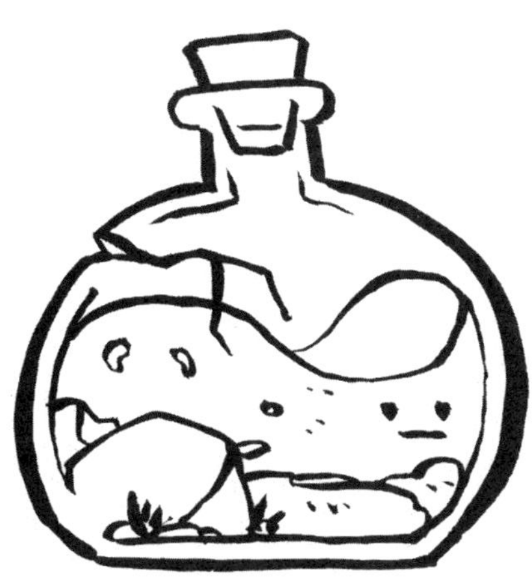
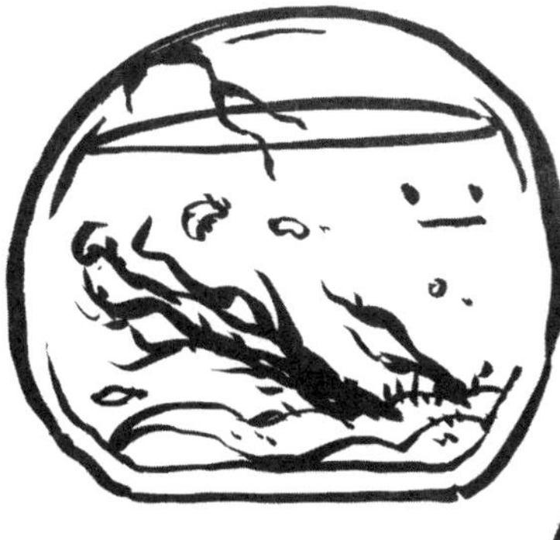
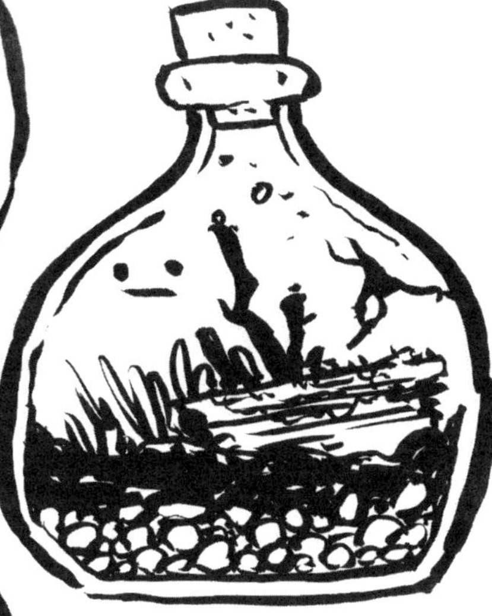
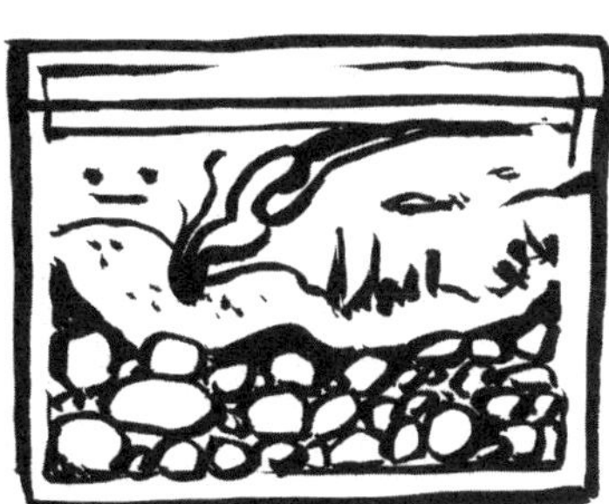
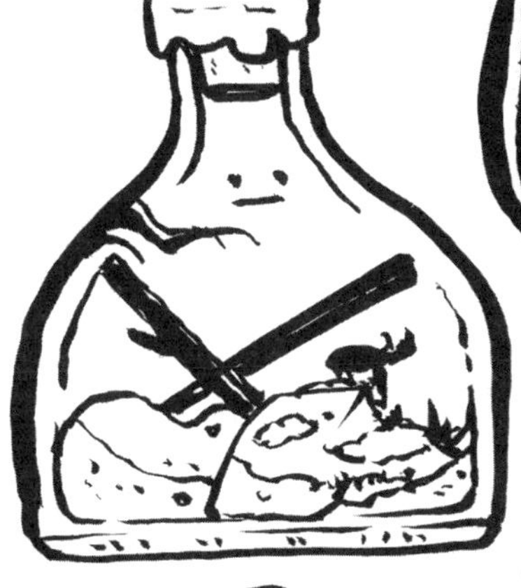
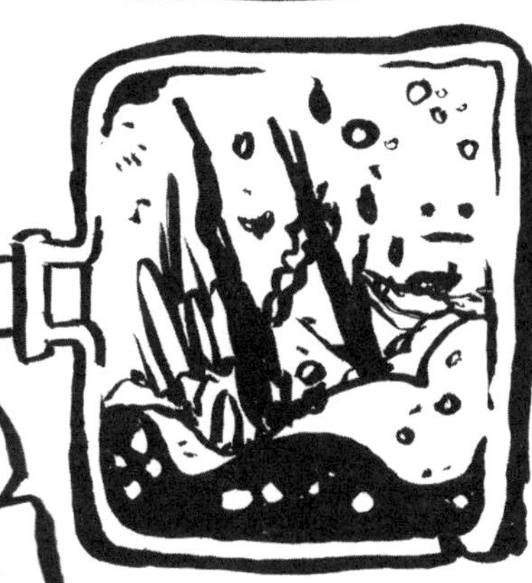
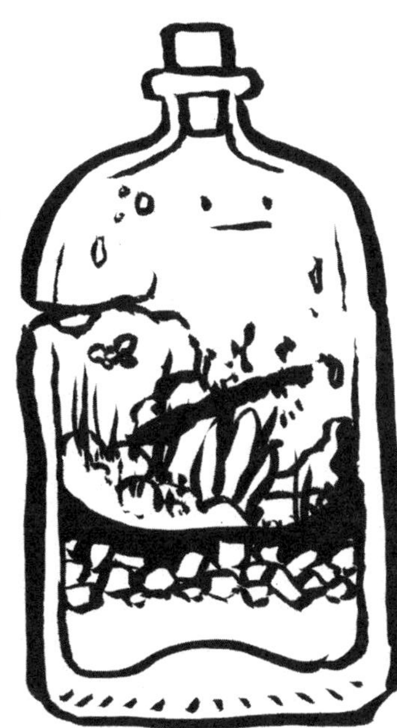

UNLESS
ESCAPING
CAPTIVITY

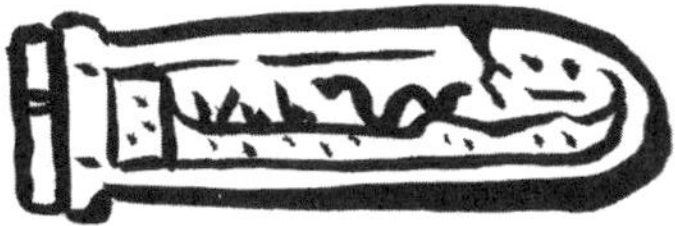
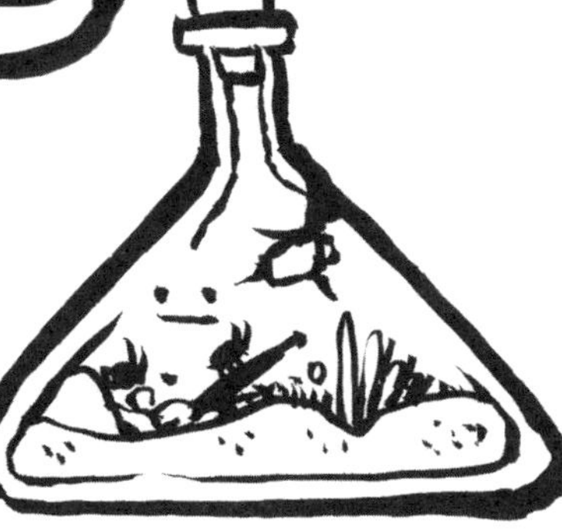

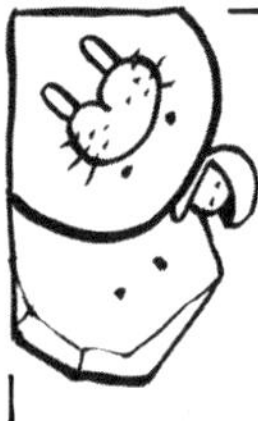

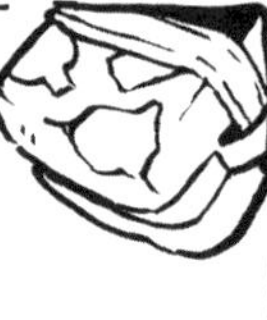

Tipping point.

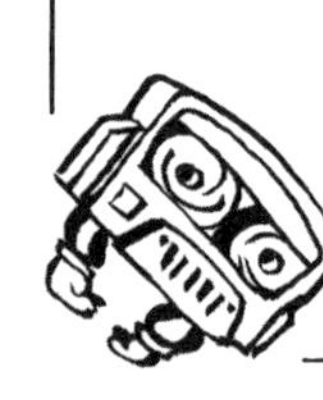

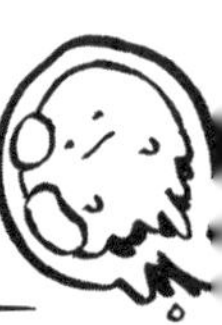

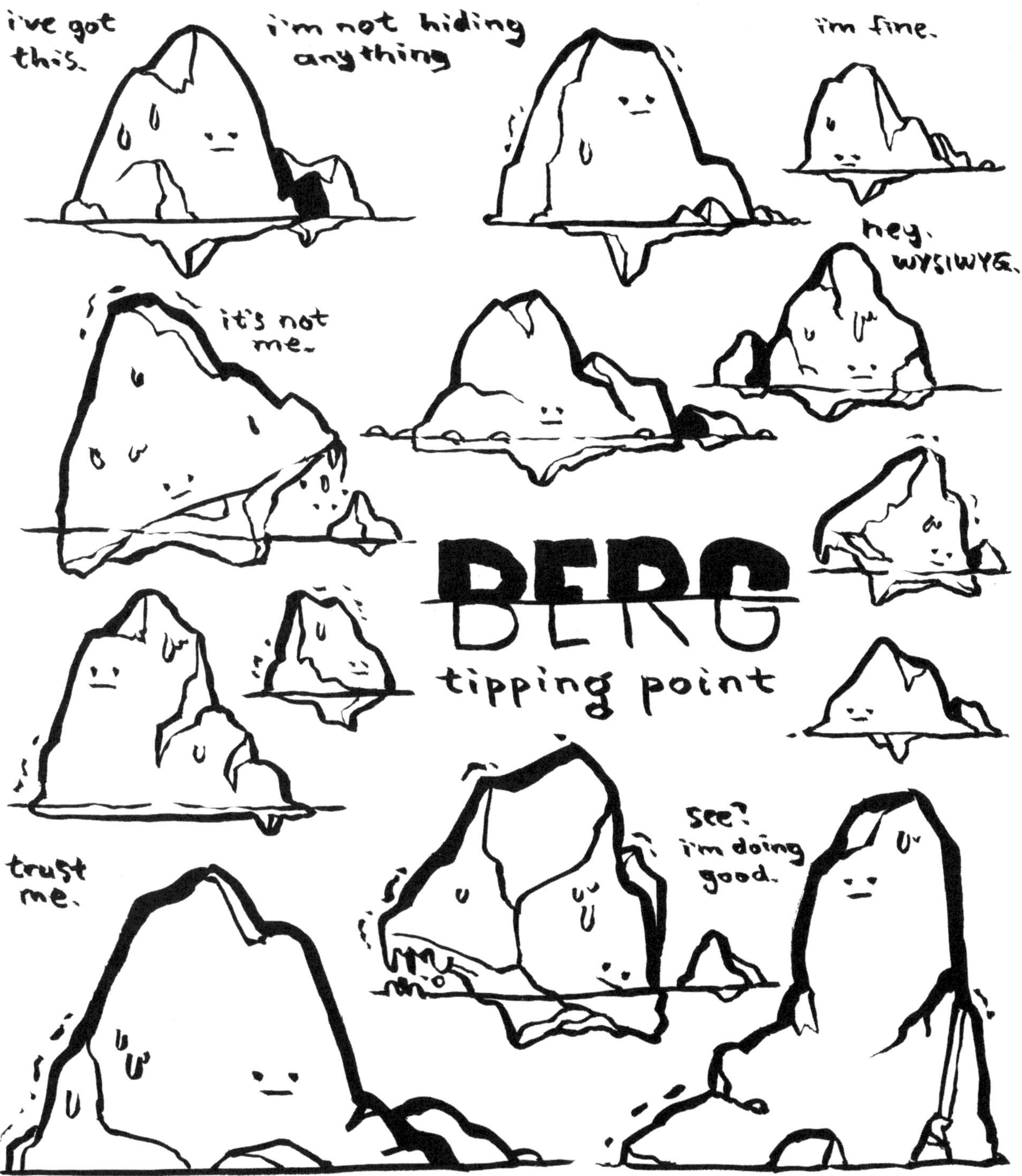

i've got this.
i'm not hiding anything
i'm fine.
hey. WYSIWYG.
it's not me.
BERG
BERG
tipping point
see? i'm doing good.
trust me.

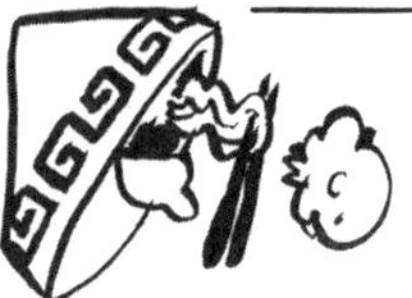

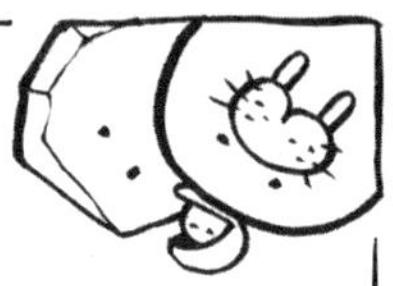

Fun falling.

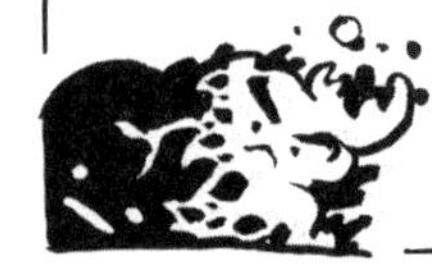

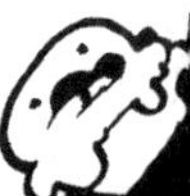

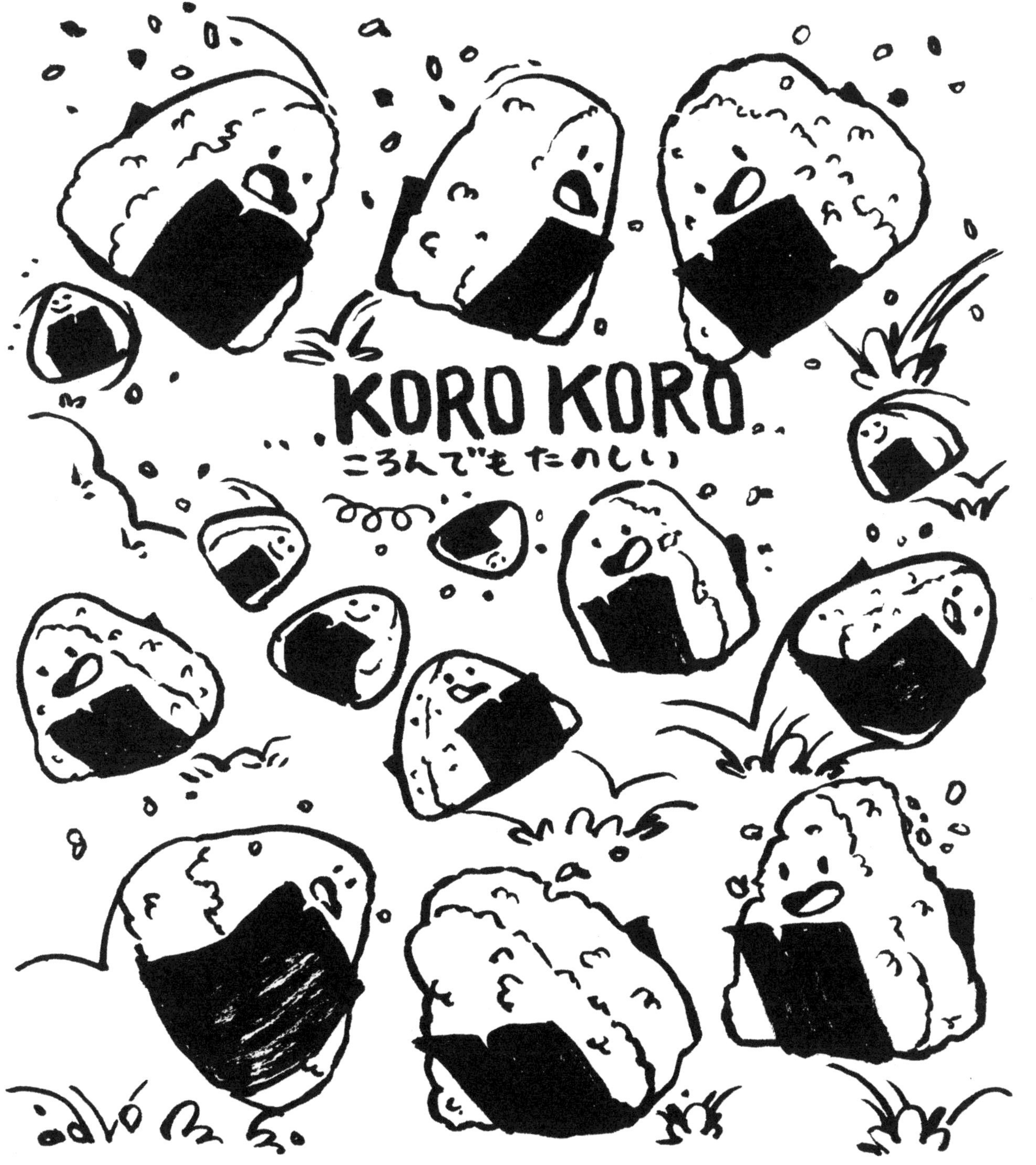
KORO KORO
ころんでもたのしい

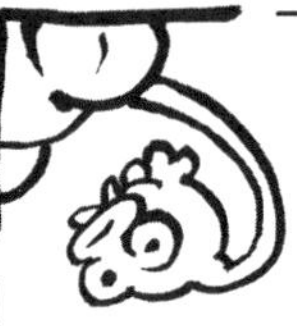

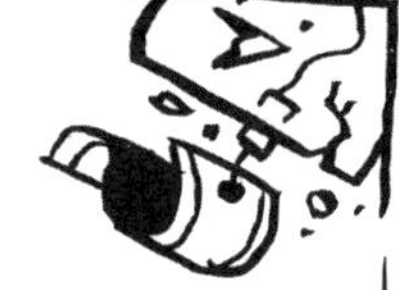

Inefficient process.

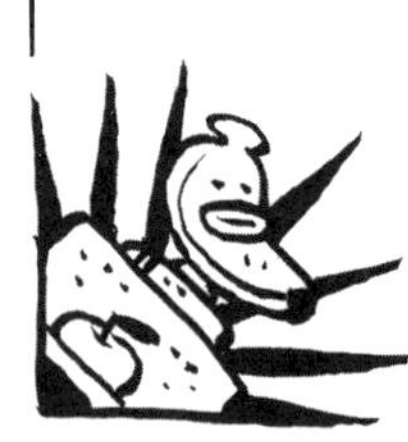

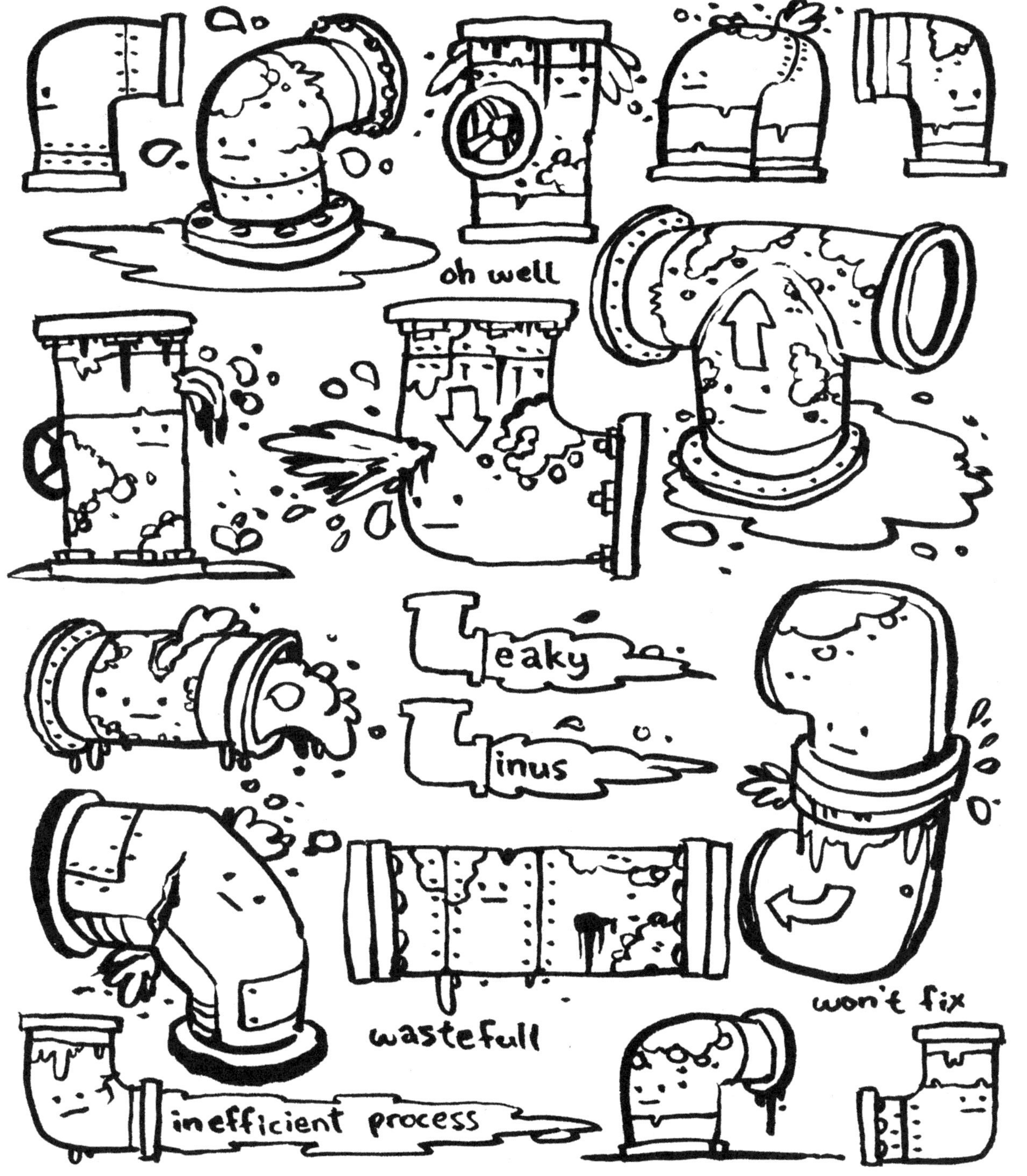
oh well
Leaky
Linus
won't fix
wastefull
inefficient process

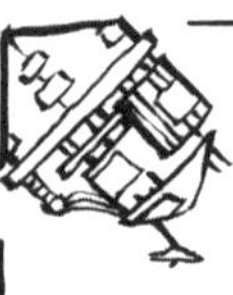

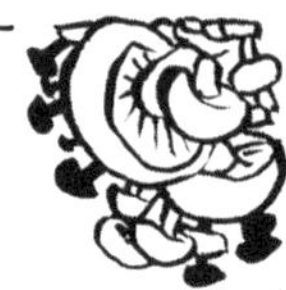

Fuzzyluscious.

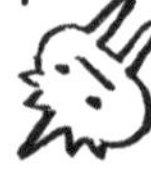

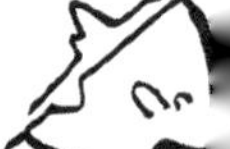

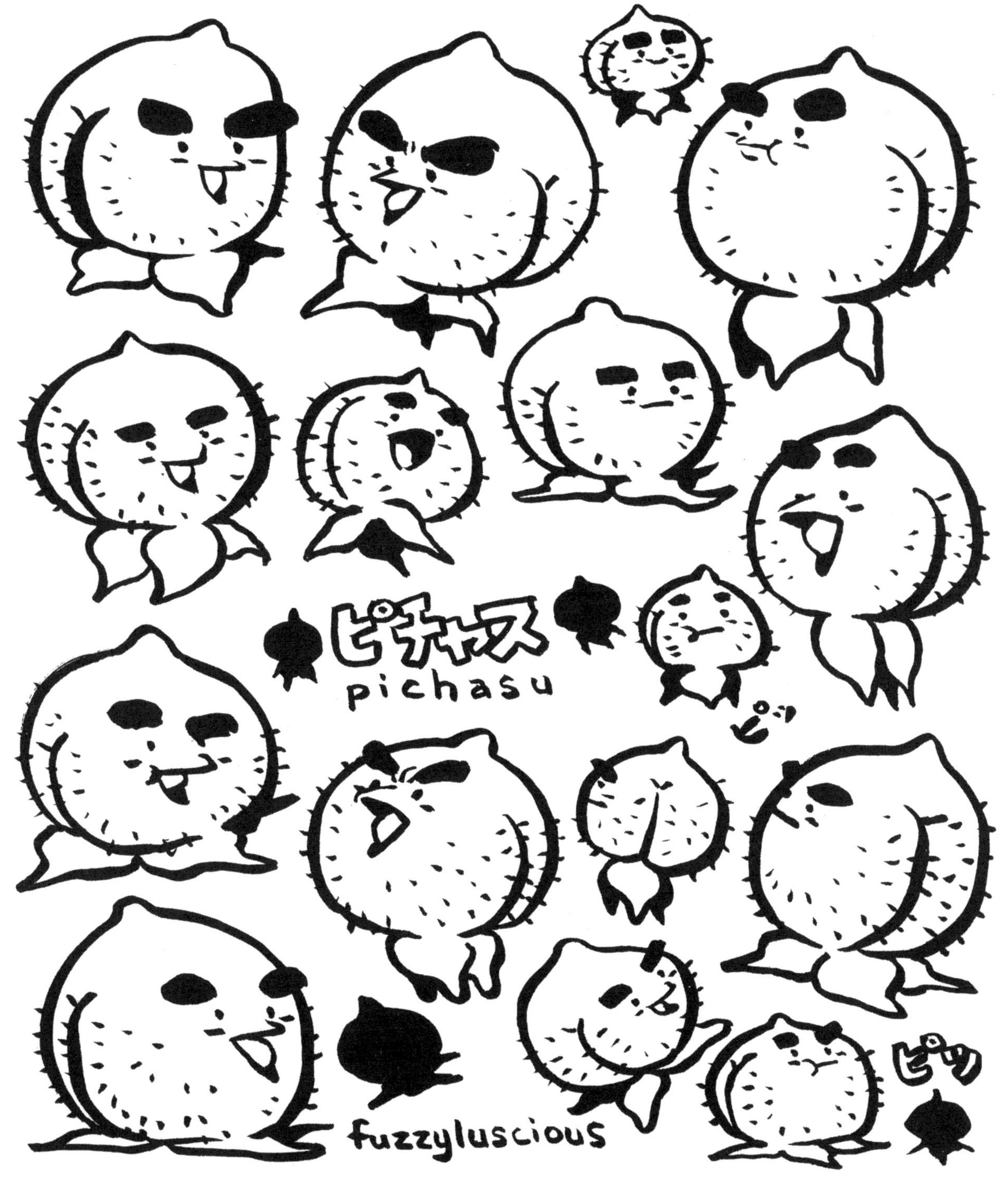
ピチャス
pichasu
ピッ
ピッ
fuzzyluscious

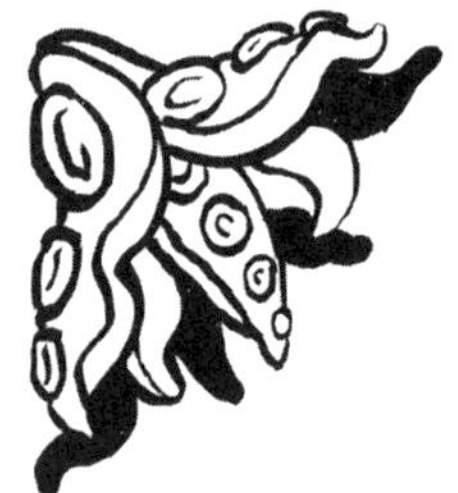

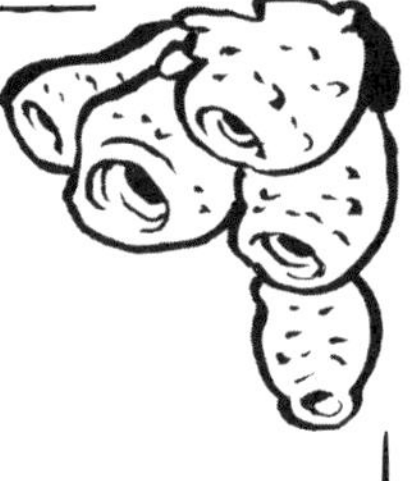

Raised on a ninja farm
and unaware of
their wounds.

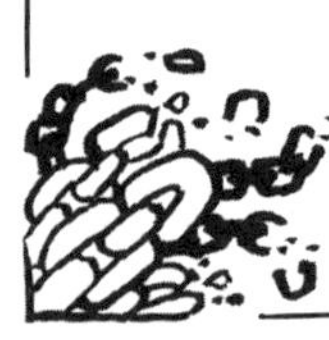

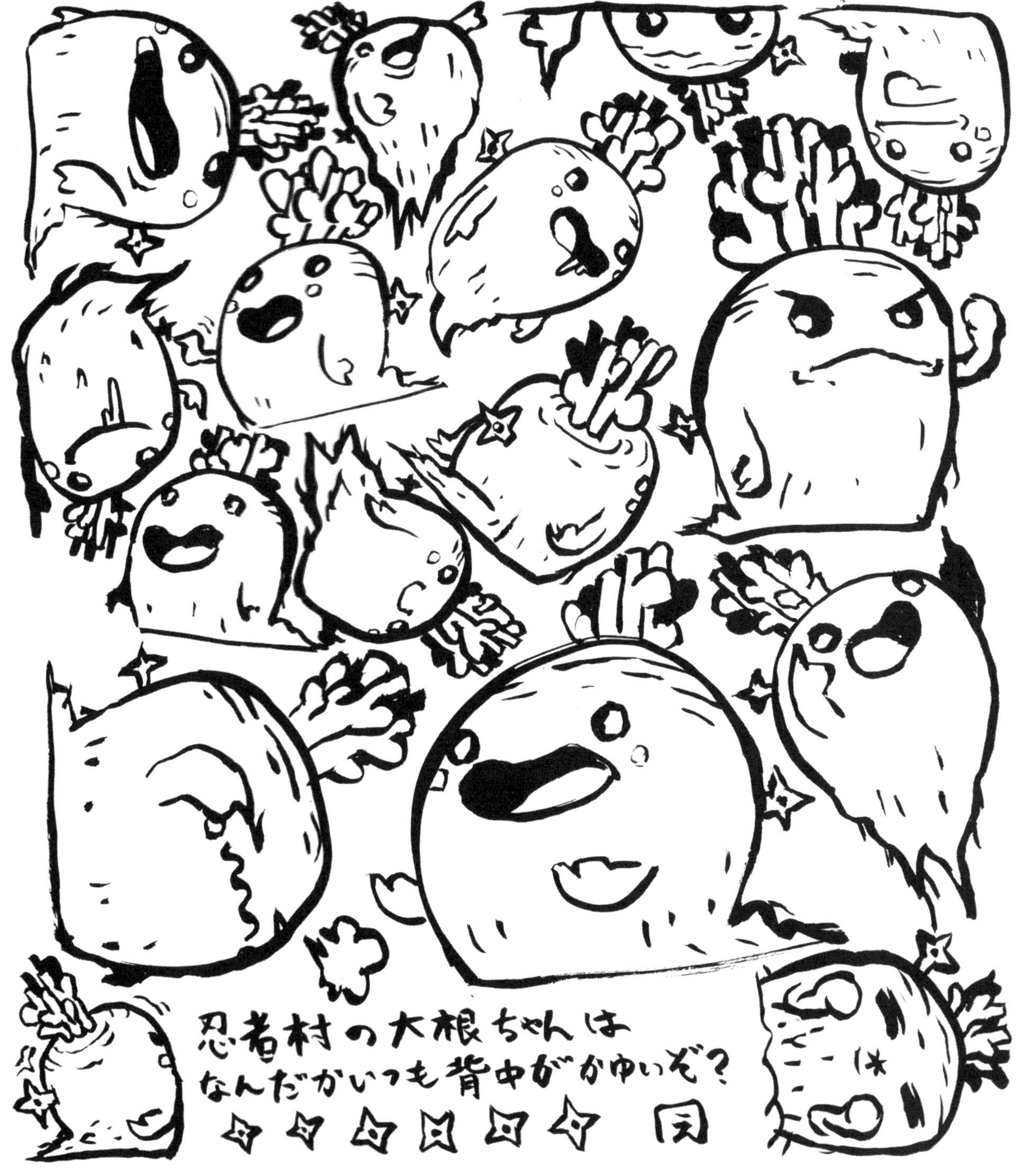

忍者村の大根ちゃんは
なんだかいつも背中がかゆいぞ？

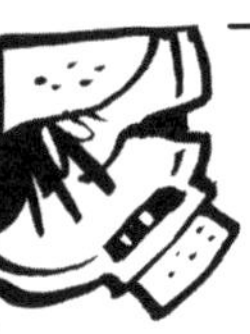

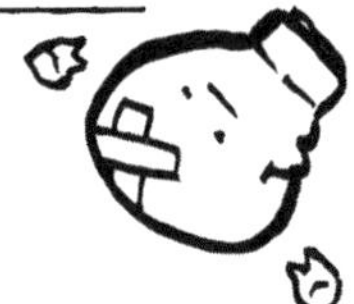

Unshared.

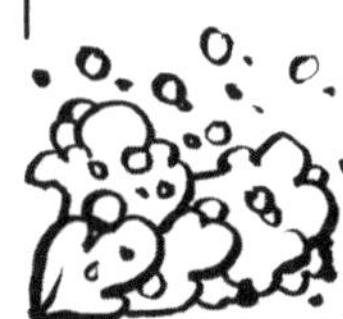

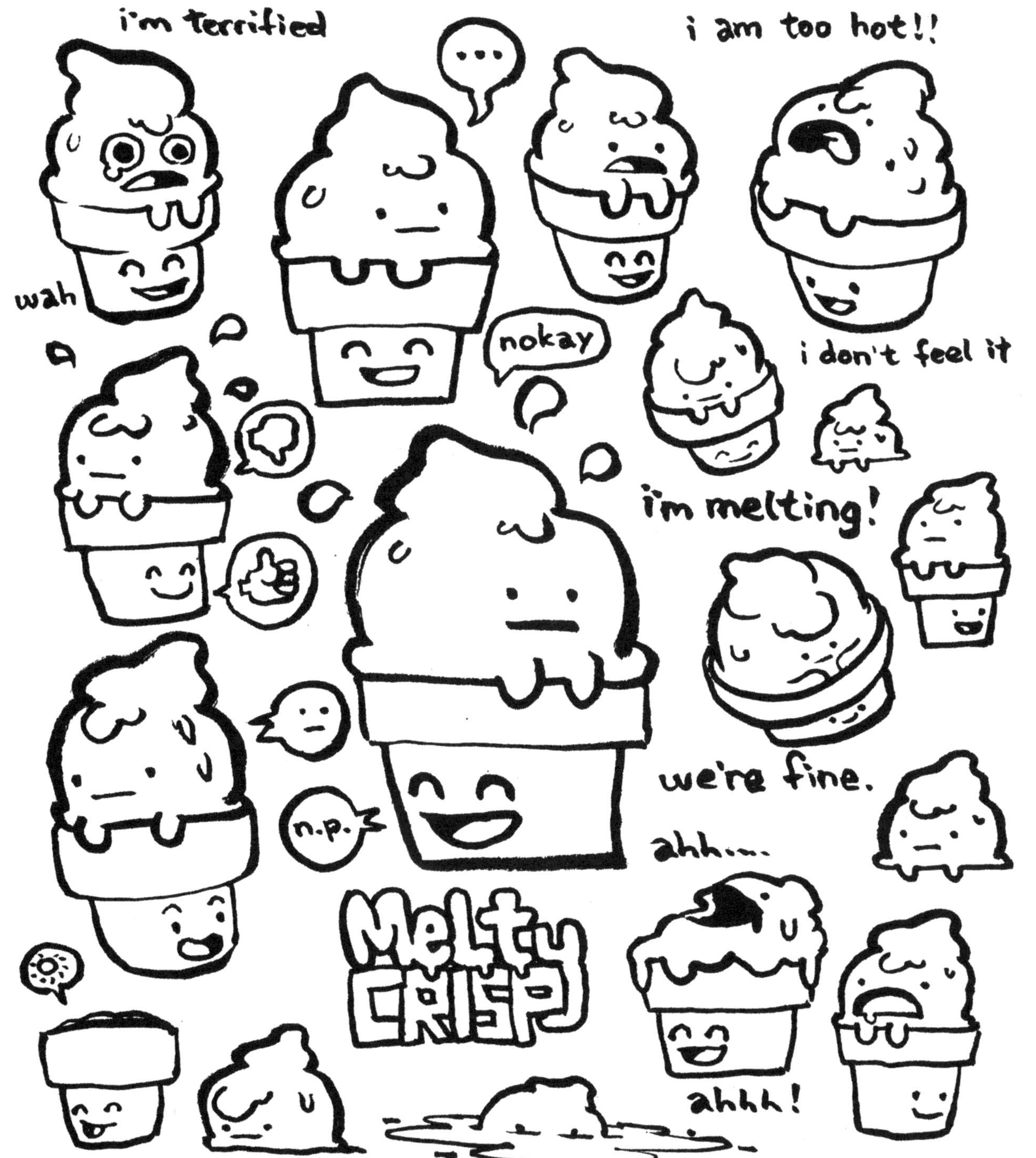

i'm terrified
...
i am too hot!!
wah
nokay
i don't feel it
i'm melting!
we're fine.
n.p.
ahh....
Melty
CRISP
ahhh!

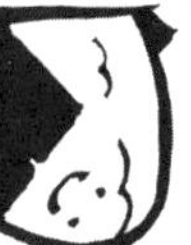

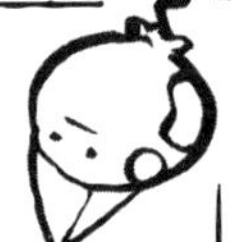

About to explode.

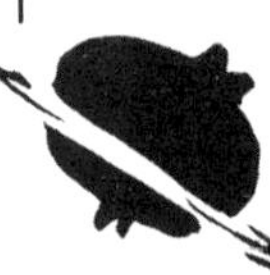

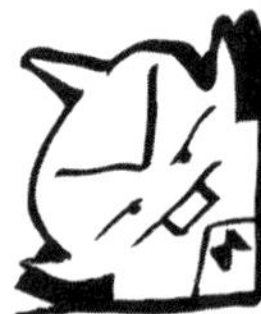

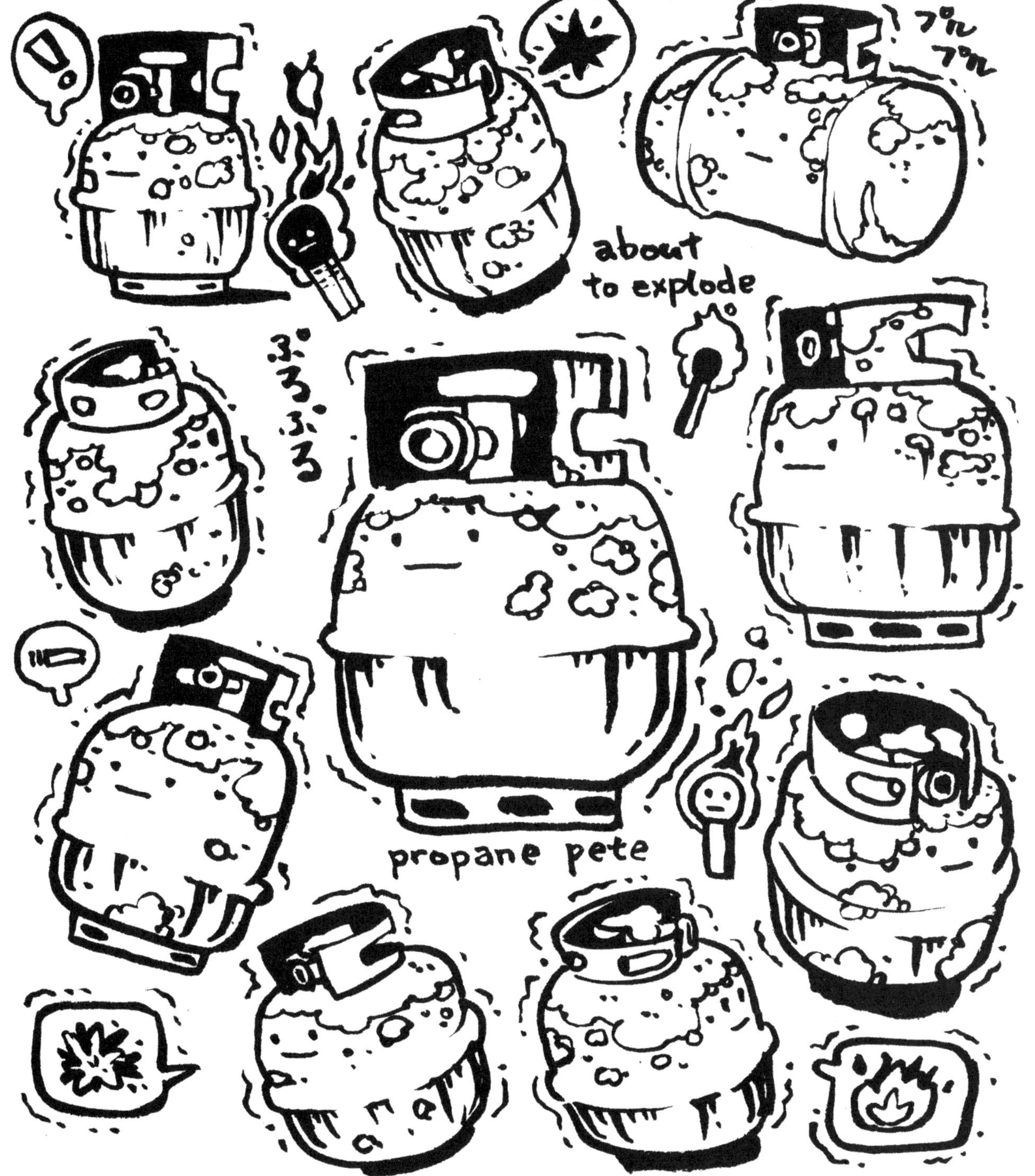

プル
プル
about
to explode
ぷるぷる
propane pete

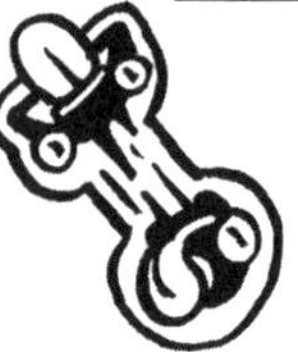
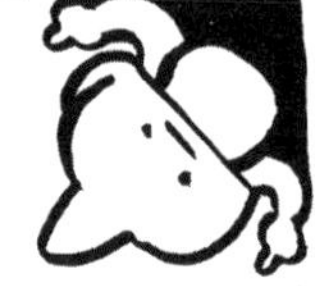

Holding the floor.

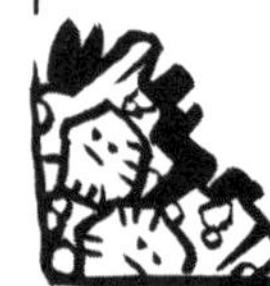
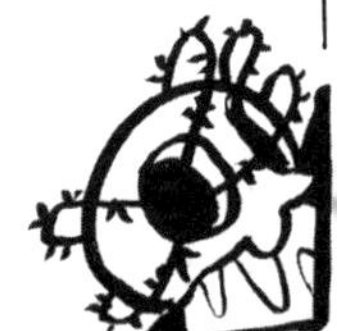

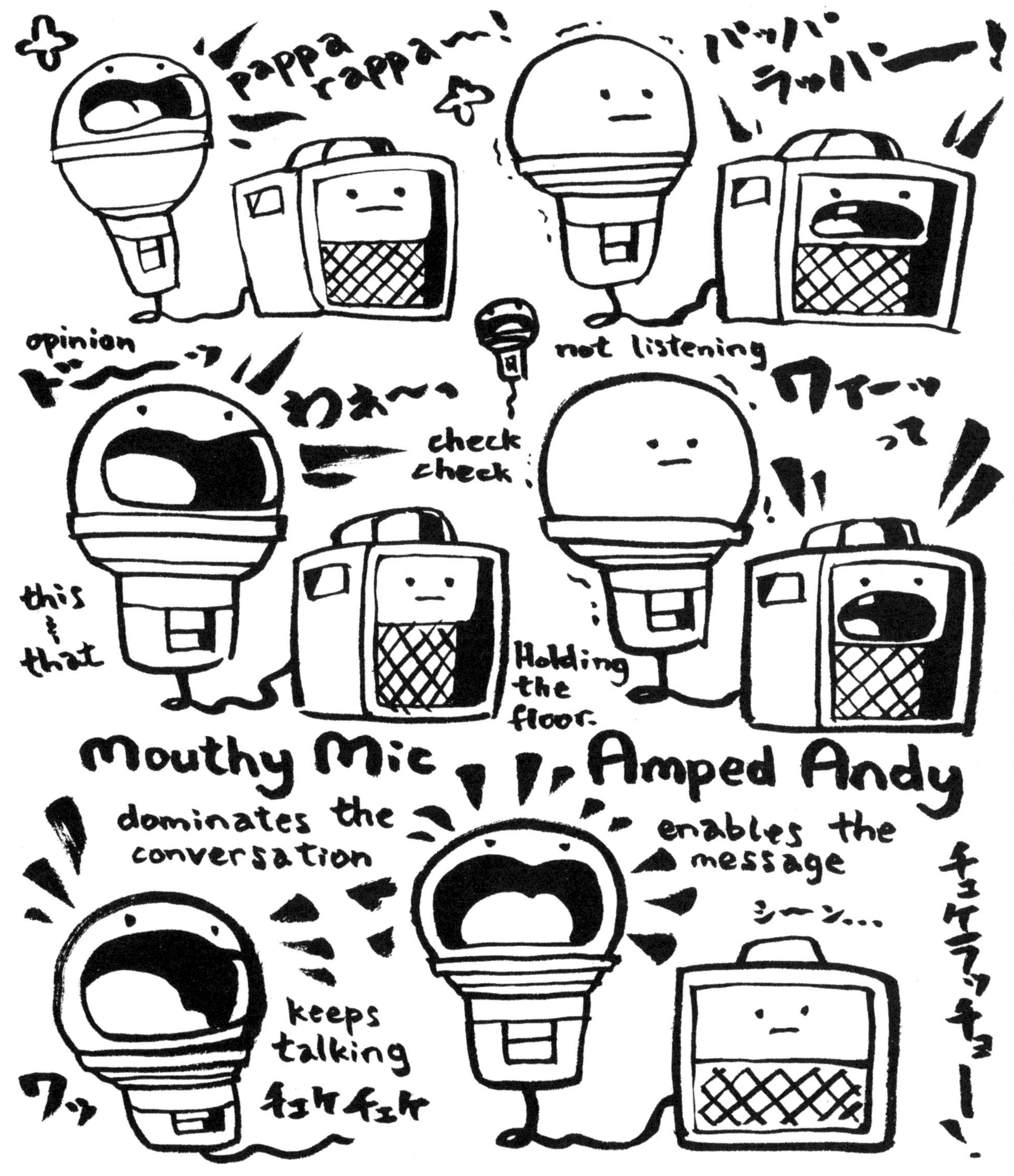

pappa rappa~!
パッパラッパー!
opinion
ド~~ッ
わぁ~っ
check check
not listening
ワァーッ
って
this & that
Holding the floor.
Mouthy Mic
Amped Andy
dominates the conversation
enables the message
keeps talking
ワッ
チェケチェケ
シーン...
チェケラッチョー!

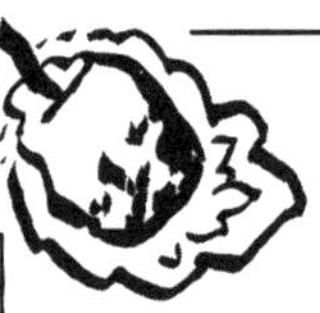

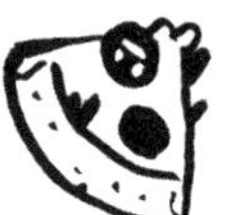

Practiced. Failed.
Practiced more.

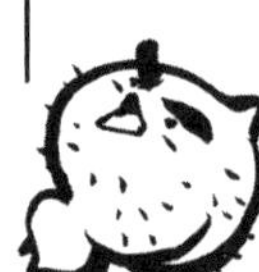

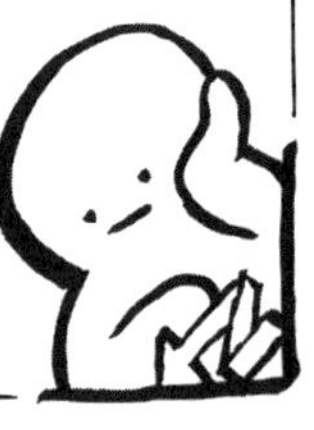

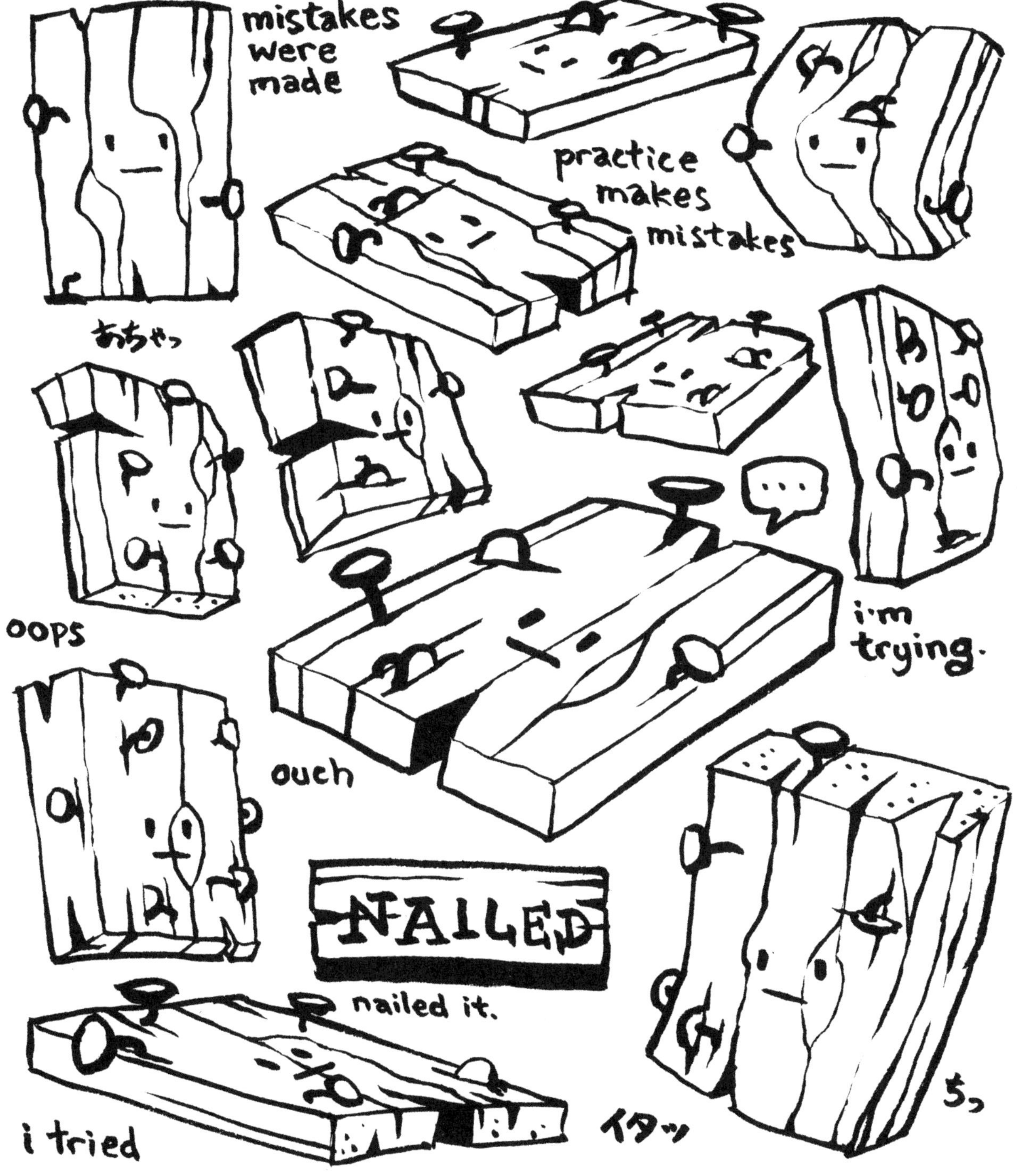
mistakes were made
practice makes mistakes
あちゃっ
oops
i'm trying.
....
ouch
NAILED
nailed it.
i tried
イタッ
ちっ

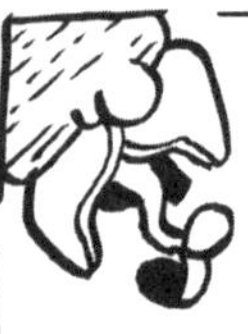

Strong opinions weakly held.

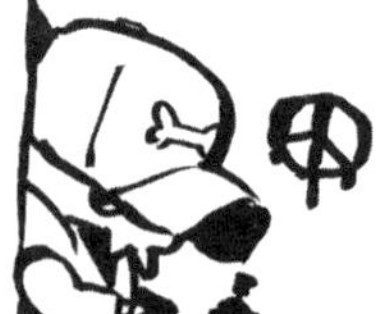
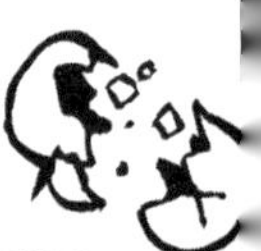

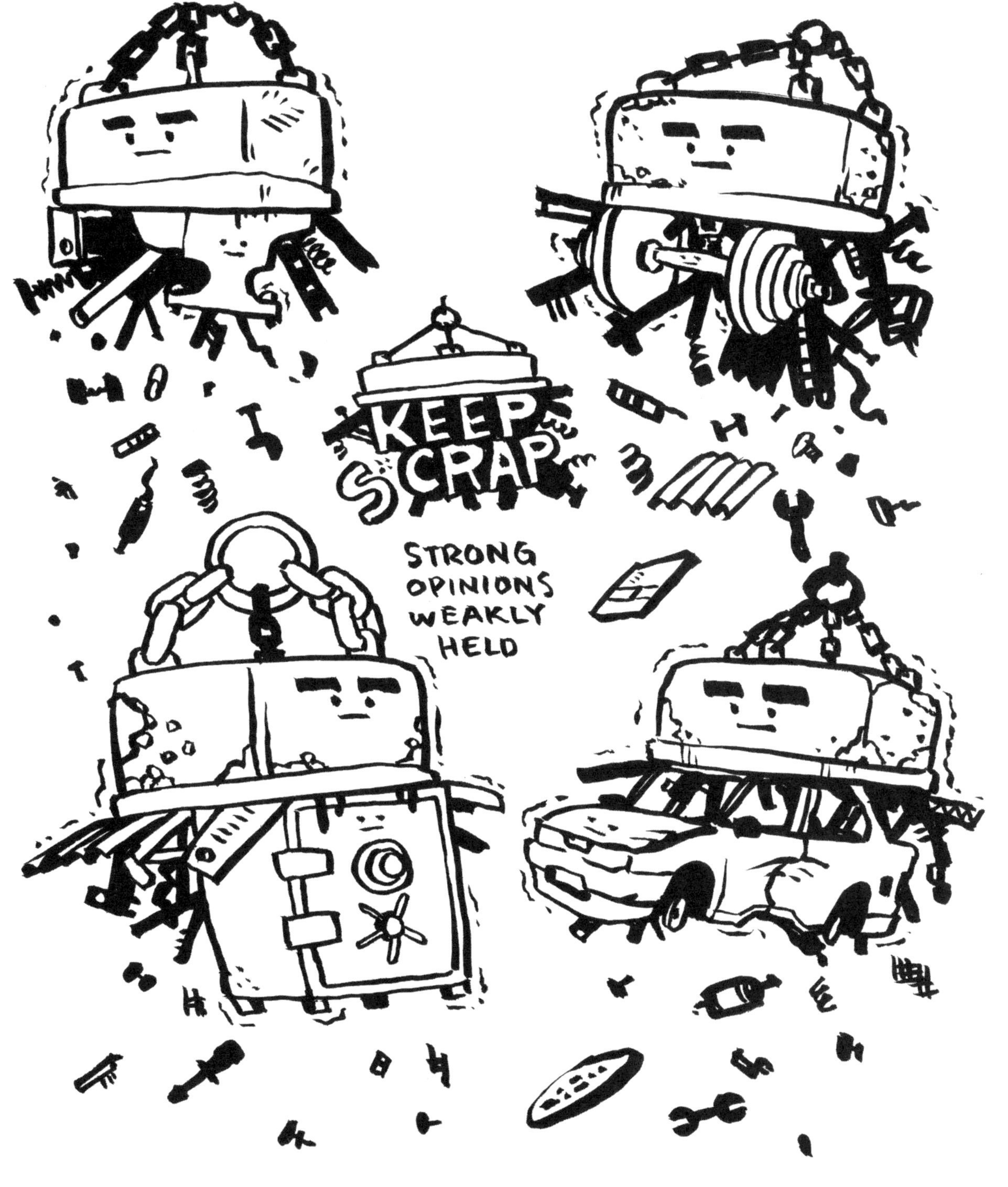
KEEP SCRAP
STRONG OPINIONS WEAKLY HELD

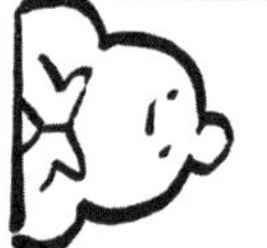

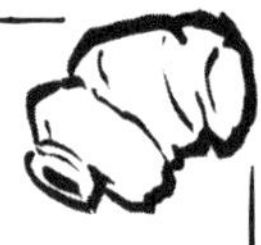

Same diff.

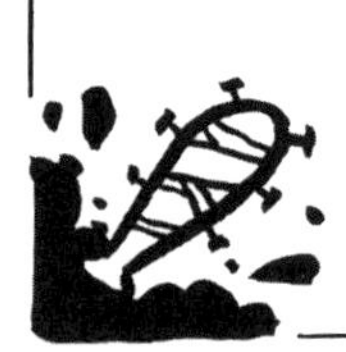

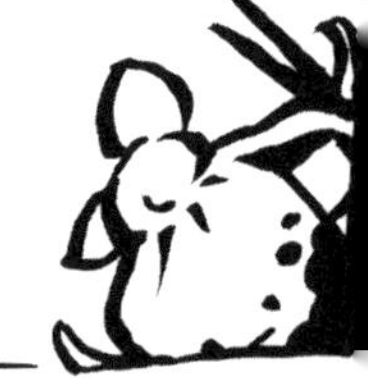

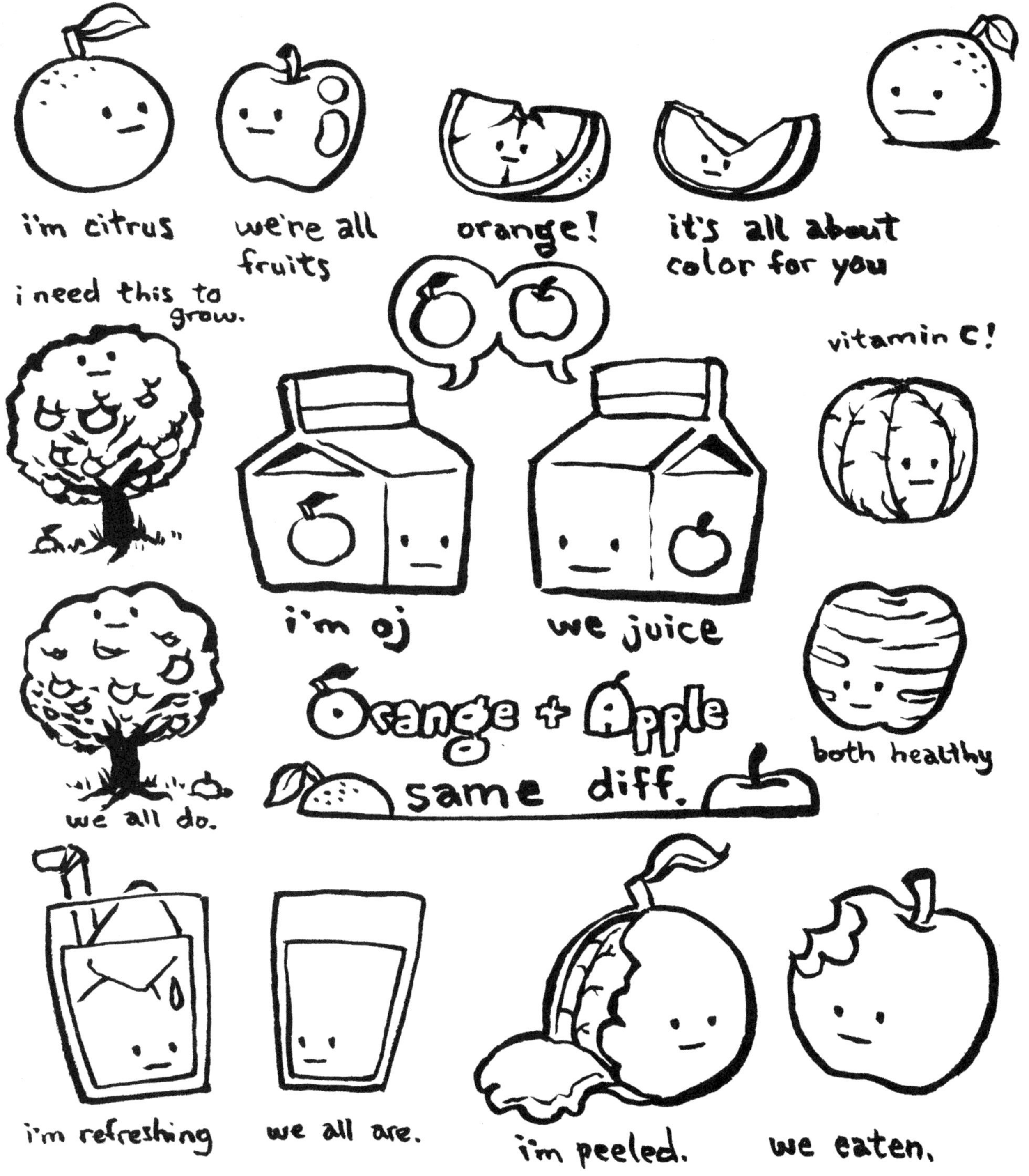

i'm citrus
we're all fruits
orange!
it's all about color for you
i need this to grow.
vitamin C!
i'm oj
we juice
we all do.
Orange + Apple
same diff.
both healthy
i'm refreshing
we all are.
i'm peeled.
we eaten.

Resource heavy.

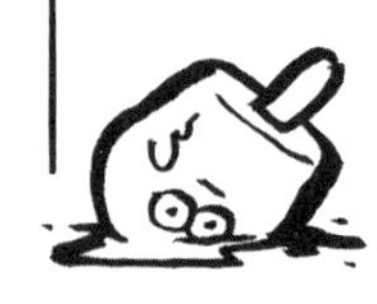
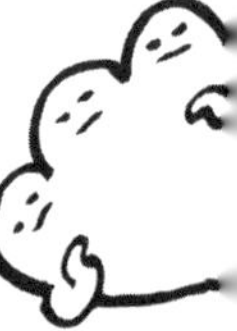

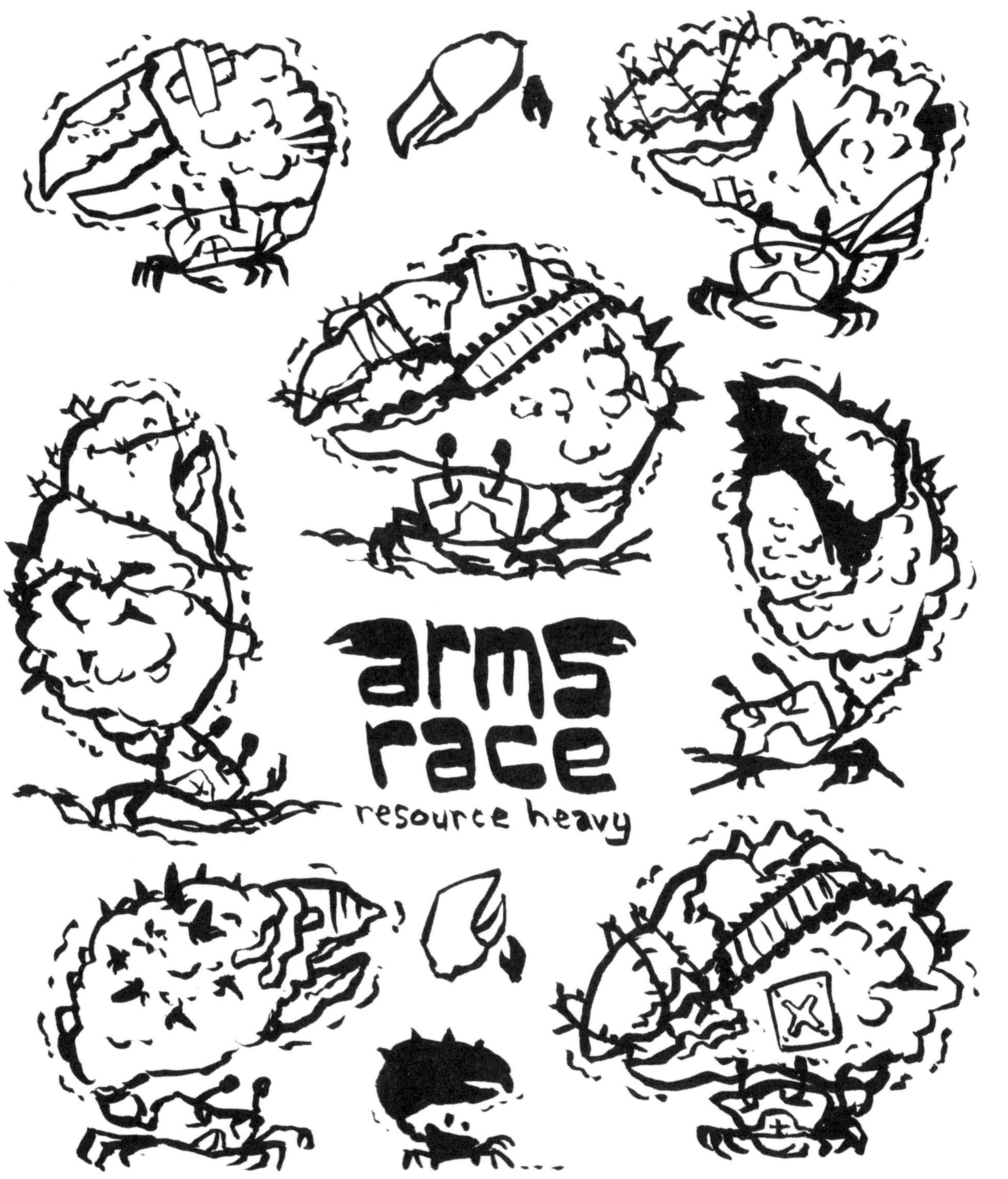
arms
race
resource heavy

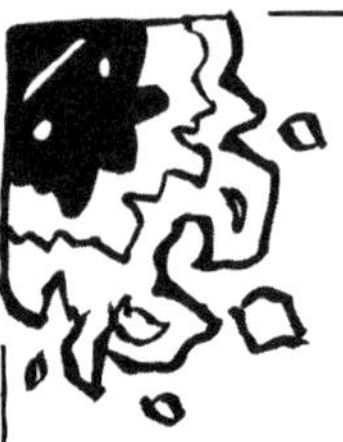

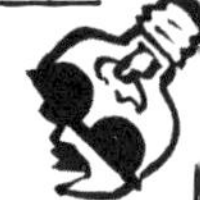

Shade.

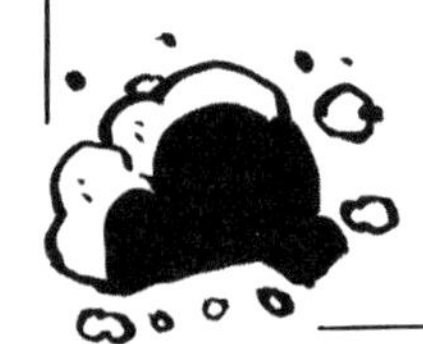

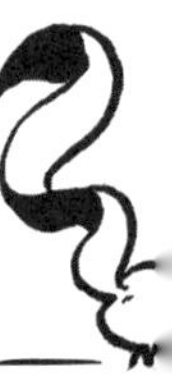

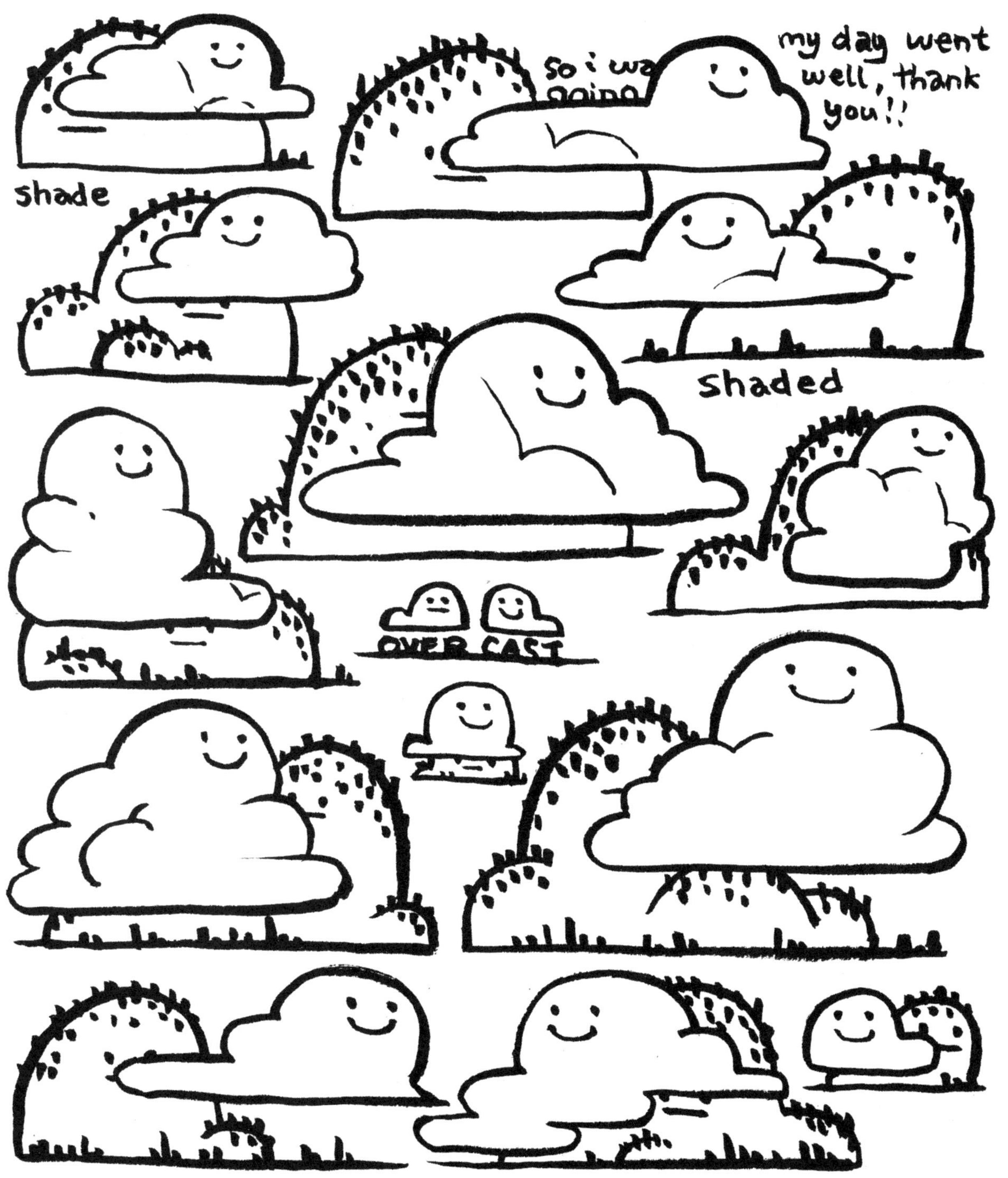
so i wa
my day went well, thank you!!
shade
shaded
OVER CAST

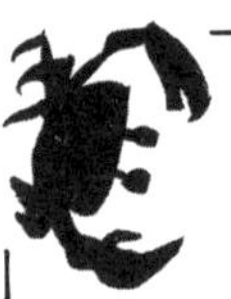

Be like water.

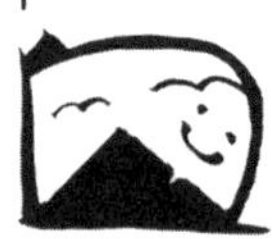

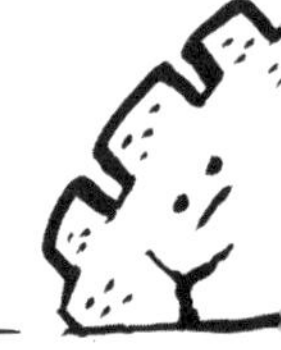

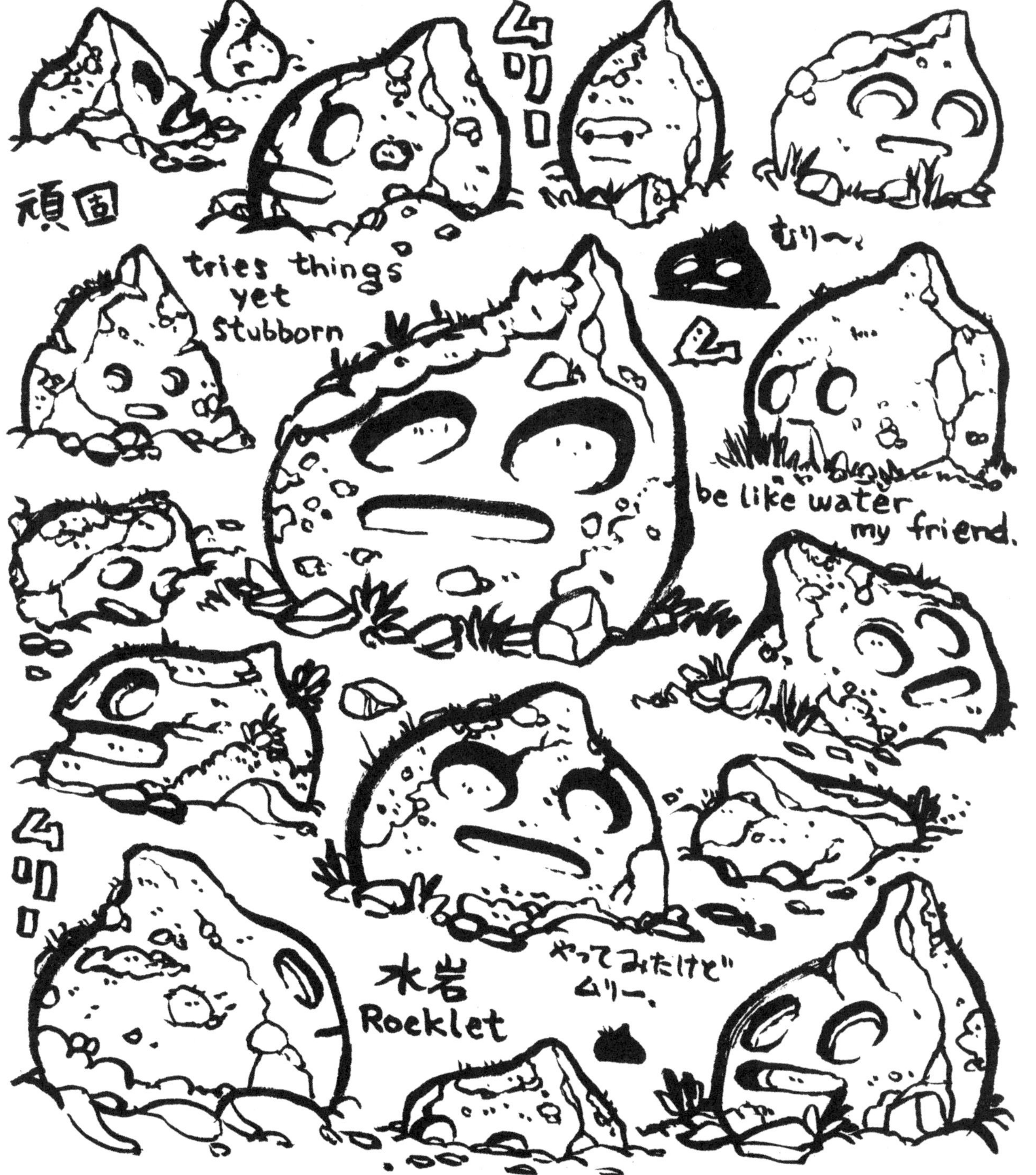

ムリー
頑固
tries things yet Stubborn
むりー。
ム
be like water my friend.
ムリー
水岩
Rocklet
やってみたけどムリー。

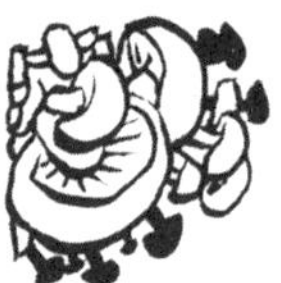

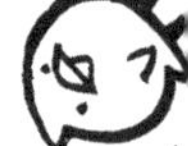

Botched delivery.

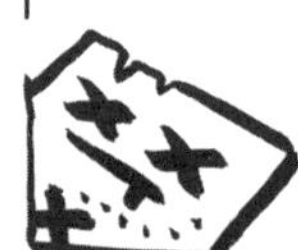

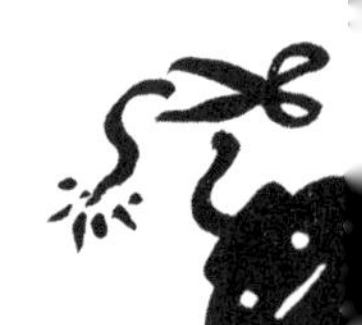

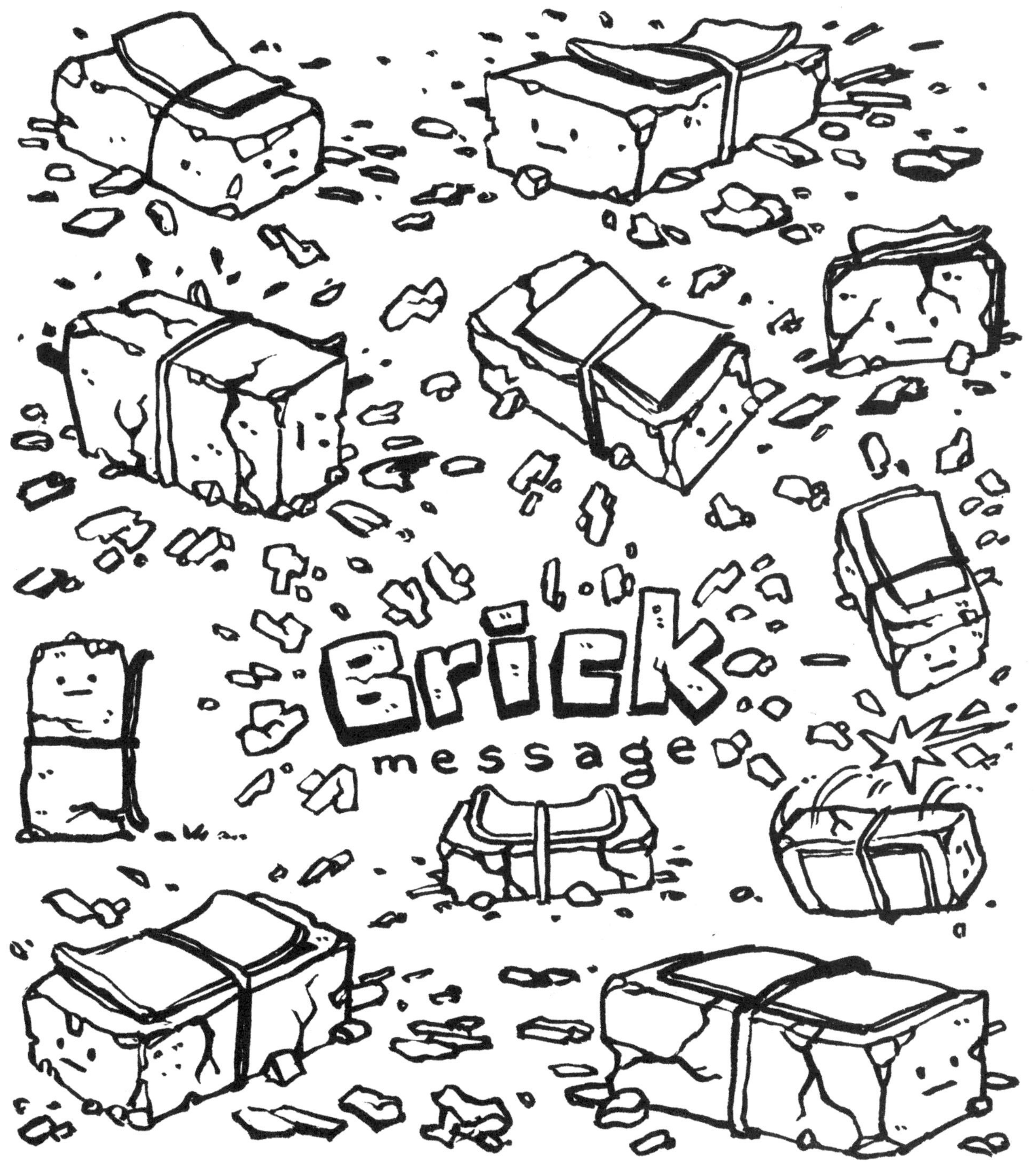
Brick
message

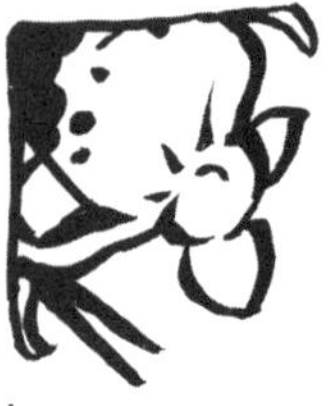

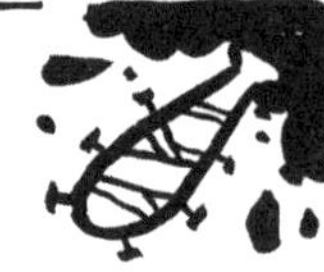

Bomb bomb.

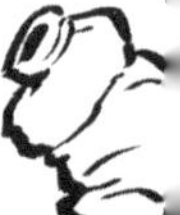

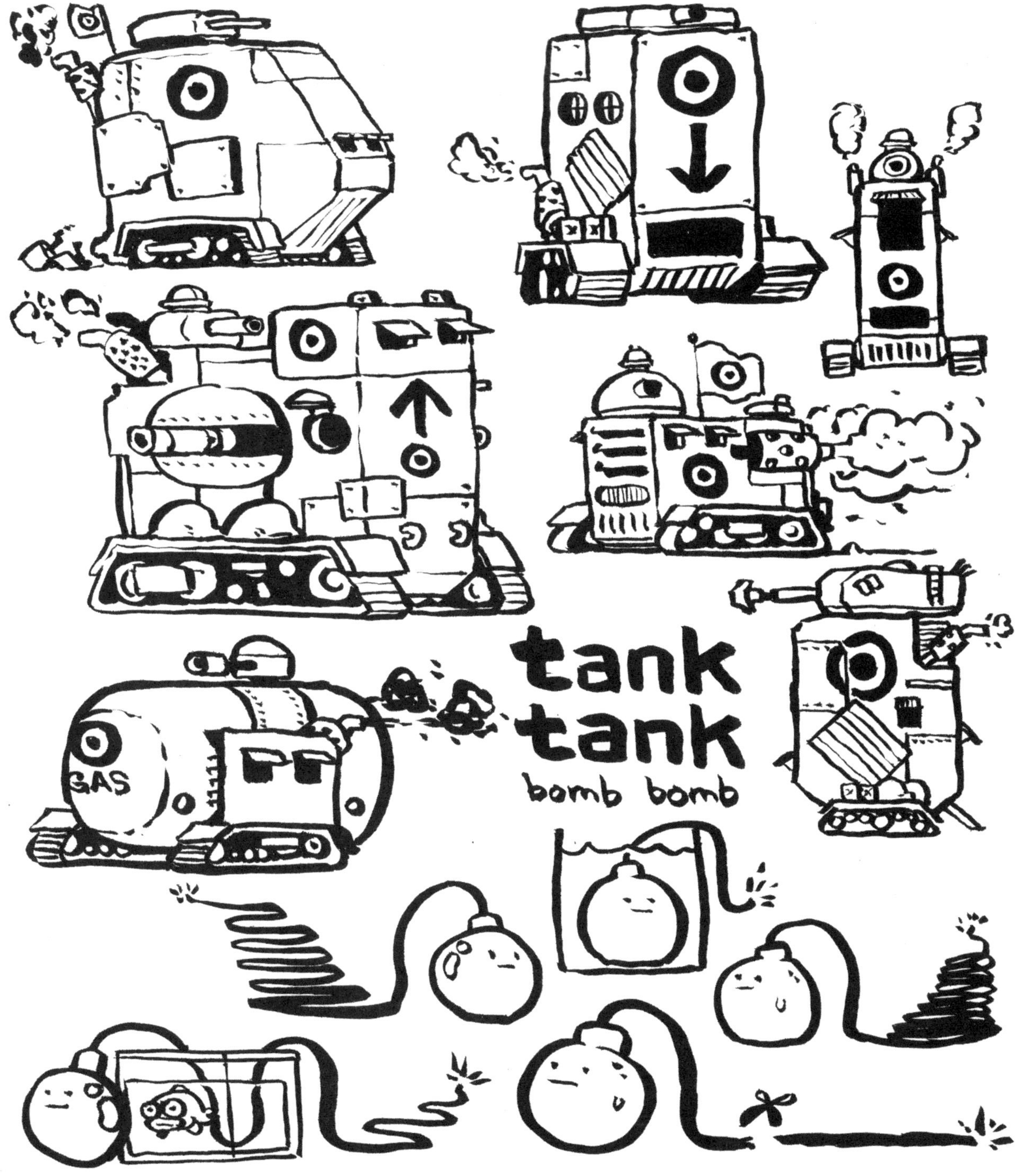
GAS
tank
tank
bomb bomb

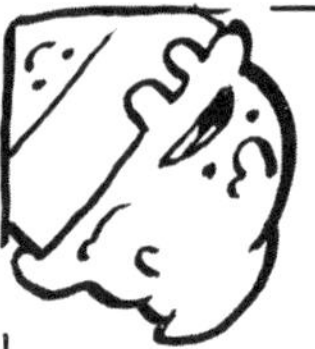

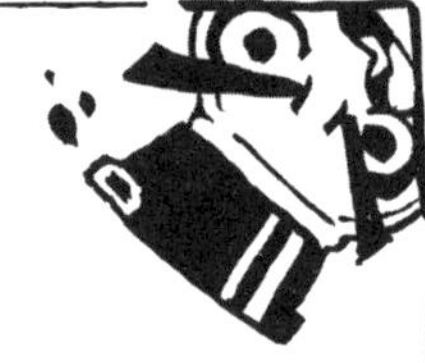

Play it from
the B Side.

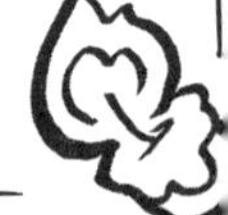

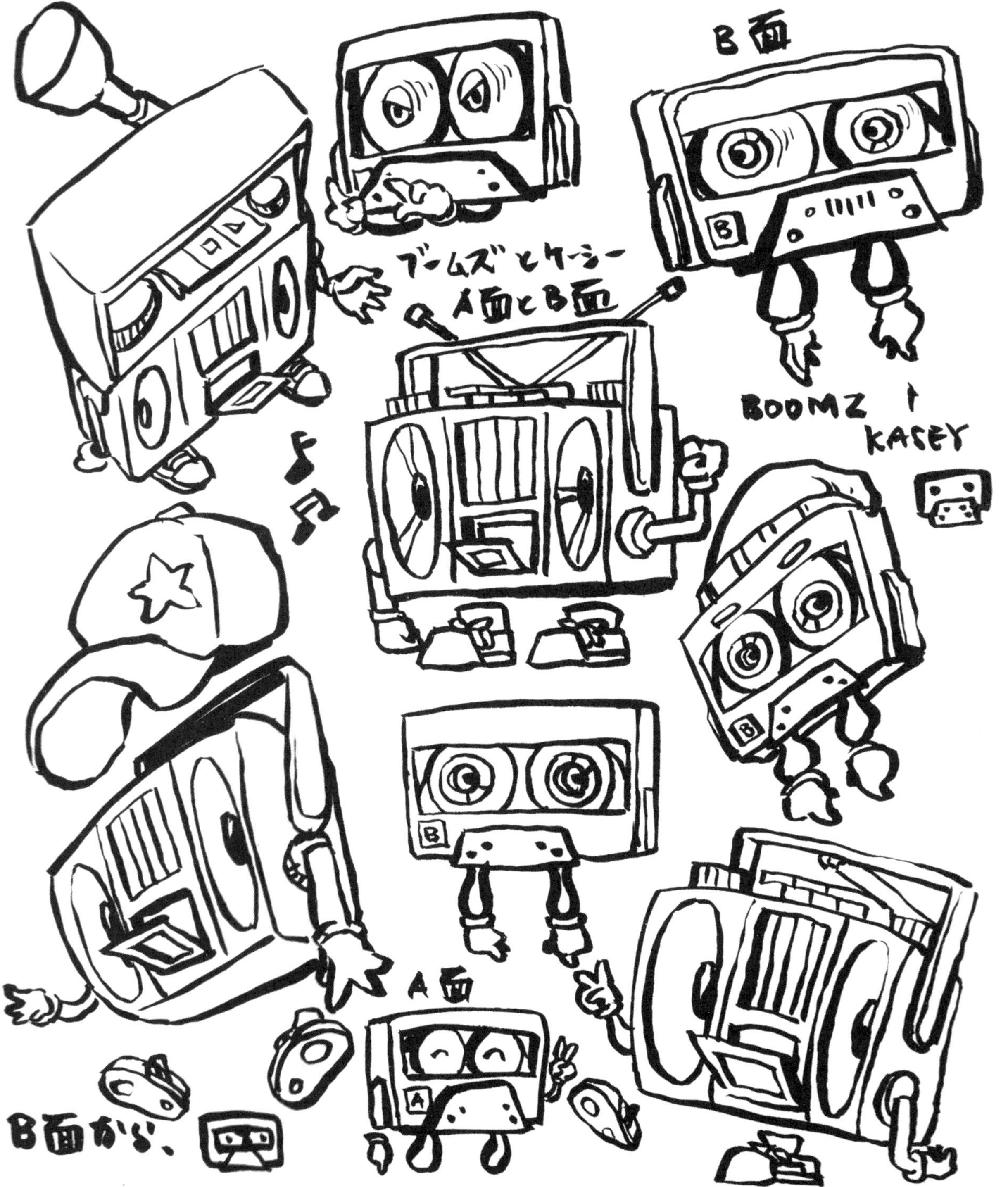

B面
ブームズとケーシー
A面とB面
BOOMZ
&
KASEY
B
B
B
A面
A
B面から、

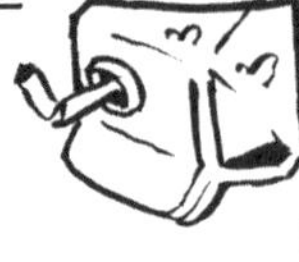

Said at a cost.

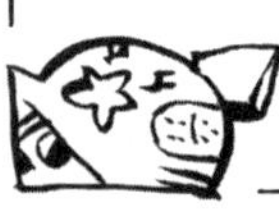

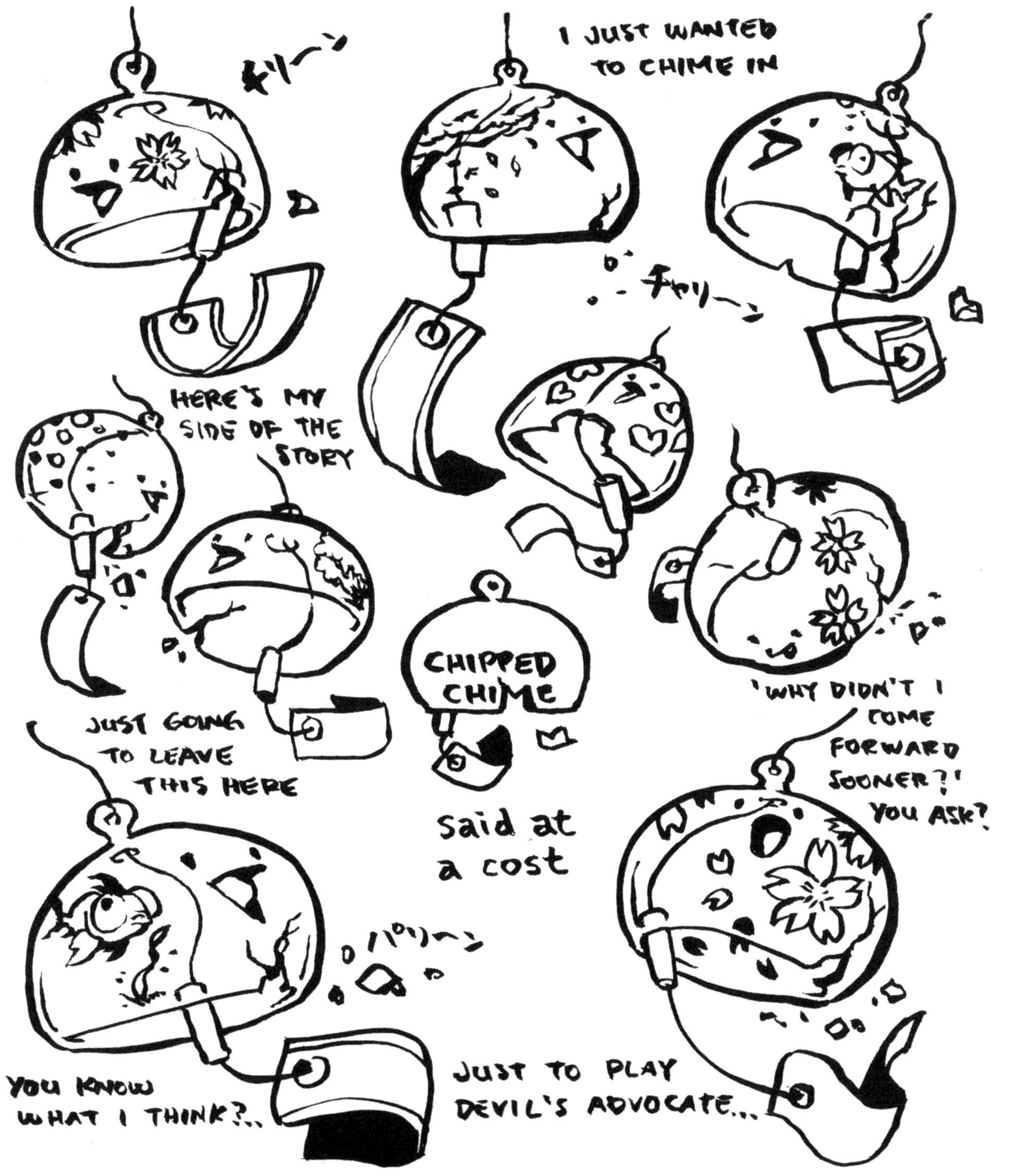
チリーン
I JUST WANTED TO CHIME IN
チャリーン
HERE'S MY SIDE OF THE STORY
JUST GOING TO LEAVE THIS HERE
CHIPPED CHIME
'WHY DIDN'T I COME FORWARD SOONER?' YOU ASK?
said at a cost
パリーン
YOU KNOW WHAT I THINK?..
JUST TO PLAY DEVIL'S ADVOCATE...

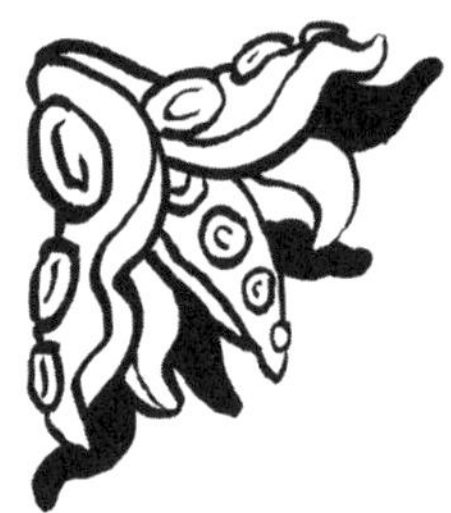

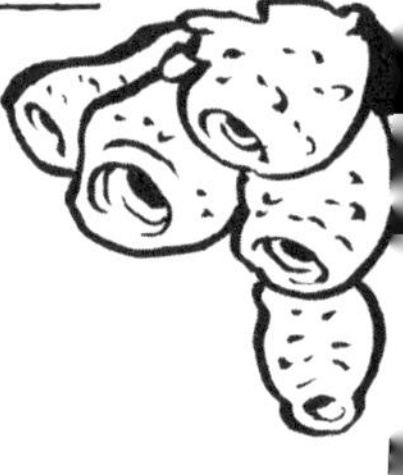

Shoulda woulda.

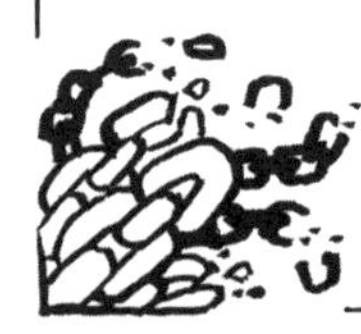

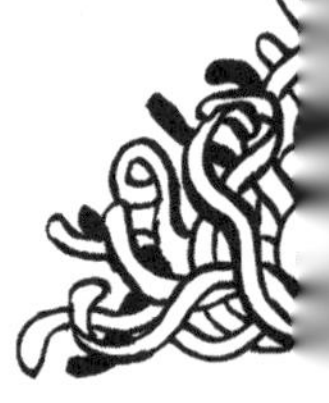

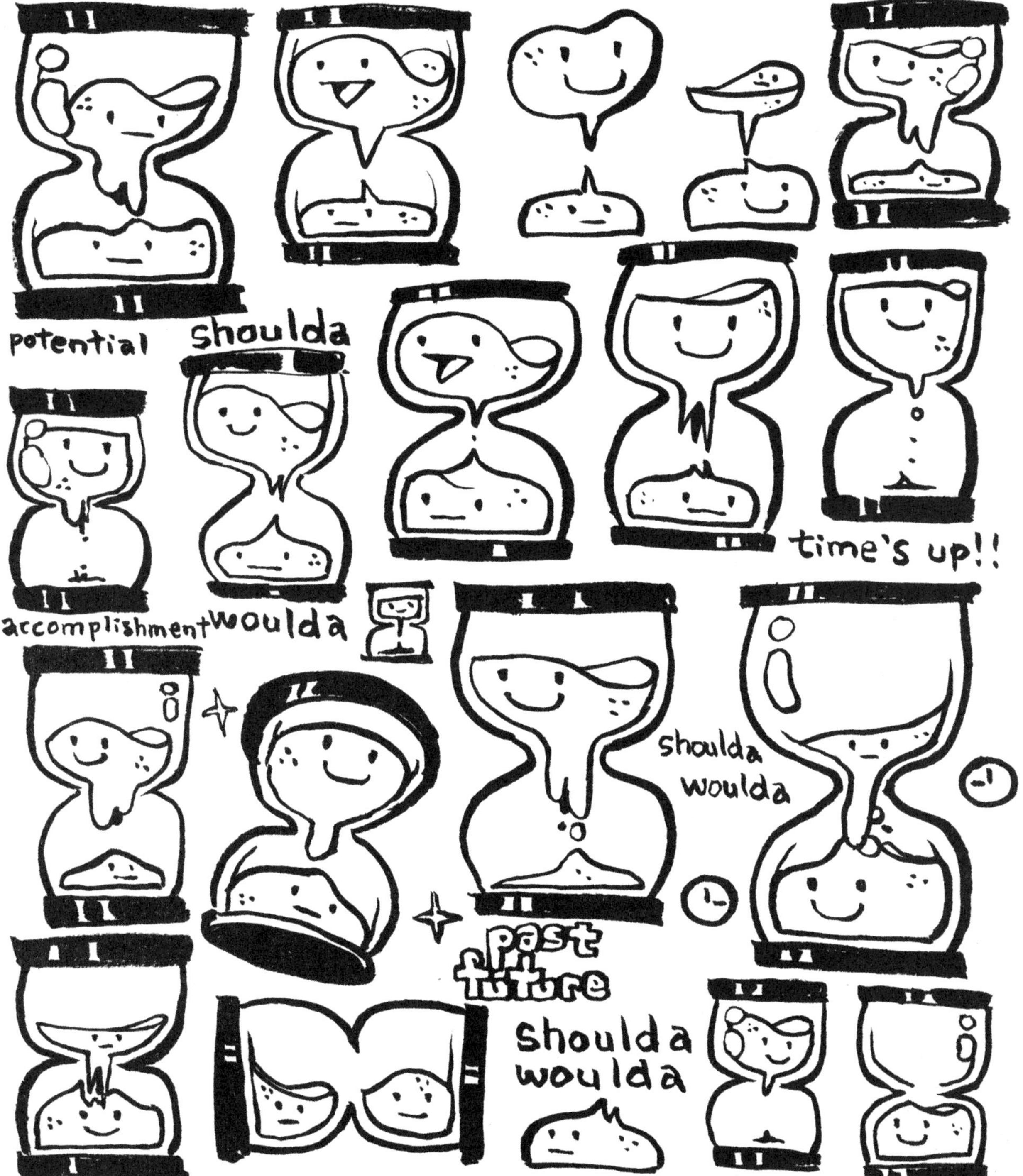
potential
shoulda
woulda
accomplishment
time's up!!
shoulda
woulda
past
future
shoulda
woulda

Staying power.

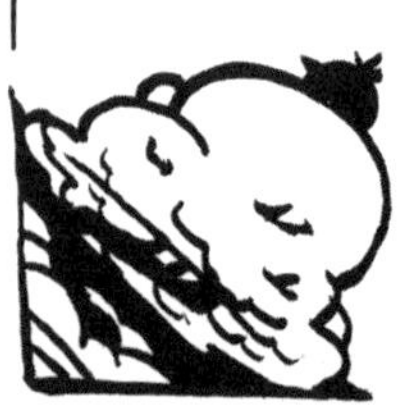

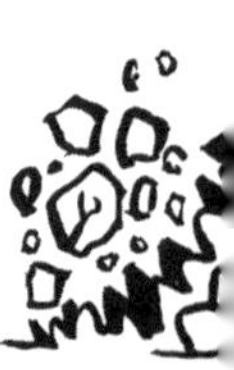

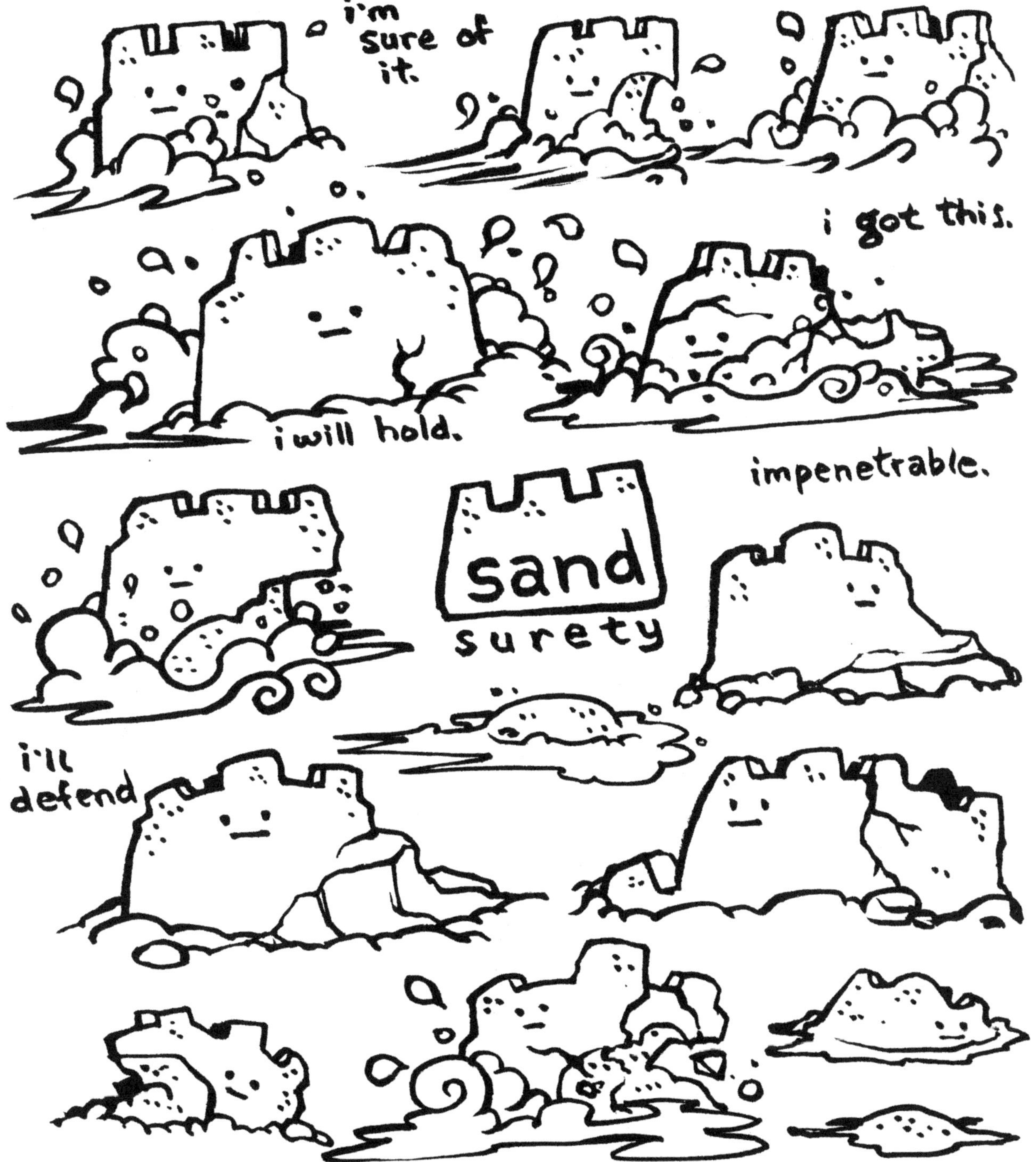
i'm sure of it.
i got this.
i will hold.
impenetrable.
sand
surety
i'll defend

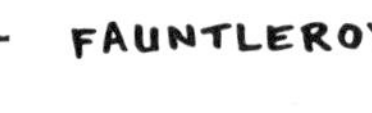

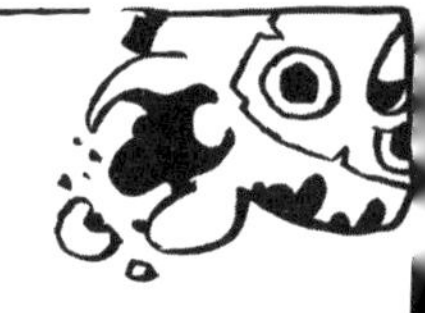

what the what?

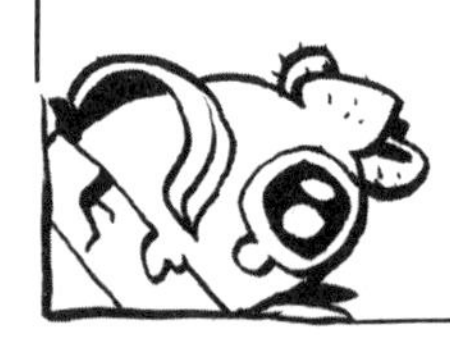

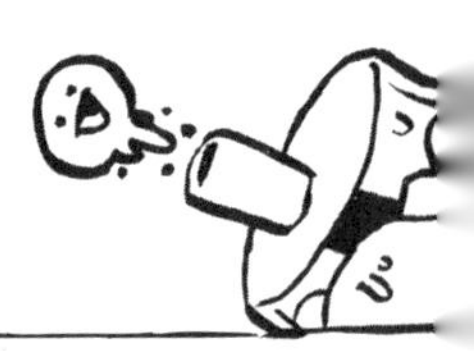

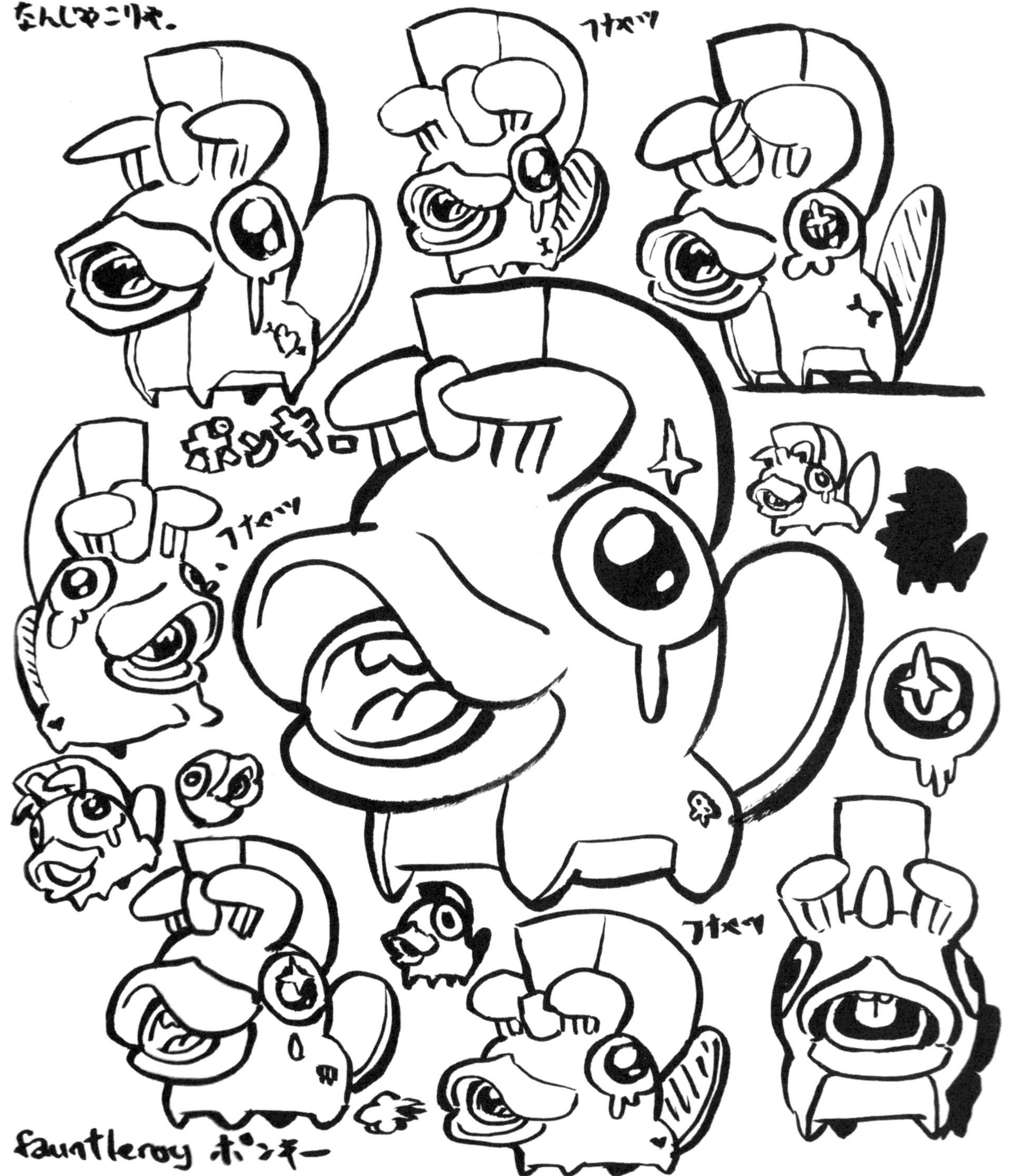
なんじゃこりゃ。
フナベツ
ポンキー。
フナベツ
フナベツ
fauntleroy ポンキー

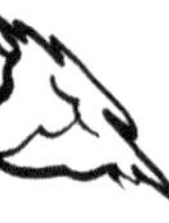

Nokay.

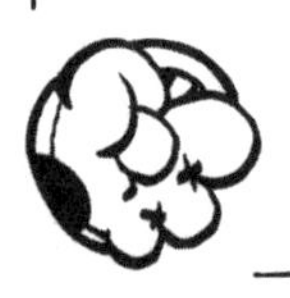

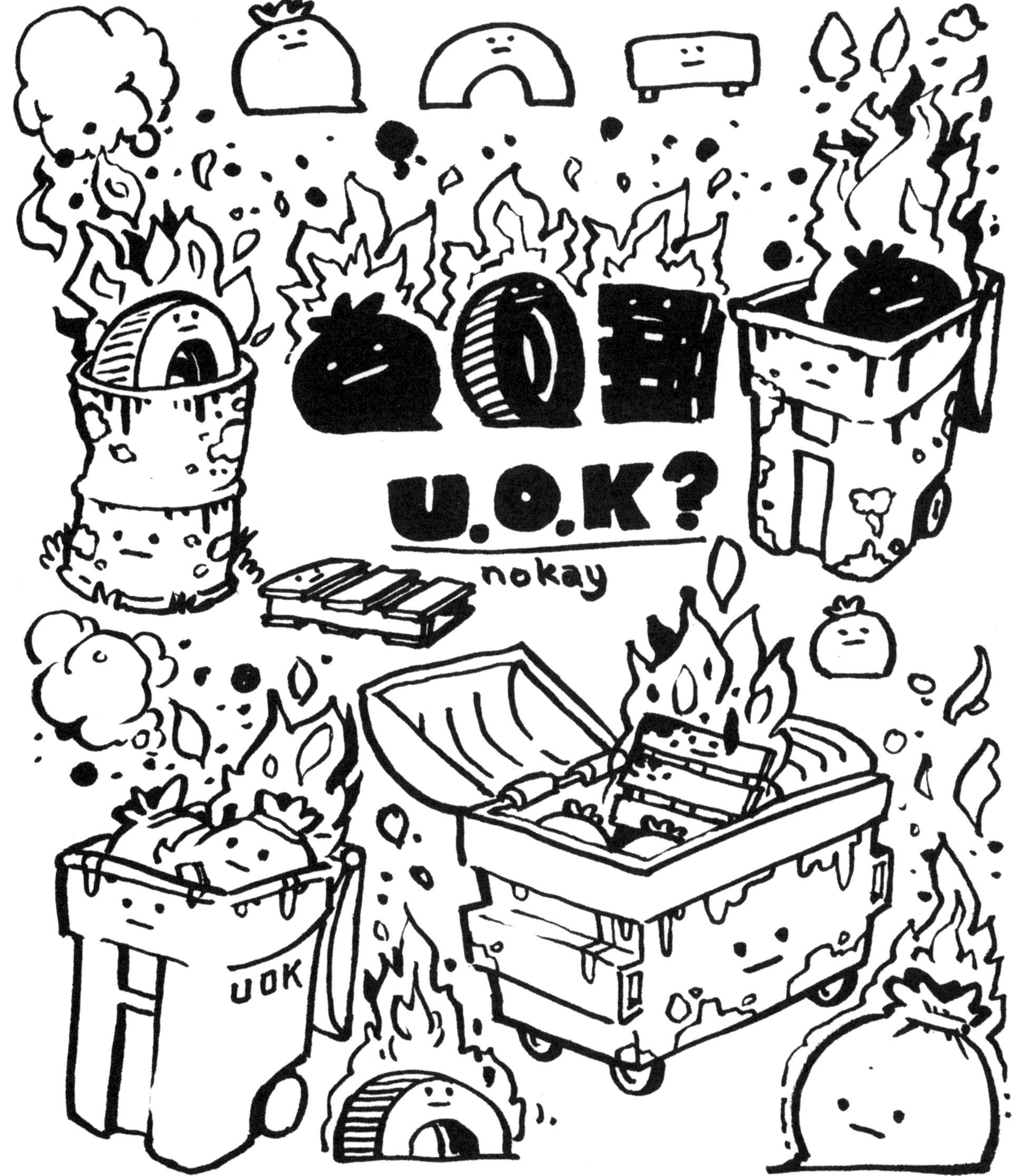
U.O.K?
nokay
UOK

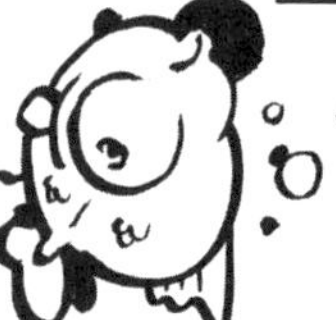

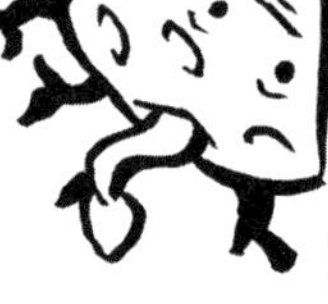

Single handed
self sufficient.

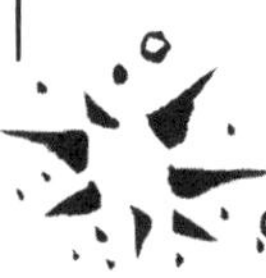

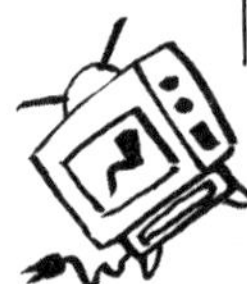

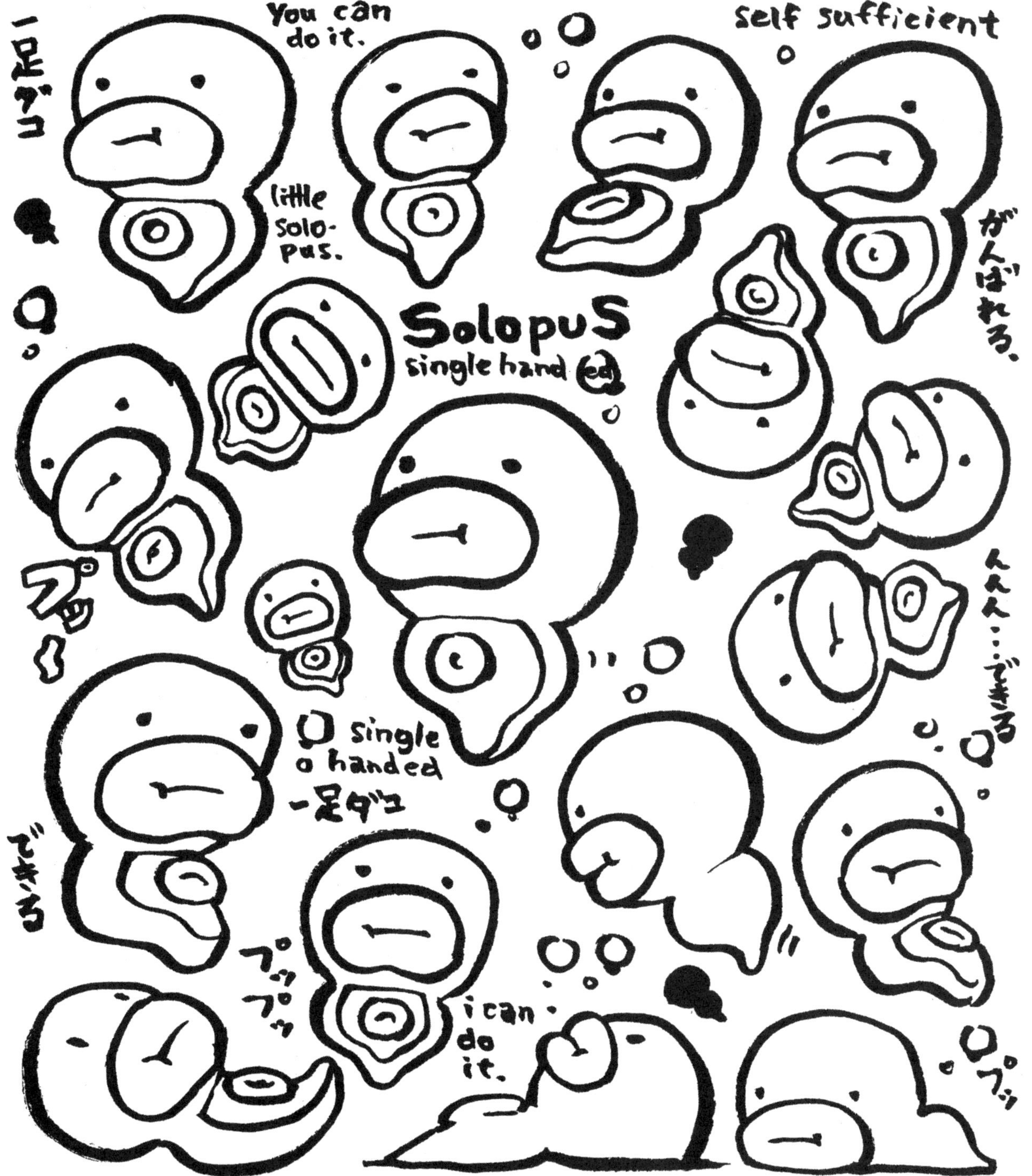

一足ダコ
You can do it.
self sufficient
little solopus.
がんばれろ。
SolopuS
single hand(ed)
プッ
んんん…できろ
single handed
一足ダコ
できろ
プップッ
i can do it.
プッ

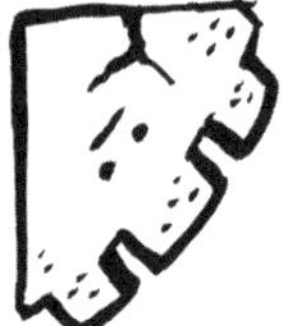

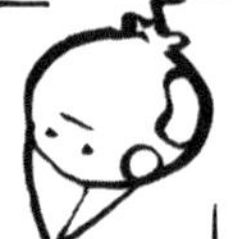

Drifted.

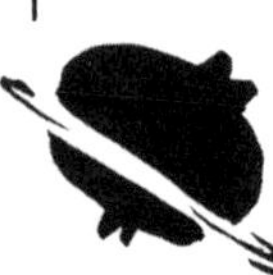

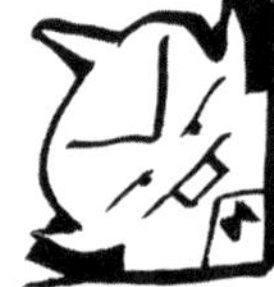

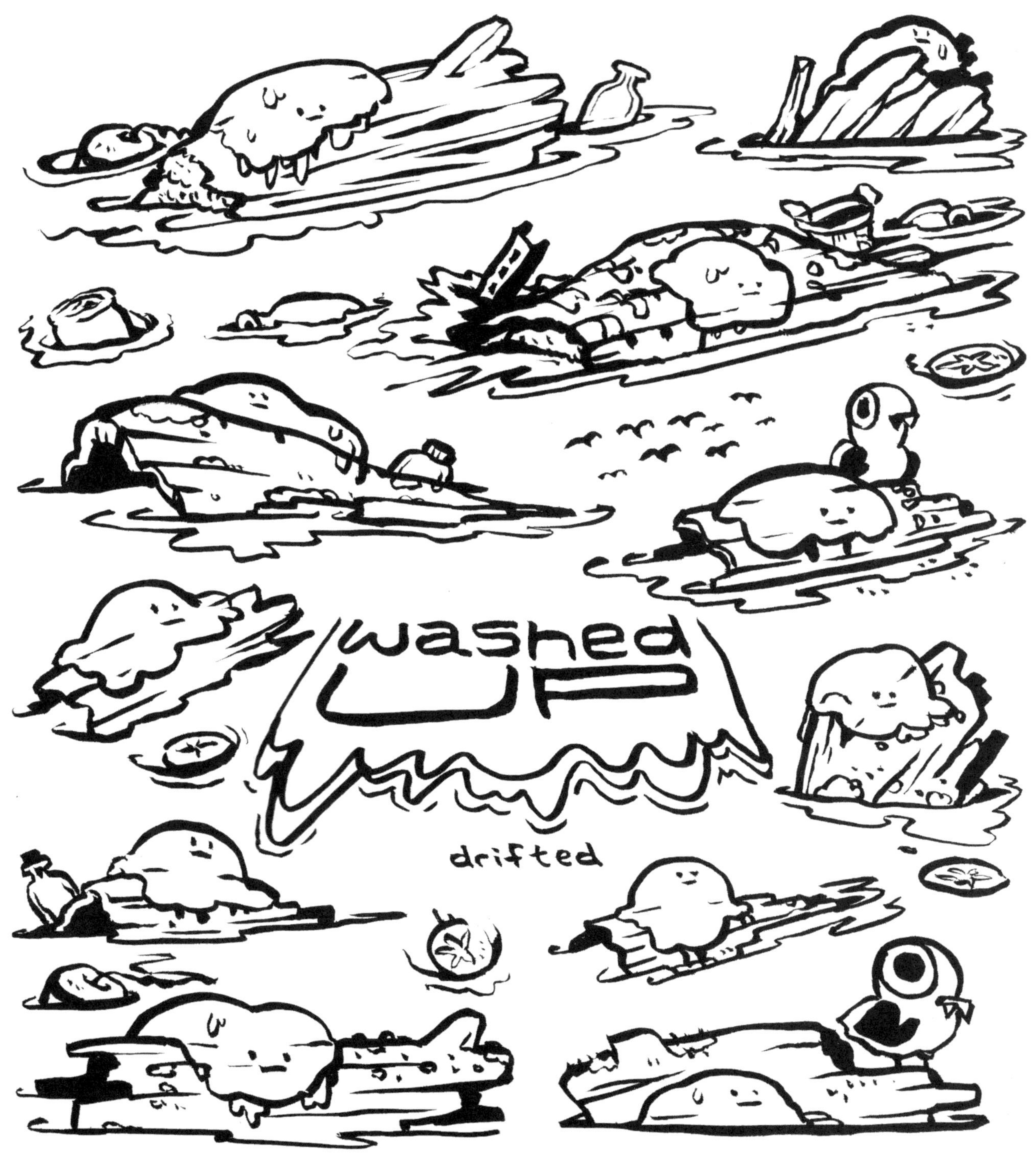
washed
UP
drifted

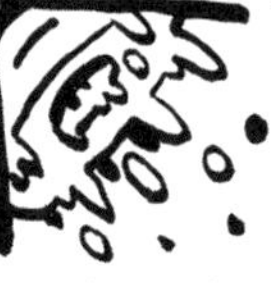

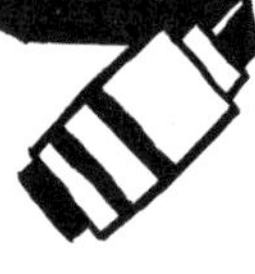

Die fast,
grow faster.

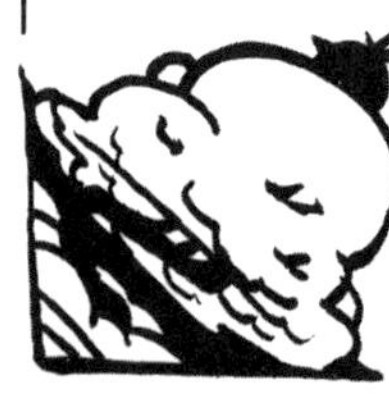

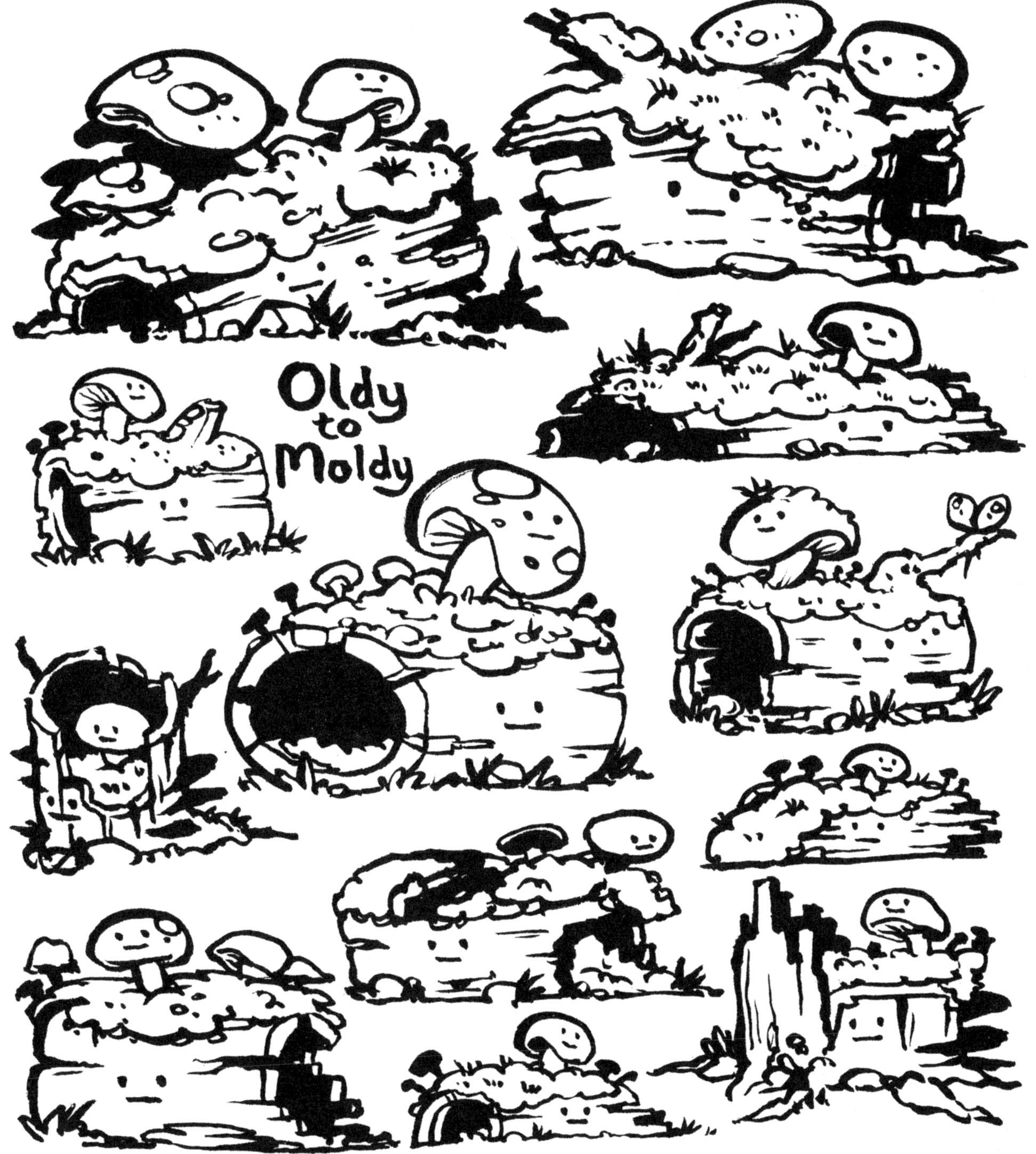
Oldy
to
Moldy

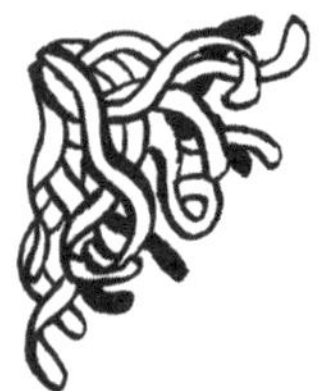

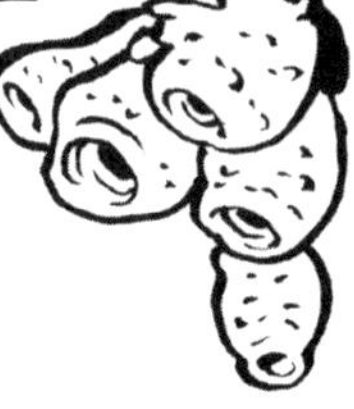

what's left of an
altruistic tree who
gave the most it could.

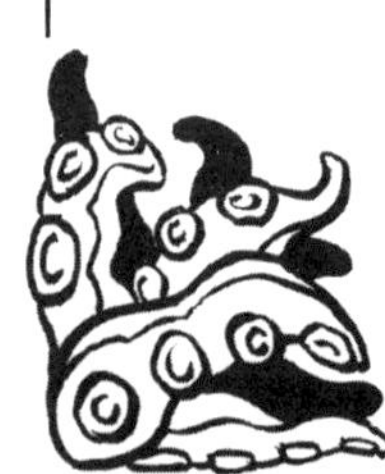

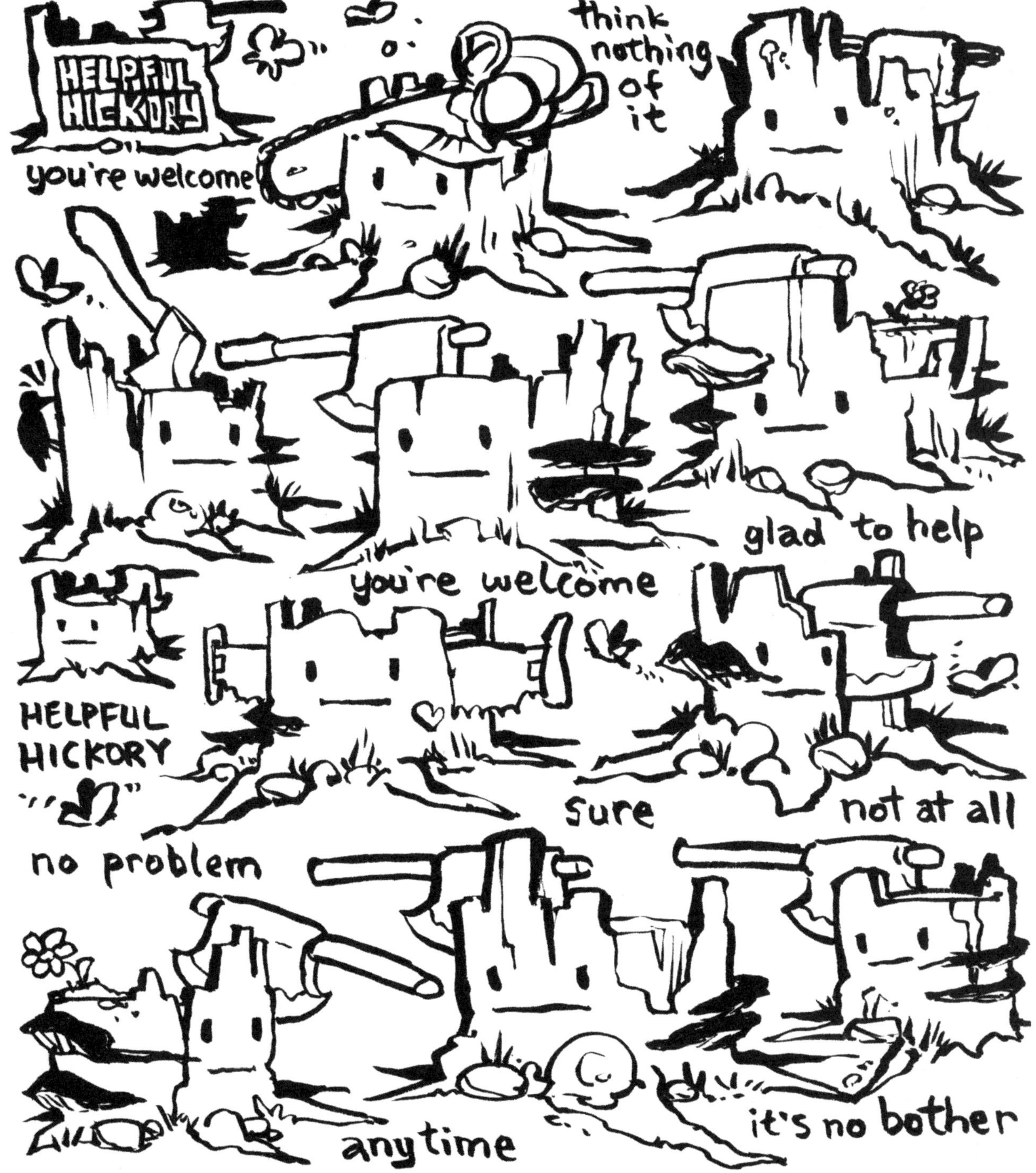
HELPFUL HICKORY
you're welcome
think nothing of it
glad to help
you're welcome
HELPFUL HICKORY
sure
not at all
no problem
anytime
it's no bother

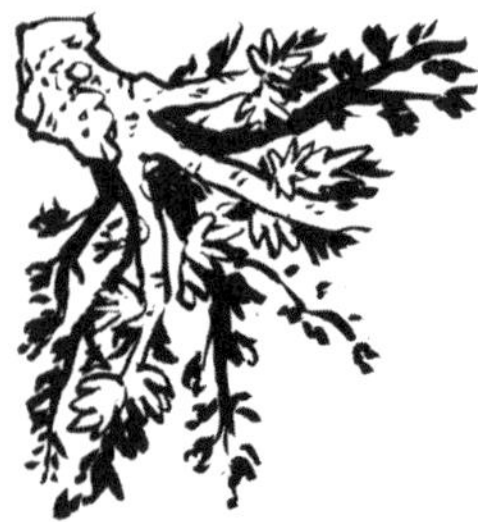

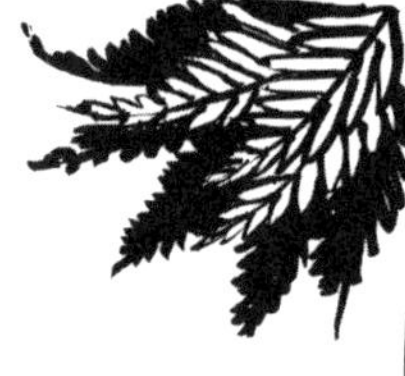

Evolved differently
but deals with it.

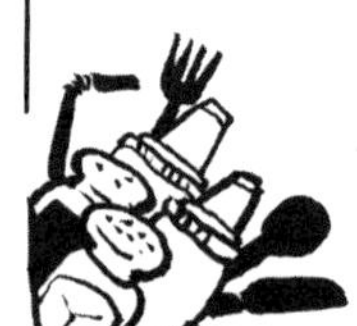

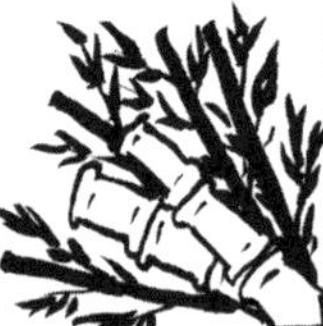

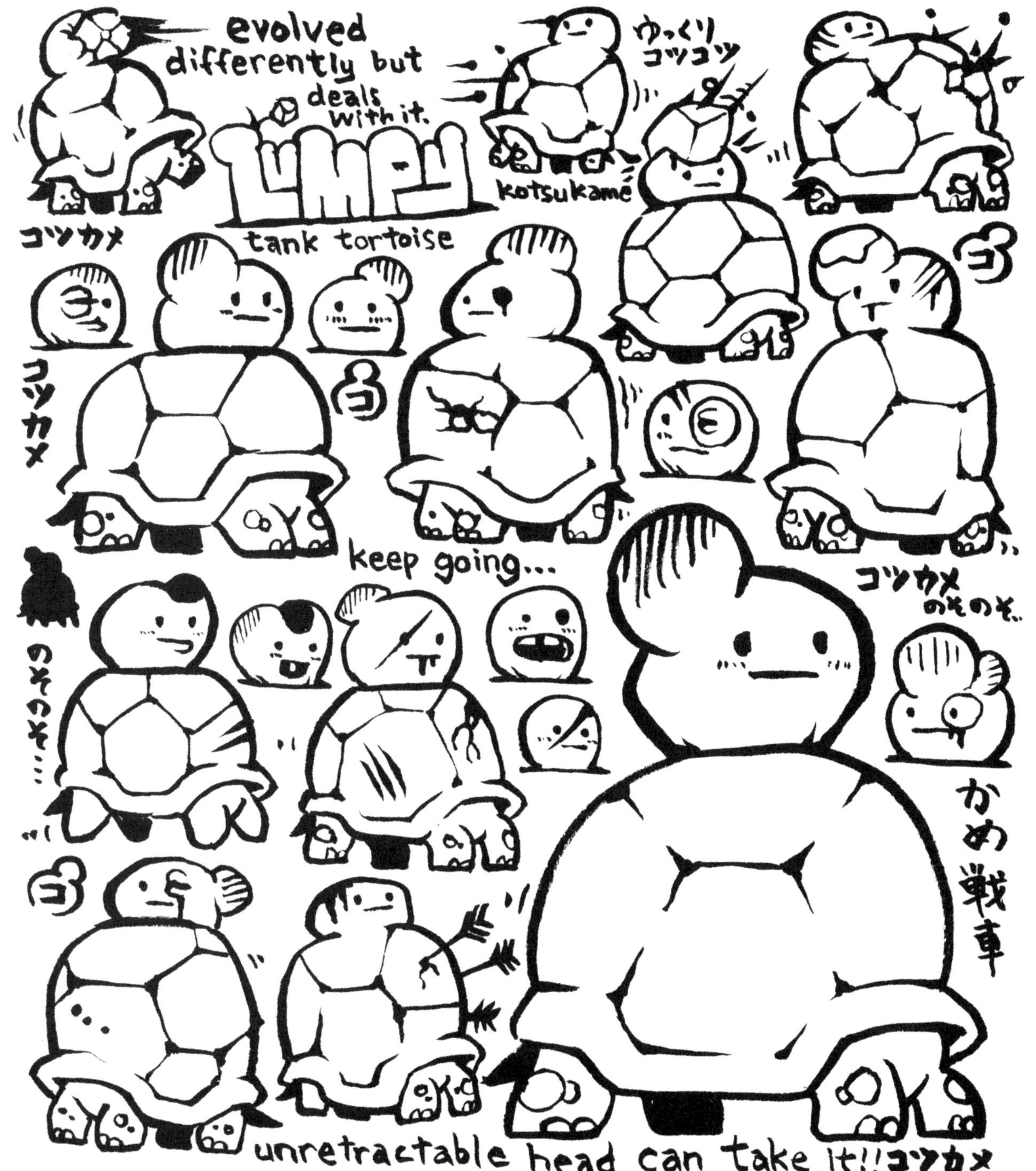
evolved differently but deals with it.
LUMPY
tank tortoise
ゆっくりコツコツ
kotsukamé
コツカメ
コツカメ
keep going...
コツカメのそのそ…
のそのそ…
かめ戦車
unretractable head can take it!!
コツカメ

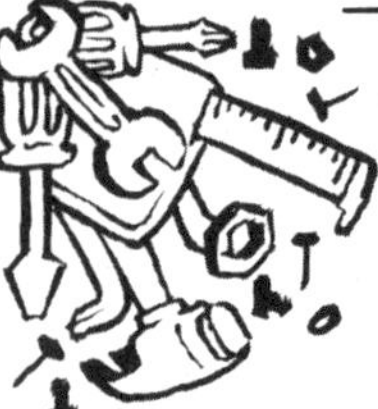

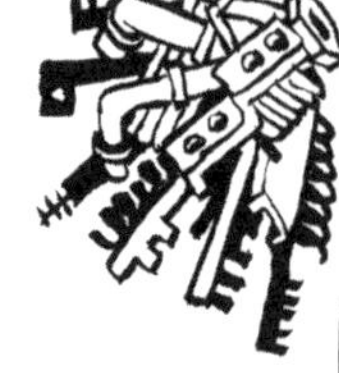

Worthy.

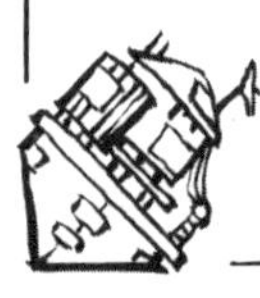

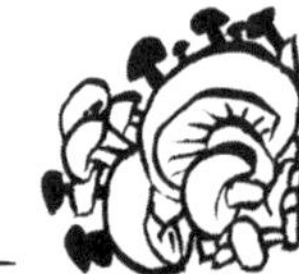

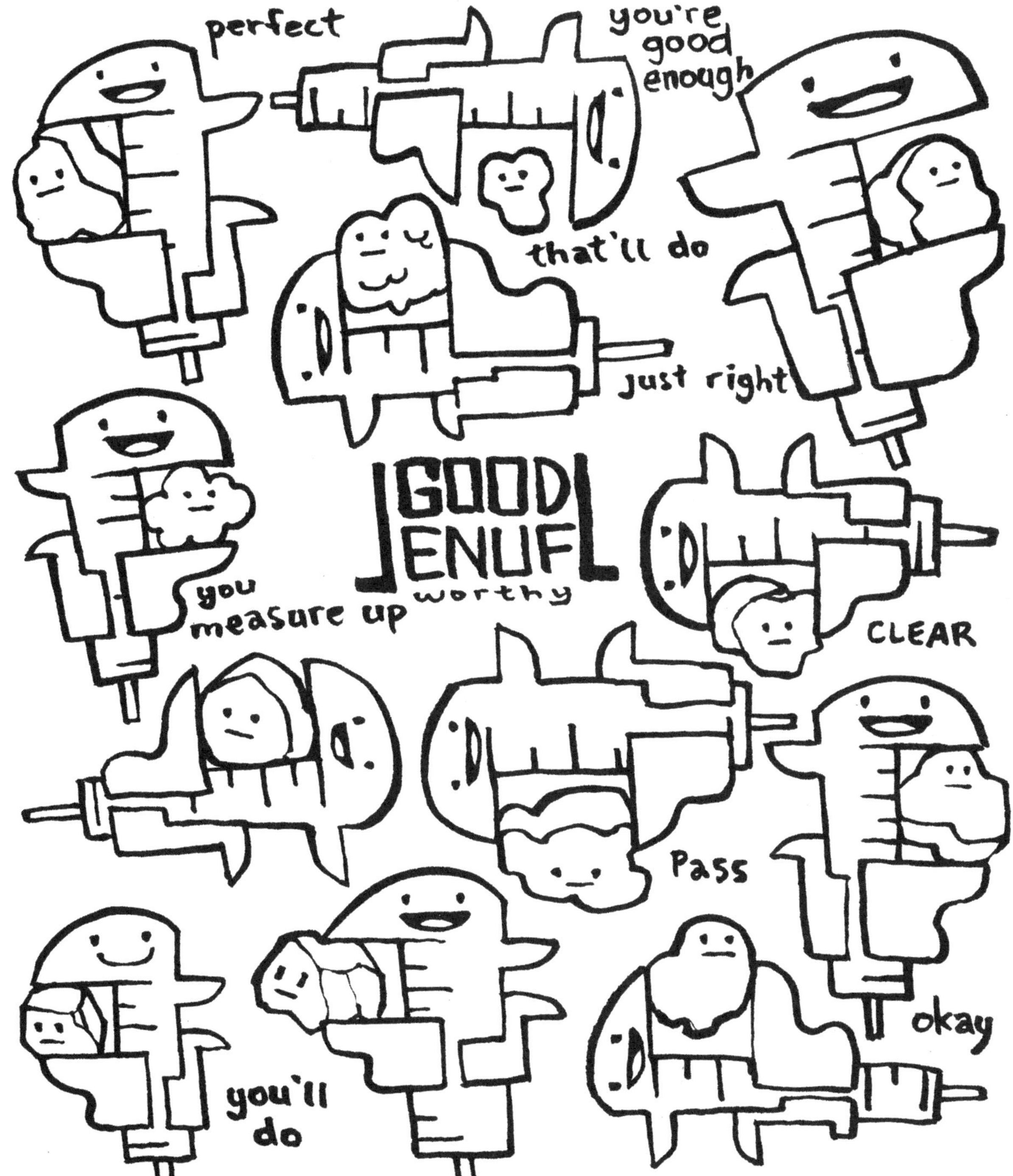
perfect
you're good enough
that'll do
just right
GOOD ENUF
you measure up
worthy
CLEAR
Pass
okay
you'll do

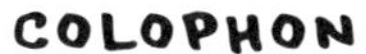

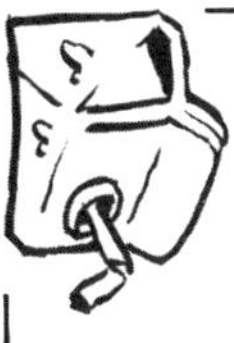

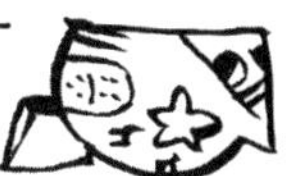

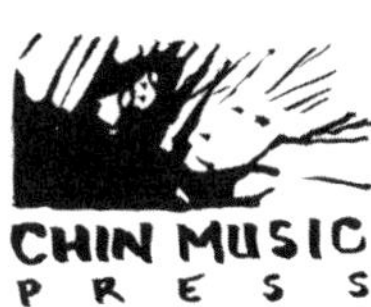

ISBN 9781634059909

Library of Congress Control Number: 2020940637

WWW.CHINMUSICPRESS.COM

This book was designed by Dan D Shafer in Seattle, Washington.

Printed and bound in China by Imago.

First printing 2020

EDITION OF 3,000

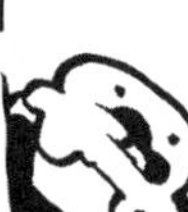

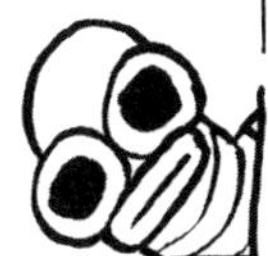

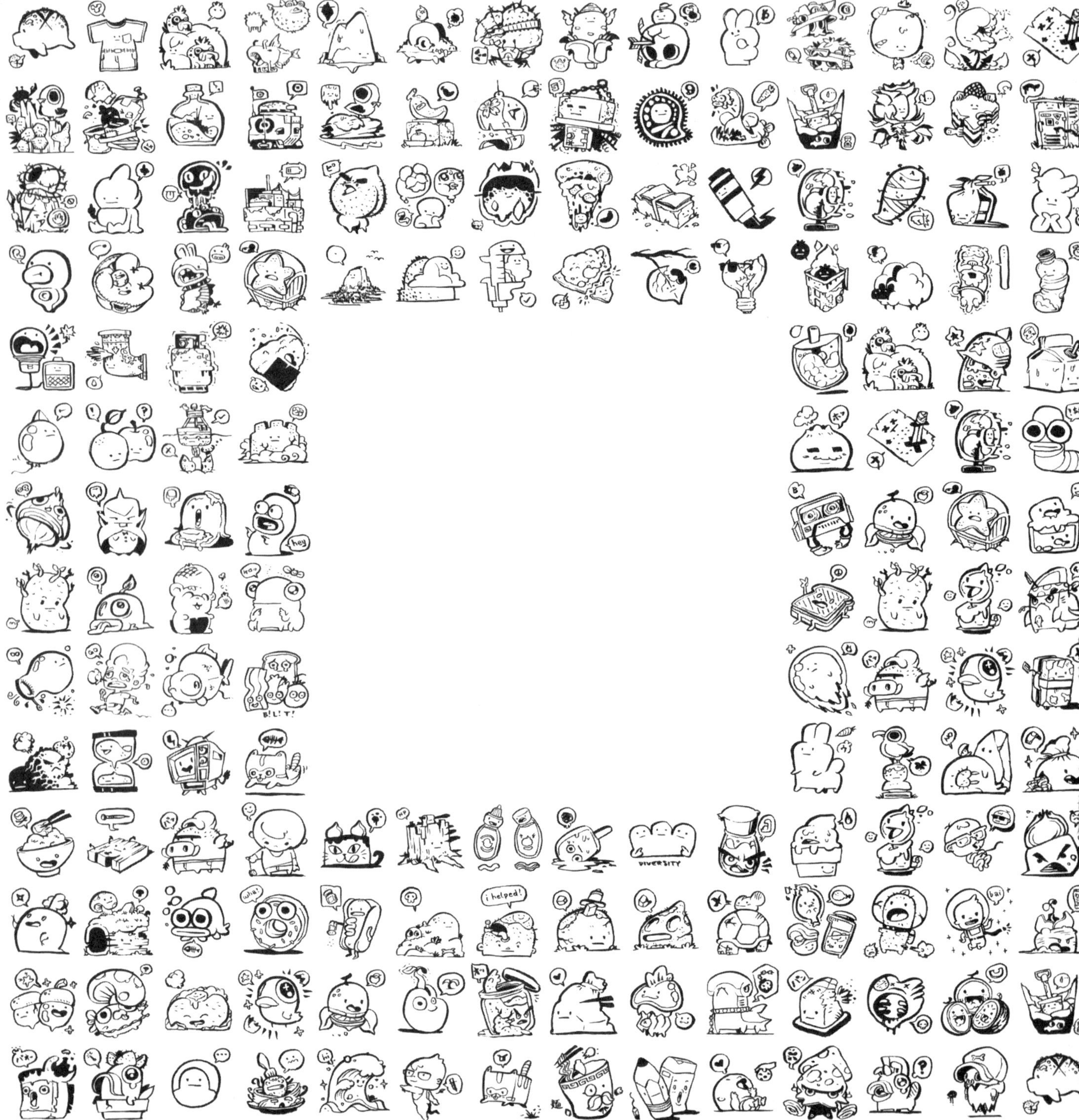
hey
B!L!T!
DIVERSITY
i helped!